Tolley's
Pensions Taxation

Tolley's
Pensions Taxation

Fourth Edition

by

Stephen Ward, BA (Econ) APFS

Members of the LexisNexis Group worldwide

United Kingdom	LexisNexis, a Division of Reed Elsevier (UK) Ltd, Lexis House, 30 Farringdon Street, London, EC4A 4HH and London House, 20-22 East London Street, Edinburgh EH7 4BQ
Australia	LexisNexis Butterworths, Chatswood, New South Wales
Austria	LexisNexis Verlag ARD Orac GmbH & Co KG, Vienna
Benelux	LexisNexis Benelux, Amsterdam
Canada	LexisNexis Canada, Markham, Ontario
China	LexisNexis China, Beijing and Shanghai
France	LexisNexis SA, Paris
Germany	LexisNexis GmbH, Dusseldorf
Hong Kong	LexisNexis Hong Kong, Hong Kong
India	LexisNexis India, New Delhi
Italy	Giuffrè Editore, Milan
Japan	LexisNexis Japan, Tokyo
Malaysia	Malayan Law Journal Sdn Bhd, Kuala Lumpur
New Zealand	LexisNexis NZ Ltd, Wellington
Singapore	LexisNexis Singapore, Singapore
South Africa	LexisNexis, Durban
USA	LexisNexis, Dayton, Ohio

Reed Elsevier (UK) Ltd 2014

Published by LexisNexis

ISBN for this volume: 9780754549352

Printed and bound by Hobbs the Printers Ltd, Totton, Hampshire SO40 2WX

Visit LexisNexis at www.lexisnexis.co.uk

Preface

In 2004 the Government of the day put in place through Finance Act 2004 a totally new and at the time refreshing tax regime for pensions. Over the previous 34 years a pensions tax system had developed that was so complex that it represented as much a barrier to pensions saving as it did an encouragement.

Suddenly on 6 April 2006 we had in the UK a single tax regime for pensions. By now in late 2014 many of the original objectives of the pensions simplification project have been lost sight of. Employers are now required to 'auto enrol' employees into a workplace pension scheme with an admitted reliance on inertia to maintain membership as once again public faith in the pension savings system has been eroded. That of course has not been helped by the turbulent economic conditions of the last few years.

The pension tax changes introduced by Finance Act 2011 and Finance Act 2013 were on the one hand about reducing the cost of pensions tax relief by around £5bn a year and on the other hand about removing what was seen as the effective compulsion to secure pension income by age 75. The latter objective has moved on to the next stage of allowing full access to pension pots effective from April 2015.

The tax rules associated with pension provision have developed over the period since 2006 into quite a complex set up. The purpose of this book is to place all the key information about pensions tax in one publication and to present it in a way that makes it accessible to practitioners, journalists and indeed anyone interested in how the pensions tax system works.

In doing that we start by looking into the past and how the UK pensions tax system developed through the twentieth century culminating in what ended up as a labyrinth of often contradictory rules and regulations.

This perhaps ought to be compulsory reading for those responsible for policy and legislation, because there are many signs of history repeating itself. One example of that is to be found in Finance Act 2011 which through approximately 60 pages of new legislation deals with what is described as 'disguised remuneration', the pension tax elements of which are dealt with in this book.

I wrote in the preface to the 2012 edition that it was hoped (certainly not expected) 'that the changes to the pensions tax system introduced by Finance Act 2011 will stand the test of time and that future Finance Acts will be silent on the subject'. This lack of expectation was not disappointed with further reductions in the annual and lifetime allowances legislated for in Finance Act 2013. The draft Taxation of Pensions Bill 2014 is one step towards implementing changes announced in the 2014 Budget speech, introducing what will be in the Chancellor's own words the biggest changes in pensions taxation since 1921.

This edition updates the book for 2014–15 with material that brings things up to date at September 2014.

Stephen Ward

Contents

Contents

Chapter 4   Benefits to members and their dependants – and their taxation

Contents

Contents

Contents

Abbreviations and References

Abbreviations

ACT	Advance Corporation Tax
AIM	Alternative Investment Market
App	Appendix
APR	Agricultural Property Relief
BES	Business Expansion Scheme
BPR	Business Property Relief
CA	Court of Appeal
CA(NI)	Court of Appeal (Northern Ireland)
CG	Inland Revenue Capital Gains Manual
CGT	Capital Gains Tax
CGTA 1979	Capital Gains Tax Act 1979
ChD	Chancery Division
CIOT	Chartered Institute of Taxation
col	column
CJEC	Court of Justice of the European Community
CRT	Composite Rate Tax
CS	Court of Session
CTO	Capital Taxes Office
CTT	Capital Transfer Tax
DTR	Double Taxation Relief
ECHR	European Convention on Human Rights
EIS	Enterprise Investment Scheme
ESC	Extra-statutory Concession
FA	Finance Act
FICO	Financial Intermediaries and Claims Offices
FOTRA	Free of tax to residents abroad

FURB	Funded Unapproved Retirement Benefit Scheme
HL	House of Lords
ICAEW	Institute of Chartered Accountants in England & Wales
IRC	Inland Revenue Commissioners
ICTA 1988	Income and Corporation Taxes Act 1988
IHT	Inheritance Tax
IHTA 1984	Inheritance Tax Act 1984
IRPR	Inland Revenue Press Release
ITEPA 2003	Income Tax (Earnings and Pensions) Act 2003
ITTOIA 2005	Income Tax (Trading and Other Income) Act 2005
KB	King's Bench Division
OECD	Organization for Economic Co-operation and Development
para	paragraph
PC	Privy Council
PET	Potentially Exempt Transfer
Pt	Part
QB	Queen's Bench Division
s	section
Sch	Sch [Sch 4 para 2 = 4th Schedule, paragraph 2]
SI	Statutory Instrument
SO	Stamp Office
SP	Inland Revenue Statement of Practice
SpC	Special Commissioners' decisions
SSCBA 1992	Social Security Contributions and Benefits Act 1992
TCGA 1992	Taxation of Chargeable Gains Act 1992
TSEM	Inland Revenue Trusts, Settlements and Estates Manual
TMA 1970	Taxes Management Act 1970
UK	United Kingdom
USM	Unlisted Securities Market

References

AC	Law Reports, Appeal Cases
All ER	All England Law Reports
EG	Estates Gazette
JLR	Jersey Law Reports
LR Sc & D	Law Reports, Scotch and Divorce (HL)
STC	Simon's Tax Cases
STC (SCD)	Simon's Tax Cases, Special Commissioners Decisions
SpC	Special Commissioners
STI	Simon's Tax Intelligence
TC	Official Reports of Tax Cases

Table of Statutes

Paragraph references printed in **bold** type in this Table indicate where the Statute is set out in part or in full.

Table of Statutory Instruments

Paragraph references printed in **bold** type indicate where the Statutory Instrument is set out in part or in full.

Table of Cases

Introduction

It was once again a privilege to be asked to update this book for its fourth edition. This edition updates the book for 2014–15 with material that brings things up to date to August 2014, following the momentous changes announced in the 2014 Budget, some of which were legislated for in Finance Act 2014. We were just in time to be able to take proper account of the (draft) Taxation of Pensions Bill 2014.

We said in the introduction to the third edition that 'changes in UK pensions tax legislation continue unabated and what was intended to be a simple new regime is now as complex as the previous set of regimes'. The changes to the pensions tax regime announced in 2014 will on the one hand introduce an element of simplification but time will tell whether this is contradicted by measures designed to obviate any unintended consequences. The publication of the (draft) Taxation of Pensions Bill 2014 does indeed incorporate such complications.

Having joined the industry in 1976 as a trainee pensions administrator and immediately pointed at sitting the Pensions Management Institute exams, preparing CHAPTER 1 of this book for the first edition took me back to an era where the starting point was pensions legislation going back to 1921.

Although until writing this book I had never actually read the relevant clauses of the 1921 Finance Act (available on the internet!) nor realized the way in which they were repeated from time to time all the way through until 1970.

It is on reflection quite astonishing that not much changed between 1921 and 1970 other than the introduction of retirement annuities in 1956. The temptation to wax lyrical in CHAPTER 1 about exempt provident funds which (if I recall correctly) were a 1947 introduction was (you will be relieved to hear) resisted. Although there is an 'in passing' reference in CHAPTER 1.

The mid 1970s was a transition between the 'old code' associated with occupational schemes and the 'new code' which replaced the old code finally in 1980. So I had to learn both in those early days. All that changed from time to time in that era were the retirement annuity contribution limits in the annual Budget. Although it is true to say that when I joined the industry pensions was something of a political football, not in the area of taxation, but in relation to the interaction between private pension schemes and State pension provision.

The State graduated pension scheme had been brought to a close and was soon to be replaced by the State Earnings Related Pension Scheme (SERPS). SERPS was introduced at a time of high inflation and I remember well at the time that those who were my mentors saw SERPS as far too generous and a scheme which could not possibly last indefinitely. So it proved.

In those days most occupational schemes, even those operated by small employers, were defined benefit schemes. Outside of what were then retirement annuity policies the concept of defined contributions was a rarity. Change was on the way though as 1973 introduced for the first time the possibility for controlling directors of director controlled companies to participate in company sponsored schemes. The development of defined contribution based small self-administered schemes for directors was at an embryonic stage.

At that time defined contribution arrangements were nearly always associated with guarantees of one form or another. With profits was the only show in town and generally associated with guaranteed annuity rates, some of which were so generous as it later turned out that they were capable of bringing down venerable institutions such as Equitable Life. Unit linking and managed funds were developments of the late 1970s onwards with life offices like Hambro Life, Abbey Life and a little later, Skandia, in the vanguard.

In 1976 or thereabouts a pension fund of £100,000 was capable for a male at age 65 of buying an annuity in the open market of around £15,000 p.a. – a far cry from the £6,000 or so it would buy today. However in today's market for annuities add in Retail Price Index based inflation protection and an ongoing pension for a surviving spouse and the annuity start point plummets to just £3,400 a year. Given that the average UK pension fund is only worth around £30,000 it is probably fair to say that the pensions timebomb that has been busy ticking away for years is at the point of detonation. Which is one of the reasons behind the 2014 changes with more to come in 2015.

Defined benefit schemes face extinction. Indeed in some instances the pension scheme tail has started to wag the dog of the corporate entity. In August 2012 Shares in Dawson International, the cashmere-making company based in the Scottish Borders, were suspended whilst the directors decided whether to place it in administration. Over the previous month the company's shares had plunged after it announced that the Pensions Regulator and the Pension Protection Fund had rejected its attempt to put its pension plans into the Pension Protection Fund. The trustees of the company's pension fund had served a notice on the employer to make contributions so as to deal with the deficit which was sufficient to threaten the survival of the company itself.

As reported in the daily Telegraph on 5 January 2012:

'Royal Dutch Shell signalled the end of an era for the UK pensions industry by announcing plans to close its final-salary scheme to new members, making it the last FTSE 100 company to do so.'

As stated in this article:

'the move is highly significant with figures from the National Association of Pension Funds estimating that only 19pc of private sector schemes are now open to new members, compared to 88pc a decade ago.'

I dare to suggest that eventually even within the public sector (where there have been strikes in order to protest about changes to pensions), the costs associated with increasing life expectancy, low gilt yields (increasing the cost of providing each pound of pension), and a falling working population as compared to the retired population make the defined benefit model surely untenable unless scheme retirement age more or less rises in line with increased life expectancy. Ongoing increases in State pension age will inevitably spill over into the private sector.

Annuities have become mired in controversy. For years, they offered the only realistic route to access retirement funds saved outside a final salary pension scheme. Insurers faced criticism for exploiting this captive market by locking vast numbers into poor-value or inappropriate contracts. Annuity rates fell so dramatically that many pension savers were forced to redraw their retirement plans. This is evidenced on a weekend visit to any large DIY store.

Savers who manage their own retirement fund face the same conundrum. Insurers estimate that people in good health live between three and six years longer than average in old age. This could indicate that a healthy 70-year-old man today will live to age 94, and a woman to age 96.

The early part of this book is a journey which with the later chapters brings us as up to date as the deadlines associated with this book permit through to August 2014.

The 2011 Finance Act for me closed yet another era and opened a new one which led to further restrictions in 2013 and no doubt there are more to follow, thoughts of which I have dared to elucidate in CHAPTER 15. The unexpected introduction of 'flexible access' from 2014 is detailed in CHAPTER 4, and how this might lead us to further change is also considered in CHAPTER 15.

This all risks taking us back full circle to a period of over complex restrictions and constraints which I for one thought we had kissed goodbye to with the passing of the Finance Act 2004.

Oh what excitement there was as the consultation documents were published which led to the pensions taxation provisions in Finance Act 2004. The condocs tended to get published just before Christmas – pensions and mince pies – joy of joys!

The radical reforms then introduced as a consequence of the painstaking work of the pensions simplification team headed by Peter Hopkins were (to start with at least) a breath of fresh air. The idea was one of a detailed framework of legislation accompanied by a few statutory instruments and a few hundred pages of HMRC guidance. Any one of us could become an expert with a few hours of devoted reading.

A decade later (no more than a blink of an eye in pensions timeline terms) and we are heading back to where we started, huge complexity, grandfathering between one set of rules and another, and so much legislation that it is probably once again almost impossible for any one person to know the whole picture inside out. The disguised remuneration legislation alone in Finance Act 2011 ran to about 60 pages last time I looked. Finance Act 2004 included a few lines about investments in pension funds and even before implementation in 2006 had been accompanied by 15 pages of legislation on taxable property.

The Finance Act 2004 provisions were about five years in the making – a set of provisions which were supposedly for the long term. But since then short-termism and a lack of proper consultation on proposed legislative change has left many of the original objectives in tatters.

The Government consultation in 2010 for example on proposals for restricting pensions income tax relief was over a period of just 6 weeks during the summer of 2010 when many who would have liked to contribute were away on some sun drenched beach. We can now see how important that was as it clearly showed the way that the wind of change was blowing. Towards reducing the cost to the Exchequer of pensions tax relief, and that wind of change is now at gale force. The (draft) Taxation of Pensions Bill 2014 is in fact a tax raising measure, as you will see from CHAPTER 15. And the period of consultation is a disgraceful four weeks, once again in August.

Although now at risk of accusations of having a rant, there remains within Government, in the view of this author anyway, a dogmatism that the privileges of tax relieved pension contributions and a (nearly) tax free pension fund must always be accompanied by complex restrictions to counter what might otherwise be seen as 'abuse', or of doing things that the 'rules did not intend'. The words 'acting outside of the spirit of the legislation' risk a falling of the red mist!

'Recycling' of the pension commencement lump sum as described in CHAPTER 4 is a classic example. Ever since the tax-free lump sum was invented it was possible in some circumstances to take it and then use it as a means of funding more pension contributions. Suddenly this became a form of 'abuse' and so 'had to be stopped'. At the end of the day a higher pension fund means more income in retirement and a greater tax take on that income for the Exchequer.

The abolition of the so called (but soon to be real) 'effective compulsion to buy an annuity' (see CHAPTER 4) was accompanied by the (soon to be changed) 'price' of a 55% tax charge on death. Yet a tax free transfer of pension rights between one generation and the next could make quite a dent in the pensions time bomb which ticks ever louder with the passing of successive generations. No wonder workplace 'auto enrolment' is seen (through inertia) as the only way of 'guaranteeing' participation in employer provided pension schemes as mentioned in CHAPTER 2 and detailed in CHAPTER 14.

One ray of hope for many associated with the 2010 discussion paper on early access to pension funds (see CHAPTER 15), was dashed very quickly when it became clear that the existence of the discussion paper arose from a Coalition Government agreement to do so, not of any real intent. So as we gradually exit the economic crisis which started in 2008 those with mediocre sized pension funds still face having their houses repossessed where some form of early albeit restricted access would save them from this and the burden on the State it represents.

The purpose of tax privileged pension savings is the provision of an income for life from a minimum age of 55 – nothing else is acceptable, or at least was not acceptable until the Chancellor's 2014 Budget speech.

It was rumoured in the run up to the 2014 Budget speech that some rabbit or other would be plucked from George Osborne's hat that would take everyone by surprise. And so it turned out as towards the end of his speech George Osborne said the following words that forever changed the nature of the UK pensions benefits system:

'We will completely change the tax treatment of defined contribution pensions to bring it into line with the modern world.'

He went on to say:

'Pensioners will have complete freedom to draw down as much or as little of their pension pot as they want, anytime they want. No caps. No drawdown limits. Let me be clear. No one will have to buy an annuity.'

Suddenly the entire pensions world was paying rapt attention. The details are set out in CHAPTER 4.

In the summer of 2011 a report by the Workplace Retirement Income Commission warned that up to 14 million workers will retire with pensions far smaller than those enjoyed by their parents as the 'golden generation' of retirement schemes comes to an end. Over half of those without a pension say that they have no spare money to invest in one, while over one in ten say that they have never thought about it seriously.

So as you use this book, as a means of understanding the UK pensions taxation rules, you may wonder if the price of income tax relief of up to 45% on member pension contributions (more if salary sacrifice is used as set out in CHAPTER 6 – how long before that becomes seen as 'abuse'?) is actually too high a price to pay. The new £40,000 annual allowance as set out in CHAPTER 3 constrains employers as well in providing decent pensions for their better paid employees, and of course time and inflation will whittle away the real value of the reduced annual allowance as there is no chance of it being uplifted for many years to come, indeed the direction of travel is obvious.

Living overseas as I and my family have done since 2005 has opened my eyes to how things work in other places. I had not before appreciated the trade off between tax privileges and constraints. The greater the former the greater are the latter immediately or over time. Perhaps the time has come to restrict income tax relief to basic rate only (or to allow none at all). But in doing that dismantle as much as possible of what once again has become a monstrosity of complexity.

Ironically the expat can escape many of the constraints associated with UK pension funds – as set out in CHAPTER 9. The changes to come in 2015 make for the expat the operation of Double Taxation Treaties of great importance, a subject which in this edition we introduce for the first time in CHAPTER 9.

On 29 September 2014 just as we were going to press the Treasury announced the abolition of the special lump sum death benefit charge with effect from April 2015.

No draft legislation has yet been published so all we can rely on is the announcement which can be found at: www.gov.uk/government/news/chance llor-abolishes-55-tax-on-pension-funds-at-death.

According to the announcement on the death of a DC scheme member before age 75 then whether or not benefit has been taken there will be no tax on the benefit received by the nominated recipient.

In this book I have tried to explain the development of the current pensions tax rules and how they currently work in a way, which I hope, makes an understanding of those rules reasonably accessible. Whether you read the whole thing or just dip into it as you need to I sincerely hope to have achieved this aim.

In the introduction to the third edition I finished off by saying 'above all though I hope there will be some food for thought as to the direction we are taking and how long it might be before the next set of major reforms are introduced'. You will see that we did not have very long to wait.

1

Introduction: the pre 2006 legacy and the post 2014 revolution

[1.1] For many years the United Kingdom has operated a system which encourages private pension provision through a system of tax reliefs. In this book we set out how the pensions taxation system works and how that system fits into the UK system of taxation generally.

The operation of the taxation system associated with pensions was radically reformed in the Finance Act 2004 which effectively disposed of a complex system that had developed since the last occasion of radical reform in 1970. This new basis was introduced with effect from 6 April 2006.

Sadly over the years between the implementation of the Finance Act 2004 reforms and the current time many of the principles associated with those reforms have disappeared. We risk once again ending up with a pensions taxation system that very few people will be able to understand. In fact we are probably there already.

This is the fourth edition of this publication and in the third edition at this point we said 'it seems insane that the ongoing "meddling" necessitates further revisions as the legislation continues to change'. However the changes announced in March 2014 and legislated for in the Finance Act 2014, with more to come in Finance Act 2015 and elsewhere, are best described as revolutionary. These are massive changes and of great importance to all who have pension rights in UK registered pension schemes and to those who offer pensions advice.

The term 'new regime' may itself therefore now need to be redefined. The 2014 Budget is recognised as heralding a game changer in that it leads to the abolition of a principle held for nearly a hundred years, that of the main purpose of a pension fund being for the provision of an income for life. Thus the inclusion of 'post 2014 revolution' in the new title of this chapter. In this chapter we introduce these forthcoming changes which are to be introduced somewhat piecemeal through a new Taxation of Pensions Bill (published in draft on 5 August 2014), a Personal Pension Schemes Bill and of course the 2015 Finance Bill.

The purpose of this book is not to cover every tiniest piece of minutiae associated with the tax regime for pensions which is introduced in this chapter and set out in detail from Chapter 2 onwards. What we hope to achieve is comprehensive coverage of the 'mainstream' which will deal with nearly all situations that practitioners will encounter from day-to-day.

Wherever applicable reference will be made to the relevant legislation, which in the main used to be surprisingly accessible and understandable. As the years since 2004 have passed the 'layer cake' style of development of the legislation has sadly taken us to a position which is no less complex than it was before the Finance Act 2004 reforms.

However firstly and in this chapter we will look at how it is we ended up with where we were before the 2006 reforms came into effect.

Pensions taxation from 1921 to 1970 – occupational pension schemes and their development from Victorian times

[1.2] In nineteenth century Britain the older generation were less visible as the percentage of the population represented by those over age 65 never exceeded 5% of the Victorian population as a whole. Life expectancy did not exceed 65 until well into the twentieth century. Those who reached age 65 were hardly likely to be able to afford to retire in the main. Continuing to work into old age was the norm until prevented by incapacity. Lighter work was often offered albeit at lower wages.

In 1901 life expectancy was 45 years for men and 49 years for women. Scientific advance and improvements in sanitation, hygiene, living conditions and nutrition of the population all contributed to a fall in deaths of infectious disease by the mid- to late twentieth century. For example, tuberculosis killed about 80,000 people in 1880. In 1997 the disease killed only 440.

The First World War, the influenza outbreak soon after, the economic depression in the late 1920s and later the Second World War all had an unfavourable impact on the life expectation of newborn children.

'Great Britain's population has increased 13 million in the past fifty years, yet the annual deaths are 50,000 more than in 1871'. These words were written in 1921. At that time life expectancy from birth for a male was 52. The writer went on to say 'It is estimated that by the end of the present century the average life of a Briton will be six years longer than it is now'. The reality was an increase of more like 26 years.

By 2012 life expectancy from birth had increased to 79 years for men and 83 years for women. Life expectancy is expected to rise further by 2032 to 83 years for men and 87 years for women. This projection is based on current trends. The precise extent of the increase will depend on patterns of disease and population lifestyle.

Whilst in 1981 a man aged 65 could expect to live for another 14 years on average, by 2012 this had risen to 19 years, and is expected to reach 25 years by 2051. For women, the corresponding increase has been even higher.

During Victorian times the percentage of the population that exceeded age 65 was never more than 5%. By 2051 the proportion of people aged 65 and over is expected to increase from the current 16% to 24%.

A few more words about life expectancy: actuaries differentiate between 'period life expectancy' and 'cohort life expectancy'. This is perhaps best illustrated by example. Period life expectancy at age 18 in 2014 is worked out using the projected mortality rate for age 18 in 2014, for age 19 in 2014, for age 20 in 2014, and so on. Cohort life expectancy is worked out using the projected mortality rate for age 18 in 2014, for age 19 in 2015, for age 20 in 2016, and so on.

So at the present time the 'period life expectancy' for a female from birth is 83 years, but the 'cohort life expectancy' is 94 years. By 2035 cohort life expectancy at birth is projected to reach 94.2 years for males and 97.2 years for females, just over 10 years longer than period life expectancy.

The foundations of an occupational pensions system are to be found in the development of the Civil Service pension scheme. For those employed in Government service various pension systems were well developed by the early nineteenth century. An office of employment was sometimes purchased from the previous job holder in return for a lump sum or periodic payments to the previous incumbent. But the Civil Service pension scheme was to become an important model in particular as it offered generous benefit levels and from as early as 1859 in a form that practitioners will recognise today. From that date the scheme offered on a non-contributory basis a pension from age 60 or later of one sixtieth of final pay for each year of service with a maximum of 40 years to count. This generous level of provision became the objective for other public sector employees and, as will be familiar, eventually spilled over into the private sector forming the origins of the framework of a maximum permitted level of benefits from an occupational pension scheme that survived until 2006.

In Victorian times private sector employer pension schemes tended to operate on an 'ex gratia' basis. But as the nineteenth century progressed there was an acceptance by some employers (in particular the Railways) and some financial institutions that it was more appropriate to put in place schemes offering set levels of benefit. These were generally achieved by a form of 'book reserve' system where funding was set aside on the employer's balance sheet. However the schemes established by the Railways were generally based upon funds that were set aside, separate from the employer and protected in the event of the employer's bankruptcy. Some schemes allowed for a part of the member's pension to be exchanged for a lump sum.

By the late nineteenth century most of the railway companies had put in place a pension scheme of one form or another for their management and clerical staff. A typical scheme would require the member to pay in perhaps 2.5% of his pay with a matching contribution from the employer. The fund would then be invested either on deposit with the employer or into fixed interest securities with the employer guaranteeing a rate of interest on the fund. The emerging pension was based on service, typically around 25% of average pay after ten years, and two-thirds after 45 years. Compulsory membership was usual.

In this early period there also existed 'money purchase schemes', where the eventual pension available depended on the contributions made by employer and employee plus interest earned.

In this period schemes were also being introduced by banks and insurance companies. However from the limited data available the membership of formal pension schemes in the private and public sector was in the region of just 5% of the workforce at that time.

One of the first known trust-based schemes was set up by Colemans (the Norwich-based mustard manufacturer) in 1900. It became accepted that the use of a pension trust was a low cost and effective vehicle for establishing a pension scheme. Not all adopted this vehicle but tax reforms in 1921 resulted in their becoming the de facto method of governance.

Until then most pension funds paid income tax on at least a part of their investment income but there was no consistency of treatment between different tax offices around the country. Lobbying Government for uniformity began in 1917 through an 11 strong Conference of Superannuation Funds. By 1919 membership had grown to 55 Superannuation Funds representing employers across industry and commerce. The pressure exerted led to the 'grandfather' of modern day pensions legislation, the 1921 Finance Act.

A quick look at the 1921 Finance Act reveals statements in the legislation that even now will seem remarkably familiar. Section 21 of the 1921 Finance Act introduces the:

> 'exemption of superannuation funds from income tax in respect of income derived from investments or deposits of the superannuation funds.'

In addition the Act provided that:

> 'any sum paid by the employer or employed person by way of contribution towards the superannuation fund shall . . . be deducted as an expense incurred in the year in which the sum is paid.'

The 1921 Finance Act introduced the concept of '*ordinary annual contributions*' and a spreading of tax relief where any contribution was not regarded as an ordinary annual contribution.

To be a superannuation fund it was necessary that the scheme be:

> 'established under irrevocable trusts in connection with some trade or undertaking carried on in the United Kingdom'.

and that

> 'the fund has for its sole purpose the provision of annuities for persons employed in the trade or undertaking either on retirement at a specified age or on becoming incapacitated at some earlier age.'

A superannuation fund (clearly the old form of words for an occupational pension scheme) was subject to approval by the Inland Revenue Commissioners.

The wordings contained in the 1921 Finance Act are repeated more or less word for word in the 1952 Income Tax Act in section 379 onwards, and again in the 1970 Income and Corporation Taxes Act in section 208 onwards.

The members of the Conference of Superannuation Funds were encouraged by the success of their lobbying and became constituted in the form of the Association of Superannuation and Pension Funds in 1923. Although self-administered pension trusts flourished an increasing number of employers took advantage of the burgeoning interest of life insurance companies in the pensions industry. Indeed for small- to medium-sized employers the specialist record keeping and investment services of a life office were felt essential. By 1934 five major UK life offices involved in the group pensions market had schemes under their management covering around 120,000 members, this growing to over 2.25 million members by 1956.

The tax efficiency of pension savings was becoming ever more apparent. The standard rate of income tax (what we would now refer to as the basic rate) was as high as 50% during the Second World War with company taxation on the margin being as high as 100%. Those employed in the insurance industry selling group pension contracts were readily able to sell their wares to employers, in particular those who were paying '100% excess profits tax', as relief on contributions to a pension scheme essentially reduced the net cost to zero.

So-called 'top hat' schemes which offered generous pension benefits for senior employees, either on a standalone basis or as a supplementary arrangement over and above the pension scheme generally operated, also became popular. Frequently these were funded by employer contributions available as a consequence of a salary reduction or foregoing a salary increase (what we would today refer to as salary sacrifice). The contributions, which would be fully tax allowable on the employer, then being used perhaps to purchase an endowment policy designed to provide a tax-free lump sum on retirement.

The tax incentives were undoubtedly effective as by 1956, according to the Government Actuary, the proportion of workers in occupational schemes was 33%, most of the growth in participation having occurred since the end of the war. By 1956–57 the annual cost to the Exchequer of pensions tax relief had reached £120 million.

Over the years as the cost of pensions tax relief increased there were the beginnings of restrictions. One of these will sound familiar as it was maintained until 2006. During the 1940s the Inland Revenue began to restrict the tax relief available on employee contributions to 15% of remuneration. In the late 1940s there came pressure for legislation to curb what was seen as abuses of the tax reliefs available in particular in relation to 'top hat' schemes for higher paid employees. Lump sums secured from such arrangements were regarded as capital when paid out and escaped tax altogether. The 1947 Finance Act introduced a provision limiting the lump sum to 25% of the total value of pension rights. Again this will sound familiar resonating with the pensions tax legislation of today.

However the 1947 Finance Act has been described as 'no more than a makeshift patchwork, covering a fundamentally rotten edifice of conflicting tax privileges for different types of pension schemes'. The system as it had by then developed was full of anomalies with different rules operational between insured pension schemes (excepting those written as trusts), and schemes subject to the 1921 Finance Act provisions.

In 1948 a committee was formed with representatives of four different trade bodies proposing pensions tax simplification. The proposals were that all reasonable contributions to pension schemes should be tax deductible and benefits on receipt should be subject to taxation. It took until 1950 however for Government to appoint a committee which took a further four years to report in the form of the 1954 Millard Tucker report. Sadly the industry-based wish for simplification was ignored with proposals limited to a little standardisation across the different types of scheme then available.

The committee proposals were only partially implemented in 1956 but with a concession to the self-employed with the introduction of retirement annuity policies. However even that concession was very limited with contributions at the time restricted to just 10% of earnings or £750 a year if less and with no tax-free lump sum provision.

An unintended consequence arose from the 1947 Act introduction of a lump sum representing up to 25% of the value of total benefits. This led to hybrid schemes developing which benefited from the tax privileges introduced in the 1921 Act, whilst another section of the scheme allowed for a lump sum up to the maximum permitted. This was highly effective even though the fund build-up of the element associated with the lump sum was not free from tax.

By 1967 occupational pension participation had reached 53% of the workforce. By the 1960s, therefore, occupational pensions had moved from a 'niche' position to a central role in Britain's system of pension provision.

As stated previously, the last occasion of major pensions taxation reform prior to Finance Act 2004 was in 1970. The 1970 Income and Corporation Taxes Act consolidated previous legislation with its provisions associated with pensions being phased out over the following 10 years. The earlier (pre 1970) provisions (consolidated in the 1952 Income and Corporation Taxes Act) became known as the 'old code'.

The 'new code' was introduced by the Finance Act 1970, and occupational pension schemes in force in 1970 were given 10 years to bring their rules into line with the 'new' legislation. This process of 'phasing in' is in stark contrast to what happened on 6 April 2006 when the Finance Act 2004 reforms were implemented and the entire pensions taxation landscape changed overnight.

The 1970 reforms weren't really about reducing complexity but more about producing a more modern system. In fact if you were to look at the legislation associated with pensions taxation as it existed before 1970 not a great deal had changed since 1921 so far as it related to the taxation rules associated with occupational pension schemes.

For the first time the 1970 Finance Act provisions were retrospective in that all new schemes had to conform by 1973 and all old schemes had to comply by 1980. These changes delivered a relatively uniform set of tax rules that operated across different types of pension schemes. The overall regime was the most generous seen to date. This generosity of tax privileges encouraged a huge growth in pension schemes which eventually accounted for around a third of the entire personal sector savings in the UK economy.

The introduction of pensions for the self-employed and those not eligible to join occupational pension schemes

[1.3] Section 226 of the 1970 Income and Corporation Taxes Act reminds us of the introduction of retirement annuity policies – originally introduced in the 1956 Finance Act which had implemented the main recommendations of the 1954 Millard Tucker No. 2 Committee on the introduction of tax efficient pension arrangements for the self-employed.

Retirement annuities were tax relieved pension arrangements available only from insurance companies (and thus often referred to as retirement annuity contracts or RACs) available to the self-employed and those who were not eligible to join superannuation schemes. These arrangements allowed the retirement annuity policy holder to pay tax relieved pension contributions of (at that time) up to 15% of 'net relevant earnings'.

Those eligible for retirement annuities included shareholding directors of director-controlled companies who indirectly or directly owned or controlled 5% or more of the shares. This was important as company directors falling into this category were not allowed to participate in an occupational pension schemes – not until 1973 anyway.

Retirement annuities and their successor, personal pensions, are considered later in this chapter.

1970 – The operation of two tax regimes

[1.4] By 1970 therefore, we had a set of rules associated with superannuation schemes (which we will from now on refer to as occupational pension schemes), and a further set of rules associated with retirement annuities.

But even in the period up to 1970 it was necessary to use some fairly complex structures to maximise the tax benefits associated with pension arrangements because of the interaction between the legislation associated with pension benefits and that associated with tax-free lump sums.

So occupational schemes established under the 1952 legislation (which provided for pensions and tax-free lump sums) were approved under sections 379 (pensions) and 388 (lump sum), the provisions of which were repeated in the 1970 Income and Corporation Taxes Act under sections 208 (pensions) and 222 (lump sum). More background to the evolution of the concept of the 'tax-free lump sum' and how the legislation dealt with it is set out later in this chapter.

Thus the 1970 Finance Act introduced the 'new code of approval'. The provisions contained in the 1970 Income and Corporation Taxes Act became known as the 'old code of approval'. Schemes generally had to conform to the new code provisions by 1980.

Occupational pensions – from 1980

[1.5] From 1980 onwards the 'new code' was all that existed so far as occupational schemes were concerned, and so the coexistence of these provisions with the retirement annuity legislation meant that now there were two pensions taxation regimes.

The occupational pension regime established in 1970 was based upon the ability of employers to provide a pension which was not allowed to exceed two thirds of final pay. The occupational scheme design principle and the accompanying tax approval based upon the principle of '60ths of final pay' astonishingly goes back to 1859 when earlier Civil Service pension schemes were replaced with a single one which provided for a pension of $\frac{1}{60}$ of final pay for each year of service with a maximum 40 years to count and a pension age of 60.

Although under the 'new code' the maximum two thirds of final pay pension could normally accrue over a period of 40 years (based upon the principle of accruing a benefit of $\frac{1}{60}$ of final pay for each year of service with the employer – generally referred to as $\frac{N}{60}$ where 'N' referred to the number of years of continuous service), a process of what was referred to as 'accelerated accrual' allowed the maximum permitted pension benefit to be achieved over just 10 years of employment.

Part of the pension earned in this way could be commuted (that is exchanged) for a tax-free lump sum of up to 1.5 times final earnings. The normal accrual of the lump sum was at the rate of $\frac{3}{80}$ of final pay in respect of each year of scheme membership ($\frac{3N}{80}$ where 'N' referred to the number of years of continuous service) but an 'accelerated accrual' basis relating to the lump sum allowed the maximum amount to be accumulated over just 20 years.

The occupational pension fund itself was exempt from taxation on its income and capital gains, and schemes were generally subject to the discretionary approval of the Inland Revenue. Schemes that provided for pension provision based on no more than the '$\frac{N}{60}$' principle (with associated dependants' benefits again not exceeding certain limits, and lump sum death benefits not exceeding twice salary at the date of death) were subject to 'mandatory approval' as the Inland Revenue were bound to approve such a scheme.

Where benefits provided were greater than those associated with 'mandatory approval' then approval of the scheme was at the discretion of the Inland Revenue. Approval was granted by the superannuation funds office (SFO) which was later renamed the pension schemes office (PSO).

In order to give practitioners, employers and scheme members alike guidance as to how the Inland Revenue would exercise their discretionary powers there was published the so-called 'practice notes' under reference IR12. These practice notes were updated periodically and supplemented by updates issued periodically by the SFO and later the PSO.

Schemes approved under the 1970 Finance Act became known as 'exempt approved schemes'. The term 'exempt' arising not because of exemption of the fund from taxation, but because of an exemption from tax as a benefit in kind on employer contributions to such schemes in the hands of the member.

The essence of the UK pensions regime is one where contributions are tax relieved and where employer contributions are not taxable in the hands of the member as a benefit in kind, where the fund is allowed to grow (more or less) free from taxation, and where the benefits (with the exception of that 'much loved anomaly' the tax-free lump sum) are taxed. This is known as an 'EET' taxation system (see CHAPTER 2) – and has operated in that way since 1921 as outlined in 1.2.

Pension planning for 'controlling directors'

[1.6] With effect from April 1973 controlling directors were allowed to join occupational pension schemes. Restrictions were later introduced in terms of how benefits had to be calculated for directors who controlled directly or indirectly 20% or more of the share capital of a director controlled company.

There were further developments as time progressed. These were introduced often as a response to perceived 'abuse', in particular following the ability of controlling directors to become members of occupational pension schemes. As controlling directors by definition had a large measure of control over their remuneration, they were able to manipulate their pattern of remuneration for the purposes of the maximum benefit rules – in particular those associated with tax-free lump sums.

Controlling directors were defined as directors of director controlled companies where the director

'either on his own or with one or more associates, [was] the beneficial owner of, or able, directly or through the medium of other companies or by any other indirect means, to control 20 per cent. or over of the ordinary share capital of the company.'

In relation to the maximum benefit rules, the definition of final remuneration for controlling directors became

'the average of any three or more years consecutive earnings ending not more than ten years before the date of which benefits were taken.'

The opening up of occupational scheme membership for controlling directors from 1973 led directly to the introduction of self-administered schemes for one or more controlling directors. These schemes allowed for 'self investment' back into the sponsoring employer and other obvious conflicts of interest between the scheme member as an individual and his capacity as a controlling director of the sponsoring employer. Additional controls were therefore introduced from 1976 that were particularly aimed at what became known as 'small self-administered schemes' (SSAS or SSAPS), containing up to 11 members. These are described in CHAPTER 6.

The evolution of the 'tax-free lump sum'

[1.7] Leslie Hannah (Inventing Retirement: The Development of Occupational Pensions in Britain – 1986) described the evolution of the tax-free lump sum of 25% of the pension fund in the following words:

'The chapter of accidents which led in absurd progression to this situation, [the tax-free lump sum] which was initially desired by no one, began in the early years of [the 20th] century' (Hannah, 1986: page 115).

Hannah notes that at the turn of the 20th century, occupational pension schemes varied widely as to whether they paid benefit as a pension, as a lump sum, or as an annuity. There were arguments that suggested a lump sum would ease the progression from working to retirement, but against this was the concern that a lump sum would be frittered away.

The Radley Commission on the Civil Service said in 1888:

'The payment . . . of a lump sum is open to the obvious objection that in the event of improvidence or misfortune in the use of it, the retired public servant may be reduced to circumstances which might lead to his being an applicant for public or private charity.'

Under the 1921 Finance Act tax-exempt occupational pension schemes were not allowed to provide lump sums by the Inland Revenue. But lump sums could be paid by the pension scheme out of non-tax exempt funds. So a structure evolved of split schemes, a tax-exempt scheme which provided for the pension benefit, and a non-tax-exempt scheme which provided for the lump sum. But as to the tax status of the lump sum (as in fact with much more of the evolution of occupational pension limits than we have alluded to above), we have to turn to what happened with the Civil Service pension scheme which began its modern day life in 1859.

The Civil Service in 1909 had negotiated a tax-free lump sum, to ensure comparability with widows' pension rights in the railways pension schemes, and in the course of those negotiations the tax-free lump sum was extended as a provision available to those who survived to retirement age. The Inland Revenue, whose workforce would of course benefit, were asked to agree to this scheme, which they (perhaps not surprisingly) did. And so the basis on which the 'tax-free lump sum' evolved was as a consequence of this deal.

The 1947 Finance Act attempted to clamp down on the proliferation of occupational pension schemes that had attempted to get round the 1921 Act, (by providing a lump sum from non tax exempt funds) and abolished all tax-free lump sums except those that were 'reasonable'. The definition of 'reasonable' adopted by those who drafted this legislation was the same level of benefits that they themselves enjoyed.

The 1956 Finance Act, which introduced retirement annuities, explicitly did not allow for tax-free lump sums, but pressure from private sector schemes to mimic the 'reasonableness' of the Civil Service scheme meant that from 1970 all pension schemes were explicitly permitted to pay tax-free lump sums from untaxed funds. By 1971 one third of private sector schemes paid a lump sum as part of the pension scheme entitlement. This proportion had risen to more than 90% by 1979.

Attempts to remove the tax-free treatment of the lump sum in the 1980s were derailed by what the then Chancellor of the Exchequer (Nigel Lawson) later described as *'the most astonishing lobbying campaign of my political career'* and, in the face of such strong political opposition, UK pension policy has since had to concentrate on limiting the anomaly of the tax-free lump sum to 25% rather than the more obvious policy of abolishing it altogether.

The run up to April 2006

[1.8] Throughout this earlier period and up to April 2006 the relationship between scheme operators, their advisers, and the Inland Revenue was generally one where the Inland Revenue were regarded as being helpful unless it was blatantly obvious that the rules were being wilfully abused. The ultimate sanction whereby the Inland Revenue could withdraw pension scheme approval with the associated and dire taxation consequences was only ever used in the most extreme of cases.

If the trustees of a particular scheme had misbehaved in some way it was usually possible to come to an agreed arrangement with the Inland Revenue with or without a trip to their offices in Nottingham. It was the discretionary basis of scheme approval by the Inland Revenue that made it possible to 'do a deal', and so the withdrawal of the approval of a pension scheme was almost unheard of.

How the UK ended up with eight pensions taxation regimes

[1.9] So far as occupational schemes were concerned the arrangements set out above continued with an ongoing process of evolution right up until 6 April 2006. The problem was that by that time we no longer had two taxation regimes associated with UK pensions – there were eight.

The purpose of the consultation process that led up to the implementation of the Finance Act 2004 was originally one of 'pensions simplification'. All the same one rarely uses that term these days in polite company.

However before outlining the pensions taxation reforms introduced from April 2006 we should consider how on earth it was that we ended up with eight taxation regimes associated with pensions by the year 2000, when in the mid-1980s there were only two. Much is owed in this regard to attempts to limit the tax-free lump sum.

As we have seen, private sector pension schemes generally gave a pension at retirement with the option to commute it for a lump sum within certain limits. The benefits of most pension scheme members were related to a fraction of final remuneration dependent on their length of service with associated benefits for a surviving spouse or other dependant following death either before or after retirement.

Schemes which adopt this basis are known as final salary or defined benefit schemes. The most common accrual rate found in scheme rules is $1/60$ of final remuneration for each year of service up to a maximum of 40. This scale of benefit is sometimes referred to as 'straight 60ths' or '$N/60$' where N is the number of years' pensionable service with the employer providing the benefit. And as we have seen it was possible through 'accelerated accrual' to be provided with the maximum permitted pension of two thirds of final pay after just 10 years' service.

By the mid-1980s money purchase or defined contribution schemes were already becoming an increasingly popular option so that employers could avoid the long-term obligations and liabilities associated with operating a final salary scheme. Exactly the same limits, with regard to the maximum permitted benefits associated with pension provision to be consistent with discretionary approval by the Inland Revenue, applied to defined contribution schemes in the same way as they applied to final salary schemes.

Small self-administered schemes for company directors had started developing in the 1970s with additional controls from 1976. Given that company pension contributions were allowed as a business expense for taxation purposes, it should come as no great surprise that schemes were often set up for the directors of director controlled businesses which, because of the generous earnings related benefits that could be provided at retirement, were able to receive large contributions. Contributions of in excess of 10 times a director's pay (bearing in mind that this was also subject to personal control in effect) were far from uncommon.

As it was possible to fund for the maximum permitted tax-free lump sum of up to 1.5 times final remuneration as a benefit that could be provided without any pension at all and after just 20 years' continuous service the scope for what was seen as manipulation of the tax rules in order to avoid high levels of personal and corporate taxation was something that was seen to merit action by government.

Thus Finance (No 2) Act 1987 introduced the first major tax reforms for pensions since 1970 – and introduced the third and fourth tax regimes.

The major changes were:

(1)   New style personal pensions from 1988 to eventually replace retirement annuity contracts;

(2)   Arrangements for members of occupational pension schemes to have the right to pay free-standing additional voluntary contributions to a separate pension plan of their choice (a FSAVCS);

(3)   The scope for manipulating pensions tax relief, particularly by very high earners, was curbed.

The latter was achieved by:

• Tightening up the definition of final pay to prevent unacceptable inflation of the figure on which benefits were based due to indexation in line with the retail prices index.

• Placing a limit of £150,000 on the tax-free lump sum available from retirement annuity policies.

• Requiring the maximum permitted pension from an occupational pension scheme to accrue over a longer period than previously (20 years instead of 10).

• An additional restriction so that the accelerated accrual of the permitted lump sum benefit was possible only to the same extent that pension benefits were uplifted. This was a major change in that it now meant the maximum permitted lump sum of 1.5 times final pay could only be achieved if firstly the maximum permitted pension of $^2/_3$ of final pay was able to be provided.

- These changes however only applied in respect of new pension schemes set up from 17 March 1987 (this was the date of the 1987 Budget), and to new members of existing pension schemes with effect from the same date. Some practitioners remembered this date as it happened to be St Patrick's Day.

So Finance (No 2) Act 1987 introduced a further two tax regimes for pensions – that associated with what was then referred to the 'post 1987' basis for occupational pension schemes, and that associated with personal pensions (see below), which were introduced from July 1988.

Unfortunately the mechanism that was adopted in order to restrict the tax-free lump sum in relation to occupational pension schemes was over complex and almost impossible to express in a way that any pension scheme member would be able to understand.

This was corrected in the 1989 Finance Act. But at the same time the opportunity was taken to introduce further measures that would further constrain permitted pension benefits, and so as a consequence restricted the ability of individuals and their employers to obtain tax relief on pension contributions.

The key provisions of the 1989 Finance Act were:

- The statutory requirement for the approval of occupational pension schemes that any other schemes of the employer must also be approved was repealed. This allowed the introduction of non-approved 'top up' schemes which quickly became known as 'funded unapproved retirement benefit schemes' (FURBS), and 'unfunded unapproved retirement benefit schemes' (UURBS).
- The introduction of a statutory limit on the maximum earnings (starting at £60,000 but indexed in line with prices) that could count for pension purposes through an approved scheme (this became known as the 'earnings cap').
- The introduction of a revised and simplified maximum basis for the limit on the accelerated accrual of lump sum retirement benefits. This amounted to 2.25 times the initial pension payable. This calculation basis arose from the fact that the maximum permitted pension was $^2/_3$ of final pay and of course 2.25 times this figure equals 1.5 times final pay.

The revised limits (and the earnings cap) only applied to new schemes set up after 13 March 1989 (budget day of that year) and to new members of existing schemes who joined after 31 May 1989.

So if a pension scheme was set up before 14 March 1989 and the member joined the scheme between 17 March 1987 and 31 May 1989, the member was then said to belong to the '1987-1989 regime'.

The earnings cap was, until its abolition in 2006, increased in line with the index of retail prices, with the resultant figure rounded up to the next £600 with the relevant figures as shown in Table 1.

Table 1 The Earnings cap 1989–2006

1989–90	£60,000	1998–99	£87,600
1990–91	£64,800	1999–2000	£90,600
1991–92	£71,400	2000–01	£91,800
1992–93	£75,000	2001–02	£95,400
1993–94	£75,000	2002–03	£97,200
1994–95	£76,800	2004–05	£99,000
1995–96	£78,600	2005–06	£102,000
1996–97	£82,200	2005–06	£105,600
1997–98	£84,000		

The Finance Act 1989 therefore had the effect of adding a further four pensions tax regimes which by now meant that the regimes comprised:

(1)   Retirement annuities (no new RACs were possible after 30 June 1988, although contributions into existing arrangements were allowed to continue).
(2)   Personal pensions – introduced 1 July 1988 (originally intended to be from 6 April 1988 but the legislation simply was not ready in time).
(3)   Occupational pensions subject to the 'pre-1987' provisions.
(4)   Occupational pensions subject to the provisions that were in place between 1987 and 1989.
(5)   Occupational pensions subject to the 'post-1989' provisions.
(6)   FURBS.
(7)   UURBS.
(8)   Regimes within the old code rules that could still apply to people who joined a scheme before 1970.

Retirement annuities and personal pensions

[1.10] To complete this historical review it is necessary to also make a mention of retirement annuities and their successor, personal pensions. Retirement annuity policies (RAPs) were the predecessors of personal pension plans. RAPs were subject to contribution limits set as an age-related percentage of earnings (the earnings that counted for this purpose were known as 'net relevant earnings', which broadly equated to earned income). From time to time the contribution limits associated with retirement annuity policies increased.

The Millard Tucker report of the 1950s made recommendations regarding the retirement arrangements for the self-employed. It was recommended that the self-employed should enjoy adequate relief under the taxation system so as to enable them to make proper provision for their old age. This led to the introduction of retirement annuity policies (RAPs) in 1956 through sections 22 and 23 of the Finance Act 1956. The original legislation set a contribution limit for tax relief purposes at £750 or 10% of net relevant earnings (with higher limits for those born before 1916). The legislation was re-enacted in 1970 (section 226 of the Income and Corporation Taxes Act 1970).

Section 20 of and Schedule 2 to Finance Act 1971 introduced cash commutation, the option to take part of the pension as a tax-free cash lump sum, and increased the maximum amount of tax relievable contributions from £750 or 10% of net relevant earnings, to £1,500 or 15% of net relevant earnings.

This legislation also enabled provision to be made, within the total allowable contributions, for a widow's pension or lump sum to be paid in the event of the policyholder's death before age 75 (originally age 70). This led to the development of so-called Section 226A insurance policies as Finance Act 1971 introduced Section 226A into the 1970 legislation. The limit of premiums payable for these policies was 5% of net relevant earnings.

The 15% of net relevant earnings limit remained in force with the overall maximum contributions increased to £2,250 in the Finance Act 1976, and to £3,000 in the Finance Act 1977. In the Finance Act 1980 the overriding monetary limit of £3,000 was abolished and the maximum contribution level was increased to 17.5% of net relevant earnings. Throughout there were higher limits for those at older ages.

'Net relevant earnings' (originally defined in section 227 of ICTA 1970) were an individual's relevant earnings (which left out of account any earned income which carried pension rights) less certain deductions. Finance Act 1980 amended the definition of net relevant earnings and it was then no longer necessary to deduct personal mortgage interest from relevant earnings when calculating net relevant earnings.

No new RAPs could be started after 30 June 1988, as personal pensions were introduced from the following day. Most existing RAPs continued to accept additional premiums, and many continue to exist to this day.

The accumulated fund from these arrangements had to be used to provide an annuity from a life office sometime between age 60 and 75. Part of the fund could be used to provide a tax-free lump sum. The extent of the permitted lump sum was based upon a formula whereby the lump sum could be up to three times the pension that remained after the lump sum had been taken. Because of the inclusion of guaranteed annuity rates in retirement annuity policies, in particular those issued up to the early 1980s, right up to the implementation of the Finance Act 2004 provisions some retirement annuity policies were able to pay out lump sums of well over 30% of the policy value.

As we have seen over the period from 1970 the permitted contributions to RAPs (expressed as a percentage of net relevant earnings in various age bands), increased from time to time.

There were additional provisions known as 'carry back' and 'carry forward'. Carry back enabled an individual to elect that the contributions paid in any tax year were treated for the purposes of tax relief as having been paid in the previous tax year. Carry forward enabled unused tax relief that had been available in up to six previous tax years to be used up. By combining 'carry back' and 'carry forward' it was possible to take advantage of income tax relief that had been available over up to seven previous tax years.

The new personal pension regime introduced from 1 July 1988 built on the RAP provisions and introduced a degree of much needed simplification. Legislation governing the approval and tax treatment of personal pension schemes is to be found in the Income and Corporation Taxes Act 1988 (ICTA 1988), Chapter IV, Part XIV and was repealed by Finance Act 2004.

Personal pensions, like their RAP predecessor, allowed the pension fund to accumulate free from capital gains tax and income tax on most forms of income received by the fund. However the range of providers able to operate personal pension schemes was (and is) much wider than that associated with retirement annuity policies. The latter were only able to be provided by life insurance companies, whereas personal pension schemes could be operated by life offices, banks, building societies and unit trust companies and the like.

A key benefit retained by those who had retirement annuity policies was that these policies remained unaffected by the later introduction of the earnings cap in Finance Act 1989. But RAPs were subject to the £150,000 limit for lump sum benefits introduced in 1987. This limit did not apply to personal pensions. And the earnings cap did not apply to RAP contributions – it did however apply to personal pensions.

There also remained a complex interaction of how the carry forward and carry back rules worked for those who had both retirement annuity policies and personal pension arrangements. Personal pensions (PPs) were therefore also designed, like their predecessor, as a pension savings vehicle for the self-employed and employees who were not members of occupational pension schemes.

A variant on the personal pension, (Stakeholder personal pensions) became available from 6 April 2001. The 1998 Pensions Green Paper, 'A new contract for welfare: Partnership in Pensions', set in train the development of stakeholder personal pensions. What started life as a pension arrangement for the low paid with a maximum contribution of £3,600 per year became a personal pension variant for medium and high earners. Stakeholder personal pensions shared the same tax regime as non-stakeholder personal pensions.

Stakeholder personal pensions were the consequence of a Government initiative to reduce the management costs associated with private pension provision. Stakeholder schemes were subject to a cap on the permitted charges but in every other respect behaved like personal pensions generally.

However the stakeholder version of personal pensions is subject to an additional layer of Department of Work and Pensions (DWP) Regulations (The Stakeholder Pension Schemes Regulations 2000, SI 200/1403, as amended), covering such areas as charges and employer access. The introduction of 'auto enrolment' into workplace pensions (see CHAPTER 14), removes the necessity for employers with five or more employees to designate and offer access to a Stakeholder personal pension scheme.

Personal pensions continue to exist today, and now fall into the post-Finance Act 2004 framework of registered pension schemes.

1989 saw the introduction of self invested personal pensions (SIPPS) enabling the SIPP member to have a much wider degree of investment control and not merely be limited to the funds offered by a typical life company provider.

Tax relief and personal pensions

[1.11] Member contributions to personal pensions are paid net of basic rate tax, which is reclaimed by the personal pension provider. Any higher rate income tax relief is claimed through the member's self-assessment tax return. Employers are also allowed to make personal pension contributions, which subject to the normal rules on deductions, will be allowable as a business expense. Retirement annuity contributions are generally paid gross with tax relief given through the self-assessment return. Retirement annuity policies could not accept employer contributions.

Personal pensions offered contracting out of the State Second Pension (S2P). Previously they were used to contract out of the S2P predecessor known as the State Earnings Related Pension Scheme (SERPS). This meant that in return for sacrificing the additional component of state pension provision it was possible for personal pensions to receive a rebate of the member's national insurance contributions. RAPs cannot be used for contracting out.

Significant tax incentives were offered to encourage contracting out through personal pensions as a means of partially privatising state pension provision. The name given to personal pensions that were capable of being used for contracting out is 'appropriate personal pensions'. These provide 'protected rights', the name given to the rights derived from the national insurance contribution (NIC) rebates which are invested in them.

The evolution of personal pensions and retirement annuities until April 2006

[1.12] Finance Act 2000 greatly widened the eligibility rules for personal pensions, but left those for RAPs unchanged. The following rules applied to personal pensions from 6 April 2001:

Individuals who were not members of an occupational scheme were eligible to join a personal pension scheme provided they were:

* Aged less than 75, and:
* Either resident and ordinarily resident in the UK at some time in the year the contribution was made, or
* A Crown servant or the spouse of a Crown servant.

The effect of this wider eligibility meant that a person who was not a member of an occupational scheme could become a member of a personal pension scheme if they had non-pensionable employed earnings, self-employed earnings or no earnings whatsoever. Contributions of up to the 'earnings threshold' (£3,600 gross) could be paid to the personal pension of anyone who satisfied the eligibility criteria, regardless of their level of earnings. Personal pensions could therefore be arranged for minor children or non-working spouses.

From April 2001 members of occupational schemes (but excluding controlling directors) could also become members of personal pension schemes with respect to the same employment (a process known as 'concurrency') in the following circumstances:

- If the individual was either resident and ordinarily resident in the UK, or was overseas as a Crown Servant or as the spouse of a Crown Servant,
- If the individual was not, and had not been a controlling director of any company at any time in the tax year or in any of the five tax years preceding it, and
- The individual had P60 remuneration not exceeding the remuneration limit (£30,000 in 2001–02 to 2005–06) for the year of contribution.

There were four other circumstances in which an occupational scheme member was eligible to become a member of a personal pension scheme:

(i)   The occupational pension scheme offered only death-in-service benefits, or

(ii) The occupational scheme was unapproved, or

(iii) The personal pension scheme was used solely for the purpose of contracting out of S2P (or, prior to 2001–02, SERPs). These arrangements were commonly known as 'rebate only personal pensions'.

(iv) The personal pension was used solely to receive transfer payments, i.e. no contributions were made.

Maximum contributions to personal pensions were a percentage of net relevant earnings (NRE), as shown in Table 2 for the final year of operating these limits in 2005–06.

Table 2: Maximum contributions as a % of NRE

Age on 6 April in tax year	Maximum percentage of NRE %	Maximum contribution in 2005–06* £
35 or less	17.5	18,480
36–45	20.0	21,120
46–50	25.0	26,400
51–55	30.0	31,680
56–60	35.0	36,960
61–74	40.0	42,240

* Based on an earnings cap of £105,600 in 2005–06

For personal pensions started before 6 April 2001, the maximum contribution to provide life cover through a term assurance policy was 5% of net relevant earnings, in line with the earlier provisions associated with retirement annuity policies.

For personal pensions that began on or after 6 April 2001, the maximum contribution in any tax year that could be used to provide life insurance cover through a term assurance policy was changed to 10% of the contributions made towards retirement benefits. The earnings cap applied and the term assurance contribution again counted towards the overall contribution limit.

The purpose of this change was to put an end (so far as future arrangements were concerned) to the concept of people using the benefit of pensions tax relief to acquire life insurance protection without there being any form of pension contribution destined to provide for retirement benefits.

An employer was able to pay contributions to an employee's personal pension:

- In respect of the employee's net relevant earnings regardless of whether the employer provided those earnings.
- Where the employee was a member of the employer's occupational scheme and was also eligible to be a member of a personal pension scheme under the concurrency rules under which the employer could also contribute.

Where an employer did pay such contributions the employee was not liable to tax on the benefit of the contributions paid to the personal pension by the employer and National Insurance contributions were not charged on the pension contributions.

However employer contributions could not be 'carried back' to the previous tax year and employee and employer contributions were aggregated when assessing whether the maximum contribution limits had been breached. Employer contributions were paid gross.

Personal pensions and retirement annuities compared

[1.13] The percentage of earnings that could be paid into RAPs above age 35 was lower than the maximum personal pension contributions, as Table 3 shows:

Table 3: Maximum contributions to retirement annuities

Age on 6 April in tax year	Maximum percentage of NRE	Maximum contribution greater than personal pension for earnings over
	%	£
35 or less	17.5	105,600
36–45	17.5	120,686
46–50	17.5	150,857
51–55	20.0	158,400
56–60	22.5	164,267
61–74	27.5	153,600

There were various other differences between personal pensions and retirement annuities which included:

- Wider eligibility rules introduced for personal pensions from 6 April 2001 did not apply to RAPs.
- The earnings threshold (see above) of £3,600 did not apply to RAPs.

- Contributions to a RAPs were also based on net relevant earnings, which were defined slightly differently from those for personal pensions.
- The earnings cap did not apply to RAP contributions.
- Tax relief on RAP contributions was not available by deduction at source. An individual could therefore receive the benefit of basic rate tax relief more rapidly with a personal pension than a RAP.
- An employer could not make contributions to a RAP.
- A RAP could not be used for contracting out of the State Second Pension (S2P) previously SERPS.
- A RAP could only take transfers in from other RAPs, not from personal pensions.
- Up until the end of the 2005–06 tax year the tax-free lump sum available at maturity from a RAP was often less than the maximum 25% of the fund that could be taken from a personal pension. The exception was if the RAP policy contained guaranteed annuity rates of greater than 11.11%.
- The tax-free cash sum was limited to £150,000 per policy for RAPs taken out after 16 March 1987.
- Pension benefits from a RAP could normally only start to be taken from the age of 60.
- RAPs could not provide pension benefits without the purchase of an annuity, unless a transfer was first made to a personal pension.

For individuals who had a retirement annuity policy already in existence this meant that by July 2008 there was a highly complex potential interaction of PP and RAP contributions.

For example where RAP and personal pension contributions were made in the same year, they were added together to determine the maximum possible contribution, but the personal pension limits applied for any year in which personal pension contributions were made.

Thus even a very small contribution to a personal pension in respect of a particular tax year had the effect of imposing the earnings cap on the calculation of the total allowable pension contributions for that year. For these purposes, a personal pension term assurance policy premium had the same effect as a pension contribution.

There is probably no better example of the lunacy that the pensions tax rules had come to. The purpose of retirement annuities and personal pensions was identical and yet the putting in place of personal pensions whilst maintaining the retirement annuity regime, created a totally unnecessary degree of complexity.

The approach to Finance Act 2004

[1.14] It is no wonder therefore that by the time we reached the end of the old millennium the position with regard to pensions tax law generally had become untenable. As the contracted out legislation associated with pensions is beyond the scope of this book except where it directly interacts with tax legislation we have not covered the additional complexities associated with this.

Suffice to say that the position had become one where it was impossible to have a clear understanding of how the entire pension system worked. There were literally thousands of pages of legislation, guidance, statutory instruments, practice notes, updates etc, and in many instances the rules just seemed contradictory and illogical.

It was therefore decided that simplification was required.

In December 2002, the then Labour Government published proposals for a radical simplification of the tax regime for pensions. Following consultation, legislation was introduced in Finance Act 2004 and came into force on 'A-day', 6 April 2006.

There were actually three documents published on 17 December 2002:

• Simplifying the taxation of pensions: increasing choice and flexibility for all (a consultation document issued jointly by HM Treasury and the Inland Revenue);
• Simplicity, security and choice: working and saving for retirement (the Green Paper);
• Simplicity, security and choice: technical paper (this paper considered the detailed technical aspects of the proposals set out in the Green Paper).

In the consultation document HM Treasury set out that there were no fewer than eight different tax regimes governing pensions. It was stated that

'As a result, pensions tax relief has become so complicated that people are put off saving for retirement and employers have become reluctant to sponsor workplace pensions. The complex rules add to the costs faced by individuals, employers and pension providers, and distort the advice people get. So they restrict what people actually save for their retirement. And that can mean they are disappointed with the income they achieve in retirement.'

The Government therefore proposed to reform the system, introducing a single set of rules stating that:

'All pension saving after implementation will follow a single set of rules which will apply to saving in all kinds of pension schemes. And there will be a single set of simple rules about how pension savings are turned into benefits.'

The Government proposed a 'clean break' with effect from a given date to be known as A-day. All pensions saving after A-day would follow a single set of rules that will apply to savings in all types of pension scheme.

The principles set out in the Green Paper were:

(1) A single lifetime limit on the total capital value of pension saving that would attract favourable tax treatment with indexation broadly in line with price inflation.
(2) If the value of an individual's overall pension fund exceeded the lifetime limit then a 'recovery charge' would apply.
(3) Pension rights built up before A-day to be valued and converted into equivalent rights under the new regime. The Government said that existing rights built up under current tax regimes would be 'respected'.
(4) Tax relief at the individual's marginal income tax rate to be available on pension contributions.

(5)   An annual limit on tax relievable inflows to an individual's pension fund – both contributions to any defined contribution scheme and growth in pension rights in defined benefit occupational schemes. Any 'inflows' above the annual limit to be subject to an income tax charge.

(6)   No restrictions on the number or types of pension scheme to which an individual may contribute.

(7)   A single, consistent set of rules about the delivery of pension benefits would be introduced.

(8)   A maximum tax-free lump sum set at 25% of the capital value of pensions savings.

(9)   When an individual dies before taking benefits, the whole value of their pension funds could be paid as a tax-free lump sum, except for any recovery charge tax on payments above the lifetime limit.

A year later, on 10 December 2003, the Government issued a further substantive document: 'Simplifying the taxation of pensions: the Government's proposals'. This developed the ideas of the 2002 consultation document and painted in more of the detail that eventually we saw enacted in the 2004 Finance Act. Implementation date, 'A Day', was 6 April 2006. By then the word 'simplification' in this context had already more or less disappeared.

The key elements that were introduced from 6 April 2006 and how they have evolved and changed since then will be explored during the remainder of this book. The words from 2002 may return to haunt:

> 'pensions tax relief has become so complicated that people are put off saving for retirement and employers have become reluctant to sponsor workplace pensions.'

The five pillars of reform

[1.15] Originally there were five 'pillars' for the new regime for 'registered pension schemes' which may be set out as:

(1)   An annual allowance for tax privileged pension savings. This started out at 100% of earned income subject to a maximum of £215,000 in tax year 2006–07, increasing in £10,000 increments to £255,000 in tax year 2010–11. (See Table 4).

(2)   A lifetime allowance limiting the extent of tax privileged pension savings. This started off as £1.5 million in tax year 2006–07 increasing progressively to £1.8 million in tax year 2010–11. (See Table 4).

(3)   A single set of investment rules applicable to all registered pension schemes.

(4)   More flexible rules in relation to death benefit provision and the abolition of the compulsion to buy an annuity or to have a secured pension.

(5)   Transitional arrangements designed to effectively 'shoehorn' the existing tax regimes into the new unified regime so that no one would be disadvantaged.

The annual allowance and the lifetime allowance as they operated until 5 April 2011 are set out in Table 4 below:

Table 4

Tax Year	Lifetime allowance	Annual Allowance
2006–2007	£1,500,000	£215,000
2007–2008	£1,600,000	£225,000
2008–2009	£1,650,000	£235,000
2009–2010	£1,750,000	£245,000
2010–2011	£1,800,000	£255,000

It was apparent from the outset to many of those in the pensions industry at the time that these amounts were set at levels that were far too generous in particular so far as the annual allowance was concerned. For a self-employed individual, for example earning £100,000 a year, we changed from a situation where tax relievable pension contributions could have been as low as £17,500 to one where they were now able to contribute up to £100,000 with income tax relief on the entirety.

HMRC estimate the net annual cost of tax relief on registered pension schemes for 2012–13 to be £22.8 billion after taking account of the tax collected on pensions in payment. The overall cost to the Exchequer of the tax privileges provided to registered pension schemes is about 2.4% of GDP.

The financial crisis of the period 2008 onwards led to the UK Government taking action to reduce the deficit and it was announced in 2010 that the cost of pensions tax relief was unacceptable and needed to be reduced. Proposals were therefore set out with the objective of reducing the cost of pensions tax relief by between £4 billion and £5 billion. These were implemented through provisions introduced in Finance Act 2011.

The most important change introduced was a reduction in the annual allowance to £50,000 in 2011–12 which (I wrote in August 2012) 'will not be reviewed for some years'. Although the £50,000 annual allowance continued in 2012–13 and 2013–14, it has reduced to £40,000 from 2014–2015. According to the Government this 'supports the objective of a system of pensions tax relief that is fair, affordable and sustainable'. The more cynical may however have spotted a trend.

Although protection was introduced for those with larger funds the lifetime allowance has also been reduced. The lifetime allowance was reduced to £1.5 million with effect from April 2012, and (once again I wrote in August 2012) 'this will not be reviewed for a considerable period of years'. The Government announced on 5 December 2012 that to 'support its objective of a system of pensions tax relief that [once again] is fair, affordable and sustainable', for 2014–2015 onwards the lifetime allowance has been reduced from £1.5 million to £1.25 million.

The post 2014 revolution

[1.16] The 2014 Budget set out radical changes to the UK pensions taxation system. Some of the changes were immediate and others will take effect from April 2015. Yet more measures are proposed to take effect from April 2015 after a process of consultation. These are massive changes and of great importance to all who have pension rights in UK registered pension schemes.

It was rumoured in the run up to the Chancellor's Budget speech that some rabbit or other would be plucked from George Osborne's hat that would take everyone by surprise. And so it turned out as towards the end of his speech George Osborne said the following words that forever changed the nature of the UK pensions benefits system:

> 'We will completely change the tax treatment of defined contribution pensions to bring it into line with the modern world.... Pensioners will have complete freedom to draw down as much or as little of their pension pot as they want, anytime they want. No caps. No drawdown limits. Let me be clear. No one will have to buy an annuity....'

> 'And we're going to introduce a new guarantee, enforced by law, that everyone who retires on these defined contribution pensions will be offered free, impartial, face-to-face advice on how to get the most from the choices they will now have. . . . What I am proposing is the most far-reaching reform to the taxation of pensions since the regime was introduced in 1921.'

The detailed changes are set out in CHAPTER 4, CHAPTER 12 and elsewhere as appropriate and the first legislative stages will be a Taxation of Pensions Bill as announced in the 2014 Queen's Speech.

The 2014 Queen's Speech

[1.17] The centrepiece of the 2014 Queen's Speech was cited as ground-breaking pensions reform. The following is adapted from the accompanying press announcement with our comment in brackets.

The reforms are claimed to be the biggest transformation in our pensions system since its inception, and (it is claimed) will give people both freedom and security in retirement. By no longer forcing people to buy an annuity (this must be at least the fourth time that government have announced the abolition of the compulsion to buy an annuity), we are giving them total control over the money they have put aside over their lifetime and greater financial security in their old age.

It's all part of a wider mission to put power back in the hands of the people who have worked hard – trusting them to run their own lives. At the same time there will be sweeping reforms to workplace pensions to give employees more certainty about their income in retirement (this is a reference to defined ambition schemes).

The legislative framework to come

[**1.18**] The Taxation of Pensions Bill will give effect to the changes to the pension tax rules as announced at the 2014 Budget, which give greater freedom and choice over how to access defined contribution pension savings. The consultation process (see CHAPTER 4) was over a short timescale and the first draft of the Bill was published in August 2014.

The main elements of the Bill are:

(1)   To introduce a new tax framework that removes the restrictions on how individuals can access their defined contribution pension savings, and allows them full access subject to their marginal tax rate.

(2)   To remove the restrictions placed on how people are able to access their defined contribution pension savings, and give them freedom and choice as to how to access their defined contribution pension fund.

(3)   To introduce anti-avoidance provisions, preventing individuals taking advantage of the new flexible arrangements for tax avoidance purposes.

The new legislation is being introduced in a huge hurry. It is seen as a potential vote winner and the Government want it legislated for well in advance of the May 2015 general election. This will undoubtedly lead to gaps and unforeseen consequences.

The Private Pensions Bill will introduce defined ambition pension schemes which it is claimed will encourage greater risk sharing between parties and allow pension savers to have greater certainty about their retirement savings.

The Bill will make provision for a new legislative framework in relation to the various categories of pension scheme. It will establish three mutually exclusive definitions for scheme type based on degrees of certainty in the benefits that schemes offer to members. Two of these will sound remarkably familiar.

(a)   Defined Benefit (DB) schemes;
(b)   Defined Ambition (shared risk or DA) schemes; and
(c)   Defined Contribution (DC) schemes.

These correspond to different types of promise – from a full promise about retirement income, a promise on part of the pension pot or income, or offering no promise at all.

The Private Pensions Bill will enable 'collective schemes' that pool risk between members and potentially allow for greater stability of pension outcomes. The Bill will contain a number of measures relating to the valuation and reporting requirements for collective schemes.

DC pensions – where individual scheme members bear the risks of longevity, inflation and investment returns – currently dominate the UK pensions market.

DB pensions – where the employer bears the risks by promising a pension usually related to salary – are in decline.

The Private Pensions Bill will enable the introduction of DA pensions, occupying a space between DC and DB pensions that will share more of the risk between parties.

And given the new flexibilities for members of Defined Contribution schemes, in order to help people make decisions that best suit their needs the Private Pensions Bill will provide that everyone with DC pensions will be offered free and impartial guidance via a 'guidance guarantee', on the range of options available to them at retirement. The Private Pensions Bill will legislate so that all individuals with a DC pension in the UK approaching retirement will be offered guidance.

Following the outcome of the HM Treasury Freedom and choice in pensions consultation, the Private Pensions Bill will allow the Department for Work and Pensions (DWP) to bring forward legislation to ban transfers out of unfunded public sector DB schemes – again see CHAPTER 12.

In the remainder of this book we will look at the UK pensions taxation system as it currently works in detail and how it continues to evolve. The purpose of this first chapter has been to set out how it is that we arrived where we are now and indeed that there is a continuing journey. How that journey might further continue is considered in the final chapter of this book.

2

The system of pensions taxation in the UK

Introduction

[2.1] In CHAPTER 1 we looked at how the previous system which operated until April 2006 had become unwieldy with eight different taxation regimes associated with pensions and set the scene for what started off as a simplification project ending up with the implementation of the provisions contained in the 2004 Finance Act which came into effect on 6 April 2006.

In this chapter we will set out the framework associated with the current system of pensions taxation in the UK.

Firstly we will look at the types of pension scheme that operate in the private sector.

Pension scheme types

[2.2] There are three main types of private pension arrangement operating in the United Kingdom:

– Occupational pensions,
– Personal pensions, and
– Stakeholder pensions.

Occupational pension schemes

[2.3] As the name suggests, occupational pension schemes are nearly always provided through an employer. The employer 'sponsors' the scheme and makes it available for employees of the employer (and possibly others) to join.

The definition of what comprises an occupational pension scheme is stated by HMRC as a:

> 'pension scheme established by an employer or employers that provides benefits to/in respect of any or all of the employees of that employer and/or any other employer and which may or may not also provide benefits to/in respect of any other persons who are not employees of any of the employers concerned.'

Since April 2006 membership of an occupational scheme has not been restricted to employees of the scheme sponsoring employer. The scheme sponsoring employer could be a limited company, a partnership, or (unusually) a sole proprietor.

The scheme rules may allow anybody who is eligible to join a registered pension scheme to participate in the scheme. The scheme sponsoring employer could therefore operate a scheme which allows people who are not employees of the sponsoring employer to join it, although this would be very unusual. Both the employer and the scheme member may make contributions. The scheme may receive transfer values in from other pension schemes, and may make transfer values out.

Benefits payable on retirement or on earlier (or on subsequent) death will either be related to the member's salary and their length of scheme membership, or based on the size of the fund that has accrued and the income that may be provided from it. So occupational pensions can either be defined contribution (DC) where either the employee, employer or both contribute, and then use the accumulated funds to provide an income at retirement, or defined benefit (DB) where an employer agrees to pay the individual a certain pension income at retirement, usually based on the number of years they have worked for the employer and their salary.

These two types of occupational pension scheme (DB and DC) are also known as final salary and money purchase schemes respectively.

There is also a variation on the defined contribution concept known as a 'cash balance scheme'.

Cash balance scheme

[2.4] A cash balance type of money purchase scheme provides the member with money purchase based benefits at retirement but based upon a guaranteed growth rate. So as with defined contribution arrangements generally the member will not know the amount of pension and lump sum that will be available at retirement age.

However under a cash balance arrangement the member will know the extent of the contributions into their pension 'pot' each year and the amount of 'interest' or 'growth' credited to those contributions.

The value of the members 'pot' when benefits become payable, only depends upon what is paid into the 'pot' and how long it remains in the scheme. The promised growth in the value of the 'pot' that is used to provide the member with benefits is fixed, but the 'form' and amount of benefits available at retirement is not. The member may for example, at retirement be able to choose the extent of the pension commencement lump sum (the new name for the tax-free lump sum); any dependants' benefits that the member wishes to attach to their own pension etc.

Finance Act 2004 section 152 defines a cash balance arrangement thus:

'(3) . . . a money purchase arrangement is a "cash balance arrangement" at any time if, at that time, all the benefits that may be provided to or in respect of the member under the arrangement are cash balance benefits . . .

(5) . . . "cash balance benefits" means benefits the rate or amount of which is calculated by reference to an amount available for the provision of benefits to or in

respect of the member calculated otherwise than wholly by reference to payments made under the arrangement by the member or by any other person in respect of the member (or transfers or other credits).'

Legal clarification of defined contribution schemes

[2.5] A recent change in the law has placed a narrower definition of what constitutes a defined contribution or money purchase pension scheme. These terms are of course freely interchangeable; they mean exactly the same thing.

The necessity to do this arose because in the case of *Bridge Trustees Ltd v Houldsworth (Secretary of State for Work and Pensions, intervener)* [2011] UKSC 42, [2012] 1 All ER 659, [2011] 1 WLR 1912 the Supreme Court concluded that benefits could fall within the definition of money purchase benefits despite there being a potential mismatch between assets and liabilities.

The judgment found that the following remained money purchase benefits:

- benefits subject to a guaranteed interest rate; and
- money purchase benefits which had been converted into a scheme pension.

This raised the possibility that a deficit could arise in relation to money purchase benefits.

The Supreme Court's finding that the benefits specified above should be treated as money purchase caused uncertainty in relation to the meaning of money purchase benefits.

The Government and many pensions industry professionals had always taken the view that the term 'money purchase benefits' should only refer to benefits where there is no risk of a funding deficit, in line with the decision of the Court of Appeal in *AON Trust Corpn Ltd v KPMG (a firm)* [2005] EWCA Civ 1004, [2006] 1 All ER 238, [2006] 1 WLR 97 in 2005.

Immediately following the Supreme Court's judgment the Government released a statement making clear its intention to introduce primary legislation to clarify the definition of money purchase benefits to ensure that a deficit could not arise in relation to these benefits.

A money purchase scheme is a pension scheme under which all of the benefits that may be provided are money purchase benefits. If a benefit is not within the new definition of a money purchase benefit, it makes the scheme subject to defined benefit scheme regulation.

Parliament enacted Part 4 of the Pensions Act 2011, which achieved this purpose. This has placed a narrower definition of money purchase benefits into Pensions Act 2011 s 29.

Pensions Act 2011 s 29 inserts a new s 181B into the Pension Schemes Act 1993 to ensure that a benefit is only money purchase when it is calculated solely by reference to the assets, meaning that the assets must always suffice to meet the liabilities. A benefit will only be treated as a money purchase benefit where the amount or rate of the benefit, other than a pension in payment, is calculated solely by reference to assets which (because of the nature of the calculation) must necessarily suffice for the purposes of its provision to or in respect of the member.

A benefit which is a pension in payment is only treated as a money purchase benefit if at all times it meets the above definition before it came into payment, and its provision is secured by an annuity contract or insurance policy taken out with an insurer. This definition ensures that a money purchase benefit cannot create a deficit.

Most schemes affected by the definition in Pensions Act 2011 s 29 are hybrid schemes. Therefore schemes providing benefits treated as money purchase where those benefits have any of the following features may be affected:

- a guarantee in the accumulation phase including, for example, a promise of an amount linked to salary, or a guaranteed interest rate; and
- a pension in payment by the scheme derived from money purchase benefits or cash balance benefits unless this is backed by a matching insurance policy.

The following are examples of benefits which may need to be reclassified as defined benefits (DB) following the introduction of the new definition of money purchase benefits:

- In-scheme annuities: many schemes offer an option for a money purchase member to secure their benefits at retirement within the scheme rather than an external annuity.
- Money purchase benefits with a DB underpin: if the value of the DB underpin exceeds the money purchase value, the member will be treated as DB. If not, they are treated as money purchase members.
- DB benefits with a money purchase underpin: if the value of the money purchase benefit exceeds the DB benefit then these will be money purchase; if not, they will be DB.
- Money purchase benefits with a guaranteed investment rate: the intention is that these benefits would be DB.
- DB benefits paid to dependents of money purchase schemes, where this will require the purchase of an insurance contract to meet the liability, even where this is expected to be funded by the employer.

The Pensions Act 2011 (Transitional and Consequential and Supplementary Provisions) Regulations 2014 (SI 2014/1711) aim to ensure that pension schemes can comply with the clarified definition of money purchase benefits in Pensions Act 2011 s 29 with minimum disruption and cost.

Although the amendments will retrospectively apply from 1 January 1997 (the earliest relevant instance of money purchase pension in existing legislation), the transitional arrangements through the above regulations remove the need to review decisions (on areas such as employer exit and scheme wind-ups) made from 1997 to 28 July 2011. They also limit the retrospective impact of the clarified definition that affected schemes have to comply with from a future date.

Personal pension schemes

[2.6] Personal pension schemes are often seen as an alternative for those who do not have access to an occupational pension scheme, for example, the self-employed and employees whose employer does not operate a pension scheme. Personal pensions can however also be used by members of occupational pension schemes in order to top up their pension provision. Personal pensions are always DC schemes.

An employer can administer a 'group personal pension scheme' (GPP). A GPP is a collection of personal pensions for a set of individuals (typically employees of the employer which has put the GPP in place) but administered for convenience through the employer who will generally collect and remit contributions to the personal pension provider.

The member's employer (if the member is employed) may make contributions to an employee's personal pension subject to the overall contributions not exceeding the member's annual allowance (£40,000 from 2014–15) as otherwise there would be a tax charge on the member.

Stakeholder personal pensions

[2.7] Stakeholder personal pensions were introduced in April 2001. They are a form of personal pension in respect of which the government set minimum standards in areas such as the costs charged by providers. Employers with five or more employees who do not offer an occupational scheme which all employees can join within one year of starting work were required to 'designate' a stakeholder scheme for their employees. Employers were not required to contribute nor was there any obligation on any employee to join a designated scheme.

A consequence of this requirement was thousands of literally 'empty' schemes, where the employer met the obligation to make such a scheme available but nobody chose to join it. Under the Pensions Act 2008 (PA 2008) the 'stakeholder designation requirement' has been removed (PA 2008 Ch 7) as a consequence of the new auto-enrolment requirements coming into force (See section **2.10** and Chapter **14**).

Pension scheme membership – definitions

[2.8] Finance Act 2004 defines pension scheme members thus in section 151:

'(1)   . . . "member" in relation to a pension scheme, means any active member, pensioner member, deferred member or pension credit member of the pension scheme.

(2)   . . . a person is an active member of a pension scheme if there are presently arrangements made under the pension scheme for the accrual of benefits to or in respect of the person.

(3)   . . . a person is a pensioner member of a pension scheme if the person is entitled to the present payment of benefits under the pension scheme and is not an active member.

(4)   A person is a deferred member of a pension scheme if the person has accrued rights under the pension scheme and is neither an active member nor a pensioner member.

(5)   A person is a pension credit member of a pension scheme if the person has rights under the pension scheme which are attributable (directly or indirectly) to pension credits. And, if a person dies having become entitled to pension credits but without having rights attributable to them, the person is to be treated as having acquired, immediately before death, the rights by virtue of which the liability in respect of the pension credits is subsequently discharged.'

Arrangements within pension schemes

[2.9] Within the pension scheme the member will have one or more 'arrangements' as described in Finance Act 2004 section 152:

'(1) . . . "arrangement", in relation to a member of a pension scheme, means an arrangement relating to the member under the pension scheme.

(2) . . . an arrangement is a "money purchase arrangement" at any time if, at that time, all the benefits that may be provided to or in respect of the member under the arrangement are cash balance benefits or other money purchase benefits.

(3) . . . a money purchase arrangement is a "cash balance arrangement" at any time if, at that time, all the benefits that may be provided to or in respect of the member under the arrangement are cash balance benefits . . .

(6) . . . an arrangement is a "defined benefits arrangement" at any time if, at that time, all the benefits that may be provided to or in respect of the member under the arrangement are defined benefits . . .

(8) . . . an arrangement is a "hybrid arrangement" at any time if, at that time, all of the benefits that may be provided to or in respect of the member under the arrangement are, depending on the circumstances, to be of one of any two or three of the following varieties—

(a)   cash balance benefits,
(b)   other money purchase benefits, and
(c)   defined benefits.'

The introduction of a compulsion to provide workplace pensions

[2.10] Under the *Pensions Act 2008* the 'stakeholder designation requirement' has been removed at the same time as new requirements were introduced on employers to automatically enrol employees into, and to contribute to, a qualifying workplace pension scheme.

The DWP confirmed the abolition of the requirement that UK employers provide employees with access to a stakeholder pension scheme with effect from 1 October 2012. Although those who are already members of their employer's designated stakeholder scheme will be protected, employers no longer need to give new employees access to a stakeholder scheme.

For employers with auto enrolment staging dates later than 1 October 2012 (see below and CHAPTER 14), there will therefore be a period during which there will not be any statutory requirement to provide access to a pension arrangement for their employees. It remains unclear how the DWP intend to remove the requirement for employers to provide stakeholder schemes to employees following certain types of TUPE transfer, as the powers to repeal the stakeholder regime do not apply to this requirement.

Until 5 April 1988 membership of an employer's pension scheme could be compulsory, literally membership could be required as a condition of employment. Now we have a situation where from October 2012 pension scheme membership will become 'automatic', the employee having to make a conscious decision to opt out. There will be a major reliance upon 'inertia', where people will simply be enrolled into a pension arrangement and accept the cost almost as if it were a form of additional taxation despite the right to 'opt out'.

The October 2010 review document (commissioned by the then incoming Coalition Government) describes this using the words:

> 'The purpose of the automatic enrolment policy is to increase the numbers of people saving for their pension by ensuring that inaction on their part will lead to pension saving occurring, just as inaction at present leads to no saving.'

Employees who have been automatically enrolled into a pension scheme have a one-month period after their automatic enrolment during which they may choose to opt out. The Department for Work and Pensions (DWP) suggests one in four of those who are eligible for auto enrolment into a pension scheme may opt out of membership.

The auto enrolment model would seem to have been built upon the Australian system, where a framework of compulsory pensions was introduced as part of a national wage bargaining exercise in 1986. Employers agreed to contribute 3% to a superannuation fund in return for reducing a 6% wage claim to 2%. This had the effect of doubling the number of workers covered by a pension scheme from 40% in 1987 to 80% by 1991. The percentage of the Australian workforce now enrolled in the pension scheme is over 90%.

Auto-enrolment began in October 2012 and will be fully phased in by 2018 so that every employee between age 22 and state pension age earning over £10,000 per year (2014–15 level) will need to be enrolled into a workplace pension scheme. Each employer will be allocated a date from when these new duties will apply to them known as their 'staging date'. The staging dates are spread over four years. Staging dates are based on the number of people in an employer's PAYE scheme. Employers with the largest numbers of workers in their PAYE schemes will have the earliest staging date.

If the employer already operates a company pension scheme that meets the relevant criteria then auto enrolment may be into that scheme. If however the relevant criteria are not met by the existing scheme or if the employer does not operate a company pension scheme then employees will be enrolled into what has been described as a 'simple low-cost pension scheme' that the Government are introducing into the pensions environment known as the National Employment Savings Trust (NEST).

NEST is a State established pension scheme with the following characteristics:

(1)   It has a public service obligation, meaning it must accept all employers who apply to participate.

(2)   It has been established by Government to ensure that employers, including those that employ low to medium earners, can access pension saving and comply with their automatic enrolment duties.

As stated by the chief executive of NEST:

> 'The Nest pension scheme is not a state pension scheme and it is not being run by Government. It has been established in UK law as a trust-based occupational pension scheme and therefore will be run like any other trust-based occupational pension scheme.'

Depending upon the size of the employer then between October 2012 and 2018 all UK employers will eventually be required to contribute a minimum of 3% of each employee's qualifying earnings to a suitable pension scheme (or NEST) unless the employee chooses to 'opt out'. Statutory minimum contributions for DC and personal pension schemes will eventually become 8% (including 3% from employers) of a band of pay from £5,772 to £41,865. These are the lower and upper limits of the qualifying earnings band for 2014–15. For example, if someone earns £18,000 a year, their 'qualifying earnings' would be £18,000 minus £5,772 which is £12,228.

The rules of a suitable DC scheme must eventually require the employer to pay an overall minimum contribution of at least 8% of the worker's qualifying earnings, of which at least 3% qualifying earnings must be from the employer. Employees themselves will eventually be required to pay a personal contribution of 4% of their qualifying earnings. This will be topped up by a further 1% representing income tax relief. Thus an overall minimum contribution of 8% of pay will be delivered but not until 2018. Earnings are defined by amounts paid in pay reference periods (week, month, etc.). Contributions are generally based on qualifying earnings (including bonuses, commission, overtime, sick pay and maternity pay).

For the first five years from 1 October 2012 combined contributions are required of 2% of which the employer must pay at least 1%; for the year after that (1 October 2017 to 30 September 2018), they move up to 5% and 2% respectively.

Suitable DB schemes must be contracted out of the State Second Pension, or meet a qualifying scheme standard. Qualifying DB schemes may defer the start of auto-enrolment until 2016 for any existing jobholders at the staging date who have previously chosen not to join that scheme despite being eligible to do so in the past.

Registered pension schemes

[2.11] The framework of occupational pensions and personal pensions etc as described in CHAPTER 1, which relied upon the discretionary approval of HMRC was replaced from 6 April 2006 by a statutory framework associated with registered pension schemes.

According to the HMRC registered pension schemes manual:

'A registered pension scheme is a pension scheme that is registered with HMRC. It qualifies for special tax privileges not available to pension schemes that are not registered.'

A registered pension scheme may be established by any of the following:

- An employer.
- An insurance company.
- A unit trust scheme manager.
- An operator, trustee or depository of a recognised EEA collective investment scheme.
- An authorised open-ended investment company.
- A building society.
- A bank.
- An EEA investment portfolio manager.

The overwhelming majority of registered pension schemes are established and operated by employers and insurance companies.

With effect from 6 April 2007 in respect of pension schemes applying for registration with HMRC, which are not occupational schemes, the scheme must be established by an entity which has permission from the Financial Services Authority (FSA) under the Financial Services and Markets Act 2000 to establish in the UK a personal pension scheme or a stakeholder pension scheme.

The registration process

[2.12] Pension schemes that were previously approved by HMRC, that is in the period up to 6 April 2006, automatically became registered pension schemes without any further action being taken. New schemes established on or after 6 April 2006 need to register with HMRC using an online process as described in the Registered Pension Schemes Manual published by HMRC.

A registered pension scheme must have a scheme 'Administrator', and it is the Administrator who will register the scheme with HMRC online. It is not necessary to provide HMRC with any scheme documentation unless requested by HMRC. Until 21 October 2013 the schemes were be registered instantly if the scheme Administrator successfully submitted an online application. HMRC could later require further information about the scheme.

As part of HMRC's ongoing review of processes to combat pension liberation, from 21 October 2013 scheme registration is not confirmed automatically. Now HMRC will review the application and may need to ask further questions or request additional information before deciding if the scheme can be registered.

If the pension scheme can be registered HMRC write and confirm the date of registration – the date the decision is made by HMRC and from which the pension scheme qualifies for tax relief and exemptions. If however the scheme cannot be registered, HMRC write and give the reason for their decision. There is a right of appeal against any decision not to register a pension scheme.

Any employer associated with the scheme (that is the sponsoring employer and any other participating employers) and the scheme members qualify for tax relief from the date of its registration. Any contributions made before the date of scheme registration, will not qualify for tax relief as contributions to a registered pension scheme as HMRC will not apply registration to a scheme retrospectively.

When a pension scheme has been registered with HMRC, it does not mean that HMRC has accepted the information provided by the scheme administrator, it only means that the registration process has taken place. Checks may be carried out by HMRC after registration in order to satisfy HMRC that the conditions to be a registered pension scheme were and continue to be met.

HMRC has the power to enquire into the scheme's affairs at a later date and may withdraw the scheme's registration from a later date. The grounds on which HMRC can consider withdrawing registration include, for example, the discovery that any information or declaration given in the registration application was materially incorrect or false.

Eligibility for participation in a registered pension scheme

[2.13] The registered pension scheme rules will specify who can join it. There are no HMRC restrictions on who is allowed to join a specific scheme, and even non-UK residents may join a registered pension scheme if the scheme rules permit.

Contributions may be paid by the scheme member, a third party on behalf of the member, or a member's employer or former employer. Where a third party pays a contribution those contributions are treated as if they had been paid by the member, so for example they count towards the member's annual allowance.

The taxation life-cycle of private pension schemes

[2.14] The taxation life-cycle of private pension arrangements can be divided into three stages. At each point there are tax implications for the member and where applicable the member's employer:

Contributions: Payments are made into a fund. These payments will be paid by the individual member and, in many cases, by their employer as well. If the scheme is funded by contributions from the employer only then it is known as a 'non-contributory scheme'.

The UK system is based upon 'tax privileges', so contributions are tax allowable on the part of both the employer and the member, this supposedly giving an incentive to make adequate retirement provision. There are however limits on the extent of tax privileged pension contributions based upon the annual allowance. And there is an overall limit on the extent of the tax privileged pension fund which can be accumulated over a working lifetime.

Investment: The fund accumulates over time. This arises from the investment activities of those who manage the fund with income and (hopefully) capital gains being generated. If the pension scheme is a DC scheme then the investment risk is entirely borne by the member. If however the scheme is a DB scheme poor investment returns can result in the employer (and possibly the members) having to pay more into the scheme than anticipated in order to meet the benefit promises associated with the scheme. The pension fund is also 'tax privileged'. As set out below it would not be right to refer to the fund as being 'tax-free' or 'tax exempt'.

Taking benefit: At a future date which can generally be from age 55 or later (there are earlier permitted benefit ages for those who traditionally retire earlier) the member will take benefit from the fund. Often there is an initial lump sum payment (now known as a pension commencement lump sum), with subsequent regular income payments either paid out of the fund or secured through an annuity purchased from a life insurance company. Income payments are taxed, but the pension commencement lump sum is (currently) free from tax.

This 'system' of pensions taxation is known as an EET system meaning 'Exempt, Exempt, Taxed', in the sense that contributions are made from pre-tax income (thus exempt from tax), the fund grows in a tax efficient manner (it would not be quite right to say it is tax-exempt), and benefits when they are taken in the form of income are taxed.

Exempt: member contributions into a registered pension scheme are given tax relief at the members marginal rate, and any employer contributions may also qualify for a deduction of corporation tax and relief from national insurance contributions;

Exempt: investment growth of the assets held in a registered pension scheme is exempt from tax;

Taxed: subject to the option to take up to 25% of a pension fund as a tax-free lump sum (the pension commencement lump sum), when an individual receives an income from their pension it will be taxed as earned income.

Employer pension contributions

[2.15] Employers receive tax relief on their contributions to a registered pension scheme on the same basis as all their other business expenditure. Tax relief on employer contributions to a registered pension scheme is given by allowing contributions made to the scheme to be deducted as an expense in computing the profits of a trade, profession or investment business, and so reducing the amount of an employer's taxable profit.

In the case of a trade or profession, employer contributions will be deductible as an expense provided that they are incurred wholly and exclusively for the purposes of the employer's trade or profession. Where the employer is a limited company this means that employer contributions are deductible for the purposes of the company's corporation tax liability. If the employer however is a partnership or sole trader then employer pension contributions are allowable against income tax.

Finally if the employer is an investment company, for example a company that invests in property, then employer pension contributions will be deductible as an expense of management.

In the period prior to 6 April 2006 there were effective controls on the extent to which employers were allowed to pay into pension schemes. This was because of a set of maximum benefit limits that applied to all forms of occupational pension scheme.

So for example where the scheme was a defined contribution occupational scheme there were rules applied in terms of the contribution limits that would be consistent with funding for the maximum permitted pension. Because of this it was accepted practice that employer contributions would always be allowable for tax purposes.

Contribution limits under the tax regime for pensions introduced from 6 April 2006 are (following the reduction in the annual allowance from £255,000 to £50,000 from April 2011, and the further reduction to £40,000 from April 2014 it may be more accurate to say 'were') much more generous than those that effectively applied before that date. Although employer contributions are in effect unlimited, any contribution made by the employer which results in the member's annual allowance being exceeded will result in a tax charge on the member on the excess. Employer contributions are only allowed for tax relief in respect of the employer's accounting period in which the contributions are paid.

In an environment where contributions made by employers are therefore without any particular limits the relevance of the 'wholly and exclusively' test associated with trading businesses becomes relevant. Much discussion on this particular point took place before guidance was finally issued by HMRC.

HMRC guidance at BIM46010 states:

> 'the payment of a pension contribution is part of the normal costs of employing staff. It will only be disallowable where there is an identifiable non-business purpose for the employer's decision to make the contribution to a registered scheme, or for the size of the contribution . . . An example of where this may occur is where the contribution is in respect of a controlling director or an employee who is a relative or close friend of the business proprietor or controlling director. If the pension contribution paid on behalf of such directors or employees is the same as that paid for a third party employee in similar circumstances . . . there is no non-business purpose . . . '.

The reality of the position is that it will be extremely unusual for some or all of an employer's pension contribution to be disallowed for the purposes of tax relief. Following the reduction in the annual allowance from April 2014, this will become even less likely.

However where an employer makes a large non regular contribution in an accounting period, tax relief will be spread over up to four accounting periods. This will generally apply where the contribution:

- Is more than 210% of the contribution paid in the previous accounting period, and
- The amount of the excess over and above that paid in the previous chargeable period is £500,000 or more.

Where tax relief is to be spread the excess contributions will be spread in accordance with Table 1:

Table 1

Excess	Spread
£500,000 – £999,999	Over 2 accounting periods
£1,000,000 – £1,999,999	Over 3 accounting periods
£2,000,000 or more	Over 4 accounting periods

In order to ensure uniformity of treatment if a local inspector of taxes is of the view that an employer pension contribution does not satisfy the 'wholly and exclusively for the purposes of the trade of the employer' test, then the local inspector is required to make a report to the HMRC Technical Team before challenging the deduction.

The purposes of this requirement is to make sure that employers generally are treated in a consistent manner for the purposes of tax relief on pension contributions being allowed against tax. The tax treatment of employer contributions will be looked at in more detail in CHAPTER 3.

Asset-backed contributions

[2.16] Legislation was introduced by Finance Act 2012 Schedule 13 that deals with the taxation treatment of asset-backed contribution arrangements including the availability of relief for employers and the impact of any changes to the arrangement over its term.

As set out by Mark Hoban (Financial Secretary to the Treasury) at the committee stage of the Bill:

'Employer asset-backed pension contributions allow an employer to put in place arrangements to reduce the funding deficit of . . . registered pension schemes. They also provide employers with flexibility around making pension contributions against sometimes volatile deficit levels without affecting their cash flow. At the same time, the arrangements give pension schemes the security required to meet their obligations to members.

The Government recognise the commercial benefits of the arrangements and want to ensure that they can be used as a way of funding pension schemes. However, some of the arrangements can give rise to unintended excess tax relief, as a result of the ways in which they are structured.

In the Budget 2011, we announced a consultation on changing the tax rules that apply to asset-backed pension contributions. The arrangements involve an employer committing to make a series of payments to the pension scheme by transferring an income-producing asset to the scheme. The arrangement will provide security to the pension scheme, because the asset will be passed to the scheme if the employer cannot make the payments during the arrangement period. On completion of the arrangement, the asset will be returned to the employer.

Following the consultation, we announced changes on 29 November 2011, with effect from that date, to prevent forestalling risks. Further changes were announced in February of this year to preserve the original policy objective following comments received on the draft legislation. Further minor changes, effective from 23 March 2011, were announced at Budget 2012.

The changes . . . ensure that up-front tax relief would be given to asset-backed pension contribution arrangements only where they meet certain conditions. The conditions ensure that at the start of the arrangement, the pension contribution promised by the employer is guaranteed to be paid by the end of the arrangement.

Where that is not the case, the provisions will ensure that up-front relief is not given. The changes will save the Exchequer nearly £2.5 billion between now and 2016-17 by preventing excessive tax relief arising to those employers who made use of particular types of asset-backed pension contributions. [Most] employers are not affected by the measure.

Schedule 13 also includes minor changes to the legislation on structured finance arrangements. This will make it easier for an asset-backed contribution arrangement to qualify for up-front relief, while reducing avoidance risks in the context of the structured finance arrangement legislation.

I will turn briefly to the amendments. It has come to HMRC's attention that some pre-existing arrangements, where the contribution was paid before 22 February 2012, may be affected in unintended ways by the transitional provisions in parts 2 and 4 of the schedule. The relieving amendments remove the unintended consequences to ensure that the relief given to the employer under such an arrangement accurately reflects, but does not exceed, payments made to the registered pension scheme. The amendments also clarify the fact that payments or determinations made in the first working day following the end of the 12-month period will not prevent any arrangement from gaining up-front relief where contributions are paid on or after 22 February 2012, provided that the arrangement meets all the other qualifying conditions. The reforms will help to protect the Exchequer against significant tax risks while at the same time providing employers with the flexibility to continue to use asset-backed pension contributions.'

Employers are generally able to claim relief for contributions paid to a registered pension scheme subject to general taxation rules. Relief is available for monetary contributions that are paid to a scheme as opposed to a contribution made in asset form.

It may be possible to structure a transaction so that a monetary contribution is achieved without the need for cash to pass between the employer and the pension scheme. With effect from 29 November 2011, employers are not able to claim relief at the time of payment if they make contributions using certain asset-backed contribution arrangements.

These changes were designed to ensure that unintended, excess tax relief could not arise in respect of such contributions. HMRC guidance explains how to identify such asset-backed contribution arrangements and how to determine whether upfront relief is available. The guidance also covers the special rules that affect asset-backed arrangements which existed at 29 November 2011 and the tax consequences of changes that are made to asset-backed arrangements.

On 22 February 2012, the Government published further legislation, which took immediate effect, with the aim of limiting the circumstances in which upfront tax relief can be given to asset-backed arrangements in line with the original policy aim.

The Government also announced further provisions, effective from 21 March 2012:

- Revenue protection provisions to recover relief when an employer ceases to be chargeable to tax, for example, when it winds up or migrates to another country;
- Anti-abuse provisions to ensure that no person will be placed in a more advantageous tax position as a result of the application of the revenue protection rules published in February 2012; and
- Related amendments to the structured finance legislation within Part 13 of Income Tax Act 2007 and Part 16 of Corporation Tax Act 2010.

What is an asset-backed contribution (ABC) arrangement?

[2.17] These are arrangements that allow an employer to use non-cash assets to underpin and/or act as a guarantee for regular income stream of payments to the pension scheme.

These arrangements do not usually result in the outright disposal of the asset to the scheme. In a simple example, an employer makes a contribution to a pension scheme. The pension scheme immediately uses the contribution to acquire from the employer a property with a predicted rental stream. The terms of the disposal contain an option by which the property reverts to the employer after, say, 15 years. The amount of the pension contribution is equal to the value of the property interest disposed of.

This will be equal to the net present value of the income stream the pension scheme expects to receive over the 15-year term. In effect, the pension scheme has immediately lent back the value of the pension contribution it received. This 'loan' will be repaid by the income stream payments over the term of the arrangement.

In a more complex arrangement, the property (or other income producing asset) is transferred into a partnership. The employer or connected persons will be members of the partnership. The employer makes a contribution to the pension scheme which the pension scheme then invests in the partnership. The amount of the employer contribution and the capital invested will be determined by the net present value of the anticipated income stream attached to the partnership interest the pension scheme acquires.

Typically, the majority of the income stream will flow through to the pension scheme's interest. This more complex structure is frequently used in pension funding arrangements due to other pensions legislation (non tax) that governs the amount of investment into employer-related assets by pension schemes. Structures can also include two tier partnership structures where the income-producing asset is held in the lower tier whilst the pension scheme acquires an interest in the higher tier.

Asset-backed contribution arrangements can be attractive to the employer as they are able to address pension scheme funding issues immediately but without having to commit cash. It also allows the employer to effectively retain the benefit of the capital growth of the asset. The pension scheme has a guaranteed income return on its investment. If the employer defaults on payment, the pension scheme is usually able to take full ownership of the asset.

This can make these arrangements more attractive to the pension scheme than a straightforward funding schedule with the employer which typically will agree the contributions to be paid over a fixed period but will not have an underlying guarantee if the employer has financial difficulty.

There was a concern that some of the structures being used to provide ABCs resulted in the employer receiving tax relief on amounts in excess of the amount that was ultimately received by the pension scheme over the term of the arrangement. The object of the changes is to ensure that such advantages are eliminated.

The tax treatment of an asset-backed contribution (ABC) arrangement

[2.18] The legislation dealing with asset-backed contributions was introduced in a number of tranches.

Legislation was introduced with effect from 29 November 2011 that dealt with the timing of relief for contributions paid via asset-backed arrangements.

That legislation was subsequently tightened with effect from 22 February 2012.

The structure of the legislation is that FA 2012 Sch 13 Part 3 contains sections 196B–196L of FA 2004 dealing with contributions paid from 22 February 2012 onwards. FA 2012 Sch 13 Part 1 contains sections 196B–196J of FA 2004 dealing with contributions paid between 29 November 2011 and 21 February 2012. So, before considering the treatment of a contribution, the date the contribution is paid needs to be determined.

Treatment of asset-backed structures that existed at 29 November 2011 and the transitional provisions

There were two main models for asset-backed pension contributions in the market when this legislation was introduced. Both were based on using assets as security for an income stream flow to the pension scheme over a significant number of years but they differed in terms of the timing of the employer relief profile over the lifespan of the arrangement.

One model accounted for the obligation to the pension scheme as a financial liability in its accounts. This meant that the legislation on structured finance arrangements (Chapter 5B of Part 13 of Income Tax Act 2007 or Chapter 2 of Part 16 of Corporation Tax Act 2010) was applicable.

This has the effect of treating the ongoing payments under the arrangement as being akin to loan repayments representing both a capital and finance cost element. The legislation ensures that the capital element is not tax relieved. Much like a repayment mortgage, the majority of each payment in the early years of the structure would consist of finance costs which are relievable for the employer. The balance of the payment would alter over the lifespan of the arrangement.

The second model was not accounted for in this way. It would provide a regular income stream over the lifespan of the arrangement but at the end point a final 'bullet' payment was due. Typically the amount of the final payment would be contingent on the pension scheme's funding position at the end of the arrangement with only a token repayment due if the scheme managed to return to a fully funded position. An analogy may be drawn with an interest only mortgage subject to the contingency around the final payment.

Whilst both models posed a risk that the employer would receive tax relief on sums in excess of what the pension scheme received, the link to the structured finance arrangement legislation in the first model produced a better match in terms of the timing of relief to the employer compared with income flows to the pension scheme. So the asset-backed contribution legislation includes this link with the structured finance legislation.

A key factor in determining whether an employer can claim upfront relief for an asset-backed contribution is whether the arrangement falls to be treated as an acceptable structured finance arrangement. A 'structured finance arrangement' is defined as being a type 1, type 2 or type 3 finance arrangement for the purposes of Chapter 5B of Part 13 of Income Tax Act 2007 or Chapter 2 of Part 16 of Corporation Tax Act 2010.

In the following references a 'disposal of an asset' includes anything constituting a disposal of an asset for the purposes of the Taxation of Chargeable Gains Act 1992 (TCGA 1992).

This definition was widened from 22 February 2012 to include the taking of any step by virtue of which a person receives an asset. This extension was included to ensure that steps such as the issue of shares or bonds on a market were within the scope of this legislation.

Asset-backed contributions paid on or after 22 February 2012

[FA 2012 Sch 13 Part 3]

The legislation identifies three forms of asset-backed contribution that mirror the three types of finance arrangement referred to in the structured finance arrangement legislation.

Section 196B – simple asset-backed contribution arrangement

Section 196D – complex asset-backed contribution arrangement involving a new partnership

Section 196F – complex asset-backed contribution arrangement using an existing partnership

Simple asset-backed arrangement

[FA 2004, s 196B as inserted by FA 2012 Sch 13 Part 3]

Example

An employer agrees to contribute £18m to a pension scheme and negotiates with the trustees to achieve this via an asset-backed arrangement. The following steps occur:

(1)   The employer enters into a legally binding debt obligation to make a contribution of £18m to the pension scheme.

(2)   The pension scheme agrees to acquire a property interest from the employer. The property has a predicted income stream of £1.5m per year and the terms of the agreement will see the property interest revert to the employer after 15 years. The pension scheme values this interest at £18m.

(3)   An agreement is entered into to offset the sum due for the acquisition of the property interest against the sum due as a pension contribution from the employer. The effective date of this agreement reflects the date the contribution is paid.

The employer is not entitled to relief for the £18m paid upfront if conditions A, B and C are met.

Condition A is that under the asset-backed arrangement:

(a)   a person (the 'borrower') receives in any period money (or some other asset, called the 'advance') from another person (the 'lender');

(b)   the borrower, or a person connected with the borrower, disposes of an asset, which is labelled the 'security', to or for the benefit of the lender, or to a person connected with the lender;

(c)   as a result of that transfer the lender is entitled to receive payments in respect of the security;

(d)   the borrower is the employer or a person connected with the employer; and

(e)   the advance is (wholly or partly) paid or provided by the lender out of the employer's contribution.

Condition B is that the asset-backed arrangement is not an 'acceptable structured finance arrangement'.

Condition C is that it is reasonable to suppose that one or more of the payments referred to in Condition A is calculated on the basis that all or some of the advance represents a loan that is to be repaid by these payments.

Conditions A and C seek to identify the essential characteristics of the arrangements being targeted.

These are arrangements where the value of the asset acquired by the pension scheme is essentially based on the value of the income stream generated by that asset where the income producing asset is not expected to remain in the pension scheme.

Although normally the arrangement has some time limit, so that the asset is transferred back to the borrower at the end of the arrangements, this is not necessarily the case. If for instance the asset is a wasting one that will be wholly depleted in repayment of the 'loan'.

Complex asset-backed contribution arrangements

[FA 2004, s 196D and s 196F as inserted FA 2012 Sch 13 Part 3]

In the simple asset-backed arrangement set out above the employer disposed of the property interest direct to the pension scheme. In the complex case, the employer transfers the property to a partnership of which it is a member.

The pension scheme joins the partnership by making a capital contribution of £18m in return for the right to receive partnership profits amounting to (say) £22.5m over the next 15 years. The partnership uses this capital contribution to finance the acquisition of the property. After 15 years, all of the rights to receive partnership profits will revert to the employer (who may be able to buy out the pension scheme's interest).

In these types of arrangements, the 'loan' is made in the form of a contribution to the partnership and a profit share is designed to repay that contribution together with interest. Once the repayment with interest has been made the lender will cease to be a member of the partnership or to share in the profits of it.

The pension contribution could be structured in a number of ways in this type of arrangement:

(1)   A straightforward cash contribution could be paid to the pension scheme on the understanding that it be used to buy the partnership interest.

(2)   The employer could be one of two or more partners in the original partnership. The employer could then dispose of its partnership interest to the scheme as part of an offset transaction.

(3)   An offset transaction involving the pension scheme, employer and partnership could be used to achieve the monetary pension contribution.

There are two variants of this complex model.

The first variant sees a partnership being created specifically to enable the asset-backed contribution to be effected.

The second variant utilises a pre-existing partnership and income stream where the existing members of the partnership are already sharing the profits attributable to that asset. Then either:

(a)   a new member (pension scheme) joins the partnership and takes a share in those profits in return for a capital contribution that is in substance a loan; or

(b)   an existing partner takes an increased share in the profits in return for a capital contribution that is in substance a loan.

Complex asset-backed contribution arrangements involving a
new partnership

[FA 2004, s 196D as inserted FA 2012 Sch 13 Part 3]

The employer is not entitled to relief for the contribution paid upfront if conditions A and B are met.

Condition A is that under the asset-backed arrangement:

(1)   a person ('the transferor') disposes of an asset to a partnership;
(2)   the transferor is the employer or a person connected with the employer;
(3)   the partnership is one of which the transferor (or a connected person) is a member immediately after that disposal. It does not matter whether it was a partner before the disposal;

(4)   the partnership receives money or another asset ('the advance') from another person ('the lender');

(5)   the advance is wholly or partly paid by the lender out of the employer's contribution;

(6)   there is a 'relevant change' (see below) in relation to the membership of the partnership; and

(7)   the share of the person involved in the relevant change in the profits of the partnership falls to be determined (wholly or partly) by reference to payments in respect of the security.

Condition B is that the asset-backed arrangement is not an 'acceptable structured finance arrangement'.

To ensure that Condition A is widely drawn, if the transferor is not the employer then any reference here to a person connected to the transferor will also include a person connected to the employer.

Complex asset-backed contribution arrangements using an existing partnership

[FA 2004, s 196F as inserted FA 2012 Sch 13 Part 3]

The employer is not entitled to relief for the contribution paid upfront if conditions A and B are met.

Condition A is that under the asset-backed arrangement:

(1)   the partnership holds an asset (the security) prior to the asset-backed arrangement being made;

(2)   the partnership then receives money or another asset (the advance) from another person ('the lender');

(3)   the advance is wholly or partly paid by the lender out of the employer's contribution;

(4)   there is a 'relevant change' (see below) in relation to the membership of the partnership; and

(5)   the share of the person involved in the relevant change in the profits of the partnership falls to be determined (wholly or partly) by reference to payments in respect of the security.

Condition B is that the asset-backed arrangement is not an 'acceptable structured finance arrangement'.

Meaning of 'relevant change' in relation to a partnership for complex arrangements

[FA 2004, s 196H as inserted FA 2012 Sch 13 Part 3]

There is a relevant change if either of the following occurs:

(a)   The lender or a person connected with the lender becomes a member of the partnership.

(b)   There is a change in a member's share in the partnership's profits and the member is the lender or a person connected with the lender. This also extends to a person who becomes connected to the lender as a result of the asset-backed arrangement.

The timing of this change in relation to the contribution being paid is not relevant. The key aspect is that the change occurs as a consequence of the asset-backed arrangement.

Meaning of acceptable structured finance arrangement

[FA 2004, s 196C, s 196E and s 196G as inserted FA 2012 Sch 13 Part 3]

There are a number of Conditions (M to Q) that an arrangement has to meet in order to be considered 'acceptable'.

Condition M

In accordance with generally accepted accounting practice, the borrower's accounts record a financial liability in respect of the advance. This should occur in the accounts for the period in which the advance is received.

For complex arrangements involving partnerships the reference to the borrower's accounts above is to the partnership's accounts.

Condition N

The lender should be a 'responsible authority'. The advance should be paid by the lender directly to the borrower (partnership in complex arrangements) entirely out of the employer's contribution. Both the advance and the recorded financial liability at the outset should be of an amount equal to the employer's contribution.

Condition O in a simple arrangement

At the time the advance is paid:

(a)   it should be the lender who is entitled to any payments referred to in Condition A;
(b)   the payments should arise at times that have been fixed and fall at intervals of no more than one year;
(c)   the payments should be received within three months of the date they arise;
(d)   each payment should, on receipt, become part of the sums held by the scheme;
(e)   the payments are all to be of the same amount;
(f)   the total amount of the payments should not be less than the amount of the contribution; and
(g)   the payments should all be expected to be received within 25 years of the date on which the employer's contribution is paid.

Condition O in a complex arrangement

At the time the advance is paid:

(a)   the lender is the person involved in the relevant change in relation to the partnership;
(b)   the lender's share in the partnership profits is determined by reference to the payments in Condition A;
(c)   determinations of the lender's share in the profits should be made at times that have been fixed and fall to be paid at intervals of no more than one year;

(d)   the lender should make a drawing from the partnership on account of its due share within three months of the determination;

(e)   each drawing should become part of the sums held by the scheme;

(f)   the drawings are all to be of the same amount;

(g)   the total amount of the drawings is not to be less than the amount of the employer's contribution; and

(h)   all drawings should be expected to be drawn within 25 years of the date on which the employer's contribution is paid.

Condition P

At the time the advance is paid, the recorded financial liability in respect of the security is to be reduced to nil by the end of the payment period by the payments to the lender.

Condition Q

At the time that the advance is made no 'commitment' should have been given in respect of the payments (drawings) to be made under the arrangement. For these purposes, a 'commitment' is one that is given to a relevant person that secures that a person receives money or another asset and that is linked to the receipt by the lender of any of the payments (drawings) referred to in Condition A.

The term 'relevant person' is widely defined to include:

(a)   The employer and persons connected with the employer.

(b)   A person acting at the direction or request or with the agreement of the employer or a connected person.

(c)   A person chosen by the employer or a connected person.

(d)   A partnership.

But it does not extend to the 'responsible authority' i.e. the person representing the pension scheme in the arrangements.

This condition is widely drawn to identify any understandings between the parties as to how the asset-backed arrangement is to operate in practical terms.

Asset-backed contributions paid between 29 November 2011 and 21 February 2012 inclusive

[FA 2012 Sch 13 Part 1]

Above we have set out Conditions A, B and C that, if met, would deny the employer upfront relief for a contribution paid from 22 February 2012 onwards using a simple asset-backed arrangement.

We have also set out Conditions A and B that, if met, would deny relief for a contribution paid using a complex asset-backed arrangement. Condition B in all those cases was that the asset-backed arrangement was not an acceptable structured finance arrangement.

For contributions paid between 29 November 2011 and 21 February 2012, the only difference is that Condition B is worded that the asset-backed arrangement is not a 'structured finance arrangement'.

The description of a structured finance arrangement still allowed ABCs to be structured so that payments to the pension scheme were loaded towards the end of the term.

This led to the tightening of the legislation by the introduction of the concept of an 'acceptable structured finance arrangement' with effect from 22 February 2012.

The effect of FA 2012 Sch 13 on existing asset-backed arrangements at 29 November 2011 and at 22 February 2012

The legislation requires that any pre-existing asset-backed arrangements be reviewed at the dates that the legislation was introduced (i.e. 29 November 2011 and 22 February 2012).

The purpose of the review is to determine whether the transitional provisions of Parts 2 and 4 of Schedule 13 of Finance Act 2012 have an impact on the tax treatment of the arrangement.

The legislation does not affect the tax treatment of any payments due under the asset-backed arrangement prior to the introduction of the legislation.

Transactions before 29 November 2011

The timing of a transaction is determined by the date that the employer contribution is effectively paid. Where a pension contribution has been effected via an asset-backed arrangement prior to 29 November 2011 (and is still in place at that date), it will need to be reviewed to determine if it falls within the transitional provisions of Part 2 of Schedule 13 of Finance Act 2012.

The aim of the legislation is to identify transactions which, if they had taken place on 29 November 2011, would not have resulted in upfront tax relief being available to the employer. These transactions will fall within the transitional provisions of Part 2.

Any transaction that would have resulted in upfront tax relief for the employer (because it is treated as a structured finance arrangement) is not immediately impacted. These transactions will not fall within the transitional provisions of Part 2. These transactions will be subject to sections 196G and 196H of Part 1 of Schedule 13 of Finance Act 2012 if an applicable event occurs.

Transactions prior to 22 February 2012

All pension contributions effected via an asset-backed arrangement before 22 February 2012 (that are still in place at that date) will need to be similarly reviewed.

The aim once again is to identify transactions which, if they had taken place on 22 February 2012, would not have resulted in upfront relief being available to the employer. These transactions will fall within the transitional provisions of Part 4.

Any transaction that would have resulted in upfront relief for the employer (because it falls within the definition of an acceptable structured finance arrangement) is not immediately impacted. These transactions will not fall within the transitional provisions of Part 4. They will remain subject to the provisions of Part 1 of Schedule 13 of Finance Act 2012 if an applicable event occurs.

Transitional provisions

There are very few asset-backed arrangements that will fall within the transitional provisions. The transitional provisions of Part 2 and Part 4 of Schedule 13 of Finance Act 2012 operate in a similar way; they simply apply to different transactions identified by date as set out above.

The transactions affected by the transitional provisions are those where the outcome of the arrangement (in terms of payment flows) for the pension scheme cannot be known until the final date. This could be due to the arrangement providing for a final bullet payment or due to a contingency in the payments provided by the design of the arrangement.

Despite this doubt over the income flows to the pension scheme, the legislation previously allowed full tax relief to the employer as and when payments were made under the asset-backed structure.

For example, a structure based on rental flows could see the employer claim relief in respect of the contribution to the pension scheme plus the annual rental flows into the structure. Under the new legislation, a pension contribution structured in this way will not result in upfront relief being available for the contribution but relief will be available for the ongoing payments into the structure (subject to other applicable legislation).

To achieve some parity of treatment between new and pre-existing contributions structured in this way, the transitional arrangements look at the tax treatment of the ongoing payments into the structure.

There are two key parts to the transitional arrangements:

(1) a review of the tax treatment of the ongoing payments into the structure; and
(2) when the arrangement comes to an end a review of the amount of tax relief given to the employer over the entirety of the arrangement.

Member pension contributions

[2.19] In order to obtain tax relief on personal contributions to a registered pension scheme, a member must be a 'relevant UK individual'.

This means that tax relief is not available to anyone who:

*   Is not resident in the UK, or
*   Has not been resident in any of the past five tax years, or
*   Does not have any earnings chargeable to UK tax.

No income tax liability applies in respect of an employee whose employer has contributed on their behalf to a registered pension scheme, so long as the overall contributions made in respect of an employee do not exceed the annual allowance.

The maximum allowable contribution payable by, or in respect of, a member for each tax year is the greater of:

- £3,600 gross, or
- 100% of 'relevant UK earnings', limited to the 'annual allowance'.

'Relevant UK earnings' are defined as:

- Income from employment.
- Income chargeable under ITTOIA 2005 Pt 2 derived from the carrying on or exercise of a trade, profession or vocation.
- Earnings of overseas Crown employees subject to UK tax (ITEPA 2003 s 28 earnings).

Unearned income does not qualify as 'relevant UK earnings'. The definition of earnings would seem to also capture income from UK furnished holiday lettings and patent income.

The concept of the 'annual allowance' was introduced in CHAPTER 1 and is limited to £40,000 in the 2014–15 tax year. How the annual allowance works in practice and in the context of the tax treatment of member pension contributions will be looked at in detail in CHAPTER 3.

Scottish Law and pension contributions

[2.20] In May 2012 the Scotland Act received Royal Assent. The Scotland Act contains provisions to devolve to the Scottish Parliament the power to set a Scottish rate of income tax for Scottish taxpayers, with effect from tax year 2016–17. The basic, higher and additional rates of income tax payable by Scottish taxpayers will be reduced by 10p in the pound for Scottish taxpayers, who will be liable in addition for whatever rate the Scottish Parliament sets each year for the following tax year, added to each of the tax bands.

The new Scottish rate will replace the Scottish Variable Rate (which allows the Scottish Government to vary the basic rate of income tax only by +/– 3p in the pound).

HMRC is currently considering the impact on the pension sector and considering the issues that could arise from the introduction of the new Scottish rate. Income tax relief on pension contributions is given at an individual's marginal rate so if UK and Scottish rates diverge, the marginal rates will diverge.

HMRC set up a Pensions Technical Group, including representatives of pension providers and insurance companies north and south of the border, to explore with them the issues that could potentially affect registered pension schemes and quantify the impact on both HMRC and those involved in administering pension schemes.

HMRC's Technical Note in May 2012 confirmed they were working with the pensions industry to try and reduce administration and costs whilst, at the same time, ensuring all pension scheme members receive the correct rate of relief, regardless of whether they are a Scottish or UK taxpayer.

In December 2013 an update to their May 2012 advice was published, having worked with the Pensions Technical Group, on the best way to deliver pension tax relief at source (RAS) at the Scottish Basic rate.

They confirmed that RAS would be given at the Scottish rate; however it was acknowledged that it might take time for the pension industry to change their systems to differentiate between a Scottish taxpayer and a UK taxpayer. Whilst HMRC intends to provide pension scheme administrators with information to allow them to make this differentiation, it has been agreed that the industry can have longer to implement the necessary changes. Therefore, the pensions industry will have to make RAS at the Scottish Basic rate available in their systems from April 2018, rather than April 2016 when there is the first possibility that the rates will diverge.

RAS tax relief will therefore be given at the UK Basic rate for these two years. In this interim period, if necessary, HMRC will identify Scottish taxpayers and make any adjustment to the tax relief direct to the scheme member. This will be done through Self-Assessment or via an adjustment to the PAYE code.

The pension fund itself

[2.21] Since 1921 UK pension funds associated with providing pension benefits have been 'tax privileged', which until 1997 meant that nearly all forms of income and capital gains were exempt from tax. However in his Budget speech on 2 July 1997 the then Chancellor of the Exchequer Gordon Brown announced the abolition of tax credits paid to pension funds and companies when they received dividend income net of advance corporation tax (ACT). The impact on pension funds has been the subject of much debate over the intervening period but it now seems very likely that it will be many years if ever before this taxation burden is reversed.

At the time this change was first introduced UK pension funds were buoyant after many years of strong investment returns. Many final salary schemes were enjoying surpluses and as a consequence contribution holidays on the part of employers and members alike were not uncommon. The introduction of a tax burden on pension funds that it was thought (or perhaps hoped) would not be well understood by the public generally and would have the effect of raising tax revenue of £5 billion (and growing) a year must at the time have seen an attractive option.

The cumulative effect in recent years of much poorer investment returns and very low interest rates now means that the overwhelming majority of defined benefit pension schemes in the private sector have been closed to new members. They are now simply too expensive for employers to afford. Private sector schemes collectively are massively in deficit by (at the time of writing) over £100 billion – a figure that is a reasonably close match to the tax take over the period associated with the abolition of the tax credits referred to above.

The taxation of pension funds is considered in more detail in CHAPTER 5.

The taxation of income and lump sum benefits

[2.22] There is a 'lifetime allowance' which limits the extent to which tax privileged pension funds may be accumulated. This was £1.8 million for the income tax year 2010–11, but was reduced from 6 April 2012 to £1.5 million and further reduced to £1.25 million from 6 April 2014. How this works in practice will be considered in detail in CHAPTER 4 as will be the protections introduced for those with larger funds who would otherwise have suffered adverse taxation consequences as a result of these changes.

In his 1985 Budget, the then Chancellor of the Exchequer Nigel Lawson described the tax-free lump sum as 'anomalous but much loved'. The principle of being able to use a part of the pension fund to provide for a lump sum has existed since at least 1921. For a detailed exposition of the 'evolution' of the tax-free status of the lump sum see CHAPTER 1.

The 'much loved anomaly' of the tax-free nature of the lump sum benefit has been one that successive Chancellors of the Exchequer have sought to restrict from time to time but never to abolish. The lump sum available when benefits are taken is now known as the 'pension commencement lump sum' (PCLS), and in value terms represents up to 25% of the member's fund.

Legislation prevents an individual withdrawing a PCLS which is then invested back into a registered pension scheme, automatically generating further tax relief on the amount invested. This is known as 'recycling lump sums'.

If recycling of lump sums does occur an individual's PCLS will be treated as an unauthorised payment. This means the individual will be liable to a tax charge of up to 55% on the PCLS.

Recycling of a lump sum is considered by HMRC to have occurred where the individual receives a PCLS and:

(1)   Because of the PCLS the amount of contributions paid into another registered pension scheme in respect of the individual is significantly greater than it would otherwise be; and

(2)   The additional contributions are made by the individual or by someone else, such as an employer; and

(3)   The recycling was pre-planned; and

(4)   The amount of the PCLS, taken together with any other such lump sum taken in the previous 12-month period, exceeds 1% of the standard lifetime allowance; and

(5)   The cumulative amount of the additional contributions exceeds 30% of the PCLS.

Income benefits whether taken as an annuity secured with a life office, or whether drawn from the pension fund are taxed as earned income. An income provided by an occupational pension scheme will generally be in the form of what is known as a 'scheme pension'. This is regarded as a form of secure pension income in the same way as where an annuity is purchased from the fund associated with a personal pension scheme or from the members fund arising within a defined contribution pension scheme operated by an employer.

With regard to all forms of DC pension schemes, there was until 5 April 2006 a compulsion to use the fund by age 75 to secure income in the form of an annuity. Only life insurance companies are allowed to provide annuities.

The abolition of the compulsion to buy an annuity (Part 1)

[2.23] In the latter part of the 19th century it was only the relatively affluent who could afford to make any personal savings for their old age. This was encouraged by the introduction as early as 1853 of tax reliefs associated with savings made by way of premiums paid towards insurance policies.

Although most of this affluent class then preferred to manage their own investments in old age, directly spending capital and income, as they needed, it was recognised even then that those who lived longer than the norm could find themselves short of funds. Those who were unwilling to take this risk stimulated what was by the second half of the 19th century a growing market for annuities provided by Government and insurance companies.

In the review of pensions taxation that took place in the run-up to the reforms introduced in Finance Act 2004 the Government wanted to take account of the views and interests of all parties including some quite small minority groups. In order to accommodate the specific objections to saving in pension schemes arising from the compulsion to purchase an annuity by members of the Plymouth Brethren this compulsion was abolished with effect from 6 April 2006.

This was achieved by allowing those over the age of 75 to continue to draw income from their pension fund in the form of what became known as an 'alternatively secured pension'. Restrictions were introduced on the amount of income that could be drawn so as to retain an apparent consistency with the HMRC position that the purpose of a tax privileged pension fund is to provide an income for life.

However 'effective compulsion' was in effect retained by virtue of the fact that a failure to secure an annuity by age 75 would, following the death of the member and any dependant who was entitled to receive income from the deceased members fund, result in a combination of tax charges which could lead to up to 82% of the fund having to be paid in tax.

This arose based on a fund of, for example, £100,000 as follows:

- Unauthorised member payment charge – 40% – £40,000;
- Unauthorised member payment surcharge – 15% – £15,000;
- Scheme sanction charge – 15% – £15,000.

These tax charges total £70,000. The remaining £30,000 was then subject to IHT at 40% – so a further £12,000, making a total of £82,000 or of course 82%.

The coalition Government was committed to abolish this 'effective compulsion' as a part of the coalition agreement. So effective was this effective compulsion that it was common practice in the press and elsewhere to refer to a compulsion associated with annuity purchase even in circumstances where that compulsion no longer existed.

Given the HMRC position that the prime purpose of a tax privileged pension fund was to provide an income for life it came as no great surprise that meeting the coalition commitment to remove the 'effective compulsion' to buy an annuity would in reality benefit only a few. For the overwhelming majority the compulsion to buy an annuity remained 'effective'.

A consultation document entitled 'Removing the requirement to annuitise by age 75' was published by HM Treasury on 15 July 2010. This document proposed that so long as an individual was able to demonstrate that they satisfied a minimum income requirement, they would be allowed to take as much income as they wanted from their pension fund even to the extent of exhausting the fund completely.

Following the responses received the Government introduced its final proposals from 6 April 2011 – the provisions being put in place within Finance Act 2011.

In summary these were:

- The compulsory transition (for those who choose not to buy an annuity) from unsecured pension income to the 'alternatively secured pension' was abolished by virtue of the abolition of the latter.
- Allowing those with DC pension savings from which they have not yet secured a pension income as at 6 April 2011 to defer taking benefits indefinitely.
- Those who have secured a lifetime pension income of at least £20,000 were able to access their drawdown pension funds without any cap on the withdrawals they may make on or after that date. This is known as 'flexible drawdown'.
- Others may instead use 'capped drawdown', where the amount drawn from the fund is subject to a set limit which approximates to the amount which could be achieved by purchasing an annuity.
- The requirement that the pension commencement lump sum must be taken by age 75 was abolished from 6 April 2011.
- The tax rate on lump sum death benefits is 55% for deaths on or after 6 April 2011 where benefits have been taken from the fund or even where benefits have not been taken if death occurs beyond age 75.
- New and reduced pension fund withdrawal limits took effect for all new drawdown pension arrangements – the term 'drawdown' replaced the previous terminology of 'unsecured' or 'alternatively secured' pension income.

A detailed consideration of these rules is set out in CHAPTER 4.

The abolition of the compulsion to buy an annuity (Part 2)

[2.24] The 2014 Budget set out radical changes to the UK pensions taxation system. The Chancellor made reference to Finance Act 1921. This introduced a trade-off whereby pension schemes, then generally referred to as superannuation funds, were able to benefit from exemption from tax on investment returns within the fund with contributions by the employer and member being tax relieved so long as the fund at retirement age was used for the sole purpose of providing an annuity.

Some of the 2014 Budget changes were effective from 27 March 2014 others will take effect from April 2015. Yet more measures are proposed to take effect from April 2015 after consultation, which ended in June 2014. Draft legislation has been published in August 2014 and more is expected later in the year.

The changes from 27 March 2014 are temporary and act as a bridge to the regime for taking benefits that is to come into effect from April 2015, which is introduced here and considered in detail in CHAPTER 4.

In summary the 27 March 2014 changes are:

- the trivial commutation limit (see CHAPTER 4) increased from £18,000 to £30,000;
- the maximum size of a small pension pot which can be taken as a lump sum (see CHAPTER 4) is increased from £2,000 to £10,000, and the number of personal pots that can be taken under these rules will be increased from two to three;
- the maximum income permitted under 'capped drawdown' (see CHAPTER 4) increased from 120% to 150% of the equivalent annuity; and
- the minimum income threshold for 'flexible drawdown' (see CHAPTER 4) changed to £12,000 from £20,000. So if a defined contribution scheme member has a secure income of at least this level the remaining fund can be cashed in but is subject to tax.

From April 2015 the Government is going to change the tax rules to allow people to access their pension savings as they wish from age 55 or later, subject to their marginal rate of income tax – rather than the current 55% charge for full withdrawal where such a withdrawal is an unauthorised member payment.

This is the unauthorised member payment charge that arises when benefit is taken in excess of the limits generally allowed from registered pension schemes and so in this context in excess of the levels permitted under capped drawdown as described earlier. Registered pension schemes generally however will not allow unauthorised member payments as if they do they risk losing their registration status.

The announcement that members of defined contribution pension schemes will be allowed to draw as much as they wish effectively abolishes the concept of capped drawdown (see CHAPTER 4) and in effect maintains the concept of flexible drawdown but in the absence of a minimum income requirement.

As these rules will be available to everybody who is a member or becomes a member of a defined contribution pension scheme then the concept of trivial commutation as it applies to defined contribution schemes becomes irrelevant.

Similarly in relation to the current provisions as they apply to small pension pots. There will be a residual need for these provisions (that is relating to trivial commutation and small pots) in relation to defined benefit schemes.

A detailed consideration of these changes and proposals is set out in CHAPTER 4.

The taxation of death benefits

[2.25] The available benefits following the death of a registered pension scheme member can be in the form of lump sums and / or in the form of pensions for dependants.

Up until 5 April 2011 the taxation of lump sum death benefits depended on whether the registered pension scheme member died before or after benefits have been taken.

In summary the pre- 6 April 2011 provisions were as follows:

- On death before benefits were taken from the pension scheme then the lump sum death benefit was free from taxation.
- Where lump sum death benefit was taken from a defined benefit scheme the maximum permitted benefit was set at four times salary at the date of death. The lump sum death benefit available from a defined contribution scheme would be limited in the same way if the scheme were an occupational scheme, but in relation to a personal pension scheme (or similar) then the lump sum payable on death would typically be represented by the fund value.
- On death after benefit had been taken in the form of unsecured income, (and thus before age 75) then where fund was paid out in lump sum form a special tax charge of 35% applied.
- On death after age 75 where an annuity had not been secured and so where benefit was being provided in the form of an alternatively secured pension, then a combination of unauthorised member payment charges and inheritance tax would lead to a total tax burden of up to 82% of the fund where the fund was used to pay a lump sum benefit (see **2.23** above).

In general terms lump sum death benefits where provided before benefits have been taken from the pension scheme are free from taxation. Lump sum death benefits in these circumstances are paid from the pension scheme to beneficiaries at the discretion of the scheme trustees. The effect of this discretionary distribution of death benefits is in order to avoid inheritance tax on the amount paid out.

Until 5 April 2011 if a pension scheme member died after the minimum pension age (55) having chosen not to exercise the right to take an income benefit there remained a possibility that the Capital Taxes Office could seek to apply inheritance tax to the fund distributed on death. This possibility was removed by the introduction of legislation to that effect in Finance Act 2011.

The taxation of lump sum benefits following the death of a pension scheme member once benefit has been taken from a registered pension scheme also changed with effect from 6 April 2011. Although inheritance tax no longer applies on any such payments (previously there was an inheritance tax charge on lump sum death benefit payments after the age of 75), a tax charge applies at the rate of 55%. This rate is expected to reduce and the reduction to be announced in the 2014 Autumn statement.

SAGA described these changes in rather blunt terms but which are difficult to counter. Namely:

' . . . the tax cut for wealthy over 75s is being financed by a tax increase on the less well-off who die early'.

As:

- Tax rates on pension funds passed on [death] after age 75 will fall from 82% to [a] maximum [of] 55%, but [the dependants of] those who die before age 75 face a tax increase [on the fund] from 35% to 55%
- The changes will help people who wish to stay in income drawdown beyond age 75, as they will not be [effectively] forced to buy an annuity
- A 55% tax relief recovery charge is penal for those who received only basic rate tax relief [on their pension contributions] and is far worse than the current 35% tax rate on [the fund following death for those in] drawdown.'

Again quoting SAGA:

'These measures are irrelevant for the vast majority of pension savers. Average annuity purchasers have [a pension fund of] just £30,000. 450,000 people every year buy an annuity and less than 1% of those buying annuities have [pension] funds above £100,000, so less than 1% of these pension savers would have enough money to benefit from flexible drawdown. For the top few, however, the benefits are substantial. Not only will they be able to take money out of their pension funds, they also face substantial tax cuts from the current level of up to 82% tax on death for pension assets that have not been annuitised by age 75, down to a maximum of 55%'.

In CHAPTER 4 these changes and their taxation consequences will be considered in detail.

In addition to, or indeed where appropriate as an alternative to lump sum death benefits, dependants' pension benefits may be provided from a registered pension scheme following the death of the scheme member.

Where the scheme is a defined benefit scheme then the rules of the scheme will normally provide that in the event of death before retirement in addition to any lump sum there will be a dependants' pension payable to a spouse, civil partner, or other financial dependant.

This will generally be expressed as a percentage (for example 50%) of the pension that the member would have been entitled to had they survived to pension age. In the event of the member's death after retirement then most defined benefit schemes will provide for a pension to continue for a surviving spouse, civil partner, or other financial dependant but expressed as a percentage of the pension income that the member was receiving at the date of death.

Where the scheme is a defined contribution scheme then it may be more tax efficient for beneficiaries to receive benefit from the fund of the deceased in the form of a lump sum, in particular where the fund is below the lifetime allowance. This would be the case in the event of death before benefits have been taken because the lump sum benefit would be paid free from tax where as income benefits would be taxable.

The tax charges as set out above relevant to lump sums paid on death after benefit has been taken from the member's pension fund may render it more tax efficient for dependants to take benefit from the fund in the form of income rather than capital. Income benefits for dependants generally are taxed as earned income.

The taxation death benefits and the changes introduced from April 2011 are covered in more detail in CHAPTER 4.

3

Taxation of contributions to registered pension schemes

Introduction

[3.1] In this chapter we look at the rules as they apply to contributions made by members and employees to registered pension schemes. As with all other taxation matters associated with registered pension schemes the relevant rules changed completely with effect from 6 April 2006.

With regard to the extent of the possible tax privileged contributions that are allowable into pension schemes this date brought radical change in that members and employees alike were no longer constrained by archaic, illogical, and inconsistent provisions.

In the era before the changes that were introduced, the rules that determined permitted contributions varied between occupational and personal schemes of one form or another. With regard to occupational schemes contributions were constrained to the extent that they were targeted at meeting benefits that could be no more than the framework of maximum permitted benefits as set out in CHAPTER 1. The occupational pension scheme member however was only able to make personal contributions (mandatory, voluntary, or a combination of the two) that could not exceed 15% of the member's remuneration.

Those who participated in retirement annuity and/or personal pension arrangements were subject to contribution limits as a percentage of earnings based upon age. The greater the individual's age then the greater the percentage of earnings they were allowed to contribute.

Occupational and personal schemes were both constrained further by the impact of the 'earnings cap' introduced in 1989, which limited the earnings which could be accounted for in both of the contexts outlined in the last two paragraphs.

For many it was apparent that the April 2006 changes went to the other extreme as far as their generosity was concerned. It came as no great surprise that the coalition Government, as a part of the UK deficit reduction proposals, put in place a significant reduction in the extent to which tax relieved pension contributions were allowed from 6 April 2011.

In this chapter we will look at the framework in detail as it started out in April 2006, bringing matters right up-to-date at the time of writing with the changes introduced as a consequence of Finance Acts 2011, 2013 and 2014.

The annual allowance 6 April 2006 to 5 April 2011

[3.2] Since 6 April 2006, all types of pension arrangement have operated within a unified tax regime for registered pension schemes. Note that changes to the annual allowance introduced with effect from 6 April 2011 are dealt with later in this chapter.

All types of registered pension scheme are subject to a contribution limit of 100% of taxable pay subject to an annual allowance which began at £215,000 on 6 April 2006, rising to £255,000 by April 2010. The annual allowance is treated as an annual limit to inflows of value, the 'total pension input amount', to an individual's pension funds within a 'pension input period'.

The progression of the annual allowance in the period 2006–07 to 2010–11 is shown in Table 1.

Table 1

Tax Year	Annual Allowance
2006–07	£215,000
2007–08	£225,000
2008–09	£235,000
2009–10	£245,000
2010–11	£255,000

To assess contributions against this inflow limit, increases in occupational defined pension benefits between one year and the next, and aggregate contributions to defined contribution schemes are valued on the basis of their inclusion in a pension input period (see below) which ends within the tax year concerned. So a pension input period which ended on 31 March 2010 resulted in contributions (or inflows) during that period that would count towards the annual allowance applicable in 2010–11 of £255,000.

For the purposes of assessing contributions against the annual allowance during the pension input period, the following were taken account of in the manner set out below:

(1)   All contributions, excluding 'contracted out rebates' allocated to provide pension benefits on a defined contribution basis. This included any funds reallocated between one member and another within the scheme.

(2)   All increases in the value of any defined benefits (using a multiple of 10) and tax-free cash sum rights – but excluding the value of any death in service benefits.

(3)   Increases in the value of deferred final salary and tax-free cash sum rights in excess of the greater of 5% and RPI. Again a multiple of 10 was used in the period up to 5 April 2011.

(4)   In assessing increases in pension rights against the annual allowance any contributions made and defined benefits scheme growth in the year during which the member took benefit were ignored in the period to 5 April 2011.

Example

> The position with regard to defined contributions is straightforward. If an individual paid defined contributions of £80,000 in a pension input period (see below) which ended on 15 May 2010, then that would have counted towards that person's annual allowance of £255,000 for the income tax year 2010–11.
>
> Another individual being a member of a final salary scheme providing a pension benefit accruing at the rate of $1/60$ of final pay for each year scheme membership would see their 'pension input' measured in the context of the increase in the number of 'sixtieths' between one year and the next, and any salary change.
>
> So in respect of an individual with ten years' pension scheme membership (and so eleven in the following year) and who between one year and the next enjoyed a salary increase from £25,000 to £28,000, his pension input was calculated as:
>
> $$\{[(^{11}/_{60} \times 28,000) - (^{10}/_{60} \times £25,000)] \times 10\}$$
>
> and thus:
>
> $$(£5,133.33 - £4,166.66) \times 10 = £9,666.70$$
>
> So based upon the new salary of £28,000, this individual could also make contributions which would be liable for income tax relief of up to a further £18,333.30 (£28,000 – £9,666.70).

These additional contributions could be made either as voluntary contributions to the occupational pension scheme, or as contributions into a separate personal pension arrangement.

Note that in these examples of how the calculations work there is no adjustment for inflation, as measured by the consumer prices index, on the starting benefit value. Such an adjustment applies from 6 April 2011 (see below) and an example with some account being taken of inflation is given later in this chapter, with further examples given in APPENDIX 6.

Pension input period (pre 6 April 2011)

[3.3] Contributions made to a registered pension scheme in a particular tax year will not necessarily count towards the member's annual allowance for that tax year.

Under **every** scheme in which an individual member participates there will be a 'pension input period'. If an individual is a member of a number of registered pension schemes then unless action is taken to change the position there will generally be a different pension input period associated with each scheme that the member is participating in.

The pension input period is defined in Finance Act 2004 section 238 as:

'(1) In the case of an arrangement under a registered pension scheme the following are pension input periods—

(a)   the period beginning with the relevant commencement date and ending with the earlier of a nominated date and the anniversary of the relevant commencement date, and

(b)   each subsequent period beginning immediately after the end of a period which is a pension input period (under paragraph (a) or this paragraph) and ending with the appropriate date.'

where . . . :

'"The relevant commencement date" means—

(a)   in the case of a cash balance arrangement or a defined benefits arrangement, or a hybrid arrangement . . . the date on which rights under the arrangement begin to accrue to or in respect of the individual,

(b)   in the case of a money purchase arrangement . . . the first date on which a contribution . . . is made'

So the first 'pension input period' in respect of membership of a particular scheme starts from the date (being on or after 6 April 2006) when contributions are first made to the scheme by the member, or on his / her behalf (for example through membership of a defined benefit scheme or as a consequence of employer contributions to a defined contribution scheme).

As is clear from the legislation it is usual that pension input periods last for 12 months and run on from each other consecutively. But the pension input period may be changed at the request of the scheme member.

Any contributions made in a 'pension input period' (other than contributions that do not attract tax relief) count against the member's annual allowance for the tax year in which the pension input period ends.

As stated, in respect of defined contribution arrangements the first pension input period starts when the first contribution to the plan is made. The end of the first pension input period is automatically set as a year later. Therefore, if the first contribution was made on 1 January 2010 then the first pension input period ran from 1 January 2010 to 1 January 2011. (See below, however, for changes introduced with effect from 6 April 2011).

So in this example the first pension input period ended on 1 January 2011. It will be apparent that the pension contribution made on 1 January 2010 was made in the 2009–10 tax year. However the pension input period associated with that arrangement ended on 1 January 2011 and so in the 2010–11 tax year. Thus the contribution made on 1 January 2010 counted for the purposes of the annual allowance towards that of the 2010–11 tax year. But the contribution received tax relief during the tax year 2009–10.

The member could change this position by requesting that the pension scheme administrator amends the date on which the first pension input period ended.

Staying with this example let's assume that the scheme member did this and requested that this pension input period ended on 31 March 2010. As a consequence the contribution made on 1 January 2010 counted towards the member's annual allowance for the 2009–10 tax year.

The second pension input period started immediately after the first one finished. So in this example the second pension input period would have started on 1 April 2010. The end of the second pension input period would have been also automatically set to end a year later. But once again it was possible to change this and nominate a new end date of the second pension input period.

The difference between the second pension input period and the first however is that the second pension input period must end in the tax year following its start date, and the second pension input period could not have a duration of more than 12 months.

Therefore in this example, the second pension input period would have started on 1 April 2010 and be set to end on 31 March 2011. The member could have asked however, to change the end date of the second pension input period so long as the end date was somewhere between 6 April 2010 and 31 March 2011.

Any subsequent pension input periods would then follow the same format in that the start date immediately followed the end of the last pension input period and the end date had to be in the following tax year.

The reason why this became a popular tax planning vehicle with high earners was that it provided the opportunity to obtain tax relief associated with two years worth of annual allowances in a single tax year. This can only be done once due to subsequent pension input periods having to end in the tax year after the start date of the input period which stops this situation from reoccurring.

Restating the example as set out above we have two pension input periods.

The first pension input period is from 1 January 2010 to 31 March 2010. Any contribution made during that period was tested against the annual allowance for 2009–10.

The second pension input period (having requested that the end date be changed) ran from 1 April 2010 to 31 March 2011 and any contribution made during that period would be tested against the 2010–11 annual allowance.

Now suppose a high earner made a £245,000 gross contribution on 1 January 2010 and a £255,000 gross contribution on 1 April 2010. The first contribution was within the first pension input period and the second contribution was within the second pension input period. However, both contributions were made in the 2009–10 tax year.

The first contribution was tested against the 2009–10 annual allowance and the second contribution was tested against the 2010–11 annual allowance. Therefore both contributions were potentially allowable against income tax.

However, as both contributions were made in the same tax year (2009–10), both will have been entered into the member's income tax return for the 2009–10 tax year and therefore the member would need to have earned income of at least £500,000 in the 2009–10 tax year in order to qualify for full income tax relief. Ideally the member would have had income in the 2009–10 tax year of much more than this in order to obtain higher rate income tax relief on the entirety of the contributions made.

This technique was used to good effect by those who received large bonuses in a particular year to mitigate some of their income tax liability. Others used it purely as a way of making contributions earlier than normal to take advantage of investment opportunities.

Pension input period – from 6 April 2011

[3.4] For new arrangements put in place on or after 6 April 2011, the first pension input period (PIP) now ends on the 5 April following (the statutory default rule), unless the scheme administrator or, in some cases, the member, nominates otherwise. Where the commencement date of the arrangement is 5 April then the pension input period is deemed to finish on the day that it started (i.e. a one day pension input period).

There was no change to the purpose of the PIP from April 2011. The PIP therefore remains as the period over which the pension input amount for an arrangement is measured against the member's annual allowance.

Each individual arrangement which has a PIP ending within a tax year contributes towards the overall total pension input amount for an individual in respect of that tax year. As set out above, the total figure is then measured against the pension scheme member's annual allowance for the tax year in question. For example a pension input period ending on 31 May 2014 would be classed as falling in the 2014–15 tax year so the input amount associated with the member would be measured against that tax year's annual allowance of £40,000.

Alterations to the PIP allow pension scheme administrators (or the member in a money purchase arrangement) to change the PIP for an arrangement so as to align it with the end of tax year, or any other date (such as a company year end), if they wish. With regard to a money purchase scheme if both the employer and the member make a nomination, it is the first nomination made which takes precedence.

Once notice has been given the second PIP begins the day after the nominated end date of the first PIP.

Nomination of a new PIP end date

[3.5] HMRC accept that a valid nomination for a particular PIP end date is made where the pension scheme administrator provides notice of this in a form that is available to all members.

This may be achieved, for example, by setting out the nominated date in the pension scheme rules, in the pension scheme handbook so long as it is made available to all the scheme members, or by a notice placed on the pension scheme's (or in the case of an occupational scheme on the employer's) website. Provided the notice is made in this way, there is no requirement to send a letter to each and every member telling them of the nominated date.

It is a matter for schemes to determine whether they have a nominated date and what that nominated date is. If no nomination has been made then the statutory default rule will apply.

A pension scheme member may nominate their own PIP end date. The member is required to give the scheme notice of this nominated date. As evidence of this, the scheme should retain whatever form of communication the member sent them by way of nomination. If the scheme does not receive any such nomination then it can assume that the scheme PIP applies.

Ending the second and subsequent PIP and starting the next

[3.6] Finance Act 2011 introduced a change which enables those who have multiple pension arrangements to bring their PIPs into line. Previously it was almost impossible to align PIPs across existing arrangements due to a limitation that it was only possible to have one pension input period ending in a tax year, and no one input period could be longer than 12 months.

The legislative change is the omission of the words *'the earlier of'* and the addition of the words *'if there is not such a nominated date, the day before'* in subsection (6) of Section 238 of Finance Act 2004.

The pension input end date for a second or subsequent PIP is now:

- A nominated date falling in the tax year immediately after that in which the last pension input period ended; or (used to be 'the earlier of');
- If no nomination has been made, the day before the anniversary date on which the last PIP ended.

So if we consider an example where an arrangement has a second or subsequent input period which started on 1 July 2013 the position is that the second PIP ends on:

- A nominated date in the 2014–15 tax year (this could be as late as 5 April 2015 meaning a pension input period of some 21 months) or
- 29 June 2014 (being the day before the anniversary of the input period that ended on 30 June 2013.

Extending the pension input period beyond 12 months does not increase the annual allowance. So in the example above it is the total input over the 21 months that is measured against the 2014–15 annual allowance.

The annual allowance charge

[3.7] There is no limit on the amount that can be invested in a registered pension scheme by a member or through their employer but there is a limit on the amount that is eligible for tax relief each year which is dealt with through the process associated with the annual allowance.

A 'pension input' beyond the annual allowance will result in a tax charge known as the annual allowance charge. The definition of the annual allowance charge is to be found in Finance Act 2004 section 227:

'(1)   A charge to income tax, to be known as the annual allowance charge, arises where—

    (a)   the total pension input amount for a tax year in the case of an individual who is a member of one or more registered pension schemes, exceeds

    (b)   the amount of the annual allowance for the tax year.

(2)   The person liable to the annual allowance charge is the individual.

(3)   The individual is liable to the annual allowance charge whether or not—

    (a)   the individual, and

(b)   the scheme administrator of the pension scheme or schemes concerned,

are resident, ordinarily resident or domiciled in the United Kingdom.

(4)   The annual allowance charge is a charge at the rate of 40% in respect of the amount by which the total pension input amount exceeds the amount of the annual allowance.'

Thus if the total inputs to registered pension schemes in respect of the registered pension scheme member exceeds the annual allowance for a particular tax year, then an annual allowance charge applied at the rate of 40% based upon the excess pension input amount. This remained in place until 5 April 2011.

How the annual allowance charge operates with effect from 6 April 2011 is set out later in this chapter.

Pensions taxation rules for high earners (Finance Act 2009)

[3.8] As we have seen, since April 2006 the tax relieved pension contribution limits have been very generous. In effect, other than the constraint of the annual allowance, up to 100% of earned income may be paid as tax relieved pension contributions.

Finance Act 2009 contained important provisions which impacted on high earning members of registered pension schemes and restricted the extent of their tax relived pension contributions. Much of this however has been repealed by the coalition Government but the provisions are mentioned here for the purposes of completeness and so that you may see the progression between the position as it maintained from April 2006 to that which maintains now.

Alistair Darling, the then Chancellor of the Exchequer, announced the proposed changes to pensions tax relief for those with relatively high incomes during his Budget speech in 2009.

The driving force behind these changes was the introduction of a new highest rate of income tax (50% on income over £150,000) effective from 6 April 2010. It was not felt appropriate that high earners would be able to avoid some or all of their income tax liability at the 50% rate by making pension contributions that would be relieved at this rate.

Under the Finance Act 2009 provisions it was set out that with effect from 6 April 2011 higher rate income tax relief on contributions to registered pension schemes would be restricted for individuals earning more than £150,000 per annum. For these individuals, tax relief was to be tapered down so that anyone earning £180,000 a year or more would only receive 20% income tax relief on their pension contributions.

These measures have been repealed and replaced by new provisions as set out later in this chapter. However the 'anti forestalling' provisions that were introduced to prevent people from accelerating their plans to make significant pension contributions so as to maximise the available income tax relief before the new rules came into effect remained unchanged.

Anti-forestalling measures

[3.9] The Government wanted to make sure that high earners did not bring forward future pension contributions so as to benefit from more tax relief on contributions that would otherwise apply if those contributions were made later, and in particular after 5 April 2011.

By so doing high earners could, without the intervention of new legislation, have benefited from the much more generous level of income tax relief that was available until the new provisions were introduced.

Regulations were also laid before Parliament to add to the list of prescribed tax avoidance schemes any new type of avoidance scheme (involving the accrual or expected accrual of pension benefits) where the main purpose was to avoid liability to the Special Annual Allowance Charge (the mechanism introduced to implement the anti-forestalling measures) as set out below.

So 'anti-forestalling' measures were put in place relating to any pension contributions made by high earners before 6 April 2011 and these measures had retrospective effect dating back to the 2009 Budget Day – 22 April 2009.

These anti-forestalling measures were set out in Schedule 35 to the Finance Act 2009. The anti-forestalling provisions applied to individuals with an annual taxable income of £150,000 or more in any of the tax years 2007–08 to 2010–11.

These anti-forestalling measures were implemented by putting in place a Special Annual Allowance of £20,000, applicable for each of the tax years 2009–10 and 2010–11. In limited circumstances, this Special Allowance could be increased to £30,000 where an individual was in the habit of making irregular pension contributions which also qualified for protection through the anti-forestalling measures.

In tandem with this Special Annual Allowance of £20,000, a Special Annual Allowance Charge of 20% was put in place which operated so as to recover the higher rate income tax relief (that is over and above basic rate income tax relief) which anyone earning more than £150,000 would otherwise have been entitled to receive. The tax charge was collected via the individual's Self Assessment tax return.

The purpose of the Special Annual Allowance was therefore to restrict the higher rate income tax relief available on registered pension scheme contributions to those earning above £150,000 per annum. How this operated in practice varied depending on the type of pension scheme that the individual was a member of.

HMRC published guidance on the anti-forestalling measures which explained in more detail the circumstances in which individuals could rely on protection from the 'Special Annual Allowance' charge and how that protection could be lost. The details are not set out here as the period associated with 'anti forestalling' has passed.

Importantly, however, the anti-forestalling measures were designed so as to permit some of those who earned more than £150,000 per annum to receive higher rate income tax relief on pension contributions or on any increase in value of their pension rights exceeding the £20,000 Special Annual Allowance limit. This was possible when the high earner's ongoing contributions or increases in the value of their pension rights fitted in with their regular pattern of pension contributions or pension benefit accrual that was already in place before 22 April 2009.

All regular pension savings under agreements which were in place before 22 April 2009 were protected and did not fall to be tested against the Special Annual Allowance regardless of their level. In addition, benefit accrual under a defined benefit scheme was protected where an individual was accruing benefits in the scheme before 22 April 2009 and where there was no material change in the rules of the scheme since that date.

The then Government introduced an amendment to the original anti-forestalling provisions as a partial concession to those who had a history of making irregular pension contributions. For those who made irregular contributions (less frequently than quarterly) to defined contribution arrangements, and where the average of those irregular contributions was more than £20,000, the special annual allowance was the average of their last three years' contributions up to a maximum of £30,000 (inclusive of any regular pension contributions).

The special annual allowance operated alongside the annual allowance. In practice this meant that all increases in pension savings, (pension input amounts), continued to be tested against the annual allowance in the usual way. Any pension input amounts made by, or in respect of, an individual in the period from 22 April 2009 to 5 April 2011 that were not protected' were tested against the special annual allowance as well, if the individual had income of £150,000 or more.

The annual allowance from April 2011

[3.10] With echoes from the 1970s pensions legislation once again became something of a political football. The Conservative/Liberal Democrat coalition came to power in May 2010, and set out in a discussion document issued on 27 July 2010 its proposals for restricting pensions income tax relief.

It was very clear that this fell within the overall framework of the Government's programme to reduce the UK deficit and was based upon an objective of reducing the cost of income tax relief associated with pensions by between £4 billion and £5 billion.

The associated urgency to get new provisions in place that would replace those already legislated for by the previous government from April 2011 was apparent by the fact that responses to the discussion document were required by 27 August 2010.

On 14 October 2010 the Government announced that, with effect from 6 April 2011, the annual allowance for tax privileged pension saving would be reduced to £50,000 and that from 6 April 2012 the lifetime allowance (covered later in this chapter) would be reduced to £1.5 million. Further reductions to the annual allowance (to £40,000) and to the lifetime allowance (to £1.25 million) are effective from 6 April 2014.

As stated by the Government:

'Taken together, these measures should generate around £4bn annual revenue in steady state, and represent a key part of the Government's deficit reduction plans.'

The pensions clauses are to be found in FA 2011 Pt 4, but the detail is in Schedules 16 to 18.

Finance Act 2011 reflects the following changes associated with the annual allowance:

(1) The annual allowance for tax years 2011–12 onwards was reduced to £50,000. (Finance Act 2011 – Schedule 17);

(2) The annual allowance charge is linked to the individual's marginal income tax rate with effect from 6 April 2011, (Finance Act 2011 – Schedule 17);

(3) Any unused annual allowance can be carried forward for three years, (Finance Act 2011 — Schedule 17);

(4) The valuation factor used to calculate the value of defined benefits pension accrual has increased from a factor of 10 to a factor of 16. (Finance Act 2011 — Schedule 17);

(5) The annual allowance rules now normally apply in the year of taking benefits, although there will be exemptions in the year of death or where the individual retires because of severe ill health;

(6) Inflation-linked increases in expected pensions for deferred members of final salary pension schemes do not count towards the annual allowance charge;

(7) Transitional rules applied from 14 October 2010 where individuals had pension inputs relating to a pension input period that started before 14 October 2010 and which ended in the 2011–12 tax year and were therefore subject to the new annual allowance limit; and

(8) Under the transitional rules where a pension input period started before 14 October 2010 and ended after 5 April 2011, the maximum pension input permitted in the pension input period without paying an annual allowance charge was £255,000. However this was subject to a maximum of £50,000 of pensions input in the period from 14 October 2010 to the last day of the pensions input period.

For members of defined contribution schemes the measure of the pension input remains straightforward, being the contributions made and / or on behalf of the member over the input period. But for final salary scheme members the calculations are (as before) based on the concept of the 'closing value' of the member's pension rights less the 'opening value' of the member's pension rights, but under the new legislation with an adjustment to the opening value based on the Consumer Prices Index (CPI).

Example

Tina is a management consultant. She is a member of a final salary scheme giving her a pension of $1/60$ of pensionable pay for each year of service. At the start of the pension input period (PIP) Tina's pensionable pay is £80,000 and she has 31 years' pensionable service.

At the end of the PIP Tina's pensionable pay has risen by 5% to £84,000 with 32 years' pensionable service.

Tina's pension input amount is the increase in the value of her pension saving over the year. This is the difference between the opening value (adjusted for CPI) and the closing value of her promised benefits.

The opening value

Tina's opening value is calculated as:

Calculate amount of annual pension accrued:
$^{31}/_{60} \times £80,000 = $ **£41,333.33**

Multiply annual rate of pension accrued by flat factor of 16
£41,333.33 × 16 = **£661,333.28**

Increase by CPI - (for this example assuming 3%)
£661,333.28 × 1.03 = **£681,173.27**

Tina's opening value is **£681,173.27**

The closing value

Tina's closing value is calculated as:

Find amount of annual pension accrued
$^{32}/_{60} \times £84,000 = $ **£44,800**

Multiply annual rate of pension by flat factor of 16
£44,800 × 16 = **£716,800**

Tina's closing value is **£716,800**

Calculating the pension input amount

The difference between the closing value and the opening value is £35,626.73. This is less than the annual allowance so Tina does not have to pay the annual allowance charge.

HMRC have provided helpful examples of how the new rules operate in the calculation of the extent to which defined benefit scheme members have utilised their annual allowance. Some of these have been incorporated into Appendix 6 for ease of reference.

The annual allowance charge from 6 April 2011

[3.11] The purpose of the annual allowance tax charge is to remove tax relief on any pension input that has been made which exceeds the member's available annual allowance.

The amount of the annual allowance charge now depends on the rate at which tax relief had effectively been given on the excess pension inputs in the first place. This therefore depends on the amount of the member's taxable income and the amount of the member's excess pension inputs. To establish the amount of the member's annual allowance charge it is necessary to add the amount of the excessive pension inputs to the amount of income on which income tax is due.

The pension inputs which exceed the annual allowance are therefore taxed at up to 45% (2014–15 income tax rates).

With effect from 6 April 2011 the annual allowance charge also applies in the year pension benefits are taken except where the member is in serious or severe ill-health. The condition for this to apply is that the individual is unable to work again in any gainful capacity before reaching pensionable age (otherwise than to an insignificant extent) or becomes entitled to a serious ill-health lump sum under the pension arrangement, or becomes entitled to a tax-free benefit provided as compensation to a member of the armed forces by reason of illness or injury. The annual allowance does not apply for the tax year in which an individual dies.

Example of the annual allowance charge calculation as applicable from 6 April 2011

Emma has £20,000 of excess pension inputs on which she has to pay the annual allowance charge.

Emma has £132,000 of income on which she is liable to pay income tax.

The total of Emma's taxable income and excess pension inputs is therefore £152,000.

For the purpose of this example the higher rate income tax limit is £150,000 and the basic rate income tax limit is £40,000.

£2,000 of Emma's excess pension input exceeds the £150,000 higher rate limit.

£8,000 of her excess pension input is above the basic rate limit but below the higher rate limit.

So Emma's annual allowance charge is calculated as:

£2,000 @ 45% = £900 and

£18,000 @ 40% = £7,200

Emma's annual allowance charge is therefore £8,100.

This example illustrates that the extent of the annual allowance charge for some could be significant. As a consequence the Government published a further discussion document in November 2010 called 'Options to meet high annual allowance charges from pension benefits'. The consultation period associated with this document ended on 7 January 2011 and the outcome is covered in **3.17** below.

2011 information regulations associated with the annual allowance

[3.12] Annual Allowance Information Regulations, SI 2011/1797 set out the requirements on pension scheme administrators and employers to ensure pension scheme members have access to the information they need to calculate and report any annual allowance charge.

The Notice of Joint Liability of the Annual Allowance Charge Regulations, SI 2011/1793 set out the requirements for a pension scheme member to notify the scheme that they want the scheme to pay their annual allowance charge in return for a reduction in their benefits.

The Modification of Scheme Rules Regulations, SI 2011/1791 provide a statutory override of existing pension scheme rules to allow pension schemes to pay a member's annual allowance charge on their behalf.

Accounting and Assessing Regulations, SI 2011/302 relate to changes to the pension scheme Accounting for Tax form to enable pension scheme administrators to report and pay any annual allowance charge they are jointly liable for.

Transitional protection relating to the 2011–12 pension input period (PIP)

[3.13] In order to avoid what would for some people amount to retrospective changes in the annual allowance, transitional protection was introduced which applied to those where their pension input started before 14 October 2010 (the date on which the lower annual allowance was announced), and ended in the 2011–12 tax year. This was known as the 'straddling pension input period'.

The annual allowance tax charge did not apply to any pension savings of more than £50,000 (subject to an overall maximum of £255,000), where the excess pension saving was built up before 14 October 2010 for PIPs ending in 2011–12.

These transitional provisions only applied where the total pension input exceeded £50,000 and operated by treating the straddling period as if it were two separate input periods – the 'pre-announcement period' and the 'post-announcement period'.

The 'pre-announcement period' commenced at the start of the PIP and ended on 13 October 2010.

Calculations for this first period were undertaken on the old basis, and so the value defined benefit increases using a factor of 10 as the multiplier. Having established the input amount for the pre-announcement period, there had to be deducted the difference between £255,000, and the lesser of £50,000 and the input relating to the 'post-announcement period'. If the result is negative it is treated as being zero.

The 'post-announcement period' began on 14 October 2010 and ended when the straddling PIP ends. Calculations for the post-announcement period were undertaken on the new basis which meant using a factor of 16 for valuing increases in defined benefits. Having established the input for the post-announcement period it was necessary to deduct £50,000 to get the post-announcement period figure (nil if the outcome was negative).

An example of the straddling pension input period

Carol is a registered pension scheme member with a PIP starting on 1 June 2010 and ending on 31 May 2011. She contributes £5,000 a month and has also made two single contributions of £20,000, one on 1 August 2010 and the other on 1 February 2011. Her total pension input for 2011–12 is £100,000 so the transitional protection rules need to be applied to see if an annual allowance charge will be payable.

Pre-announcement period (period 1)

Pension contributions: (5 × £5,000) plus £20,000 = £45,000.

Post-announcement period (period 2)

Pension contributions: (7 × £5,000) plus £20,000 = £55,000

The figures to be used therefore are:

In respect of the pre-announcement period:

£45,000 – (£255,000 – £50,000) = NIL (as result is negative)

In respect of the post-announcement period:

£55,000 – £50,000 = £5,000

An annual allowance charge based on £5,000 applies unless Carol is able to carry forward unused relief.

The annual allowance from April 2014

[3.14] The annual allowance has reduced to £40,000 from 2014–15. Legislation to implement this was contained in Finance Act 2013 where section 49 amends FA 2004 s 228. According to the Government this 'supports the objective of a system of pensions tax relief that is fair, affordable and sustainable'.

There are no changes to the carry forward rules (see **3.18** below). This means that the amount of any unused allowances arising from the tax years 2011–12 to 2013–14 and available for carry forward to 2014–15 and subsequent years will still be based on the £50,000 limit.

The annual allowance for those in flexible drawdown and flexi-access drawdown from April 2015

[3.15]

If a member of a defined contribution scheme receives a flexible drawdown payment (see CHAPTER 4) before 6 April 2015, then under the pre-6 April 2015 (current) rules they have a nil annual allowance for all types of pension savings (both money purchase and defined benefit).

On 6 April 2015, the fund will automatically become a flexi-access drawdown fund (see CHAPTER 4) and the member will be subject to the new money purchase annual allowance rules from that date (see below).

The normal annual allowance will apply for those who trigger the money purchase annual allowance rules. Therefore for tax years 2015–16 onwards, a £40,000 overall annual allowance will apply with a £10,000 limit on tax relieved money purchase savings where the money purchase annual allowance rules apply. The balance could of course be used if the member were a member of a defined benefit scheme.

The money purchase annual allowance from 6 April 2015

[3.16] The new money purchase annual allowance rules have been introduced to ensure that individuals do not use the new flexibilities, which are intended to provide people with greater access to their retirement savings (see CHAPTER 4), to avoid tax on their current earnings by diverting their salary into their pension with tax relief, and then immediately withdrawing 25% tax-free.

The money purchase annual allowance rules will apply if any of the following occurs in a tax year, on or after 6 April 2015:

(1)   drawdown of funds from a flexi-access drawdown fund, including receiving payments from a short-term annuity provided from a flexi-access drawdown fund;

(2)   receipt of an uncrystallised funds pension lump sum (see CHAPTER 4);

(3)   notification of conversion of a pre-6 April 2015 capped drawdown pension fund to a flexi-access drawdown fund and subsequently taking a drawdown pension from that fund;

(4)   taking more than the permitted maximum for capped drawdown from a pre-6 April 2015 drawdown pension fund; or

(5)   receiving a stand-alone lump sum and not being entitled to enhanced protection.

In addition the money purchase annual allowance rules will apply from 6 April 2015:

(6)   on receipt before 6 April 2015 of a flexible drawdown payment from a pre-6 April 2015 drawdown pension fund.

If the money purchase annual allowance rules are triggered then a £10,000 annual allowance will apply for money purchase pension savings. Depending on whether or not this £10,000 limit is exceeded, either a reduced £30,000 annual allowance will apply on any defined benefit scheme benefit accrual, or the normal £40,000 annual allowance will apply less any money purchase pension savings.

If the money purchase annual allowance rules are triggered and the £10,000 money purchase annual allowance is exceeded in any tax year then an annual allowance charge will apply on the excess over £10,000, and the annual allowance for the remainder of pension savings (defined benefit scheme benefit accrual) will be reduced to £30,000 (the 'alternative annual allowance') plus any unused annual allowance carried forward from the three previous tax years.

To ensure that the same savings are not subject to the annual allowance twice, any pension savings tested against the £10,000 money purchase annual allowance will not be tested against the reduced £30,000 annual allowance.

If the £10,000 money purchase annual allowance is not exceeded then the total annual allowance, for money purchase and defined benefit arrangements, will continue to be £40,000 plus any unused annual allowance carried forward from the three previous tax years.

It will not be possible to carry forward any unused money purchase annual allowance.

If there is a trigger event in a tax year then the money purchase annual allowance rules apply from the day after the trigger event occurred. The amount of any annual allowance charge due will depend on whether total money purchase pension savings exceed £10,000, and whether in addition the alternative chargeable amount is more than the default chargeable amount.

For the purpose of the annual allowance generally, pension savings in a particular arrangement count for the pension input period for the arrangement that ends in a particular tax year. Each successive pension input period must end in consecutive tax years, but pension input periods do not have to match tax years.

So when a trigger event occurs in a tax year there are a number of possible situations for pension input periods that may be affected:

(1)   There may have been a pension input period that has already ended in the tax year. For example a pension input period runs from 1 October 2015 to 30 September 2016 and a trigger event occurs on 1 November 2016.

(2)   There may be a pension input period that will end in the tax year but hasn't ended when the trigger event occurs. For example a pension input period runs from 1 January 2015 to 31 December 2015 and a trigger event occurs on 1 December 2015.

(3)   There may be a pension input period ending in the next tax year, for example a trigger event occurs on 1 March 2016 where the pension input period runs 1 January to December.

In the first year that the money purchase annual allowance rules apply any money purchase savings made prior to triggering the rules will not be subject to the money purchase annual allowance.

So where the first situation arises then for the purposes of the £10,000 money purchase annual allowance the pension input amount for a money purchase arrangement is treated as nil. However any pension input amount for this arrangement is tested against the full annual allowance, even if other money purchase savings would have exceeded the money purchase annual allowance.

Where the second or third situation arises, the pension input amount is split into two, the amount that arose up to and including the date of the trigger event, and the amount that arose after the trigger event. Only the latter is tested against the money purchase annual allowance. The way that the pension input amount is split depends on the type of arrangement:

(a)   Where the money purchase arrangement is a defined contribution arrangement this split is based on the contributions for each period.

(b)   If the arrangement is a cash balance arrangement, then the pension input amount for the arrangement is split proportionally so that if the pension input period is 365 days and the trigger event occurred 100 days before the end of the pension input period, then the pension input amount that is tested against the money purchase annual allowance is 100/365 times that pension input amount.

Paying the annual allowance charge

[3.17] Until 6 April 2011, the much higher level of the annual allowance meant that it was relatively unusual for an individual to be subject to an annual allowance charge. Where an annual allowance charge was payable it would be dealt with through the pension scheme member's self-assessment tax return.

However the Government recognised that a consequence of the much lower annual allowance introduced from 6 April 2011 would mean that for some people (in particular members of defined benefit occupational schemes), difficulties could arise associated with settling the tax liability that the annual allowance charge could result in.

Thus since 6 April 2011 individuals can elect for their pension scheme to pay their annual allowance charge out of their pension benefits.

All the same and as stated in the discussion document referred to in **3.11**:

'Average annual pension contributions are significantly below £50,000. Only around 100,000 individuals are currently saving more than that, around 80 per cent of whom are on incomes of over £100,000.

The Government anticipates that most individuals and employers will look to adapt their pension saving behaviour and remuneration terms to ensure that their pension contributions remain below the annual allowance. This will mean that few people will actually face a tax charge for exceeding the annual allowance.'

And in recognition of the nature of the issue:

'It is relatively simple for individuals who are members of defined contribution schemes to identify and control contributions into their pension pot. However, the Government recognises that this is more difficult for members of defined benefit schemes, particularly traditional final salary schemes.

This is because DB pension-holders receive a future pension promise determined by various factors including length of service, scheme accrual rate, level of salary, and rate of salary increase. In particular circumstances, the combination of these factors could create uneven, and potentially sizeable, annual increases in pension in certain years.'

One of the measures was to introduce the possibility of carrying forward unused lifetime allowance accrued over the previous three years. The relevant provisions are set out below in **3.18**. Although this provision will for many significantly reduce or eliminate an annual allowance charge there is still likely to be a problem

'especially . . . . for high earners and long servers in final salary schemes with generous accrual rates.'

Scheme Pays

Payment of the annual allowance charge from the member's pension benefits has been allowed since 6 April 2011 where the individual has an annual allowance charge of more than £2,000. Individuals who are eligible to opt for their annual allowance charge to be met from their pension benefits can report this choice on their self-assessment tax return. The individual also needs to inform the pension scheme of which they are a member of their election.

The pension scheme will then have to make an offsetting adjustment to the individual's pension benefit, to reflect the value of the tax due. The Government stipulated that the associated reduction to an individual's pension benefits to account for the payment of an annual allowance charge must be broadly fair and accurate, so that the individual and other members of the same scheme cannot be advantaged or disadvantaged as a result. Because of the complexities associated with defined benefit schemes in particular it was decided that it would be left to the scheme to determine how the member's pension benefits would be reduced to take account of the payment of the annual allowance charge from the pension fund.

The responses to a discussion document indicated that some pension schemes may choose to use a variant of the pension debit approach as used for divorce cases.

Others indicated that they would look to reduce any defined contribution benefits held within a defined benefit scheme, such as those associated with additional voluntary contributions. Another suggested approach was that schemes could hold a debit against the defined benefits in the form of a 'negative defined contribution' (or loan) made to the individual to account for the annual allowance charge paid by the scheme.

The view expressed by the Government was that, in general terms, these approaches could be appropriate for schemes to use. But it was also recognised that there may also be circumstances where a deduction of a period of service could be appropriate, for example if there are unlikely to be future changes in salary that could otherwise lead to volatile outcomes.

The Government concluded that it should be for pension scheme trustees, having taken advice from actuaries, to ensure that any offsetting adjustment made to a member's benefit delivers a just and reasonable outcome to that individual and to other scheme members. As a consequence pension schemes will be able to make adjustments that fit best for their own scheme design and individual circumstances.

This is the approach that has been legislated for. However, if it materialises that there are later concerns about the way that schemes act in practice in this regard then the Government has made it clear that it will ask the Government Actuary to lead work on developing a more prescriptive regime, which will be legislated for subsequently.

Normally when a member wants to use 'scheme pays', the member must give notice to the scheme no later than 31 July in the year following that in which the tax year ends in which the charge arises (FA 2004 s 237B(5) as inserted by FA 2011 Schedule 17, para 15). So for an annual allowance charge arising in tax year 2014–15, the notice must be given no later than 31 July 2016.

This deadline is subject to s 237B(6) which applies in the tax year the member becomes entitled to all their benefits under the pension scheme. This sets out that the notice must be given before the date they become actually entitled to all their benefits under the pension scheme. The intention here was to ensure that any reduction to benefits could be calculated before benefits came into payment.

However the current legislation refers to when the individual becomes entitled to all of their benefits in the tax year for which the annual allowance charge relates. Because the member's pension input period (PIP) does not have to align with the tax year, in some circumstances this can mean that their final annual allowance charge does not arise in the tax year the individual has taken all their benefits. In these circumstances they cannot give notice for that annual allowance charge before they take benefits because the annual allowance charge relates to the following tax year. Regulations will be made to amend s 237B(6) to address this issue and the regulations will be retrospective.

Carrying forward unused annual allowance

[3.18] Paragraph 5 of FA 2011 Sch 17 inserted a new section 228A in Finance Act 2004.

This provides for any unused annual allowance for the three years preceding the current year to be added to the annual allowance for the current year for the purposes of determining whether an annual allowance charge is applicable in relation to the pension scheme member for the current year.

Unused annual allowance is only available for carry forward where it arises during a tax year in which the individual is a member of a registered pension scheme, but applies in respect of a tax year even if the pension input amount for that year is nil.

Quoting from the new legislation (s 228A inserted by FA 2011 Sch 17 para 5):

'(1)   This section applies if the individual has unused annual allowance available for the tax year ("the current tax year").

(2)   The annual allowance for the current tax year in the case of the individual is to be treated as increased by the amount of the unused annual allowance available for the current tax year.

(3)   The individual has unused annual allowance available for the current tax year if:

(a)   the amount of the annual allowance (before any increase under this section) for the immediately preceding tax year exceeded the total pension input amount in the case of the individual for that tax year, or

(b)   the amount of the annual allowance (before any such increase) for either or both of the two tax years immediately preceding that immediately preceding tax year exceeded the total pension input amount in the case of the individual for the tax year concerned and the excess (or, where there is an excess for both of those tax years, the excess for both tax years) has not been used up, or both.

(4)   Subsection (3):

(a)   does not apply in relation to a tax year preceding the current tax year unless the individual was a member of a registered pension scheme at some time during that tax year, but

(b)   subject to that, applies in relation to such a tax year even if the total pension input amount in the case of the individual for that tax year was nil (in which case the excess within paragraph (a) or (b) of that subsection is the whole amount of the annual allowance before any increase under this section).'

Where the member is in a defined benefit scheme the carry forward calculations can be quite complex. An example is shown in APPENDIX 6.

There is a strict order in which any available annual allowance must be used up. The annual allowance for the current tax year should be used first. The unused annual allowance from earlier years is then used, beginning with any available annual allowance from the earliest tax year.

However, the position for tax years 2008–09, 2009–10 and 2010–11 (where a deemed annual allowance of £50,000 applies) is treated differently as set out in the next section.

Unused annual allowance can be carried forward automatically and does not need to be notified by the individual to HMRC or the scheme administrator.

Valuing pension inputs made before 6 April 2011 for carry forward purposes

[3.19] The amount of the annual allowance for 2011–12 and thereafter is lower than the annual allowance was for previous tax years. Because of this there were special rules for working out how much annual allowance could be carried forward from the tax years 2008–09, 2009–10, and 2010–11. The annual allowance for each of 2008–09, 2009–10 and 2010–11 is deemed to have been £50,000.

So if an individual's total pension input amount in each of those tax years was £20,000 then they were deemed to have up to £30,000 of unused annual allowance to carry forward in respect of each year. If their total pension input amount was £50,000 or more in respect of any of these tax years then they would not have any annual allowance left to carry forward from that tax year.

The calculations are based on the new valuation methods in respect of final salary schemes. So, for a defined benefit arrangement the new factor of 16 is used (rather than the previous factor of 10). And the opening value is increased by the CPI (see section **3.10**). The method of working out if the individual had to pay an annual allowance charge, and how much, for the tax years 2008–09, 2009–10 and 2010–11 has not changed.

Normally, if one of the previous three years has an input amount of more than the annual allowance then that excess is treated as using up any amount of available annual allowance from the preceding year(s) first and this will reduce the available annual allowance to be carried forward.

The lifetime allowance – 6 April 2006 to 5 April 2012

[3.20] A lifetime limit on the total amount of pension value that could benefit from tax relief was introduced with effect from 6 April 2006.

At outset this was £1.5 million. The lifetime allowance increased to £1.6 million for 2007–08, then to £1.65 million for 2008–09, £1.75 million for 2009–10 and £1.8 million for 2010–11. This remained unchanged for 2011–12. The intention at the time of the introduction of the lifetime allowance was that the amount of the lifetime allowance would then be reviewed with subsequent reviews every five years.

Testing against the lifetime allowance takes place at a benefit crystallisation event. Generally a benefit crystallisation event will occur when benefits are taken. The full range of benefit crystallisation events is however described in Appendix **4**.

At the time of its introduction it was recognised that there were some people who had accrued pension rights that already exceeded the lifetime allowance and that without protecting them in some way they would become subject to a lifetime allowance charge (see below) when benefits are taken.

Two forms of protection were introduced. Primary protection was designed for those who at 5 April 2006 already had pension rights that exceeded £1.5 million. So long as they registered for primary protection before 6 April 2009 they receive the benefit of an enhanced lifetime allowance.

So if an individual for example had pension rights which as at 5 April 2006 were valued at £3 million, that individual would (on registration for primary protection) be entitled to an enhanced annual allowance which would be double the normal annual allowance. So in the tax year 2011–12 for example no annual allowance charge would apply if benefits were taken in that tax year and the value of such an individual's pensions rights did not exceed £3.6 million.

The second form of protection, enhanced protection, was available to anybody whether or not the value of their pension rights at 5 April 2006 already exceeded the then lifetime allowance. By undertaking not to accrue additional pension rights (other than a limited exemption associated with defined benefit scheme membership), the individual with enhanced protection benefits from an unlimited lifetime allowance.

Registration was necessary in order to benefit from one of or both forms of protection. The way that registration for both forms of protection works is on the basis that if an individual who has registered for enhanced protection loses that protection by virtue of additional pension accrual then the benefit of primary protection (if applicable) takes over. This would however only be relevant for an individual who at 5 April 2006 had pension rights which already exceeded £1.5 million.

The lifetime allowance from 6 April 2012

[3.21] As a part of the strategy associated with the desire to reduce the taxation costs associated with registered pension schemes it had already been announced by the previous Labour administration that the lifetime allowance would be frozen from 6 April 2011 for at least five years.

The coalition Government decided to take this further. Finance Act 2011 included provisions to reduce the lifetime allowance to £1.5 million with effect from 6 April 2012.

The legislation that puts this in place is set out in FA 2004 s 218 as substituted by FA 2011 Sch 18 para 2, thus:

'(2) The standard lifetime allowance for the tax year 2012-13 and, subject to subsection (3), subsequent tax years is £1,500,000.

(3) The Treasury may by order provide that the standard lifetime allowance for any tax year subsequent to the tax year 2012-13 is such amount, not being less than the standard lifetime allowance for the immediately preceding tax year, as is specified in the order.'

Anyone however with existing primary or enhanced protection is unaffected by the reduction in the lifetime allowance, in the sense in particular that so far as primary protection is concerned, the enhanced lifetime allowance is based upon the original £1.8 million figure and not the new £1.5 million level of the lifetime allowance.

A similar association with the previous level of the lifetime allowance is introduced in relation to 'trivial commutation', with a fixed threshold in that regard of £18,000 (1% of the previous lifetime allowance). Similarly in other instances where the 1% of lifetime allowance threshold has relevance a fixed figure of £18,000 now applies.

Fixed protection

[3.22] Alongside the reduction in the lifetime allowance is a form of protection called 'fixed protection'. This protection is available to people who expect the value of their pension savings to exceed £1.5 million when they come to take their benefits. An application for fixed protection had to be made by 6 April 2012.

The Registered Pension Schemes (Lifetime Allowance Transitional Protection) Regulations, SI 2011/1752, set out the requirements for an individual to apply for the new fixed protection from the reduced lifetime allowance. The purpose of fixed protection is to protect pension rights with a value of up to £1.8 million from the lifetime allowance charge.

However, to retain fixed protection it is necessary that:

(1)   No new contributions are paid to a defined contribution arrangement.
(2)   The amount of benefits that can continue to be accrued in a defined benefit scheme or a cash balance scheme will be limited (see below),
(3)   Participation does not take place in a further registered pension scheme unless it is only for the purpose of receiving a transfer of rights from an existing pension arrangement.

Entitlement to fixed protection will not be available if the member already benefits from enhanced or primary protection.

For defined benefits or cash balance arrangements the benefit of fixed protection will be lost if in any tax year from 2012–13 onwards, the value of the individual's pension rights over the tax year have gone up by more than the 'relevant percentage'.

The benefit accrual test for fixed protection is a forward looking test that begins immediately after midnight on 6 April each year. If the pension and lump sum rights of a scheme member with fixed protection are increased by an amount exceeding the relevant percentage at any time during a tax year, the member will lose their fixed protection at the point the relevant percentage was exceeded, irrespective of what happens subsequently during the tax year.

The relevant percentage is either:

(a)   The annual rate used to increase the member's pension rights as specified in the scheme rules at 9 December 2010 or, if none,
(b)   The percentage by which the consumer prices index (CPI) increased in the year ending in September of the previous tax year. So for the tax year 2014–15 it will be the percentage increase in the CPI for the 12-month period ending September 2013. That increase was 2.7%. If there is no increase or a fall in the CPI in the relevant period, then the percentage rate is nil.

Defined benefits schemes normally specify a percentage rate by which deferred benefits will increase each year until the time when the member takes their benefits. At the start of any tax year a member will be able to find out the relevant percentage applicable to them because it is either specified in the scheme rules or has already been published as the annual increase in the CPI.

For an active member, benefits will normally increase in value by reference to years of service and pensionable salary rather than by a percentage rate. So the relevant percentage for an active member of a defined benefits scheme will be the increase in CPI.

This will allow scheme members to calculate by how much their pension and lump sum rights can increase during the tax year before they lose fixed protection.

It is for the scheme member to decide on the frequency of the test during the tax year based on their own circumstances, bearing in mind they have an obligation to notify HMRC if they have lost fixed protection, with possible penalties for not doing so.

Pension scheme rules may include an earnings cap. This means that the definition of final pensionable salary includes a cap on the amount of a member's earnings that counts as pensionable salary. The cap may change with the tax year (for example the continued operation of the earnings cap under pre A-day tax legislation). Where a member has applied for fixed protection and the scheme rules include an earnings cap, an increase in the cap may lead to a loss of fixed protection where this results in benefit accrual.

The Government announced in the 2012 budget papers that a regulation making power would be introduced to allow changes to be made to the fixed protection legislation. This power was included in Finance Act 2013 and allowed regulations to be made to help prevent an individual losing fixed protection in certain specific circumstances.

Paragraph 14 of FA 2011 Sch 18 provided for when fixed protection applies and when it ceases to apply. However, this legislation could not be amended other than through changes in a future Finance Act. The new power allows regulations to be made retrospectively back to April 2012, providing they do not increase any person's liability to tax.

Thus FA 2004 Sch 28 defines what a 'scheme pension' is for the purposes of FA 2004 Part 4. Subject to certain specific exceptions, extended by the Pension Schemes (Reduction in Pension Rates) Regulations 2006 (SI 2006/138), these rules ensured that if a pension in payment were reduced, that the pension will not remain a scheme pension and future payments will be unauthorised payments. However a 'scheme pays' facility was introduced in 2011 when the annual allowance was reduced to £50,000, so that annual allowance charges could be met by scheme administrators out of scheme members' pension funds.

Regulations were introduced in 2013 to amend the Pension Schemes (Reduction in Pension Rates) Regulations 2006 (SI 2006/138). This amendment ensures that a reduction to a member's pension in payment made because the member's annual allowance charge has been paid by the pension scheme out of the member's accrued benefits, will not affect the tax treatment of the pension.

These regulations also amend the Registered Pension Schemes (Accounting and Assessment) Regulations 2005 (SI 2005/3454) by extending the information that scheme administrators must provide to HMRC where annual allowance charges are paid out of a scheme, to include the tax year to which the charge relates.

The amending regulations referred to are the Registered Pension Schemes (Reduction in Pension Rates, Accounting and Assessment) (Amendment) Regulations 2013 (SI 2013/1111).

The lifetime allowance from 6 April 2014

[3.23] The Government announced on 5 December 2012 that to 'support its objective of a system of pensions tax relief that is fair, affordable and sustainable', for 2014–15 onwards the lifetime allowance would be reduced from £1.5 million to £1.25 million.

Legislation was introduced in Finance Act 2013 amending section 218 of FA 2004.

Fixed protection 2014 and individual protection 2014

[3.24] In relation to fixed protection 2014, legislation was introduced in section 47 of Finance Act 2013 and in Schedule 22. The Government also consulted on a new form of protection – individual protection.

Fixed protection 2014 ('FP14')

This entitles individuals with pension savings of £1.4 million or more at 6 April 2014 to a lifetime allowance of £1.5 million. Any new pension savings made by or on behalf of the individual on or after 6 April 2014 will generally lead to the loss of FP14. Individuals must apply for FP14 before 6 April 2014.

An individual with FP14 therefore has a lifetime allowance of £1.5 million. Any new savings made on or after 6 April 2014, however, would mean that the individual would revert to the standard lifetime allowance of £1.25 million and any tax relieved pension savings above £1.25 million would be subject to the lifetime allowance charge. In effect, this means individuals with FP14 are likely to need to opt out of active membership of all UK tax relieved pension schemes if they want to maintain this protection.

Individual protection ('IP14')

In order to offer individuals greater flexibility in protecting any pension rights they have accrued before 6 April 2014 from the lifetime allowance charge, (subject to an overall maximum of the current lifetime allowance of £1.5 million), the Government announced in the 2013 Budget that it will offer an individual protection regime in addition to the fixed protection (2014) regime.

A consultation document was issued on 10 June 2013 (see https://www.gov.u k/government/uploads/system/uploads/attachment_data/file/205777/130607_ IP14_Condoc_Final.pdf).

Legislation was introduced in Finance Act 2014 to provide further transitional protection ('individual protection 2014' or simply 'IP14') from the pensions lifetime allowance charge.

The effects of IP14 are that:

- IP14 gives individuals a personalised lifetime allowance based on the value of their pension savings at 5 April 2014 (up to £1.5 million). It allows individuals to continue pension saving after 5 April 2014 whilst protecting tax relieved pension savings that have accrued up to that date, subject to an overall maximum of £1.5 million.
- Individuals have until 5 April 2017 to apply for IP14 if they don't have existing primary or enhanced protection.
- The option of IP14 will therefore be of particular benefit for those who want to continue saving in their pension scheme after 5 April 2014, albeit that they would normally have a lower lifetime allowance than with FP14 and will be subject to lifetime allowance charges on the additional savings.
- IP14 may also be beneficial to an individual whose employer normally contributes towards their pension scheme but, if the individual opted out of the pension scheme, they would not be able to receive the value of those employer contributions in another form such as higher pay. In such cases they may prefer to remain an active member of the scheme and continue to receive the benefit of the employer contributions, albeit that these will be subject to an LTA charge when benefits are taken.
- Individuals will be able to apply for both FP14 and IP14, subject to meeting the eligibility conditions.

Calculation of the lifetime allowance

[3.25] For the purposes of determining whether the lifetime allowance has been exceeded the following factors are and continue to be used:

- A factor of 20:1 to convert each £1 of a member's benefit from a defined benefits scheme to a capital sum. This factor applies irrespective of the age and sex of the member and their retirement date.
- This 20:1 factor can be used where the member's scheme benefits provide for dependants' pensions of no more than the member's own pension and where pensions in payment increase by no more than the greater of 5% per annum compound or RPI. Where a scheme provides for a benefits structure in excess of this, then a separate conversion factor must be agreed with HMRC.
- A factor of 25:1 to convert each £1 of a member's benefits in payment prior to 6 April 2006 to a capital sum. This higher factor is to take account of the assumption that a pension commencement lump sum will have been taken.

• Where a member is in receipt of income withdrawal benefits, which started before 6 April 2006, the income being withdrawn will be assumed to be at the maximum permitted level as calculated on the commencement of income withdrawal or at the most recent review. A factor of 25:1 will then be used to convert the income/assumed income to a capital sum.

Retirement age – and its impact on the lifetime allowance

[3.26] The minimum age from which benefits may normally be drawn for those in good health from a registered pension scheme has been 55 since 6 April 2010. There are, however, two circumstances where benefits may be taken whilst the member is in normal health before age 55.

(1) Where members of occupational schemes have a contractual right to draw benefits before age 55. This right will be honoured where it was in force before 10 December 2003 - and where it continued to apply from 6 April 2006. This right must be capable of being exercised by the employee or ex-employee unilaterally. There must not be the operation of any trustee's discretion to enable this provision to apply.
All the benefits from the scheme in question must be taken when this right is used and the individual must no longer be employed by the employer when benefits commence. Thus if they have not already left they must retire from the service of that employer.

(2) Where individuals are members of a personal pension/stakeholder scheme, or a retirement annuity policy at 6 April 2006 from which they were entitled to draw benefits early because they are in a 'special occupation' (e.g. professional footballer). So long as benefits are taken in full from the scheme at the permitted lower age, then this facility remains.

In each of the above cases the member's lifetime allowance is reduced by 2.5% for each complete year before age 55 that the benefit is taken. For example, if the benefit is taken at age 35 for a professional footballer in 2014, the reduction in his/her lifetime allowance would be 50% (i.e. 20 × 2.5%).

Further pension rights may accrue. However, the individual in this example would only be able to use the remaining 50% of their lifetime allowance for the purpose of accumulating further tax privileged savings.

Benefits from the registered scheme may also be taken before age 55 where the member is in ill health (see CHAPTER 4). To pay benefits in these circumstances the scheme will need a written opinion from a registered medical practitioner that the member is incapable of continuing their current occupation because of ill-health.

Testing against the lifetime allowance

[3.27] Funds will be tested against the lifetime allowance when:

- A benefit comes into payment (is 'crystallised') from a registered scheme.
- When there is an increase to a pension in payment above that assumed by the conversion factor used to value the benefit against the lifetime allowance.
- The scheme member reaches age 75 with unvested funds.
- The member dies and a lump sum death benefit is payable - other than a lump sum arising from vested benefits.

If the registered scheme member has previously taken benefit from any scheme whether before or after 6 April 2006, these benefits must be taken into account when determining the benefits that may be drawn within the member's lifetime allowance at the time further benefits are vested.

When benefits 'crystallise' for lifetime allowance purposes, what is then measured is the level of the member's lifetime allowance that is represented by the member's crystallised benefits. It is then necessary to calculate the percentage of the member's lifetime allowance (as applies for the tax year in which the crystallisation event occurs) that the capital value of the benefits 'crystallising' represents. This is the extent to which the member's lifetime allowance has been used - measured as a percentage of the lifetime allowance.

When the individual next draws or 'crystallises' benefits, the same process repeats. But this time the measure that is looked at is the level of the member's lifetime allowance represented by the member's newly crystallised benefits (as a percentage of the then lifetime allowance) against the 'available' percentage of the member's lifetime allowance when the subsequent 'crystallisation' occurs.

In order to ascertain the percentage of lifetime allowance used at a benefit crystallisation event (BCE) the registered pension scheme Administrator needs to establish the capital value of the benefits coming into payment. This is the amount 'crystallised' at that event. Where benefit is crystallising from a defined contribution arrangement then we only have to consider the lump sum value of the pension fund that is being used. When dealing with a defined pension benefit a capital value of that benefit is established by multiplying it by 20 or 25 (see previous section) depending on whether a lump sum has been taken.

There are 11 types of BCE which trigger a lifetime allowance test, each covering a different circumstance (for example the payment of a lump sum, the payment of a scheme pension etc). A different valuation method for each type of BCE is described in the legislation, to obtain an accurate or transparent value of the capital worth of the benefit rights being tested. The benefit crystallisation events are described in APPENDIX 4.

The lifetime allowance charge

[3.28] At any time when benefits are taken (a benefit crystallisation event), whether on retirement or otherwise taking benefit), or following the death of the registered scheme member, there must be a check to ensure that the lifetime allowance has not been exceeded.

If the lifetime allowance has been exceeded, then the excess fund (the 'chargeable amount') will be subject to a lifetime allowance charge of 25%. Income drawn from the excess fund will then be subject to income tax in the usual way, generally at 40%.

The excess fund may instead be taken as a lump sum, but becomes subject to a 40% tax charge.

If for example the excess fund when benefits are taken is £100,000 and the member prefers to pay the tax and receive the balance as a lump sum the calculation is as follows:

- The lifetime allowance charge reduces the fund to £75,000 (by 25%).
- The remaining fund of £75,000 is then taxed at 40% – a further £30,000.

Thus the member after the tax has been paid will be in receipt of a total of £45,000. Thus, the total tax charge works out at 55% if the excess fund is taken in lump sum form.

The lifetime allowance charge is intended to compensate for the tax reliefs that the excess fund will have attracted over time, both on the contributions and the fund growth.

The excess fund as shown above may be taken as a lump sum, but subject to a 40% tax charge. Thus, the total tax charge works out at 55% if the excess fund is taken in this way.

4

Benefits to members and their dependants – and their taxation

Introduction

[4.1] The purpose of a registered pension scheme is to provide retirement and death benefits for its members and their financial dependants. The UK pensions taxation system is predicated upon tax privileges through relief on contributions on entry, a tax privileged pension fund which grows largely free of taxation, and benefits on retirement which are subject to taxation with the exception of the pension commencement lump sum which is (currently) free from tax.

£19.5 billion was contributed to personal pensions in 2012–13, lower than the £19.9 billion in 2011–12 and below the peak of £20.9 billion contributed in 2007–08 ahead of the financial crisis and downturn in the UK economy.

Gross pension tax relief in 2012–13 is projected to be £34.8 billion, broadly unchanged from 2011–12. The absence of any growth is largely due to the reduction in the pension annual allowance that occurred in April 2011. Relief given on pension contributions in 2012–13 was around three times the corresponding tax on private pensions being paid out.

HMRC estimate the net annual cost of tax relief on registered pension schemes for 2012–13 to be £22.8 billion after taking account of the tax collected on pensions in payment.

There is however a further cost to the Exchequer in respect of National Insurance contributions which are not chargeable on contributions to pension schemes made by employers. This relief was estimated to be worth £15.2 billion in 2012–13.

This suggests, therefore, that the overall cost to the Exchequer of the tax privileges provided to registered pension schemes amounted to some £38 billion for the tax year 2012–13. This represented about 2.4% of GDP.

The proportion of payments contributed by employers has risen consistently since 1990–91 from around 9% in the early 1990s to 51% in 2012–13.

The taxation of benefits is an important mechanism by which the Government can seek to recover at least part of the cost of the pensions tax relief allowed on entry.

Detailed current and historical statistical information about the value of the tax reliefs afforded UK pension funds may be found at www.gov.uk/government/uploads/system/uploads/attachment_data/file/285063/pensions-intro.pdf.

As stated in CHAPTER 3 members may generally take benefit from a registered pension scheme any time after the age of 55. Up until 5 April 2010 this had been possible from age 50. Benefits however may be taken earlier by those in occupations which are traditionally subject to an early retirement age and by those in serious ill health.

The most well-known benefit is of course the anomalous 'tax-free lump sum'. This term is however no longer contained within the legislation and is called the 'pension commencement lump sum' (PCLS), which is (currently) free from tax.

IHT anti-avoidance charges that apply to registered pension schemes and Qualifying Non UK Pension Schemes (QNUPS) (see CHAPTER 9) where the scheme member omits to take their retirement entitlements (e.g. a failure to buy an annuity) were removed from 6 April 2011.

The 2014 Budget speech

[4.2] Later in this chapter we will set out the changes to the ways that benefits may be taken from defined contribution pension schemes from April 2015 with transitional changes from 27 March 2014.

These were unexpected by the pensions profession generally and were announced by the words of the Chancellor of the Exchequer thus:

'We will completely change the tax treatment of defined contribution pensions to bring it into line with the modern world. There will be consequential implications for defined benefit pensions upon which we will consult and proceed cautiously.

So the changes we announce will not today apply to them.

But 13 million people have defined contribution schemes, and the number continues to grow. We've introduced flexibilities. But most people still have little option but to take out an annuity, even though annuity rates have fallen by a half over the last 15 years.

The tax rules around these pensions are a manifestation of a patronising view that pensioners can't be trusted with their own pension pots. I reject that.

People who have worked hard and saved hard all their lives, and done the right thing, should be trusted with their own finances. And that's precisely what we will now do. Trust the people. Some changes will take effect from next week.

We will:

- cut the income requirement for flexible drawdown from £20,000 to £12,000;
- raise the capped drawdown limit from 120% to 150% [of the GAD rates];
- increase the size of the lump sum small pot five-fold to £10,000; and
- almost double the total pension savings you can take as a lump sum to £30,000.

All of these changes will come into effect on 27 March [2014].

These measures alone would amount to a radical change. But they are only a step in the fundamental reform of the taxation of defined contribution pensions I want to see. I am announcing today that we will legislate to remove all remaining tax restrictions on how pensioners have access to their pension pots.

Pensioners will have complete freedom to draw down as much or as little of their pension pot as they want, anytime they want. No caps. No drawdown limits. Let me be clear. No one will have to buy an annuity.

And we're going to introduce a new guarantee, enforced by law, that everyone who retires on these defined contribution pensions will be offered free, impartial, face-to-face advice on how to get the most from the choices they will now have.

Those who still want the certainty of an annuity, as many will, will be able to shop around for the best deal. I am providing £20 million over the next two years to work with consumer groups and industry to develop this new right to advice.

When it comes to tax charges, it will still be possible to take a quarter of your pension pot tax-free on retirement, as today. But instead of the punitive 55% tax that exists now if you try to take the rest, anything else you take out of your pension will simply be taxed at normal marginal tax rates – as with any other income. So not a 55% tax but a 20% tax for most pensioners.

The OBR confirm that in the next fifteen years, as some people use these new freedoms to draw down their pensions, this tax cut will lead to an increase in tax receipts.

These major changes to the tax regime require a separate act of parliament – and we will have them in place for April next year.

Mr Deputy Speaker, what I am proposing is the most far-reaching reform to the taxation of pensions since the regime was introduced in 1921.'

Minimum pension age and the 2014 Budget proposals

[4.3] Before April 2006 those taking benefit from an occupational pension scheme had to retire from employment of the scheme-sponsoring employer in order to do so. Occupational schemes had a normal retirement age defined in the scheme rules. Normal retirement age as defined was applicable both to active members who reached that age whilst remaining in the employment of the sponsoring employer as well as those with deferred pension rights who had previously left service.

Permitted normal retirement ages were in the range of 60 to 75 and so long as the trustees of the scheme consented then benefits could be taken on early retirement from age 50 onwards.

The first standalone defined contribution arrangements were retirement annuities introduced from 1956. The relevant legislation was then re-enacted in 1970 (FA 1970 s 226) with benefits able to be taken between the ages of 50 and 70, which became between ages 50 and 75 from 1976.

The wide-ranging reforms effective from April 2006 abolished, with regard to occupational schemes, the necessity to retire from service before taking benefit, and therefore created for all the opportunity to take benefit at the time of a registered pension scheme member's choosing between age 50 and age 75. This was subject to the caveat that so long as the scheme rules so permitted, or where the exercise trustee discretion was required, it was applied in that way.

In April 2010 there was a change in the minimum permitted pension age from 50 to 55. There was no particular logic to this overnight change other than the argument that it reflected increases in life expectancy over previous decades.

Although it is possible in theory to take benefits before age 55 this would, when taken from a UK registered pension scheme, be an unauthorised member payment and attract tax at a penal rate of 55%. Generally registered pension schemes will not permit unauthorised payments within the framework of their rules.

The April 2014 consultation document proposed that minimum pension age will increase to 57 from 2028. This begins to create a link between the minimum permitted benefit age and private pension arrangements and state pension age. 2028 is a point at which minimum pension age so far as the state pension is concerned will increase to 67.

It was further proposed that as state pension age continues to increase beyond age 67 then so will the minimum benefit age permitted from registered pension schemes maintaining a gap of ten years between one and the other. The exception as is the case now is in the event of serious ill health.

It is also worth reinforcing the point that the current rules associated with trivial commutation and 'small pension pots' limit accessibility to age 60 or later.

Once the new reforms are implemented in April 2015 then these provisions will disappear with full access available from age 55 or later and the excess over 25% of the fund value being subject to tax. This however will rely upon benefit being taken from a defined contribution scheme.

Benefits available from registered pension schemes

[4.4] A registered pension scheme is authorised to pay out benefits to or in respect of a member in two forms, as a pension or as a lump sum (or of course both). The legislation (Finance Act 2004 ss 164–168 and Schedules 28 and 29) lists all the 'authorised' forms of pensions and lump sum payments, the circumstances in which they can be paid, and sets out the conditions and restrictions that these payments must meet or follow in order for them to be 'authorised'.

The legislation authorises a registered pension scheme to provide pension benefits for its members that comply with 'the pension rules', and lump sum payments that comply with the 'lump sum rules'. If a pension benefit or a lump sum payment do not comply with these rules it is an 'unauthorised member payment', and the payments made will be taxed. A list of the pension rules and of the lump sum rules can be found in Appendix 1.

Unauthorised member payments (that is to say payments made outside of these rules) will result in a tax charge of up to 55% of the unauthorised payment, and in addition a scheme sanction charge will become payable by the administrator of the pension scheme that has granted the unauthorised member payment, this being 15% of the payment made, or deemed to have been made.

Authorised member payments of themselves however will frequently be subject to taxation as set out below.

There were originally seven 'pension rules' dealing with the payment of pension benefits during the lifetime of a scheme member, and these prescribe the various ways that pension benefits may be paid. Following the provisions of Finance Act 2011, pension rules 6 and 7 have been abolished (see APPENDIX 1).

If the benefit payment, or part of such a payment, does not meet all the conditions and restrictions imposed through the 'pension rules' or 'lump sum rules' then, unless it meets the conditions associated with any of the other 'authorised member payments', it will be an 'unauthorised member payment' and taxed as set out above.

The position is the same where dealing with benefits paid on the death of the member by a registered pension scheme, although the rules governing payments in these circumstances are referred to as the 'pension death benefit rules' and the 'lump sum death benefit rule'. These rules are listed in APPENDIX 2.

Member pension and lump sum payments

[4.5] So as set out above two of the forms of authorised member payments permitted are:

- Pensions permitted by the pension rules or pension death benefit rules, and
- Lump sums permitted by the lump sum rule or lump sum death benefit rule.

There is no maximum pension that can be paid from a registered pension scheme. Pensions must be paid at least annually and taxed at source. In general, income arising from sources within the UK (and therefore from UK pension arrangements) to a non-resident individual remains liable to UK tax. However, the member may be entitled to relief from UK tax under the terms of any double taxation agreement between the UK and the pension scheme member's country of residence.

Pension benefits may be taken in one of three ways:

Scheme pension – the pension is provided from the registered pension scheme, or from an insurance company selected by the scheme Administrator. This is the only option available to members of defined benefit schemes as a consequence of pension rule 3.

Lifetime annuity – this is an annuity payable as a consequence of the annuity being secured through an insurance company which the scheme member has the opportunity to choose. This is an option for example for a member of a personal pension scheme. From 6 April 2015, some of the current restrictions on a lifetime annuity will be removed. Firstly the annual rate of the lifetime annuity will be allowed to go down as well as up. Secondly there will no longer be a requirement that the member must have been given the opportunity to select the insurance company provider, although schemes may still offer the member this opportunity should they wish. Finally the current ten-year restriction on the maximum period for paying the income from a lifetime annuity after the member's death will be removed. A lifetime annuity may from April 2015 continue to be paid after the member's death for any period that is set out in the annuity contract.

Drawdown (referred to as 'unsecured income' until 5 April 2011) – this option was, until April 2011, only available before and until age 75 (with an extension to age 77 whilst the Government's proposals were being finalised).

Since 6 April 2011 drawdown may continue beyond age 75 without having to secure income by that age. Benefits drawn down may be provided either directly from the member's pension fund through income withdrawal or in the form of a short-term temporary annuity (i.e. up to five years duration).

Until 6 April 2011 where an annuity from a defined contribution scheme had not been secured by age 75 then the member's fund would fall into an **Alternatively Secured Pension (ASP)** – this was originally introduced from April 2006 and was a restricted form of income withdrawal, only available to those aged 75 and over. ASP was abolished with effect from April 6 2011.

It will be clear from the above that significant changes from the original structures that were put in place in April 2006 have been effected from 6 April 2011. Further changes are effective from 6 April 2015 as introduced in **4.2** above. These are detailed later in this chapter.

Pension Benefit structures in general terms

[4.6] Pensions paid direct from the scheme (**a scheme pension**) or through the purchase of a lifetime annuity are collectively referred to as 'secured pensions'. This is because both forms of pension are guaranteed for the life of the member.

A scheme pension may be guaranteed for a certain term not exceeding ten years. So if the member dies before that term has ended the scheme pension will continue to be paid regardless to the end of the guarantee period, but to another person or to the deceased's estate. The ten-year maximum term-certain period runs from the date the member first becomes entitled to that scheme pension.

This maximum period for guaranteeing a scheme pension is to be removed from 6 April 2015 as provided for in the (draft) Taxation of Pensions Bill 2014.

Alternatively a registered pension scheme may provide a member with 'pension protection' associated with their scheme pension. This means the scheme guarantees that if the member dies before their 75th birthday, and has not received a certain total level of scheme pension by that time, the scheme will pay the balance as a lump sum on the member's death. The lump sum paid in this circumstance is referred to as a 'pension protection lump sum death benefit'. No such benefit can be paid if the member dies on or after reaching their 75th birthday.

Members of a defined contribution scheme may take pension benefits in the form of a scheme pension (available from occupational schemes only), a lifetime annuity, or in the form of income drawdown (known as unsecured income until 5 April 2011).

In respect of the period to 6 April 2011 benefits from age 75 (77 whilst the Government were finalising the revised arrangements) could not continue to be provided on an unsecured basis.

The option of an Alternatively Secured Pension then became available for those who did not wish to secure an annuity. Thus, as a consequence, the concept of a compulsion to annuitise by age 75 was abolished with effect from 6 April 2006 – but there were tax implications. ASP was abolished with effect from 6 April 2011.

The provisions as they now apply are set out later in this chapter with additional information about ASP as it operated in the period to 5 April 2011 for those who are interested in the process that led to its implementation and subsequent abolition.

The pension commencement lump sum

[4.7] When a member first becomes entitled to a pension benefit a registered pension scheme may, within set limits, pay the member a lump sum which is free from UK tax. Such a payment is referred to as a 'pension commencement lump sum' (PCLS).

The size of the PCLS which comprises an authorised payment is limited by reference to the capital value of the pension benefit the lump sum is linked to.

The PCLS is linked to the entitlement to:

- A scheme pension – which is only available from an occupational scheme;
- A lifetime annuity – most usually provided from a personal pension scheme or similar;
- Unsecured pension – where income is 'drawn from the fund' instead of being secured by a scheme pension or through an annuity.

The basic rule is that 25% of the aggregate value of the pension/lump sum entitlements arising at that point may be paid as a pension commencement lump sum. As these three pension benefit types work very differently, the legislation specifies how the maximum PCLS is calculated in each of the three scenarios.

Where the registered pension scheme is a defined contribution arrangement the extent of the permitted PCLS is straightforward. It is simply 25% of the fund value.

Where however the registered pension scheme is a defined benefit scheme the calculation methodology is little more complex. The starting point is to consider the member's pension entitlement and then to give that a lump sum value by multiplying by 20. It is then 25% of this figure that is available as a PCLS. The multiple of '20' is referred to in the legislation as the 'relevant valuation factor' and will apply unless a higher factor has been agreed with HMRC associated with a particular scheme.

So if an individual is entitled to a pension from a registered pension scheme of say £15,000 a year that is deemed to have a value of £300,000. 25% of that is £75,000, which represents the maximum, permitted PCLS.

This is however subject to this basis being permitted by the rules of the scheme. Occupational schemes in existence before April 2006 generally provided for a tax-free lump sum benefit (the predecessor of the PCLS), based upon the member's salary at the date of retirement, and years of scheme membership. The maximum permitted lump sum being up to 1.5 times final remuneration.

In our example of such a pension scheme member being entitled to a pension of £15,000 a year, if in the period up to 5 April 2006 that individual's final pay from his employer was (say) £25,000 a year, then his maximum lump sum entitlement would have been up to £37,500.

Most pension schemes have adapted their rules so as to allow for the potentially greater lump sums that the post 5 April 2006 regime can allow.

Following the benefit reforms introduced from 6 April 2011 it is no longer necessary for any PCLS to be taken by age 75. It may be taken beyond that age without any maximum age limit.

Temporary changes to the rules relating to the PCLS – various temporary changes have been introduced to enable people who wish to do so to take a PCLS at age 55 or later but wait for longer than would otherwise be permitted to take benefit from the balance of the fund so as to be able to access the more flexible benefit regime that comes into effect from April 2015. These were included in the Finance Act 2014.

Normally any PCLS paid from pension savings must be taken in connection with a pension no more than six months before the pension and must be paid from the same scheme.

Where these conditions are not met the intended tax-free lump sum is an unauthorised payment and subject to the associated tax charges.

Finance Act 2014 Schedule 5 amends these provisions to enable individuals to take a PCLS and wait until April 2015 to decide how they want to access their pension savings, or whether to transfer the rest of their pension savings to another pension provider to enable them to access their pension savings.

Legislation has been included in Schedule 5 to:

(a)   allow the pension associated with a PCLS paid before 6 April 2015 to be paid no later than 5 October 2015, from a money purchase arrangement;

(b)   allow the funds intended to provide a pension associated with a PCLS paid before 6 April 2015 to be transferred to and paid from a different scheme to the PCLS, in respect of a money purchase arrangement;

(c)   ensure that where the associated pension is paid from a different scheme to the PCLS under (b) above, any right to a protected pension age or protected lump sum is preserved as part of the transfer;

(d)   ensure that where an intended PCLS received before 6 April 2015 from a money purchase arrangement is repaid to the scheme before 6 October 2015, it is treated for tax purposes as if it had never been paid;

(e)   allow a member who has received a PCLS before 27 March 2014 to commute the uncrystallised expected pension to a lump sum under the trivial commutation or small pots rules providing they meet the other conditions;

(f)   ensure that where a member receives a PCLS in respect of a money purchase arrangement and dies before taking the expected pension under these transitional provisions, the PCLS will continue to be an authorised payment;

(g)   modify the scheme administrator reporting and scheme sanction charge rules relating to the above changes.

Transitional protection and lump sums

[4.8] A member of an occupational pension scheme where the scheme was subject to HMRC discretionary approval before 6 April 2006 may have had the right under the provisions of the scheme to a tax-free lump sum that on calculation in accordance with the scheme rules exceeded the 25% pension commencement lump sum limit. In order to avoid the possibility of a tax charge on the excess lump sum benefit the legislation gave protection against such tax charges applying.

No form of registration of this protection is required with HMRC, the appropriate records are retained by the pension scheme Administrator.

Additional provisions apply for those with larger funds who (by 5 April 2009) registered with HMRC for either (or both of) primary or enhanced protection. The rules introduced with effect from 6 April 2006 meant that the member, in the absence of such protection, would not be able to benefit from total pension commencement lump sums exceeding 25% of the standard lifetime allowance – £375,000 in 2006–07.

If on 5 April 2006 the registered pension scheme member had total lump sum rights of more than £375,000 then registration for transitional protection (enhanced or primary) enabled protection of these lump sum rights at the same time. The protection certificate provided by HMRC records the value of the member's protected lump sum rights.

Recycling of pension commencement lump sums

[4.9] The Government took action in 2006 to stop what was perceived as the potential abuse of the new pensions taxation rules by means of a device designed to boost the amount in a registered pension scheme through the (perceived) artificial generation of tax reliefs. The 'device' was in fact not in any way new nor in any way associated with the new pensions taxation rules. 'Recycling' had been possible for many years.

The legislation is to be found in paragraph 3A of Schedule 29 to the Finance Act 2004, as inserted by Finance Act 2006 s 159.

The concept of 'recycling' operates by virtue of the pension scheme member withdrawing a PCLS which is reinvested back into a registered pension scheme. The reinvestment automatically generates further income tax relief on the amount reinvested. This in turn would allow a further PCLS to be paid out, so that the cycle can be repeated. This became known as 'recycling'.

So if an individual has a pension fund of £160,000, and is 57 years of age, they could theoretically have taken a PCLS of £40,000, and so long as they had earned income of at least this amount (and were not benefiting from any other contributions or pension accrual – post 5 April 2011 rules), this on being reinvested into (say) a personal pension scheme would represent a contribution made net of basic rate income tax relief of £50,000 gross. £10,000 (representing the tax relief due at basic rate on a £50,000 contribution) would be claimed by the pension provider from HMRC and credited to the member's pension fund. If the member also happened to be a higher rate taxpayer then additional tax relief would be claimed through the member's self-assessment tax return.

If benefit is taken immediately or shortly afterwards then a further PCLS would become available of £12,500 which (in this example say during the following tax year) could be used as the means for funding a further (net of basic rate) pension contribution.

Given that pension income is taxed at a member's marginal rate of income tax, anyone recycling in this way would effectively be exchanging a tax-free PCLS in part for a potential future stream of taxed income and therefore the potential benefits are unlikely to be large. However, this device was seen as 'abusive' as it is intended to do nothing more than generate artificially high amounts of tax relief through a circulation of money.

To prevent individuals from artificially boosting their pension funds by recycling tax-free lump sums in this way an anti-avoidance rule was inserted into schedule 29 Finance Act 2004 to take effect from 6 April 2006. The legislation targeted cases where lump sums were taken with the sole or main purpose of reinvesting them in a pension scheme to create additional pensions savings through the additional tax relief granted.

As is often the case a relatively simple concept has resulted in complex legislative provisions. The legislation associated with recycling covers less than one page in the 2006 Finance Act but it originally came accompanied by 28 pages of guidance notes issued by HMRC which has since been refined into 15 pages in the registered pension schemes manual.

In a specific instance it can be the case that the conclusion reached is 'it might be recycling but then again it might not'.

If a recycling of the PCLS does occur then the entirety of the PCLS (that is all of it not just that element of the PCLS which has been recycled) will be treated as an unauthorised payment. This means the individual will be liable to a tax charge of up to 55% on the whole of the PCLS.

In straightforward terms recycling of a lump sum is considered by HMRC to have occurred where the individual receives a PCLS and:

(1)   because of the PCLS the amount of contributions paid into another registered pension scheme in respect of the individual is significantly greater than it would otherwise be; and

(2)   the additional contributions are made by the individual or by someone else, such as an employer; and

(3)   the recycling was pre-planned; and

(4)   the amount of the PCLS, taken together with any other such lump sum taken in the previous 12 months exceeds 1% of the standard lifetime allowance; and

(5)   the cumulative amount of the additional contributions exceeds 30% of the PCLS.

A change will be made from 6 April 2015 (as proposed in the (draft) Taxation of Pensions Bill 2014) so that this rule applies where the amount of the pension commencement lump sum, taken together with any other such lump sums taken in the previous 12-month period, exceeds £10,000, not 1% of the lifetime allowance as at present.

Pension commencement lump sum recycling considerations in more detail

[4.10] Recycling may perhaps be defined as an individual deciding in a structured and pre-planned way, to take a PCLS from a Registered Pension Scheme in order to use that lump sum directly or indirectly to pay significantly greater contributions into a pension arrangement. The significantly greater contribution is paid 'because of' the PCLS'.

As far as HMRC were concerned 'very few lump sum payments should be affected by the recycling rule, in particular a PCLS would not be caught if it was paid as part of an individual's normal retirement planning.'

The limits themselves (as set out above) are easy enough to interpret but a number of questions arose in relation to the wording of the legislation:

•   How to determine the intentions of the individual with regard to pre-planning?

•   What did HMRC mean by significantly increased contributions?

•   What constitutes normal retirement planning?

Probably the most important condition that must apply in order for PCLS recycling to have occurred is the pre-planning condition – that is the individual must intend from the outset to take a PCLS in order to enable significantly greater contributions to be paid into a registered pension scheme and so benefit from further income tax relief.

The order in which the PCLS is taken and the contribution made will not affect the pre-planning consideration. Recycling would be deemed to have occurred in both the following circumstances:

Recycling example 1

- The individual decides to use the PCLS as a means to increase contributions
- The individual receives the lump sum
- The individual pays an increased contribution into a pension arrangement

Recycling example 2

- The individual decides to use the PCLS as a means to increase contributions
- The individual pays an increased contribution into a pension arrangement
- The individual receives the lump sum from the first arrangement.

There are numerous other possible variations on the same theme.

However, where the individual takes a PCLS and subsequently decides to pay a further pension contribution the onus will not be on that individual to prove the absence of an intention when the lump sum was taken to use the PCLS to pay a fund a further contribution, but it will be up to HMRC to prove intent.

HMRC generally take the view that a significant increase occurs where, because of a PCLS, the amount of additional contributions is more than 30% of the contributions that might otherwise have been expected to be paid.

HMRC guidelines go into some detail as to exactly what the expected contribution might have been and great care is taken to exclude increases as a result of contractual obligations, earnings increases through promotion, and other naturally occurring events outside an individual's control.

The amount of additional contributions is measured on a cumulative basis to determine if there has been a significant increase.

The period of time over which contributions are measured is:

- The two tax years immediately preceding the tax year the individual took the lump sum;
- The tax year in which the lump sum was taken;
- The two tax years following the tax year in which the lump sum was taken.

HMRC have specified what is considered to be 'normal retirement planning' in that the recycling rule is not intended to apply to individuals who simply increase contributions to a pension schemes (or who have increased contributions paid in respect of them such as by their employer) with the intention of increasing the benefits that will ultimately be paid from those schemes, particularly a PCLS. This is provided no PCLS is actually used as the means to increase those contributions, whether directly or indirectly.

This is because the recycling rule applies only where contributions are significantly increased because of the lump sum. When the recycling rule is triggered the whole of the PCLS is treated as an unauthorised payment regardless of how much of it was actually recycled. The unauthorised payment charge is 40% of the pension commencement lump sum, payable by the member, plus possibly an additional 15% surcharge, if the lump sum was more than 25% of total funds, also payable by the member.

The scheme administrator who paid the lump sum will also be liable for a scheme sanction charge of between 15%–40% depending upon how much of the unauthorised payment charge is paid by the member. There is however a right of appeal for the scheme administrator where it can be proved that they made the original payment in good faith and on the understanding that it was not to be used to fund recycling.

Trivial commutation lump sum

[4.11] This benefit option is available where the total capital value of all the member's retirement benefits does not exceed £30,000 (the commutation limit) and where the member of the pension scheme is aged 60 or over. This figure was increased from £18,000 with effect from 27 March 2014.

The age 75 limit for trivial commutation was abolished from 6 April 2011.

Trivial commutation is only available as an option if the value of the member's benefit entitlements under all registered pension schemes valued on a nominated date do not exceed £30,000. The value here includes rights that have previously crystallised for lifetime allowance purposes (including any pensions in payment on 5 April 2006).

The £18,000 limit for trivial commutation applicable until 26 March 2014 originally started out as 1% of the lifetime allowance but remained at a fixed £18,000 until 26 March 2014 despite the reduction in the lifetime allowance to £1.5 million from 6 April 2012 and to £1.25 million from 6 April 2014.

Legislation introduced in Finance Act 2014 (s 42) amends Finance Act 2004 from 27 March 2014 to allow members over 60, with total pension savings of £30,000 or less, to take out all of those savings as one or more trivial commutation lump sums and thus to increase the limit in regulation 10 of SI 2009/1171 to £30,000.

In these circumstances, the entire sum may be commuted for a lump sum. 25% of the trivial commutation lump sum is free from tax and the balance is taxed, normally, at basic rate.

There is a window of one year within which to take all the benefits on triviality grounds. This period is set by reference to the first trivial commutation lump sum payment. An individual can only have one 12-month commutation period in their lifetime. So the member needs to use this period to commute any trivial benefits they hold in multiple registered pension schemes, as once a commutation period has been set and then ended no further trivial commutation lump sum payment can be made. Trivial commutations that occurred before 6 April 2006 do not count for this purpose.

All the benefits held under a registered pension scheme (including any in payment) must be commuted this way if a trivial commutation lump sum is to be paid. However, if the individual holds benefits under more than one scheme they are not required to commute their benefits under every scheme.

Other small lump sums – 'small pots'

[4.12] One effect of the rules introduced in April 2006 was that it was no longer possible to commute for a lump sum small pensions that could previously have been commuted. Previously, it had been possible to commute a pension if it was less than £260 per annum and no account had to be taken of any other pensions in payment.

In the 2008 Budget it was announced that changes would be made to help more members of occupational pensions with small pensions. Regulations under these widened powers made it possible to commute some small 'stranded pots' valued at less than £2,000 in occupational pension schemes. These provisions were put in place over and above the trivial commutation rule.

In April 2011, the Government said it would explore ways to allow personal pensions of less than £2,000 to be taken as a lump sum so extending the 'stranded pots' provision so that it was not just limited to the occupational pensions sector.

In December 2011, the Government announced that Regulations would be introduced to enable individuals to access those savings held in small personal pension schemes (i.e. £2,000 or less) by way of a lump sum payment. These were the Registered Pension Schemes (Authorised Payments) Regulations 2009 (SI 2009/1171) ('the 2009 Regulations').

The Registered Pension Schemes (Authorised Payments) (Amendment) Regulations 2012 (SI 2012/1881) ('the 2012 Regulations') amended the 2009 Regulations.

The 2012 Regulations inserted a new regulation 11A into the 2009 Regulations, which prescribed a new category of payment as an 'authorised payment' for the purposes of FA 2004 s 164(1). This extended the ability to commute a pension fund or benefit value of £2,000 or less to personal/stakeholder pensions (group and individual), retirement annuity contracts and buyout contracts so thus to sums held in any registered pension scheme rather than occupational and public service pension schemes only.

Unlike the occupational 'small lump sum' rule, the requirement to extinguish the member's entitlement to benefits did not extend to the scheme as a whole. As the personal pension 'small lump sum' rule is arrangement specific, an individual was able to commute up to two arrangements from the same pension scheme, or one arrangement from two different pension schemes, leaving further pension rights in the scheme(s) to come into payment at a later date.

Tax charges are applied in the same way as a normal trivial commutation payment with 25% of payment normally being tax free (to reflect the tax-free lump sum which would have been paid had the pension rights been crystallised to provide retirement benefits), with the remainder taxed under PAYE. If however commutation was of a pension in payment then the whole payment is taxable under PAYE.

The legislation thus allowed further small lump sums to be paid from a registered pension scheme without having to follow the conditions associated with a trivial commutation lump sum. Where a member receives one of these small lump sum payments, the payment will not be classed as a trivial commutation lump sum.

Such one-off small lump sum payments are allowed as authorised member payments in circumstances prescribed in the regulations.

The conditions that needed to be met for a small lump sum to be commuted under Regulation 11A are that:

- The payment is made on or after 6 April 2012,
- The payment is made to a member who has reached the age of 60,
- The 'small lump sum' payment does not exceed £2,000,
- The payment extinguishes the member's entitlement to benefits under the arrangement, and
- The member has not previously received more than one payment under Regulation 11A.

The last condition meant that an individual was allowed up to two such small lump sum payments each not exceeding £2,000 during their lifetime if all the other conditions are met. The regulation applies at arrangement level rather than at scheme level. So payments can be made from two separate registered pension schemes or from the same scheme where the payments are made under different arrangements in that scheme.

As one of the conditions is that the payment extinguishes the member's entitlement to benefits under the arrangement from which the payment is made but not their entitlement under the scheme as a whole, a member can take such a small lump sum even though they may still have an entitlement to benefits under another arrangement in that scheme.

From 27 March 2014 the maximum size of a small pension pot which can be taken as a lump sum has been increased from £2,000 to £10,000, and the number of personal pension pots that can be taken under these rules is increased from two to three.

Thus legislation has been introduced in Finance Act 2014 to:

- increase the other small pots limits in Part 2 of SI 2009/1171 to £10,000;
- increase the number of lump sums that can be taken under regulation 11A of SI 2009/1171 to three; and
- increase the small pot limit in article 23C of SI 2009/1172 to £10,000.

Effect of the 2014 changes to trivial commutation and 'small pots'

[4.13] The plight of those with pension funds of small value was highlighted in an article in the Financial Times on 17 January 2014. Although the 'average' pension pot (according to the Association of British Insurers (ABI)) used to purchase an annuity is about £33,000, a large number of people were effectively forced to buy an annuity with smaller pension funds which attracted significantly lower annuity rates.

Data from the ABI shows that in the first nine months of 2013, 41,010 customers bought an annuity with a purchase price of less than £5,000. There were a further 36,925 who bought an annuity with a pension pot of between £5,000 and £10,000. Combined, these accounted for nearly one-third of all annuity sales in 2013.

Around 75% when taking benefit from a defined contribution pension arrangement have used the fund to purchase an annuity. Clearly the new trivial commutation and 'small pots' limits have the potential to be a great benefit to a large number of people.

Trivial commutation and 'small pots' from April 2015

[4.14] The main change to the small pots rules is that from 6 April 2015 this type of lump sum may be paid to an individual from their normal minimum pension age (55), not age 60 as at present. So those with total pensions worth up to £30,000 or three personal pensions worth less than £10,000 each will be able to access the full amount from 55.

But from 6 April 2015 it will not be possible to receive a trivial commutation lump sum from a money purchase arrangement. The introduction of the uncrystallised funds pension lump sum provides a way to withdraw all of the funds from a money purchase arrangement from 6 April 2015, so the trivial commutation rule falls away.

The trivial commutation and small pot rules will continue to apply to defined benefit schemes. The age at which an individual can make use of these rules will be lowered from 60 to 55 – as set out in the (draft) Pensions Taxation Bill 2014. These rules allow individuals to take up to £30,000 of total pension savings as a lump sum, or a £10,000 small pot as a lump sum regardless of total pension wealth.

Short service refund lump sum

[4.15] If an occupational pension scheme member leaves the scheme having been a member for less than two years and so does not qualify for a statutory short service benefit under Department of Work and Pensions (DWP) legislation, they may if the scheme rules so provide be able to get a refund of any contributions they made to the scheme. This is a short service refund lump sum and must be paid before age 75.

The rate of tax charged on a short service refund lump sum made in the 2011–12 tax year or in a later tax year is:

20% in respect of the first £20,000 refunded, and

50% in respect of any remainder.

The relevant DWP legislation is Chapter I and Chapter 5, Part IV Pension Schemes Act 1993 (particularly section 71) and sections 101AA to 101AI, as introduced by section 264 of the Pensions Act 2004 and the Occupational Pension Schemes (Preservation of Benefit) Regulations, SI 1991/167.

The Pensions Act 2014 withdraws the facility to refund employee pension contributions to members who leave a money purchase scheme before completing two years of pensionable service. The impact of this reform will primarily be on individuals whose period of membership extends beyond 30 days' qualifying service. Instead of being refunded, their pension contributions will remain in their former employers' schemes and will continue to be invested on their behalf.

Individuals may instead request to have their 'pot' transferred to their new employers' scheme.

Refund of excess contributions lump sum

[4.16] If a pension scheme member paid contributions which would otherwise qualify for tax relief but the amount paid exceeded 100 per cent of the member's earnings (or £3,600 if greater) then the excess amount may be refunded.

The rules for paying a refund of excess contributions lump sum have not changed from 6 April 2011. Excess relievable contributions can be refunded up to six years after the end of the tax year in which the contributions were paid even if the claimant is over the age of 75 when a refund is sought.

The definition of a refund of excess contributions lump sum limits the amount of actual excess contributions made by the member. But the rules of a registered pension scheme may allow for the payment of interest on refunded contributions. In some cases, the payment of such interest is treated under the scheme rules as being additional to the refund of excess contributions lump sum payment itself.

Should a scheme wish to pay interest in circumstances where the interest is not part of the lump sum itself, such interest may be treated as a scheme administration member payment. Such payments should be made on an arm's-length, commercial basis. So any interest paid by a scheme on a refund of excess contributions should be no more than a reasonable commercial rate if it is to be regarded as a scheme administration member payment.

Winding up lump sum

[4.17] A member of an occupational pension scheme that is winding up with a value of their pension rights of less than £18,000 may receive the entire payment as a lump sum. There is no lower or upper age limit for receiving a winding-up lump sum.

The maximum amount that can be paid as a winding-up lump sum from a registered pension scheme is £18,000. If the member has not previously taken benefits from the scheme paying the lump sum only 75% of the lump sum will be taxable, otherwise the entirety will be taxable.

To qualify for tax treatment as a winding-up lump sum the payment must:

- be paid only where the member has available lifetime allowance. Although the winding-up lump sum payment is not tested against the member's available lifetime allowance, this requirement is there to discourage this payment method being used to avoid the lifetime allowance charge where the member has used up the entirety of their lifetime allowance,
- extinguish the member's entitlement to benefits under the scheme, and
- only be paid where benefits are deemed trivial.

Serious ill-health lump sum

[4.18] If the member of a registered pension scheme is so ill that they are not expected to live for more than a year (which must be confirmed by medical evidence), they can receive any remaining uncrystallised pension entitlement from the scheme that remains in the form of a lump sum.

There is no lower or upper age limit for paying a serious ill-health lump sum. However if it is paid beyond age 75 it will be taxable at 55% through a 'serious ill-health lump sum charge'.

One of the conditions for paying a serious ill-health lump sum is that there remains sufficient unused lifetime allowance. Payment of a serious ill-health lump sum before age 75 triggers a test against the member's lifetime allowance. Any amount by which the lump sum exceeds the lifetime allowance will be liable to the lifetime allowance charge at 55%.

There are additional conditions that all must be met in order for a payment to be treated as a serious ill-health lump sum. These are:

- Before making the payment the scheme administrator must receive written evidence from a registered medical practitioner confirming that the member is expected to live for less than one year.
- The payment extinguishes the member's entitlement to benefits under the arrangement so all of the benefits under the arrangement must be commuted and paid as a serious ill-health lump sum.
- The payment is made in respect of an uncrystallised arrangement.

The rules associated with Unsecured Income through income withdrawal – 6 April 2006 to 5 April 2011

[4.19] This section is incorporated in this chapter for the purposes of completion, and because the rules as apply from 6 April 2011 onwards evolved from these provisions. This section therefore needs to be read in that context.

Introduced through the Finance Act 1995 pension drawdown (also known as income drawdown or pension fund withdrawal) allowed members of both personal and occupational pensions to take withdrawals from their pension as opposed to acquiring a pension annuity.

The intention behind the original concept was to give defined contribution based pension scheme members the maximum possible flexibility over deciding when and how their benefits would finally be secured through the purchase of an annuity. As a consequence and followed through in the provisions of Finance Act 2004, pension benefits under a money purchase arrangement could be taken before the member attained age 75 in a flexible and unsecured form, direct from the scheme within certain limits (an 'unsecured pension' using the terminology of Finance Act 2004).

The pre- April 2006 basis was to determine the extent of the amount that was allowed to be drawn by reference to notional annuity rates published by the Government Actuary's Department – which became universally known as the GAD rates.

The GAD rates varied by age and sex, and the correct GAD rate for a particular individual at a particular point in time would be determined by their age, and the 15 year Gilt yield. The maximum permitted income that could be drawn was the GAD rate multiplied by the size of the member's fund, and the minimum income that had to be drawn was 35% of the maximum. A review had to take place generally every three years.

The principles behind pension fund withdrawal continued into the new 'unsecured pension' regime. Pension income had to be taken annually or more frequently. But Finance Act 2004 did not specify a minimum level of required income which therefore became zero.

The maximum unsecured pension income was increased from 6 April 2006, as compared to the previous drawdown rules, to 120% of the 'relevant annuity', or 'basis amount'. The original intention was to specify the relevant annuity (or basis amount), by reference to the FSA comparative annuity tables. HMRC eventually bowed to pressure (not least from the FSA) and reverted to the well-understood Government Actuaries Department (GAD) rates – which were reviewed and revised from 6 April 2006. The definition of the 'relevant annuity' was simply therefore the GAD rate multiplied by the member's fund.

The maximum income had to be reviewed at least every five years (as compared to the previous 3 year rule), based on the then value of the fund and the level of the then 'relevant annuity'. In addition to the five-year review mechanism certain additional events triggered a review.

A review would be required for example where part of the fund value available for unsecured income was 'lost', due to part of the unsecured pension fund being used to purchase a lifetime annuity (or surrendered to provide a scheme pension), and hence there would need to be a reduction in the maximum unsecured income to reflect the reduced unsecured pension fund.

A review would also be required where the unsecured pension fund was boosted by the member 'designating' that any unvested funds held in the arrangement were brought in to form a part of the unsecured pension fund. The maximum unsecured income would then need to be reset at a higher level to reflect the increased unsecured fund size.

Transitional provisions introduced in Schedule 3 to Finance Act (No 2) 2010 enabled scheme members who reached age 75 on or after 22 June 2010 to withdraw income from their drawdown fund of between nil and 120% of an equivalent annuity after reaching the age of 75 and before age 77.

The rules associated with Alternatively Secured Pension withdrawal – 6 April 2006 to 5 April 2011

[4.20] Once again this section is included for the purposes of completeness. The Alternatively Secured Pension was abolished with effect from 6 April 2011.

In the period up to 6 April 2011 once a member of a registered pension scheme reached age 75 there were stricter rules on how a pension had to be provided. HMRC expected any pension paid on or after this date to be provided for in a more secure manner, with a guarantee that pension income would last for the individual's lifetime, no matter how long that may be (so a 'secured pension' or in this case 'alternatively secured' pension). So a pension for life had to be provided in a secure and guaranteed manner from age 75 onwards, either through the purchase of a guaranteed lifetime annuity from an insurance company or direct from the scheme as a guaranteed scheme pension, or using this alternative method.

Alternatively secured pensions were developed in recognition of the fact that some religious groups (in particular the Plymouth brethren) objected to annuities due to their concerns about insurance and the pooling of mortality risk, or because they simply saw the purchase of an annuity as a form of gambling on the duration of human life.

Under money purchase schemes HMRC allowed pension income to be provided beyond age 75 through the 'alternatively secured pension', but given the lack of a pension guarantee the rules associated with the 'alternatively secured pension' provided for a more conservative annual maximum payment than was permitted before age 75 (as 'unsecured pensions'). In addition a yearly review of that limit was required, to ensure the individual did not exhaust their pension fund before death.

The maximum amount that could be withdrawn under the alternatively secured pension was calculated in exactly the same manner as with unsecured pensions with the registered pension scheme administrator calculating a basis amount by reference to the GAD tables. The 'relevant annuity' was based on the assumption that the member was aged 74 years and 364 days – irrespective of their actual age simply because the GAD tables did not extend any further.

Unlike with the payment of an unsecured pension the maximum level of alternatively secured pension was recalculated at the beginning of each new pension year based on the level of alternatively secured pension fund held in the arrangement at that point. The scheme member could at any time of course choose to purchase an annuity.

Alternatively secured pension arrangements had to pay as an income at least 55% of the 'relevant annuity' with a maximum of 90% of the relevant annuity. Unless the remaining fund was left to charity on the death of the member and of any dependants entitled to a 'dependant's alternatively secured annuity', the total tax charges applicable through a combination of unauthorised member payment charges and inheritance tax were up to 82% of the remaining fund.

The rules associated with 'flexible drawdown' and 'capped drawdown' from 6 April 2011 to 5 April 2015

[4.21] Because of the tax treatment of the remaining fund on death (referred to as the 'left over fund') if a registered pension scheme member had not used the unsecured pension fund to buy an annuity by age 75 or later death – recalling that a total tax burden of up to 82% could apply, this was regarded as being an effective compulsion to buy an annuity prior to that age.

The Government undertook to change this position, and did so by introducing new rules effective from 6 April 2011. Whether or not these provisions actually removed the 'effective compulsion to buy an annuity' is something that the reader may wish to dwell on.

The arrangements put into effect from 6 April 2011:

- Enabled individuals with defined contribution pension rights from which they have not yet taken benefit pension to defer a decision to take benefits from their scheme indefinitely. So the requirement to take benefit in some form by age 75 (including the pension commencement lump sum) has been removed.
- Set the maximum permitted income that may be drawn down at 100% of the GAD rate applying. (So taking us back to the position where we were before April 2006). (Note however that the 120% of GAD rate basis was restored from March 2013).
- Required the maximum amount that may be withdrawn to be determined at least every three years until the end of the year in which the member reaches the age of 75, after which reviews will be carried out annually. So once again taking us back to the position which applied before April 2006.
- Do not differentiate between benefits being drawn down before and after age 75 so the minimum annual withdrawal amount which previously applied beyond the age of 75 through the alternatively secured pension was abolished.
- Enabled individuals with a secure annual lifetime pension income of at least £20,000 (£12,000 from 27 March 2014) to gain access to some or all of their remaining pension fund without any cap on the withdrawals they may take.

- Set the tax rate on lump sum death benefits where benefit has been taken at 55%. But unused drawdown pension funds of a member who dies with no living dependants may be donated tax free to a charity. This is referred to as a 'charity lump sum death benefit'.
- Set the tax rate on lump sum death benefits payable beyond the age of 75 where the member has not taken benefit once again at 55%.

The term '**capped drawdown**', refers to those who do not have secure pension income of at least £20,000 a year (£12,000 from 27 March 2014) and so who are unable to gain access to the remaining fund. Capped drawdown may continue beyond age 75 but on the member's 75th birthday the value of the drawdown pension fund will be tested against the member's lifetime allowance.

The term '**flexible drawdown**' refers to those who have secure pension income of at least £20,000 a year (£12,000 from 27 March 2014) and so have the opportunity to gain access to the remaining part of the pension fund albeit subject to taxation.

In respect of drawdown pension arrangements put in place before 6 April 2011, the altered withdrawal limits take effect from the start of the next reference period. The GAD tables have been extended to show equivalent annuities for each birthday from 76 to 84, and for age 85 and over.

It should be noted that the tax rules do not require the maximum income to actually be available for drawdown from a particular scheme. The statutory calculations only serve to determine whether a given level of drawdown pension is an authorised payment for tax purposes. Scheme administrators are free to provide more modest calculations suggesting recommended maximum withdrawals, to avoid the possibility of prematurely exhausting the drawdown pension fund.

Where an individual who is aged under 23 is in receipt of a drawdown pension (most likely in the form of a dependent childs pension), the maximum amount that may be paid is calculated by reference to the 5-year UK gilt yield shown in the FTSE UK Gilts Indices, rather than the 15-year UK gilt yield which is used for those aged 23 or over. The drawdown pension is payable only until a 'child's' 23rd birthday and so the tables are drawn up on the basis that income withdrawals deplete the fund by that time.

In late 2012 the 5-year UK gilt index yield was less than 2%, and the GAD tables only provide a basis amount for gilt rates down to 2%, so HMRC confirmed that, if the 5-year UK gilt index yield is below 2%, the scheme administrator should calculate the basis amount for anyone aged under 23 using the gilt yield figure of 2%.

In August 2014 the 5-year gilt index yield was at 1.88%, so the basis amount is calculated using the 2% yield level.

Note that until March 2013 the maximum permitted drawdown, known as capped drawdown, was at 100% of the GAD rate. Those drawing income at 100% of the GAD rate will be able to increase their income and draw 120% of the GAD rate at the next anniversary of their drawdown review date falling on or after 26 March 2013.

From 27 March 2014, the 120% of GAD rate limit is increased to 150%.

Sixty-day window for the review of the Maximum Capped Drawdown Limit

[4.22] Where a formal review of unsecured pension limits is being undertaken the scheme administrator does not necessarily have to make the calculation on the first day of the pension year concerned (the 'reference date'). The calculation may be made on any day within a 60-day window ending on that first day of the pension year, i.e. within the 60 days running up to the reference date. This relaxation also applies where the scheme administrator has agreed to a member's request for a new review to be carried out before the expiry of the five-year reference period.

The date the scheme administrator chooses to do the review in that 60-day window is referred to in the legislation as the 'nominated date'. The calculation will be carried out by reference to the value of the unsecured pension fund on the nominated date, and the member's age on the nominated date.

The 60-day window gives the scheme administrator time to ascertain the fund value and liaise with the member. It is therefore up to the scheme administrator to choose on which day they do the calculation.

Use of the 60-day window does not change the timing of the forthcoming pension year. These periods are set from outset, and cannot be disrupted, although they may be shortened in the event of the member dying or where the member reaches age 75. The new limit calculated still only comes into effect on the first day of the relevant pension year, even though it is effectively calculated in the earlier year.

The 60-day window cannot be used where:

- an initial calculation is made when the fund is first designated as available for unsecured pension, and
- an additional review is triggered because:
    - of a lifetime annuity purchase or the provision of a scheme pension,
    - additional fund designation occurs, or
    - of the application of a pension sharing order.

How to use the GAD tables

Step 1

[4.23] Establish the date for calculation purposes. For the time the calculation is made this is the date the member first designates some of the funds held in her or his pension arrangement to be used to provide a drawdown pension (using Finance Act 2011 terminology). That is, when entitlement to a drawdown pension first arises.

Where the member is under age 75, this is the first day of the first 'reference period'.

Where the member is 75 or over when they first take benefits, (under the Finance Act 2011 provisions), it is the first day of the first drawdown pension year. The recalculation is done annually so there is no reference period.

Step 2

Calculate the age in complete years of the pensioner at the point of calculation.

Step 3

Obtain the yield on UK gilts (15 years) from the FTSE UK Gilt Indices, as published daily in the Financial Times, for the 15th day of the month before the month in which the point of calculation falls.

If the 15th day is not a working day, obtain the corresponding yield for the working day immediately preceding the 15th. The yield obtained is rounded down to the next 0.25%. For example, 3.12% is rounded to 3.00%, and 2.39% is rounded to 2.25%.

Step 4

Obtain the basis amount per £1,000 of fund from the GAD tables.

Step 5

Perform the calculation by reference to the member's fund value.

Capped drawdown example

Lynne originally designated £150,000 into drawdown pension on 1 September 2011. The reference period for calculating her maximum capped drawdown pension ends on 31 August 2014.

The scheme administrator can carry out the calculation of the revised maximum drawdown pension on any day in the period of 60 days ending on the new reference date. This means that the calculation can be done on any day in the period starting on 4 July 2014 and ending on 1 September 2014. The date the scheme administrator uses to do the calculation is the 'nominated date'. The new reference period starts on 1 September 2014.

To work out the maximum drawdown pension the scheme administrator needs to know:

how old Lynne is on the nominated date;

the yield on 15-year UK gilts from the FTSE UK Gilt Indices on the 15th day of the month before the nominated date, and

the value of Lynne's drawdown pension fund on the nominated date.

The scheme administrator chooses to use a nominated date of 31 July 2014.

Lynne is 61 on 31 July 2014 and the value of her drawdown pension fund on that day is £145,000.

The scheme administrator looks up the 15-year UK Gilt index for 15 June 2014. This we will assume is 3.75%.

- According to the GAD tables this gives an amount of £59 pension per £1,000 of drawdown pension fund.*
- The new maximum pension is £12,832 (145 × 59 = £8,555, which is multiplied by 150%). This new maximum drawdown pension will take effect from the start of Lynne's new reference period on 1 September 2014.

* Note that the GAD rate used is the male rate — see **4.24** below

Amendments to the use of the GAD rates

[4.24] The maximum amount that may be paid as a drawdown pension for individuals over the age of 22 is calculated by reference to the 15-year UK gilt yield. The basis amount for these individuals is then worked out using Table 1 or 2 of the drawdown pension tables that have been published by HMRC. Table 1 is for men and Table 2 is for women.

The 15-year UK gilt index yield was less than 3% for November 2011 and remains so now (2.94% as at 6 August 2014).

Tables 1 and 2 only provide a basis amount for gilt rates down to 2%. HMRC have confirmed that 2% should be regarded as the minimum level to be used when calculating the maximum drawdown pension payable. Consequently, if the 15-year UK gilt index yield were to fall below 2%, the scheme administrator should calculate the basis amount using the gilt yield figure of 2%.

On 1 March 2011 the European Court of Justice ruled that insurers using gender as a risk factor in ways which resulted in individual differences in premiums and benefits for men and women should not be permitted for insurance transactions covered by Council Directive 2004/113/EC implementing the principle of equal treatment between men and women in the access to and supply of goods and services ('the gender directive'). The judgement is however binding in UK law and the Government is therefore legally required to implement it.

The ECJ ruling covers annuity rates for men and women where the annuity purchase is covered by the gender directive. The calculation of the maximum drawdown pension is based on the notional annuity that could have been bought with the drawdown pension fund.

HMRC updated its guidance about drawdown pensions with an instruction that the same rate should be used for women as for men to determine their maximum drawdown pension from 21 December 2012. This increased the maximum permitted drawdown pension for women with effect from that date. The maximum drawdown pension for both men and women aged 23 and over is now calculated using the higher male GAD rates.

Flexible drawdown to 5 April 2015

[4.25] The pension scheme member may gain access to their remaining pension fund through 'flexible drawdown' if there is a secured pension in place of at least £20,000 a year. The figure of £20,000 a year is described in the legislation as the minimum income requirement. The minimum income requirement has reduced to £12,000 from 27 March 2014.

Secondary legislation (The Registered Pension Schemes (Relevant Income) Regulations, SI 2011/1783), makes further provision about what counts as relevant income for the purposes of the minimum income requirement in paragraphs 14A and 24C of Schedule 28 to the Finance Act 2004.

These regulations were put in place as a consequence of new regulation-making powers in paragraph 14B and paragraph 24D of Schedule 28 to the Finance Act 2004. Legislation included in the Finance Act 2011 inserts paragraphs 14A, 14B, 24C and 24D into Schedule 28 with effect for tax years beginning on or after 6 April 2011.

Relevant income means income from any of the following:

- Payment of a scheme pension or dependants scheme pension provided by a registered pension scheme but excluding income of this type where paid from a defined benefit or money purchase scheme with less than 20 pensioner members (see below);
- Payment of a lifetime annuity or dependants annuity made by a registered pension scheme;
- Payment from an overseas pension scheme which, if the scheme were a relevant non-UK scheme, would (by virtue of Schedule 34 Finance Act 2004) fall within the definitions of the first two points above;
- Payment of a social security pension.

Any new pension savings put in place by or in respect of an individual once they have accessed the whole of their drawdown pension fund will be liable to the annual allowance charge on all pension input amounts.

The Registered Pension Schemes (Relevant Income) Regulations, SI 2011/1783 Regs 2–4 provide that three types of payment are not to be regarded as 'relevant pension income'.

The first category is payments of scheme pensions made in respect of defined benefit arrangements where there are fewer than 20 pensioner members in the pension scheme.

The second category is scheme pensions under money purchase arrangements where the pension scheme has less than 20 pensioner members entitled to such pensions.

The third category is payments of lifetime annuities or dependants' annuities exceeding the higher of (a) the minimum amount of income that an annuitant may draw determined in accordance with condition 3 of regulation 2(4) of the Registered Pension Schemes (Prescribed Manner of Determining Amount of Annuities) Regulations 2006 (SI 2006/568) or (b) the minimum amount.

Flexible drawdown in practice

[4.26] If a pension provider wishes to offer flexible drawdown then, in order to ensure they are not subject to a scheme sanction charge, the scheme administrator needs to take reasonable steps to satisfy themselves that the individual satisfies the minimum income requirement ('MIR'). If the scheme administrator keeps an audit trail to show this, then although each case would have to be considered on its merits, HMRC would expect a good faith 'let out' from any scheme sanction charge to apply.

However, it is up to the pension scheme administrator to assess the extent to which they need to make further enquiries following receipt of an MIR declaration from a scheme member seeking to use this facility.

There is no prescriptive definition of the evidence that the pension scheme administrators should obtain, if anything, beyond the statutory declaration made by the scheme member.

In addition to the possibility of false declarations, there is also the capacity for some members to misunderstand what constitutes the MIR and to include elements that should not be included. Clearly not all scheme pensions and lifetime annuities qualify (including dependants' pensions and lifetime annuities) so pension scheme administrators will routinely seek to obtain more specific details of the relevant income sources.

If the declaration made by the scheme member relies on any non-UK pension income, the scheme administrator should bear in mind that as a UK provider they are likely to be in the best position to determine whether the particular income counts as relevant income.

Neither the non-UK pension scheme nor the individual is likely to be able to say with any confidence whether such a source of income meets the statutory test, that is whether or not it would be a 'relevant income' scheme pension if it were being paid by a registered pension scheme. Such cases might therefore call for more detailed enquiries about the characteristics of the pension and/or scheme than in relation to payments from other sources with which they are more familiar.

Regulations

[4.27] The Registered Pension Schemes (Provision of Information) (Amendment) (No 2) Regulations, 2011/1797 are made under regulation-making powers in sections 251(1)(a),(2) and 282(1A) of Finance Act 2004. They prescribe what information the scheme administrator is required to deliver to HMRC when a registered pension scheme pays a flexible drawdown pension.

The Registered Pension Schemes (Prescribed Requirements of Flexible Drawdown Declaration) Regulations, SI 2011/1792 prescribe the requirements for a 'valid declaration' that a scheme member or dependant meets 'the flexible drawdown conditions'.

'Flexible drawdown' and 'capped drawdown' from 27 March 2014 in summary

[4.28] Legislation was introduced in Finance Act 2014 effective from 27 March 2014 to reduce the minimum income threshold for flexible drawdown to £12,000 and to increase the maximum income permitted under 'capped drawdown' from 120% to 150% of the GAD rate.

These are transitional provisions in the run up to the introduction of flexi-access drawdown funds with effect from April 2015. At the time of writing in August 2014 draft legislation in the form of the Pensions Taxation Bill has just been published.

'Flexi-access drawdown funds' – from 6 April 2015

[4.29] From April 2015 the Government is changing the tax rules to allow people to access their pension savings as they wish from age 55 or later, subject to their marginal rate of income tax – rather than the current 55% charge for full withdrawal where such a withdrawal is an unauthorised member payment.

This is the unauthorised member payment charge that arises when benefit is taken in excess of the limits generally allowed from registered pension schemes and so in this context in excess of the levels permitted under capped drawdown as described earlier. Registered pension schemes generally however will not allow unauthorised member payments as if they do they risk losing their registration status.

The legislation will include a scheme rules override. This will allow scheme trustees or managers to make payments within these new rules should they wish without having to change the scheme rules. However scheme trustees or managers will not have to make these payments if they choose not to do so. In such a case, the member may wish to consider whether to transfer to another money purchase arrangement that offers the flexibility the member may require.

As these rules will be available to everybody who is a member or becomes a member of a defined contribution pension scheme then the concept of trivial commutation as it applies to defined contribution schemes becomes irrelevant.

Similarly in relation to the current provisions as they apply to small pension pots. There will be a residual need for these provisions (that is relating to trivial commutation and small pots) in relation to defined benefit schemes.

Members of defined contribution pension schemes will from 6 April 2015 be able to access any amount they require from year-to-year through flexi-access drawdown. Thus if required up to the entire pension fund may be taken from a defined contribution scheme from age 55 with UK tax payable at the individual's marginal rate on the excess over the pension commencement lump sum.

To access defined contribution pension funds (other than through buying an annuity or receiving a scheme pension) there will be two main choices:

(1)   use a flexi-access drawdown fund, from which can be drawn down any amount over whatever period chosen; or

(2)   take a single lump sum or a series of lump sums from uncrystallised funds (known as an uncrystallised funds pension lump sum). Any payment of an uncrystallised funds pension lump sum will be 25% tax free, with the remainder taxable as if it were a pension.

Flexible access payments on or after 6 April 2015 will trigger the money purchase annual allowance rules (see CHAPTER 3). This will limit the amount of tax relief available on future contributions to any money purchase arrangement.

But the changes will also ensure that for those who have already taken (or 'crystallised') their pension from a money purchase arrangement, the current tax rules can continue to apply to any payments of pension that are received on or after 6 April 2015 without triggering the money purchase annual allowance rules – unless or until benefits are taken under the new rules.

If before 6 April 2015 benefit was being taken as flexible drawdown, the drawdown pension fund will convert automatically to a flexi-access drawdown fund on 6 April 2015. The money purchase annual allowance rules will apply from that date. Any further designations under the arrangement holding the drawdown fund will go into the converted flexi-access drawdown fund.

If on 5 April 2015 the member's existing drawdown fund was paying capped drawdown and new funds are designated under the same arrangement there will be two options.

(1)   Before designating the funds the capped drawdown pension fund can be converted into a flexi-access drawdown fund. Then the newly designated funds will be designated to the converted flexi-access drawdown fund. When accessing any of these funds this will trigger the money purchase annual allowance rules.

(2)   If the existing capped drawdown pension fund is not converted into a flexi-access drawdown fund, then the newly designated funds will be designated to the existing capped drawdown pension fund. The GAD based limit (at 150%) on the maximum amount of pension that can be drawn each year will continue to apply to that fund.

As long as the drawdown pension taken is not more than the maximum capped drawdown amount, or the member has not flexibly accessed pension funds under another arrangement or as an uncrystallised funds pension lump sum, then the money purchase annual allowance rules won't apply.

If the scheme member does not have an existing drawdown pension fund on 5 April 2015, then before going into drawdown they must designate those funds to a new drawdown fund, known as their flexi-access drawdown fund. It will be apparent that for those who are not in drawdown before 6 April 2015 the option of capped drawdown no longer exists.

On designating these funds as available for drawdown, the member will be able to receive at the same time (in addition that is) a tax-free pension commencement lump sum of one third of the value of the funds placed into the flexi-access drawdown fund. This is of course 25% of the total funds being 'used'.

For example if £75,000 is designated to the flexi-access drawdown fund a further £25,000 may be taken as a PCLS. Thus 25% of a total of £100,000.

Following the designation of funds as available for drawdown through a flexi-access drawdown fund, and subsequent access of any of those funds, whether in the form of income withdrawal or a short-term annuity, then the member will be subject to the money purchase annual allowance rules and will receive tax relief only on money purchase pension savings of up to £10,000 a year. This is the 'money purchase annual allowance', see also CHAPTER 3.

The fact that members of defined contribution pension schemes will be allowed to draw as much as they wish from newly designated flexi-access drawdown funds effectively abolishes the concept of capped drawdown except for those in capped drawdown as at 5 April 2015 and who do not choose to change to flexi-access drawdown.

The use of flexi-access drawdown funds opens up much by way of tax planning opportunities.

Example

James is 60 and has taxable income of £50,000. He has £250,000 in his pension pot and takes all this money out on 7 June 2015. He will receive £62,500 without tax (25% of the fund as a pension commencement lump sum) and the balance will be taxed at a mixture of 40% and 45%. He also loses his personal allowance because his total taxable income is over £100,000. James would have paid less tax if he had spread the withdrawals over several years.

Uncrystallised funds pension lump sums – from 6 April 2015

[4.30] From 6 April 2015, if a defined contribution scheme member want to access some or all of their money purchase pension savings without first designating funds as available for drawdown, they can instead take an 'uncrystallised funds pension lump sum' (UFPLS).

Normally 25% of the amount paid will be tax free, with the remainder taxable as pension income.

To qualify as an UFPLS:

(1)   it must be payable from uncrystallised rights held under a money purchase arrangement;

(2)   the member must have more lifetime allowance remaining than the amount of the lump sum if the member is under age 75 when it is paid;

(3)   if the member is aged 75 or over when the lump sum is paid, they must have at least some lifetime allowance remaining at that time; and

(4)   the member must have reached normal minimum pension age (55) or meet the ill-health conditions.

An UFPLS cannot be paid from a drawdown fund.

The member cannot be paid an uncrystallised funds pension lump sum if immediately before the lump sum is paid:

(a)   the member has either primary protection and/or enhanced protection with protection of lump sum rights of more than £375,000; or

(b)   the member has a lifetime allowance enhancement factor (due to primary protection, pension credits from previously crystallised rights, non-residence, transfers from recognised overseas pension schemes or pre-commencement pension credits) and the available portion of the lump sum allowance is less than 25% of the proposed UFPLS.

This provision ensures that the member cannot get an UFPLS that would give a greater tax-free amount than could be paid as a pension commencement lump sum.

If the member takes an UFPLS on or after 6 April 2015, they will be subject to the money purchase annual allowance rules from that date. Any excess money purchase pension savings over £10,000 will not benefit from tax relief and the annual allowance charge would apply.

If the member is under age 75 when an UFPLS is paid, the full amount of the lump sum is tested against the remaining lifetime allowance as a benefit crystallisation event 6 (BCE6) (see APPENDIX 4). The amount of a BCE6 is the amount of the lump sum paid. Any lump sum paid in excess of the individual's remaining lifetime allowance will not be UFPLS, but will be a lifetime allowance excess lump sum.

If the member is aged 75 or over when the lump sum is paid, they must have at least some remaining lifetime allowance remaining otherwise the lump sum is not an UFPLS. If the lump sum is fully within the member's remaining lifetime allowance, they receive 25% of the lump sum tax free and the remainder is taxable as pension income.

But if the amount of the UFPLS is more than the remaining lifetime allowance, there is a restriction on the amount that can be taken tax free. The tax-free part of the lump sum will be an amount equal to 25% of the amount of lifetime allowance remaining. The rest of the lump sum is taxable as pension income.

Unsecured Income through a short-term annuity contract

[4.31] A member may choose to provide part (or all) of their drawdown pension through the purchase of a short-term annuity contract from an insurance company. This would in effect 'secure the drawdown'.

The idea of the short-term annuity contract option is to give people the opportunity to reassess their pension needs periodically and to choose alternative types of annuities, so long as (in relation to the period up to 5 April 2011) they secured an income for life by age 75.

With effect from 6 April 2011 a short-term annuity is regarded as a form of drawdown pension. The amendments effective from this date provide that payments under a short-term annuity do not have to end when the member reaches the age of 75.

So in contrast to direct withdrawal from the fund the drawdown secured through the short-term annuity is paid to the member direct by an insurance company (rather than through the registered pension scheme administrator), as dictated by the terms of an annuity contract. A proportion of the drawdown pension fund held in the arrangement will therefore be lost when the contract is purchased by virtue of the purchase price of the short-term annuity.

The term of the annuity contract purchased for this purpose cannot be more than five years, and the maximum amount of income provided through the short-term annuity is limited by exactly the same rules as applies to income drawdown payments.

So where a short-term annuity is bought using funds from a capped drawdown pension fund the relevant upper limit on the amount the short-term annuity can pay applies. The amount payable from a short-term annuity contract plus the amount of any income withdrawal from the capped drawdown pension fund in a pension year cannot be more than the permitted maximum drawdown pension.

However if a short-term annuity is purchased from a drawdown pension fund to which flexible drawdown applies there is no upper limit on the amount the short-term annuity can pay.

The term of the annuity originally could not extend beyond the member's/annuitant's 75th birthday until the changes effective from 6 April 2011 (as set out above) were introduced. A dependants' short-term annuity is a form of dependants' drawdown pension. The amended provisions also provide that payments under a dependant's short-term annuity payments may carry on beyond the age of 75.

From 6 April 2015, members of defined contribution schemes may choose to buy a short-term annuity with some or all of the funds in their flexi-access drawdown fund.

Also from 6 April 2015, the income received from a short-term annuity may go down as well as up, and there will no longer be a requirement that the member must have been given the opportunity to select the insurance company provider, although schemes may still offer this opportunity should they wish.

Flexible annuities

[4.32] These are annuities whose amount is determined in accordance with Regulation 2(4) of the Registered Pension Schemes (Prescribed Manner of Determining Amount of Annuities) Regulations, SI 2006/568. The annuity may be capable of being varied between a minimum and a maximum figure, and the flexible annuity is designed for a lifetime, not a fixed, or limited term. The concept is therefore to utilise the annuitant's fund to provide an income for the rest of their life.

The annual amount payable to an annuitant from a lifetime annuity may vary from year to year but the circumstances in which the annual amount payable in any year can fall below the amount paid in the previous year are limited. If the rate of pension payable to an individual is reduced in any circumstance other than those set out below then all future payments will be unauthorised member payments, and be taxed as such. However providing the annual amount is determined in accordance with one of the following alternative methods HMRC will not consider any reduction in the annual amount to result in tax charge:

Method One – Indexation

Where after allowing for any contractual charges, the 'variation' in the annuity is by a percentage which does not exceed changes in RPI, the market value of any 'freely marketable assets', or an index reflecting the value of 'freely marketable assets'. 'Freely marketable assets' means assets which are sold on the open market at a price not determined by the member.

Method Two – With profits

Where the variation in the annual amount from year to year reflects variable bonuses added because the annuity contract participates in an insurance company's with profits fund.

Method Three – Indexation/with profits combination

Using any combination of Methods One and Two.

Method Four – Selected rate of growth linked to Methods One, Two or Three

Where the variation in the annual amount paid from year to year is dependent on the factors used in Methods One, Two or Three but the member selects the starting level of the annuity based on an assumed annual level of growth of between 0% and 5%.

So if increases above the starting level of the annuity are dependent on bonuses being added by an insurance company with profits fund, then if the with profits fund delivers less than the assumed annual level of growth , the amount paid could fall below the level payable in the previous year.

Method Five – Flexible withdrawals

Here variations in the annual amount paid from year to year must be determined in accordance with the following conditions:

(a) Where the amount of the annuity payable is linked to any one or more of the factors specified in Methods One, Two, or Three.

(b) A review must be conducted by the insurance company providing the annuity at least once every three years.

(c) At the time of the review the maximum and minimum amount of income that may be drawn in each year until the next review must be determined.

The maximum amount of income which the annuitant may receive is 150% of a level annuity based on the provider's own annuity rates or if the insurance company does not offer annuities, the average of three current market annuity rates. In this context a 'level annuity' is defined as a single life level annuity if a single life annuity has been purchased. If a joint life annuity has been purchased, then it means a joint life level annuity. The minimum amount of income which the annuitant may receive is 50% of the level annuity.

Flexible annuities do not as a matter of course offer the lump sum death benefits payable by drawdown pension funds. They do, however, provide the annuitant with the benefit of a mortality cross-subsidy, sharing longevity risk between different annuitants.

The mortality cross subsidy from flexible annuity contracts protects the annuitant against the risk of outliving his or her fund in a way that is not available under drawdown pension arrangements.

Transfers

[4.33] For those who are members of defined benefit schemes, in order to avail themselves of the enhanced flexible drawdown opportunity through flexi-access drawdown they would first need to be able to transfer to a defined contribution scheme offering the new flexi-access drawdown facility as described.

Although there is a statutory right to transfer between one registered pension scheme and another this only applies until 12 months before scheme pension age. After that it is a matter for the scheme trustees to decide whether they will allow such a transfer or not.

Those that historically have chosen to transfer out of defined benefit schemes into defined contribution arrangements have been those with deferred pension rights generally having ceased service with the scheme-sponsoring employer many years earlier.

The flexi-access drawdown facility may well, in the ordinary course of events, make it much more common for people to want to transfer from defined benefit schemes to defined contribution schemes at or near the point at which they wish to take benefit (but subject to the 12–month restriction being addressed as suggested above).

However this will not be possible for members of defined benefit public sector pension schemes as discussed in CHAPTER 12.

Death Benefits – before benefits have been crystallised

[4.34] There are only two lump sum death benefit payments that trigger a check against the lifetime allowance.

These are:

*   A defined benefits lump sum death benefit, or
*   An uncrystallised funds lump sum death benefit

These benefits can only be paid where the member dies before taking benefits (lump sum and/or pension) from the registered pension scheme of which they are a member. If the member died before 6 April 2011 these benefits can only be paid where the member died before the age of 75.

Where a member of a defined benefit scheme dies before taking benefits a lump sum death benefit of a set monetary amount or, as a multiple of salary, may be paid – a defined benefits lump sum death benefit.

There is no limit to the level of the defined benefits lump sum death benefit that can be paid from a scheme, but it will be tested against the (deceased) member's lifetime allowance. Schemes may promise to pay a set amount of money on death or a lump sum death benefit linked to the salary of the member, or by some other measure. It is entirely a matter for the scheme to decide.

A defined benefits lump sum death benefit must be paid within two years of the date the member died. If it is paid later than this date then it will no longer be a defined benefits lump sum death benefit, and (unless it falls within the definition of one of the other 'authorised' lump sum death benefits) will be an 'unauthorised member payment'.

The reasons for this restriction are to ensure that the funds backing up the liability within the scheme are not retained indefinitely in a tax-free environment, and to ensure the lifetime allowance test that is triggered by the payment is carried out within a reasonable timescale. A similar provision applies to uncrystallised lump sum death benefits (see below).

Where a member of a defined contribution scheme dies before taking benefits death benefits can be paid as:

(1)   A lump sum, (an uncrystallised funds lump sum death benefit) which is payable at the discretion of the scheme administrator/trustees to the members' dependants or legal personal representatives. The lump sum will be tested against the lifetime allowance applicable on the members' death. If there is any excess fund over and above the lifetime allowance it would be subject to tax at 55%, payable by the recipients of the lump sum death benefit.

(2)   'Pension' to one or more dependants. Dependants' pensions benefits do not count towards the lifetime allowance of the deceased member. Dependants' pensions are taxed in the hands of the recipient as earned income.

An uncrystallised funds lump sum death benefit can only be paid:

*   From a money purchase arrangement,
*   Where unvested funds are held in the arrangement at the time the member died, and
*   Where the member died before taking benefit from the fund.

A term-assurance policy that pays out, say, a set monetary amount on the death of an individual is regarded as providing a 'cash-balance' benefit. The payment represents an uncrystallised funds lump sum death benefit. However, a term-assurance policy that pays out a benefit on the death of an individual by reference to the individual's salary will be providing a defined benefits lump sum death benefit.

In addition a 'pension' may be paid to one or more dependants. The value of the available dependants' 'pension' benefits will not count towards the lifetime allowance of the deceased member.

Death Benefits – after benefits have been crystallised

[4.35] Where the member dies whilst in drawdown the residual fund may be used to provide:

- A lump sum subject to tax at 55%.
- Dependants' pension benefits. This could be paid as an annuity, as drawdown, or as a scheme pension or with effect from 6 April 2015 as a dependants' flexi-access drawdown.

With regard to a drawdown pension, which could be provided through a short-term annuity contract, or by direct withdrawal from the fund, the maximum amount that could be drawn from a fund designated to a dependant would be based upon the age of the dependant at the date of the pension scheme member's death. The calculation method determining the 'basis amount' (as described above by reference to the GAD rates), and the maximum permitted income withdrawal being (now) 150% of the basis amount.

Where the dependant dies while in receipt of drawdown benefits, the residual fund can be used to provide a lump sum, again subject to tax at 55%. This is called the special lump sum death benefit charge and a reduction in the level of it is due to be announced in the 2014 Autumn statement.

Where the member dies while taking secured income (or an annuity) the nature of the available death benefit will depend on the form of death benefit selected by the member when the secured income was set up. In the event of the member's death then the annuity (or secured income) could provide for a continuing pension for a surviving dependant (a dependants' annuity), or there could be ongoing payments for the balance of any guaranteed minimum period associated with the member's pension. Either would be subject to tax in the hands of the recipient.

Where payments are continuing to be made under a guaranteed payment period any dependant's pension can be deferred until the end of the guaranteed payment period.

Where the member was in a defined benefit scheme and elected for 'pension protection' or was in a defined contribution scheme and elected for 'annuity protection' a lump sum death benefit can be paid. The lump sum death benefit will be equivalent to the fund value used to provide the secured income less the actual amounts of income/pension paid to the member before death. A tax charge of 55% will apply. Provision can be made for payment to be made to a dependant.

A member cannot elect both 'pension/annuity protection' and a guaranteed payment period in respect of their secured income. Only one or other of these options may be selected.

Dependants' pensions to 6 April 2015

[4.36] There are four forms of pension benefits that a money purchase arrangement can potentially provide to any surviving dependants of the member on the death of that member.

These mirror the four types of pension benefit such an arrangement can provide the member in their lifetime and are as follows:

- A dependants' annuity,
- A dependants' scheme pension,
- A dependants' drawdown pension, or
- A dependants' scheme pension – this option may only be offered (other than from a defined benefit scheme) if the member or the dependant was given the choice of an annuity instead.

If a dependant's pension entitlement is deemed to be trivial, it may be paid as a trivial commutation lump sum death benefit or where appropriate as a winding-up lump sum death benefit (see below).

There is only one form of pension that a defined benefit scheme can provide to any surviving dependants of the member on the death of that member – a dependants' scheme pension. This mirrors the position applying to the member during their lifetime.

A dependant is defined as:

- A person who was married to the member (or a civil partner) at the date of the member's death,
- A child of the member who is aged under 23 at the date of the member's death,
- A child of the member and aged 23 or over who, in the opinion of the scheme administrator, was at the date of death of the member, dependent on the member because of physical or mental impairment,
- A person who at the date of the member's death was, in the opinion of the scheme administrator financially dependent on the member or in a financial relationship with the member involving mutual dependence or was dependent on the member because of physical or mental impairment. This provision is primarily designed to provide for opposite sex or same-sex partners.

The dependant's pension must normally be payable for the lifetime of the dependant – or until the recipient ceases to be a dependant. A dependants' scheme pension does not have to come into payment immediately following the death of the member.

As with a member's scheme pension, there is no upper limit imposed on the level of dependants' scheme pension payable (both generally, or in relation to the level of benefits provided previously to the member from the arrangement). Once in payment the level of pension in payment cannot generally be reduced.

A dependants' annuity contract can only be purchased by a money purchase arrangement. Such a contract may be purchased following the death of the member from any remaining unvested funds, or drawdown funds remaining on the death of the member.

A dependants' annuity may also be subsequently purchased from a dependants' drawdown pension fund following a period of dependants' drawdown pension. Alternatively, provision for a continuing dependants' annuity may be provided for when the member purchases a lifetime annuity (so the contract is written on a 'joint life' basis). Such contracts should only provide a continuing dependants' annuity to a person (or persons) who is (or are) dependent on the member at the time of their death.

As with a dependants' scheme pension, a dependants' annuity cannot always be paid for the lifetime of the dependant. Where the dependant is a child the annuity must cease when the child stops meeting the 'dependency' definition. The contract may provide for the annuity to stop earlier if the dependant marries.

Where the dependant is not a child the annuity must be payable for the lifetime of the dependant, although again the contract may provide for the annuity to stop earlier where that dependant marries (or remarries). Payments under a dependants' annuity cannot cease before the above points are reached or before the dependant dies.

The term dependants' drawdown pension replaces the terms dependants' unsecured pension and dependants' alternatively secured pension that were used before 6 April 2011.

From 6 April 2011 dependants' drawdown pension may be paid:

- directly from the scheme (called dependants' income withdrawal),
- from an insurance company using a dependants' short-term annuity, or
- as a mix of payments direct from the scheme and from a dependants' short-term annuity.

Dependants' income withdrawal comes in two forms – capped drawdown and flexible drawdown. So in practical terms a dependants' drawdown pension can be paid in one or more of three ways:

- dependants' capped drawdown;
- dependants' flexible drawdown; or
- through a dependants' short-term annuity.

Dependants' pensions from 6 April 2015

[4.37] From 6 April 2015, similar changes to the rules for dependant's annuities and dependants' drawdown pensions are being made to those for a lifetime annuity, and a member's drawdown pension.

For dependant's annuities purchased on or after 6 April 2015 there will no longer be a requirement that:

(1) the member or the dependant must have been given the option to choose the insurance company providing the annuity;

(2) the annual rate of the annuity cannot go down; the annual rate of a dependant's annuity will be able to go down as well as up.

Dependants will have the same options as members for drawdown pensions, as follows:

(1) designations after 5 April 2015 under an arrangement where there is no pre April 2015 dependants' drawdown pension fund will be to a dependants' flexi-access drawdown fund;

(2)   existing dependants' drawdown pension funds paying flexible dependants' drawdown pension will convert to a dependants' flexi-access drawdown fund on 6 April. Any designations to that pre-existing drawdown pension fund will be into the converted dependants' flexi-access drawdown fund;

(3)   dependants may convert existing dependants' drawdown pension funds paying capped dependants' drawdown pension into dependants' flexi-access drawdown fund in a similar way to members. That is they either notify their scheme administrator they intend to convert the fund or take dependants' drawdown pension of more than the annual maximum amount for capped drawdown. Any designations to the fund after it has converted will be to a dependants' flexi-access drawdown fund;

(4)   dependants can choose not to convert their existing capped dependants' drawdown pension funds. Any further designations under the arrangement will be to the existing capped dependants' drawdown pension fund. The cap on the maximum amount of dependants' drawdown pension that can be paid will continue to apply. Scheme administrators will still need to carry out regular reviews and calculations of the maximum annual amount in line with the existing requirements.

However there is one significant difference between members' drawdown and dependants' drawdown. Payment from a dependant's flexi-access drawdown fund on its own will not trigger application of the money purchase annual allowance rules.

Only if the individual has also received an uncrystallised funds pension lump sum or is also receiving member's flexi-access drawdown benefits will the money purchase annual allowance rules apply.

Winding up lump sum death benefit

[4.38] If a pension scheme is winding up, the scheme administrator can choose to convert a small dependant's pension into a one-off lump sum payment. This is a winding-up lump sum. The maximum winding-up lump sum death benefit that can be paid from any scheme is £18,000.

The whole lump sum is taxable as pension income of the dependant.

Schemes will no longer be able to pay a winding-up lump sum death benefit from the date Royal Assent is given to the 2014 Taxation of Pensions Bill.

All payments that could prior to this date be paid as a winding-up lump sum death benefit will still be able to be paid from the date the 2014 Taxation of Pensions Bill comes into effect as an authorised payment, but as a trivial commutation lump sum death benefit.

Trivial commutation lump sum death benefit

[4.39] The maximum trivial commutation lump sum death benefit that can be paid from any scheme is £18,000. This is a maximum amount per scheme, not the maximum across all schemes.

A trivial commutation can be paid whatever age the member was when they died and there is no time limit for making the payment. A dependant's pension that is about to start or one that is already being paid can be commuted. The dependant in receipt of or who was due to be paid the dependant's pension is the person who should get this lump sum and the lump sum is taxable as pension income of the dependant.

Where the member dies after the day on which Royal Assent is given to the 2014 Taxation of Pensions Bill a trivial commutation lump sum death benefit may also be paid to an individual in respect of any entitlement they had to receive any guaranteed payments of an annuity due to be paid after the member's death.

The limit for a trivial commutation lump sum death benefit is also being raised from £18,000 to £30,000 in respect of members who die after the day on which Royal Assent is given to the Bill.

The special lump sum death benefit charge

[4.40] The concept of drawdown instead of annuity purchase was available from the mid-1990s. At that stage this was really about the deferral of annuity purchase where the obligation to secure an income for life to an annuity operated from age 75 at the latest.

Consideration was then given as to the appropriate burden of taxation that should apply in the event of the pension scheme member's death in drawdown before an annuity was purchased. At the time the conclusion was that there needed to be some element of additional taxation above basic rate to take account of the fact that the pensions fund had accrued income and growth without the burden of taxation. Although there was no particular logic to it, it was deemed that a 'fair' assessment of the value of the tax-free accumulation was 10%. Therefore the tax charge on the fund following the death of a member in drawdown was set at the then basic rate of income tax (25%) plus 10%, giving of course a 35% tax charge in total.

However the legislation implementing this did not formally create a link between the basic tax rate and the additional 10%. Therefore as over succeeding years the basic rate of income tax fell back the 35% tax charge remained in place and did so until the implementation of Finance Act 2004 on 6 April 2006.

From April 2006 until now in the event of death whilst drawing unsecured income (now once again referred to as drawdown) if benefit were taken in the form of a lump sum then the special lump sum death benefit charge applies at the rate of 55%.

At the time the then Government proposed that any unused funds remaining upon death should be taxed at a rate designed to recover past relief given unless they were used to provide a dependant's pension. This attracted particular criticism from many who argued it was unfairly high, particularly for basic rate taxpayers and existing unsecured pension holders. However, the Government remained of the view that 55% was appropriate.

The then Government estimated that 75% of individuals currently in draw-down would have received most of their tax relief at the higher rate. It thus rejected calls for a lower charge (such as the previous 35% rate) on the grounds that this would not fully recover the relief provided for many people, and would create an incentive for some people to save into a pension in order to avoid inheritance tax.

A surviving spouse or other dependant can of course as an alternative draw an income benefit from the fund and pay income tax on it, but any residual fund following the death of the last dependant able to draw from the fund remains subject to the special lump sum death benefit charge.

Following a change in the law in 2011 the obligation to secure pension income at age 75 or later, through annuity purchase or through an alternatively secured pension, was abolished. Although the option of an alternatively secured pension was introduced in April 2006 as an alternative for people with principled objections to annuitisation, it was never intended to be widely used.

No longer was it necessary to take benefit at all by age 75, but beyond that age whether or not benefit has been taken the special lump sum death benefit charge applies on any remaining fund.

The March 2014 consultation document only devoted a few words to this issue:

> 'The government believes the tax rules that apply to pensions on death need to be reviewed to ensure they are appropriate under the new system. In particular, the government believes that a flat 55% rate will be too high in many cases given that everyone with defined contribution pension savings will now have the freedom to enter into drawdown rather than an annuity. We will engage with stakeholders to review these rules to ensure that taxation of pension wealth at death remains fair under the new system.'

These words as quoted from the consultation document are somewhat ingenuous in that anybody with defined contribution pension savings already had the option to enter into drawdown. What has not been possible until the changes due to come into force in 2015 is the option for the individual in drawdown to drain off the entire fund unless he was particularly unlucky with the underlying investments of the fund.

The reality is an acceptance, it seems, that if there is a choice between withdrawing the entirety of the fund and paying income tax (the burden of which can be managed by taking withdrawals over time), then no sane person is going to leave a substantial fund behind to then be taxed at 55%. There is no suggestion in the consultation document elsewhere as to what a fair rate of tax might be. But there seems to be an overwhelming logic in favour of a 40% rate given the synchronisation of that rate between higher rate income tax and the inheritance tax rate. We would be surprised if any other rate than 40% was in the Government's mind as an outcome.

An announcement of the Government's decision has been promised for the 2014 Autumn statement.

Where funds have been designated as available for drawdown on or after 6 April 2015 to a flexi-access drawdown fund, any unused funds on the death of the member can be paid as a flexi-access drawdown fund lump sum death benefit.

Any unused funds on the death of the member on or after 6 April 2015 from a pre-6 April 2015 capped drawdown pension fund that has not converted to a flexi-access drawdown fund can be paid as a drawdown pension fund lump sum death benefit as at present.

The conditions for the payment and the taxation of a flexi-access drawdown fund lump sum death benefit are the same as for the payment of a drawdown pension fund lump sum death benefit.

Scheme rules override

[4.41] The rules of many pension schemes will not allow payments to be made using the new flexible access provisions.

The legislation will include a permissive scheme rules override in connection with the following payments:

- drawdown pensions;
- purchase of a short-term annuity;
- dependants' drawdown pensions;
- purchase of a dependants' short-term annuity;
- an uncrystallised funds pension lump sum.

The scheme trustees or manager will be able to choose whether or not to make any of these payments even if the scheme rules do not allow for this. Scheme trustees or managers will not be compelled to provide benefits using the new flexible access provisions.

5

The taxation of UK pension fund investments and defined benefit scheme investment strategy

Introduction

[5.1] If this chapter were being written in the mid-1990s it would be very short. Until 1997 it was normal practice for pensions advisers to simply say that the income and capital growth received by a UK pension fund was tax-free. There was a pretty much universal acceptance of the term 'tax-free pension fund'. There were some exceptions (for example associated with trading income), but other than that our mid-1990s chapter about the taxation of pension funds would more or less have ended here.

The 1997 tax attack on UK pension funds by the then Chancellor of the Exchequer Gordon Brown is infamous, and took place at a time when UK defined benefit schemes were frequently in surplus (that is their assets exceeded their liabilities), with the sponsoring employer and sometimes even the members enjoying a contribution holiday. At the time introducing tax on pension funds was seen as something of a soft target. The position as a consequence is that the Advance Corporation tax withheld on UK dividends cannot be reclaimed by the pension fund. This rather innocuous sounding statement has resulted in the Exchequer over the period since its introduction in 1997 benefiting to the tune of perhaps £120 billion.

Coincidentally this is a pretty close match to the extent that defined benefit pension schemes collectively are in deficit at the time of writing in mid 2014. It is worth noting that most defined benefit pension schemes are now closed to new members.

In this chapter we also consider the implications that may apply to private sector defined benefit schemes as a consequence of the changes announced in the 2014 Budget and the implications for such schemes given the ability of members to transfer out to defined contribution schemes is going to remain as announced in July 2014 (see CHAPTER 14).

It is possible that an increased level of transfers out from private sector defined benefit schemes to defined contribution schemes in respect of those who want to avail themselves of flexi-access drawdown from April 2015 (see CHAPTER 4) may have some impact on scheme investments.

The application of VAT to pension funds is outlined in APPENDIX 3, which also includes a short note on stamp duty land tax.

The evolution of Pensions taxation reform and pension fund investment

[5.2] As we have seen before the eight historic taxation regimes associated with UK pension schemes were replaced with a single uniform regime with effect from 6 April 2006.

So far as pension fund investment was concerned the reforms originally introduced the ability of UK pension funds to invest without restriction including for example in residential property, fine wines, jewellery etc, with a tax charge on the member who enjoyed a personal benefit from any such 'unconventional' investments.

It became apparent in the run-up to April 2006 that there was going to be huge demand associated with the investment of pension funds in residential property in particular. The proposed removal of the ban on investment in residential property by self-invested personal pension schemes (SIPPs) and small, self-administered schemes (SSASs) encouraged a great deal of speculation that this would lead to significant distortions in the housing market and to people using their pension funds to buy their own homes as well as holidays in the usual exotic overseas locations.

And as a consequence in the December 2005 pre-budget report the Government said:

> 'To prevent the potential abuse of the simplification rules, where people could claim tax relief in relation to pension contributions into Self Invested Personal Pensions (SIPPs) for the purpose of funding purchases of holiday and second homes for their or their family's personal use, from 6 April 2006 SIPPs and all other forms of self-directed pensions will be prohibited from obtaining tax advantages when investing in residential property, and certain other assets such as fine wines.'

As a result Finance Act 2006 made amendments to Finance Act 2004, which introduced the concept of 'taxable property', to the pensions taxation vocabulary.

Pension fund taxation in 2014

[5.3] It would now be correct to say that UK pension funds are largely free from the burden of taxation.

(1) With regard to income tax pension funds are exempt (FA 2004 s 186). There is an exception however in relation to income derived from investments or deposits held by a registered pension scheme as a member of a property investment based limited liability partnership.

(2) However income arising from a trading activity undertaken by a registered pension scheme is not investment income and so is not exempt from tax.

(3) With regard to capital gains arising from the disposal of investments held for the purposes of a registered pension scheme – there is an exemption from capital gains tax (TCGA 1992 s 271 as amended by FA

2004 s 187). The exception once again relates to property investment limited liability partnerships, where gains arising from the disposal of assets remain liable to capital gains tax.

Investment regulated pension schemes and taxable property

[5.4] The pre-budget report published on 5 December 2005 within an accompanying technical paper removed for practical purposes the ability of member directed pension schemes to invest in residential property and in other types of asset that were prohibited in the pre Finance Act 2004 regime, including gemstones, fine wines, etc.

Now it would be more appropriate to use the term 'effectively prohibited' as the practical implications of investing in such assets would be to open up the possibility of tax implications that could in the worst-case scenario arise at a rate of 70%.

The technical paper said:

'The new pensions tax regime, in Chapter 4 of the Finance Act 2004, takes effect from A-Day and provides a single investment regime for all registered pension schemes. As part of this single set of investment rules registered pension schemes were given the right to invest in residential property and other tangible moveable assets. This rule extended to self-directed pension schemes which are, under the current rules prohibited from investing in certain assets.

However, to prevent the potential abuse of these rules by people directing the scheme to acquire assets from which a personal benefit will be derived, rather than directing the acquisition of those assets and the associated generous tax reliefs for their intended purpose of building a fund that will ensure a secure income in retirement, the Government has decided to tighten the rules governing allowable investment by certain types of registered pension scheme – notably those where investment can be member-directed – to prohibit tax advantages arising where there is investment in residential property and certain tangible moveable property.'

The consequences for anyone who invests in taxable property through a registered pension scheme are draconian indeed. Over 40 pages of Finance Act 2006 (in particular Schedule 21), made amendments to Finance Act 2004 relating to investment by member directed registered pension schemes in what is referred to as taxable property. Schedule 21 (by inserting FA 2004 Sch 29A) set about this as follows.

Schedule 29A has an introductory section which sets out the taxation consequences of an 'Investment regulated pension scheme' owning taxable property.

Part 1 defines Investment regulated pension schemes and refers to occupational pension schemes (in this context small self-administered schemes – see CHAPTER 6) and non occupational schemes – namely self-invested personal pension schemes (SIPPs – again see CHAPTER 6). Paragraph 1 of new FA 2004 Sch 29A inserted by Sch 21 means by definition that a SIPP is an investment regulated pension scheme.

'1(1)

For the purposes of the taxable property provisions a registered pension scheme which is not an occupational pension scheme is an investment-regulated pension scheme if one or more of its members meets the condition in sub-paragraph (2).

(2)

The condition is that either–

(a)   the member, or

(b)   a person related to the member,

is or has been able (directly or indirectly) to direct, influence or advise on the manner of investment of any of the sums and assets held for the purposes of an arrangement under the pension scheme relating to the member.'

In relation to occupational pension schemes paragraph 2 of new schedule 29A says:

'(1)   For the purposes of the taxable property provisions a registered pension scheme which is an occupational pension scheme is an investment-regulated pension scheme if–

   (a)   there are 50 or fewer members of the pension scheme, and one or more of those members meets the condition in sub-paragraph (2), or

   (b)   at least 10% of the members of the pension scheme meet that condition.

(2)   The condition is that either–

   (a)   the member, or

   (b)   a person related to the member,

is or has been able (directly or indirectly) to direct, influence or advise on the manner of investment of any of the sums and assets held for the purposes of the pension scheme.'

An investment regulated pension scheme is defined therefore as one where the member is able (whether directly or indirectly) to direct or influence the manner of investments the scheme makes.

Part 2 of Schedule 29A is concerned with taxable property. Taxable property being 'residential property' or 'tangible movable property'.

Residential property

[5.5] The definition of residential property in paragraph 7 (1) of Schedule 29A is 'a building that is used or is suitable for use as a dwelling'. This subparagraph goes on to include the land associated with such a building, hotels, and astonishingly a beach hut.

Residential property can be in the UK or elsewhere and includes any related land that is wholly or partly the garden in respect of the building. Also caught is any related land that is wholly or partly the grounds of the residential property and which is used or intended to be used for a purpose connected with the enjoyment of the building. This could for example include an orchard and also includes any building or structure on any related land.

Even investment in a hotel may be treated as taxable property where it provides accommodation rights such as time-share. The term 'building (or structure)' includes some part of a building or structure. So within a block of flats for example each flat is treated as a separate building. If the building is a shop with a separate flat above (meaning it has a separate entrance) then it is treated as two separate buildings. The flat is then treated as residential property and the shop as commercial property.

Ground rents held in relation to residential property will also be treated as residential property.

Time share and hotels

[5.6] Time-share accommodation is residential property whether or not it relates to a particular property, for example a self contained apartment on the Costa del Sol, or accommodation rights in a hotel. However if a pension scheme owns the entirety of a hotel or is a joint owner with others of all of the hotel then this does not constitute residential property. Here the hotel is treated as commercial property.

Hotels, inns, and the like are only defined as residential property where the interest which the pension scheme holds directly is only part of the accommodation and the member or his family has a right to use that or any other part of the accommodation.

For example this would include the purchase of a long lease on a single hotel room by a registered pension scheme and where as a result the pension scheme member has the right to use the hotel.

Property converted or adapted as residential property

[5.7] The definition of residential property does not apply to property or land which is not residential property when the investment regulated pension scheme acquires it. But of course the building or land may later become residential property whilst owned by the pension scheme as a result of being subsequently developed.

Whilst under construction or in the process of conversion the land or property is not residential property as during that period it is not habitable. The residential property treatment applies from the point when the property becomes suitable for use as a dwelling.

As a consequence a property which is sold before the development is substantially completed never becomes residential property.

'Job Related' Residential Property

[5.8] Two types of 'job related' residential property will not be treated as taxable property. These are where the property is occupied by an employee who, not being a member of the pension scheme nor connected with such a member, is required as a condition of employment to occupy the property. The most commonly cited example is a caretaker's flat. If however the property is later let out to a person who is not in that position it will be deemed to have been acquired by the scheme at that point and an unauthorised payment charge will arise.

Another example of property which is not regarded as taxable property is a flat above a shop that is leased from the pension scheme which owns it along with the shop and where the flat is occupied by the trader.

Property which is not treated as residential property

[5.9] The following are defined as not being residential property for this purpose in Schedule 29A Finance Act 2004 which Schedule 21 inserts:

'(a)   a home or other institution providing residential accommodation for children;

(b)   a hall of residence for students;

(c)   a home or other institution providing residential accommodation with personal care for persons in need of personal care by reason of old age, disability, past or present dependence on alcohol or drugs or past or present mental disorder;

(d)   a hospital or hospice;

(e)   a prison or similar establishment'

In addition Paragraph 20 of Schedule 21 sets out exceptions to indirect holdings in property so that the tax charges do not apply through vehicles which carry on trading activities, real estate investment trusts, etc.

Tangible movable property

[5.10] This is not specifically defined in the 2006 Finance Act but generally refers to any type of property that can be moved (i.e. it is not attached to real property or land), touched or felt. HMRC (Registered Pensions Schemes Manual RPSM71091200) describe tangible movable property thus:

'These are things that you can touch and move. Examples are art, antiques, jewellery, fine wine, boats, classic and vintage cars, stamp collections, rare books.'

Part 3 of schedule 21 is concerned with the acquisition and holding of taxable property and covers direct and indirect ownership.

Certain tangible movable property is not regarded as taxable property if it is of a type that is normally held as an investment where there is no possibility of personal use. Investment grade gold bullion is not regarded as taxable property. The definition of investment grade is gold of a purity not less than 995 thousandths that is in a form of a bar or a wafer, of a weight accepted by the bullion markets.

Exceptions to the taxable property rules

[5.11] Paragraph 20 of Schedule 29A sets out exceptions with regard to indirect holdings in property so that the tax charges do not apply to vehicles which carry on trading activities, real estate investment trusts, etc. This is considered in more detail below.

But from paragraph 21 of Schedule 29A, the indirect holding by an investment regulated pension scheme in taxable property includes holding such property held through a shareholding by the scheme in a company where the scheme itself together with controlling directors of the company (being scheme members) have control over the company.

This seems to be a backdoor way of preventing member directed registered pension schemes investing in private enterprises with which they are concerned if the company being invested in owns tangible movable property. There is however a sensible provision exempting assets with a value of less than £6,000.

So changes which were introduced to deter indirect investment in residential property and tangible moveable assets, effectively prohibit investment in shares in a pension scheme member's own company.

Where a SSAS or a SIPP invests in shares in a connected company the pension scheme administrator will be obliged to check whether the company owns residential property or works of art or any other tangible moveable property including assets used in the day-to-day operation of the company which exceed £6,000 in value. Such assets would include office furniture, plant and machinery but would also include directors' cars and commercial vehicles, if owned by the company.

Paragraph 23 of Schedule 29A enables syndicated ownership of what would otherwise be taxable assets. Paragraph 24 in Condition C means that there must be at least 11 participants because of the use of the term '10% or more'.

The amendments introduced into FA 2004 included the introduction of Sections 174A, 185A to 185I, 273ZA and Schedule 29A.

The taxation consequences of a registered pension scheme investing in taxable property

[5.12] If an investment regulated pension scheme directly or indirectly acquires taxable property (residential property or tangible moveable property) it is regarded as an unauthorised payment. This will create an unauthorised payment charge on the member whose pension arrangement acquires the asset.

So the member is then subject to the unauthorised member payment charge at 40% on the value of the unauthorised payment. The scheme administrator is liable to a scheme sanction charge, generally an amount of 15% of the value of the unauthorised payment. If certain limits are exceeded the member may also be subject to the unauthorised payments surcharge at 15%.

In addition the registered pension scheme administrator will be liable to a scheme sanction charge on any income arising from the taxable assets and on any capital gains on their disposal. Income received from taxable property will be charged on the scheme administrator. This will be represented by a scheme sanction charge at a rate of 40% on the income received.

If however the income arising from the taxable property is less than 10% of the value of the property then instead of being taxed on the actual income received the registered pension scheme administrator will be taxed on a deemed level of income. The amount of the deemed income will be 10% of the value of the property.

Capital gains arising on the disposal of taxable property will also be taxed on the scheme administrator in the form of a scheme sanction charge at 40%. The capital gain will not benefit from any annual exempt amount as would apply in the case of an individual.

These provisions however it should be remembered only apply to investment regulated pension schemes as described in 5.13 below.

Investment regulated pension schemes in more detail

[5.13] In order to determine whether a scheme is investment regulated or not HMRC set out separate tests for occupational pension schemes and other forms of regulated pension scheme.

With regard to registered pension schemes which are not occupational pension schemes an investment regulated pension scheme is one where one or more of its members is able (or has been able) directly or indirectly, to direct, influence, or advise on the nature of the investments that are held by the scheme relating to the member. This condition is also satisfied where that level of control as defined is satisfied by a person related to the scheme member.

In respect of occupational pension schemes an investment regulated pension scheme is one where:

(a)   The scheme has less than 50 members and has at least one member who meets the self-direction condition as set out above, or

(b)   The scheme has at least 10% of its membership as members who meet the self-direction condition irrespective of the size of the scheme.

A further category of occupational pension scheme is also regarded as an investment regulated pension scheme for the purposes of the tax charges set out above.

This is where the scheme is an occupational pension scheme that is not itself an investment regulated pension scheme, in the sense of satisfying either condition (a) or (b) as set out above, but where one or more of its members is or has been able (whether directly or indirectly) to direct, influence or advise on the manner of investments linked to an arrangement under the scheme relating to the member.

In this case the arrangement as it relates to the member is treated as an investment regulated pension scheme. The purpose of this provision is to prevent large occupational schemes setting up separate sections of the scheme that permit particular classes of member to direct that their funds are invested in taxable assets. This is in terms of specific assets held just for the purposes of the member's arrangement within the scheme.

These provisions also catch a pool of taxable assets which are held for a collection of arrangements where those arrangements effectively form a separate section of the scheme designed to allow investment in residential property and/or other forms of taxable property.

Within the above the term 'related to the member' has been used. This applies if the person exercising control over the investments and the member are connected persons. The term connected person is defined in ITA 2007 s 993 thus:

'An individual ('A') is connected with another individual ('B') if—(a) A is B's spouse or civil partner, (b) A is a relative of B, (c) A is the spouse or civil partner of a relative of B, (d) A is a relative of B's spouse or civil partner, or (e) A is the spouse or civil partner of a relative of B's spouse or civil partner.'

[ITA 2007 s 994(1)] Section 839(8) states that, in this context:

'"relative" means brother, sister, ancestor or lineal descendant.'

Married or civil partners are thus connected with each other. In effect the taxable property provisions are not avoided if a connected persons acts with regard to the investment of the scheme on behalf of the scheme member.

Indirect investment in taxable property via genuinely diverse commercial vehicles

[5.14] Such investment will not be subject to the tax charges on taxable property. Indirect investments held through genuinely diverse commercial vehicles will not be subject to tax charges when held as a scheme investment by an investment regulated pension scheme (FA 2004 Sch 29A Pt 3).

There are three categories of genuinely diverse commercial vehicle, UK REITS, other kinds of vehicle, and Trading Concerns.

With regard to a REIT this is provided that the pension scheme does not directly or indirectly hold an interest in the UK REIT for the purposes of enabling a pension scheme member or a connected person of such a member to occupy or use the property.

Genuinely diverse commercial vehicles which meet certain conditions, and where the pension scheme, with associates, directly or indirectly owns 10% or less of the vehicle and where there is no right to have private use of any taxable property are also not subject to tax charges when held as a scheme investment by an investment regulated pension scheme.

The vehicle must meet the following conditions:

(1)   The total value of the assets held by the vehicle is at least £1 million, or the vehicle holds at least three assets which are residential property, and (in either of these cases) no asset held by the vehicle being taxable property has a value which exceeds 40% of the total value of the assets.

(2)   If the vehicle is a company, it must be resident in the United Kingdom and not be a close company, or is not resident in the United Kingdom and would not be a close company if it were resident in the United Kingdom.

(3)   The vehicle does not have as a main purpose the direct or indirect holding of an animal used for sporting purposes.

(4)   The pension scheme must not directly or indirectly hold an interest in the vehicle for the purposes of enabling a member of the pension scheme or a connected person of a member to occupy or use the property.

(5)   The pension scheme may not hold directly or indirectly an interest in the vehicle that exceeds:

    –   10% or more of the share capital or issued share capital of the vehicle,

    –   10% or more of the voting rights in the vehicle,

    –   a right to receive 10% or more of the income of the vehicle.

With regard to trading concerns the conditions to be met are:

(a)   The vehicle's main activity is the carrying on of a trade, profession or vocation.

(b)   The pension scheme either alone or together with associated persons does not have control of the vehicle.

(c)   Neither a pension scheme member nor a person connected to such a member is a controlling director of the vehicle or of any other vehicle which holds an interest in the vehicle directly or indirectly.

(d)   The pension scheme does not directly or indirectly hold an interest in the vehicle for the purposes of enabling a pension scheme member or a connected person of such a member to occupy or use a property.

The term 'control' has the meaning given by section 416 Income and Corporation Taxes Act 1988 (now CTA 2010 ss 450, 451).

The term 'associated person' in relation to the pension scheme means:

•   any member of the pension scheme,
•   any person connected with such a member,
•   any arrangement (under that or another pension scheme) relating to a member of the pension scheme,
•   any arrangement (under that or another pension scheme) relating to a person connected to such a member,
•   any associated pension scheme.

The term 'controlling director' means a director to whom paragraph (b) of section 417(5) Income and Corporation Taxes Act 1988 applies (now CTA 2010 s 452(2)(b)), broadly 20% controlling directors.

The purpose is to enable pension schemes to invest commercially in trading concerns without worrying about tangible moveable property that is being used by the company for its trade.

Transitional Protection

[5.15] Under the rules that applied up to 6 April 2006 pension schemes were permitted to hold interests both directly and indirectly in some types of residential property and in some cases tangible moveable property. The taxable property provisions will not generally apply therefore to taxable assets that were legitimately held under the rules operating before 6 April 2006 and where the taxable assets are not improved.

The basic test for transitional protection to apply is that the holding of the relevant interest immediately before 6 April 2006 would not have given grounds for the withdrawal scheme of approval by HMRC of the relevant scheme.

If these conditions are met then the tax charges relating to the holding of taxable property by an investment-regulated pension scheme will not apply to that property or to any indirect holding.

Other investment related rules associated with registered pension schemes

[5.16] The employer-related investment restrictions are set out in section 40 of the Pensions Act 1995 and in the Occupational Pension Schemes (Investment) Regulations 2005, SI 2005/3378 (the Investment Regulations).

With regard to occupational pension schemes (that is employer sponsored schemes) there is a limit on holdings of shares in a sponsoring employer amounting to 5% of the registered schemes assets, or 20% of the scheme assets where they relate to more than one sponsoring employer.

The Occupational Pension Schemes (Investment) (Amendment) Regulations 2010, SI 2010/2161 (the Amendment Regulations), were laid before Parliament on 2 September 2010. They introduce technical changes to the Investment Regulations that were necessary to ensure compliance with Directive 2003/41/EC of the European Parliament and of the Council of 3 June 2003 (the IORP Directive). Article 18(1)(f) of that Directive imposed a 5% limit on the amount of resources an occupational pension scheme may invest in the sponsoring employer.

The Investment Regulations already imposed this restriction in most circumstances, but they provided an exception for investments by the operator of a collective investment scheme, and a transitional provision which allowed certain schemes to retain employer-related investments in excess of the 5% limit required by the IORP Directive.

Both the exception and the transitional provision relied on Article 22 of the IORP Directive which permitted Member States to postpone until 23 September 2010 the application of Article 18(1)(f) to occupational pension schemes operating in their territory. From that date, in order for the Investment Regulations to be EU compliant, it was necessary to revoke the exception for collective investment schemes and the transitional provision which allowed certain schemes to hold investment in excess of 5% and this was the effect of the Amendment Regulations.

Under the Investment Regulations there are further restrictions relating to the investment approach associated with occupational pension schemes which have 100 or more members. These restrictions are set out in paragraph 4 et seq of the Investment Regulations:

(1)   The assets must be invested in the best interests of members and beneficiaries; and in the case of a potential conflict of interest, in the sole interest of members and beneficiaries.

(2)   The powers of investment, or the discretion, must be exercised in a manner calculated to ensure the security, quality, liquidity and profitability of the portfolio as a whole.

(3)   Assets held to cover the scheme's technical provisions must also be invested in a manner appropriate to the nature and duration of the expected future retirement benefits payable under the scheme.

(4)   The assets of the scheme must consist predominantly of investments admitted to trading on regulated markets and investment in assets which are not admitted to trading on such markets must in any event be kept to a prudent level.

(5)   The assets of the scheme must be properly diversified in such a way as to avoid excessive reliance on any particular asset, issuer or group of undertakings and so as to avoid accumulations of risk in the portfolio as a whole. Investments in assets issued by the same issuer or by issuers belonging to the same group must not expose the scheme to excessive risk concentration.

(6)   Investment in derivative instruments may be made only in so far as they contribute to a reduction of risks; or facilitate efficient portfolio management (including the reduction of cost or the generation of additional capital or income with an acceptable level of risk).

As a self-invested personal pension scheme is not, by definition, an employer sponsored scheme then no such limits or restrictions apply to self-invested personal pension schemes. However as self-invested personal pension schemes are regulated by the Financial Conduct Authority the trustees of such schemes are in practice becoming subject to investment constraints that limit the investment choices that scheme members can make. For example it is rare indeed for a self-invested personal pension scheme provider to allow any form of collective investment that is unregulated.

Loans to members of any form of registered pension scheme are not permitted in the sense that they are treated as unauthorised payments.

With regard to employer sponsored schemes, loans to employers directly from the registered scheme must be secured by way of a first charge on assets that are at least equal to the loan. Borrowing by the scheme is limited to 50% of the scheme assets.

Subsequent falls in the value of the security are permitted, provided these are not the result of actions taken by the employer or connected persons. Interest must be charged on loans to employers, of at least the Corporation Tax Self Assessment Rate (currently base rate plus 1%). The loan must not last for more than five years and may be no more than 50% of the market value of the scheme assets. The loan to the employer must allow only one opportunity for the loan to be rolled over into a new loan where there remains an amount owing after five years and then for a maximum extension period of five years.

Final salary pension schemes and investment strategy

[5.17] As set out in CHAPTER 1 the investment management needs of pension schemes were recognised in the first half of the 20th century by insurance companies who were able to offer a comprehensive package of administration and investment management services to occupational pension schemes generally. By the 1950s insurance companies had an overwhelming market share of the financial management associated with occupational pension schemes.

In the pre-war period the investment strategies associated with almost all pension schemes were based upon fixed interest securities and primarily investing in government stock and fixed interest bonds issued by public utilities. It was rare for there to be a departure from this approach thus a more aggressive strategy involving investment in equities in a quest for better returns was unusual. Many pension funds were prohibited by the provisions of the trust deed from investing other than in a conservative manner and many actuaries and financial advisers accepted the conventional wisdom that the liabilities of a final salary scheme were best matched by the fixed returns to redemption of gilt-edged securities and other fixed interest stocks rather than by taking risks in the equity market.

However those funds that in the post-war period invested in equities produced a much better return not surprisingly bearing in mind that after allowing for inflation the real return from equities averaged 12.6% a year in the 1950s and 5.4% a year in the 1960s. Over the same two decades government stock gave a negative or just a barely positive real return. By the 1960s commercial property investment was also becoming a major feature of the investment strategy of some final salary pension funds. Amongst insurance companies one of the market leaders, Legal and General was investing about 25% of its funds in commercial and industrial property. Pension funds also began to enter into partnerships with property developers.

During the second half of the 20th century large pension funds gradually deserted insurance companies in favour of adopting a self-administered approach. Life companies began to see their marketplace as being more confined to schemes offered by small- and medium-sized employers. Insurance companies began to compete with self-administered schemes managed either in-house or by merchant banks and introduced their own 'managed funds'. Large pension funds could choose to invest in asset-backed funds managed by life offices choosing from a range of funds involving equities, fixed interest and property. Other services including actuarial advice and administrative services could be purchased on a fee paying basis. This was an approach best described as unbundling the services required by a typical final salary pension scheme.

The stock market crash of 1973–74 was a reminder that equities can fall as well as rise. The much held opinion that equity-based investment was the key to providing a hedge against inflation was particularly damaged in 1974 when the average return on pension fund assets was −31%, yet wage inflation was running at 29%. Final salary funds in the 1970s showed large deficits often requiring additional employer contributions to restore the finances of such schemes.

It remains the case that large pension schemes will tend to adopt a reasonably diverse investment management approach and pension funds are probably the single largest source of funds available for investment in stock markets. In the current era government policy through quantitative easing has artificially lowered the returns to redemption on fixed interest securities, increasing the attraction of equities and property as investments. These latter sectors have given strong performance in recent years. The increasing obligation of schemes over time to provide index linking of benefits has placed the final salary scheme sector under enormous pressures. Not surprisingly outside the public sector such schemes are in terminal decline with a rapid move towards defined contribution schemes where the investment risk is taken not by the employer but by the scheme member.

Final salary pension schemes – investment strategy and the possible impact of the 2014 Budget proposals (updated to August 2014)

[5.18] As stated in CHAPTER 4 and elsewhere, the 2014 Budget proposals to be implemented from 6 April 2015 will remove the obligation of defined contribution pension scheme members to use the accumulated fund for the purpose of providing an income for life from age 55 or later.

As this flexibility will not extend to defined benefit schemes, defined benefit scheme members will only be able to avail themselves of the new additional flexibility if they first transfer out to a defined contribution scheme, typically to a life office provided personal pension or to a Self-Invested Personal Pension Scheme.

In its consultation document the Government's position was one of suggesting that for most people retaining membership of and therefore taking benefit from a defined benefit scheme will remain the best option. It is therefore hard to say whether going forward the best option for defined benefit scheme members is to take benefit from the scheme by way of a scheme pension.

Because of what is in effect for many a necessity of 'opting out' of a defined benefit scheme in order to transfer to a defined contribution scheme, those who are active scheme members will generally not have the opportunity of considering an alternative option as things currently stand. This really only extends to those who have left the service of the scheme's sponsoring employer and have deferred benefit rights.

The consultation document asked whether it is possible to extend the new freedom of access that will become available to members of defined contribution schemes to members of private sector defined benefit pension schemes and states: 'in principle, the government would like to find a way to do so. However, in practice this decision is finely balanced and the government intends to proceed with caution.'

Private sector defined benefit pension schemes are significant investors in equities and not least in gilts and corporate bonds. More mature schemes typically favour investment in long-dated government bonds and highly-rated corporate bonds so that there is a closer match between scheme assets and liabilities.

The consultation document considered the implications carefully in stating:

> 'if members of defined benefit schemes were to continue to be permitted to transfer to defined contribution schemes, then the stock of assets currently held by defined benefit schemes could potentially be affected . . . that might affect the demand for long dated and index linked government and corporate debt in particular.

> Given that the stock of defined benefit liabilities and assets exceeds £1.1 trillion, even relatively small changes to this stock could have a significant impact on financial markets. In turn this could impact on the wider economy, particularly through the gilts, corporate credit and equities markets. By comparison, a reduction in annuity purchases would only affect the way in which around £11 billion of new funds are invested each year.'

Of the £1.1 trillion of assets held by private sector final salary schemes, some £290 billion is held in government bonds and £200 billion in corporate bonds. These holdings represent something like a quarter and a half respectively of the entire market for these bonds.

So here lay something of a conundrum. The Government is unwilling to allow the additional benefit flexibility accommodated through transfers from un-funded public sector schemes to defined contribution schemes because of the immediate direct cost to the exchequer associated with each and every such transfer (see CHAPTER 9).

And so far as the private sector is concerned if the volume of transfers from private sector defined benefit schemes became disproportionate then there would be unwelcome side effects in terms of stock markets but in particular possibly affecting the Government's ability to fund its borrowing requirement as pension fund investors as institutions are major participants in the market for government stock.

The dilemma is expressed clearly in the following words: 'whilst the govern-ment would in principle welcome the opportunity to extend greater choice to members of private sector defined benefit pension schemes, it will not do so at the expense of significant damage to the wider economy – for instance, if doing so were to make it materially harder or more expensive for UK companies to finance long-term investment.'

However in its response to the consultation (published in July 2014) there was a significant softening of tone:

> 'Taking into account the exclusion of pensioners from the right to transfer; the limited number of active and deferred scheme members for whom it would be in their best interests to transfer; and the likelihood that those transferring would do

so when they reach the scheme's normal age for crystallising their pension pots, the government believes that the overall impact on the existing defined benefit asset base is likely to be limited if private sector defined benefit to defined contribution transfers continue to be allowed.'

From a market perspective the impact of maintaining defined benefit flexibility will at the margins necessitate greater liquidity in asset holdings. However the main driver underpinning portfolio restructuring in the future is likely to continue to be increasing maturity of defined benefit schemes and corresponding de-risking, irrespective of any decision on defined benefit flexibility.

6

Pensions taxation and the higher paid – SIPPs and SSASs

Introduction

[6.1] Following Finance Act 2004 the need to consider types of pension arrangements for the relatively well-paid other than traditional (that is registered) pension schemes became less acute.

This was because of a step change in the possible level of contributions that could go into a registered pension scheme and which would enjoy the benefit of tax relief on the part of the employer and the member. This maximised at an annual allowance of £255,000 in respect of the tax year 2010–11.

From 6 April 2011 however the annual allowance reduced to £50,000 and we wrote in the 2012–2013 edition of this book 'it may be several years before it increases again (if ever)'. From 6 April 2014 the annual allowance reduced to £40,000.

These changes have severely curtailed the ability of individuals to use contributions to a registered pension scheme as a means of tax mitigation. All the same the fact that it is possible for those who were members of an existing registered pension scheme at the appropriate time to carry forward unused pension relief relating to the three previous tax years retains pension contributions as a useful tax planning tool for the higher paid.

In the economic and political environment of 2014 however, fundamental and even moral objection to any mechanism that is associated with 'tax avoidance' is such that one has to wonder whether such objections have now extended to what are perceived as large pension contributions.

According to HM Treasury average annual pension contributions are significantly below £50,000 and only around 100,000 individuals were (before the introduction of the lower annual allowance) saving more than that, around 80% of whom were on incomes of over £100,000. Hardly surprising given that the average value of an individual's UK pension fund is only in the region of £30,000.

Although not necessarily confined as a planning tool for the higher paid we also cover the subject of salary sacrifice in this chapter.

For some who want to ensure they make adequate provision for their retirement the constraints introduced by reductions in the annual allowance may force consideration of other forms of savings.

One possibility is that of contributing to a Qualifying Non-UK Pension Scheme (QNUPS). Although there is no tax relief on the contributions, there is immediate protection from inheritance tax on the accumulated fund in the event of the member's death, and a greater degree of benefit flexibility will generally be available depending on the overseas jurisdiction where the arrangement is established.

SIPPs and SSASs

[6.2] There is a pre-April 2006 legacy of schemes that developed with the higher paid, and in particular directors of smaller companies, in mind. Here we are referring to Small Self Administered Pension Schemes (SSASs) which in this chapter we will look at with a brief historical perspective, then consider how they fit into the current framework for registered pension schemes.

Although not confined to the 'higher paid' the concept of Self Invested Personal Pensions (SIPPs) was introduced from 1989, and gave those who wished it the ability to have some control over the way in which their personal pension fund is invested. The average SIPP fund is considerably more than the average fund in a more traditional type of personal pension. The ability to accumulate a fund that is sufficient to justify investment control is not necessarily confined to the higher paid however.

All the same it seems that the average 'true' SIPP has approximately £280,000 invested – nearly 10 times the size of the average UK pension fund.

A survey published in the March 2013 edition of *Money Management* shows that in respect of the providers who responded to the survey request, the total assets under SIPP administration grew by 16.5% compared to the previous survey, increasing to £103.2bn from £88.6bn. The survey, which assessed data submitted by 60 providers covering 88 schemes, captures most of the estimated 110 active SIPP operators. The survey shows there to be 928,465 SIPPs in existence.

The vast majority, around 80%, of the SIPPs in force, are operated by six or so providers with the rest accounted for by a 'long tail' of smaller providers.

The average SIPP value also improved, rising to £227,573 from £203,684. This figure is lower than the size of the fund associated with what we have above referred to as a 'true' SIPP, as the survey includes life office providers where the SIPP 'container' is used as the means of holding investment funds offered by the life office provider.

Suffolk Life's 'survey of surveys' has been maintained over many years and analyses published data and supplements it with industry knowledge, estimating a total of 913,000 SIPPs with total assets of £104.7bn. Of these there are an estimated 184,000 'full-range bespoke SIPPs' (what we have above referred to as 'true' SIPPs), accounting for total assets of £51.6bn and an average fund size of £280,000.

The earnings cap

[6.3] In the years prior to April 2006, there was a limit on the extent to which pension contributions could be made for the higher paid constrained by the so-called 'earnings cap'.

The earnings cap was introduced to set a ceiling on the amount of benefits that could be paid from occupational pension schemes. So this included defined contribution and defined benefit company pension schemes, public sector pension schemes, as well as SSASs and other forms of individual occupational scheme.

It applied to those who joined an occupational pension scheme set up since 14 March 1989, or who joined an occupational pension scheme from 1 June 1989 (which was set up before 14 March 1989).

The same limit applied to all personal pension schemes for tax years 1989–90 onwards.

From 6 April 2006, the limit set by the earnings cap was replaced. Since then the earnings cap has been replaced by the lifetime allowance and the annual allowance limits.

However, it is important to understand that many company and public sector defined benefit pension schemes continue to use the 'Notional' Earnings Cap in order to restrict benefits payable. Other employers and pension schemes may of course choose to set their own earnings cap instead in order to restrict the extent to which benefits accumulate, and of course to control costs – in particular of course associated with the relatively high paid.

To assist the pensions industry with the transition into the post 5 April 2006 pensions tax regime, and those schemes whose rules still restricted benefits by reference to the earnings cap, HMRC agreed to publish details of a notional earnings cap setting out what the earnings cap would have been, had it still been in existence, each year until 2010–11. (Pensions Tax Simplification Newsletters No 11, March 2006 and No 25, 28 February 2007, HMRC Internet Statements 15 February 2008, 19 February 2009, 29 January 2010.)

The Registered Pension Schemes (Modification of the Rules of Existing Schemes) Regulations 2006 and 2009 (SIs 2006/364 and 2009/3055) ('the modification regulations') modified the rules of pension schemes that automatically became registered pension schemes on 6 April 2006 for a certain period, called the 'transitional period'.

The transitional period ended on the earlier of the first date after 5 April 2006 on which rule amendments in relation to such schemes took effect which stated that the modifications no longer applied to the scheme, and 5 April 2011. This effectively gave pension schemes up to five years to make suitable amendments to their scheme rules.

One of the features of the modification regulations was to preserve the effect of the earnings cap on existing pension schemes to which the modification regulations applied during the transitional period. The modification regulations continued to apply the earnings cap during the transitional period as if the pre 6 April 2006 provisions associated with the earnings cap had remained in force.

If any schemes still need to know what the Earnings Cap would have been for tax years after the 2010–11 tax year they will need to calculate it themselves by adjusting the previous year's figure in line with RPI as published in September of the preceding tax year.

The method by which to do so is to be found in S590C of the Income and Corporation Taxes Act 1998. Historic levels of earnings cap (including the notional earnings cap from 2006–07 onwards) are shown in Table 1 below.

The calculation is not difficult as it is simply a matter of uprating the previous year's cap in line with the change in RPI from September to September (i.e. 12-month period ending with the September of the tax year in which the cap is required) and then rounding that figure up to the nearest amount divisible by 600.

Table 1 – The Earnings cap 1989 – 2006 extended to 2014–15 (Notional)

1989–90	£60,000	2002–03	£97,200
1990–91	£64,800	2003–04	£99,000
1991–92	£71,400	2004–05	£102,000
1992–93	£75,000	2005–06	£105,600
1993–94	£75,000	2006–07	£108,600
1994–95	£76,800	2007–08	£112,800
1995–96	£78,600	2008–09	£117,600
1996–97	£82,200	2009–10	£123,600
1997–98	£84,000	2010–11	£123,600
1998–99	£87,600	2011–12	£129,600
1999–2000	£90,600	2012–13	£137,400
2000–01	£91,800	2013–14	£141,000
2001–02	£95,400	2014–15	£145,800

Additional provision over and above the earnings cap

[6.4] Additional pension provision in the period to 5 April 2006 could be made using unapproved schemes of either a funded (Funded Unapproved Retirement Benefit Schemes – FURBS) or unfunded nature (Unfunded Unapproved Retirement Benefit Schemes – UURBS). From 6 April 2006 additional provision could be made through Employer Financed Retirement Benefit Schemes (EFRBS).

We will consider these particular types of pension arrangements in CHAPTER 7.

Small self administered pension schemes – 5 April 2006

[6.5] This term relating to a specific type of occupational pension scheme is usually abbreviated to the term SSAS. SSASs are a form of occupational pension scheme predominantly intended for the membership of 'controlling directors' (as defined below). It is often the case that private family operated companies opt for a SSAS and there are typically only 2 or 3 members.

It was only from 1973 onwards (following provisions in the 1973 Finance Act) that controlling directors were allowed to participate in an occupational pension scheme, and the upsurge in interest that then took place in establishing pension schemes for 'controlling directors' led to additional controls being introduced in relation to them from 1976 onwards.

For many company directors more traditional insurance company provided pension arrangements operating under occupational pension scheme rules were perfectly satisfactory (known as Individual Pension Arrangements or Executive Pension Plans). But as substantial funds accumulated or as (for tax planning reasons) there was scope to make large contributions the wish for more direct investment control became apparent. Thus the concept of an occupational pension scheme for a small number of members evolved.

It was considered that special requirements were necessary associated with the Inland Revenue approval of such schemes because under trust law (and in particular the case of *Saunders v Vautier* (1841) Cr&Ph 240 [1835]–[1842] All ER Rep 58) it was possible for a trust with a small number of beneficiaries to be broken (or busted) regardless of the terms under which the trust was constituted.

Definitions

[6.6] The official definition of a SSAS is:

'a scheme with less than 12 members where at least one of those members is connected with another member, or with a trustee or with the employer in relation to the scheme'

Inland Revenue memorandum 109, issued in August 1991, also added the term 'a scheme is defined as self-administered if some or all of the income or other assets are invested otherwise than in insurance policies' . . . (see below).

The Inland Revenue's discretion to approve a SSAS became limited by the Retirement Benefit Schemes (Restriction on Discretion to Approve) (Small Self-Administered Schemes) Regulations, SI 1991/1614 – the SSAS regulations.

The SSAS regulations defined a SSAS as a small self administered scheme with less than 12 members where least one of the members was connected with another member or with a trustee or employer in relation to the scheme. In the language of the SSAS regulations (to aid understanding a few keywords are in bold) 'small self-administered scheme' means a scheme:

'(a)   some or all of the income and other assets of which are invested otherwise than in insurance policies, **and**

(b)   **which, if** a scheme member is connected with:

159

  (i) another scheme member,
  (ii) a trustee of the scheme, or
  (iii) a person who is an employer in relation to the scheme, has less than
     12 members'

The meaning of the term 'controlling director' is given by paragraph (b) of section 417(5) of Income and Corporation Taxes Act 1988 (rewritten to CTA 2010 s 452(1), (2)). Broadly, it is any person concerned in the management of the company's trade or business who, either alone or with associated persons, is able to control, directly or indirectly, not less than 20% of the overall capital of the company.

The term 'associated person' in relation to the pension scheme means:

- Any member of the pension scheme;
- Any person connected with such a member;
- Any arrangement (under that or another pension scheme) relating to a member of the pension scheme;
- Any arrangement (under that or another pension scheme) relating to a person connected to such a member;
- Any associated pension scheme.

A pension scheme is associated with another pension scheme if members representing at least 10% by value of one pension scheme are members of the other pension scheme or connected with such members.

As a SSAS is an occupational pension scheme it is subject to the provisions of the Pensions Act 1995. Certain provisions of the Pensions Act 1995 were applied to all SSASs, such as the jurisdiction of the Occupational Pensions Regulatory Authority (OPRA), [Note that OPRA was replaced by the Pensions Regulator from April 2005], limited price indexation (LPI), disclosure of information, trustee duties, and equal treatment provisions.

If the SSAS met certain conditions then it could be exempt from other provisions of the Pensions Act 1995. To benefit from such exemption the trust rules had to provide that decisions were made by unanimous agreement of the trustees. In most cases the trustees were all the members of the scheme plus the 'pensioneer trustee'.

SSAS in operation

[6.7] Given that SSASs are established in order to provide benefits primarily for the directors who control the scheme sponsoring employer, and who are also trustees of the scheme, this leads to the obvious possibility of conflicts of interest.

These conflicts could lead to actions being taken relating to the scheme for reasons other than the provision of benefits on retirement. From as long ago as 1976 SSASs were required to deal with this potential conflict of interest by requiring that one of the trustees be a 'pensioneer trustee'. The Pension Schemes Office (PSO) introduced the concept of the pensioneer trustee with the Association of Pensioneer Trustees (APT) being formed in 1979. The PSO issued memorandum no. 58 in 1976 which introduced the requirement for there to be a pensioneer trustee.

Memorandum 58 provided the main guidance for the operation of a SSAS until August 1991 when the SSAS regulations (see above), came into force. The PSO was replaced on 1 April 2001 by the Inland Revenue Savings, Pensions, Share Schemes (IR SPSS). IR SPSS could consider a scheme with 12 or more members to be a SSAS if it deemed the numbers had been increased to avoid the SSAS regulations. Only one SSAS is permitted per company and it is possible for a single SSAS to be available for a number of associated companies.

Abolished as a requirement associated with a SSAS with effect from 6 April 2006, the pensioneer trustee was an individual recognised by the Inland Revenue as being widely involved with occupational pension schemes and who had regular dealings with the then PSO. The pensioneer trustee was required to give an undertaking to the PSO that they would not consent to the termination of a SSAS other than in accordance with the winding up rule associated with the scheme.

PSO Update 69 later required the pensioneer trustee to be a co-owner of all assets and to be a co-signatory on the SSAS bank account. This meant that the SSAS could not purchase or sell assets without written authority from the Pensioneer Trustee. This therefore strengthened the role of the Pensioneer Trustee and expanded their role to beyond that associated with the winding up of a SSAS. It is important to establish a bank account in the name of the trustees so that the assets of the company are kept separate from those of the SSAS members.

SSASs were considered by controlling directors as a useful means of sheltering company profits in that company contributions were allowable against Corporation tax subject to the usual provision of being wholly and exclusively for the purposes of the trade. The latter constraint in the period to 5 April 2006 was not difficult to satisfy because of specific limits on the benefits that a SSAS, as an occupational pension scheme, could provide with associated constraints on contributions.

In order to ensure however that a SSAS did not become overfunded the scheme was required to have an actuarial valuation undertaken every three years. In addition contributions could not be made to the scheme unless they were justified by the most recent actuarial report.

The other key area in which the Inland Revenue had an interest in monitoring the activities of SSASs related to scheme investments. This began with the statutory condition of approval (relevant at that time) that the scheme should be 'bone fide established for the sole purpose of providing relevant benefits'. There were concerns that the nature of the scheme membership and the relationship with the principal employer could lead to tax-exempt investments being held for the purposes of later providing pension scheme benefits that could be of a type such as to produce a 'non relevant benefit' for the beneficiaries of the scheme or the sponsoring employer.

Thus the SSAS regulations made provisions to limit the power of the trustees to borrow money, hold certain assets as investments, lend money, and purchase shares in the sponsoring employer, and the purchase, sale, or lease of assets. For example SSASs were prohibited from investing in residential property and what were then described as 'personal chattels'. The SSAS was also limited in the extent to which it was allowed to invest in voting shares of the sponsoring employer, not to exceed a shareholding limit of 30%. Scheme trustees were specifically prohibited by virtue of the SSAS regulations from making loans to a member of the scheme or to any person (other than an employer) connected to (meaning in essence related to or in business with) a member of the scheme.

Loans were however permitted as an investment of the scheme to the principal employer.

During the first two years of the scheme's existence the limit was 25% of the fund's assets increasing to 50% of the fund's assets after that time period. There were also specific provisions about the rate of interest that the employer needed to pay to the scheme in relation to a loan, and the timescale within which loans needed to be repaid bearing in mind the need for the scheme to have sufficient liquidity to pay members benefits at the appropriate time.

The SSAS regulations notwithstanding there was a general requirement that scheme trustees should act in the best interest of the members considering those interests in that capacity alone and not in the capacity of employee, shareholder, et cetera. As a consequence, a loan could not be made to an employer for the purpose of keeping an ailing business afloat or to employers who were technically insolvent.

There was a general expectation that a loan should not be made to an employer unless the trustees would be prepared to lend the same amount on the same terms to an unconnected party of comparable standing. The SSAS regulations also required that loans to a sponsoring employer of the scheme should not be of such amount or frequency as to suggest that the employer were only partly funding the scheme whilst claiming a tax deduction on pension contributions made. The minimum term of a loan could not therefore be less than 364 days and from a commercial perspective an interest rate of at least 3% above bank base rate was required unless it could be demonstrated in writing that a similar loan could be obtained from a bank or other financial institution at a lower rate than this.

Limits were also set on the extent to which a scheme being a SSAS was allowed to borrow for the purposes of making scheme investments. This limit was set at a multiple of three times the ordinary annual contributions paid by the employer and membership, plus 45% of the value of the scheme investments.

In the pre-April 2006 regime a SSAS was the only type of pension scheme that was able to enter into a transaction with a 'connected person'. For example the employer sponsoring a SSAS could sell a commercial property to the scheme or buy a commercial property from it. No transactions of this type could however take place between the scheme and its members.

SSAS since 6 April 2006

[6.8] It is interesting that one or two elements of the conditions that related to SSASs in the period before 6 April 2006 have found their way into the legislation associated with registered pension schemes generally.

For example a registered pension scheme which is an occupational pension scheme may make a loan to a sponsoring employer.

There are five tests that a loan to a sponsoring employer from a pension scheme such as a SSAS must satisfy to qualify as 'an authorised employer loan'.

If a loan fails to meet one or more of these tests an unauthorised payment charge will apply.

The five key tests relate to:

(1)   **Security** – the amount of the loan must be secured throughout the full term as a first charge on any asset owned by the sponsoring employer.

(2)   **Interest rates** – the interest-rate charged must be at least 1% over bank base rate.

(3)   **Term of loan** – which must not exceed five years.

(4)   **Maximum amount of loan** – Section 179 (1)(a) of Finance Act 2004 restricts the amount of a loan which can be made to a sponsoring employer to 50% of the fund value.

(5)   **Repayment terms** – All loans to employers must be repaid in equal instalments of capital and interest for each complete year of the loan.

There is no 'small' scheme association so far as HMRC are concerned in relation to 'less than twelve members' as used to exist (see the previous section).

However schemes with less than 12 members and where all decisions are made unanimously (or have an independent trustee), are exempt from the trustees' knowledge and understanding requirements of the Pensions Act 2004 and the member-nominated trustee requirements. If every member of the scheme is a trustee, the scheme will also be exempt from the Internal Disputes Resolution Procedure requirements.

Thus although since April 2006 there has been no requirement for such a scheme to have a pensioneer trustee, many have chosen to retain a pensioneer trustee in place.

In the same way as applies to registered pension schemes generally SSASs may borrow to invest and to provide a member's benefit which has become payable. The maximum amount that can be borrowed is 50% of the net asset value of the scheme.

The ongoing attraction of a SSAS remains for company directors as business-owners who wish to use existing accrued pension rights (in the form of transfers in) and/or future pension monies (in the form of contributions) to interact with their business. The pension fund could for example be used to buy commercial property which is then leased back on commercial terms to the sponsoring employer.

Self invested personal pension schemes (SIPPs) – evolution to 5 April 2006

[6.9] A Self Invested Personal Pension (SIPP) is simply a type of personal pension plan and so as a consequence is a registered pension scheme. A SIPP operates in exactly the same way as any other registered pension scheme with regard to contributions, tax relief and eligibility.

SIPPS are perhaps the most flexible form of pension scheme available. They provide access to a wide range of investments from individual shares to unit trusts, traded endowment policies and commercial property, including farmland and forestry. A SIPP is an arrangement within a personal pension scheme, in which the member has the power to direct how the contributions are invested. Members may make choices about what assets are bought, leased or sold, and decide when those assets are acquired or disposed of.

The idea of SIPPs was first voiced in the 1989 Budget. The then Chancellor of the Exchequer Nigel Lawson 'proposing to make it easier for members of personal pension schemes to direct their investments'. This 'new product' then emerged following the publication of Joint Office memorandum 101 (that is the joint office of what was then the Superannuation Funds Office and the Occupational Pensions Board) – 'Personal pensions (investment of members' contributions, use of scheme funds)', in October 1989. This set out rules and conditions for a broader range of investments associated with personal pension schemes. The first SIPPs were introduced into the market and the first business written by around March 1990.

Until then personal pension arrangements were generally locked into life company products, often with a limited range of funds from which to choose, relatively high and unclear charges, and penalties if the policyholder transferred to another pension provider. A conventional personal pension generally involves the plan holder paying money to an insurance company for investment in an insurance policy. This means the money is invested with relatively little choice on the part of the policyholder.

SIPPs may all the same take the form of member's arrangements that are wholly invested in insurance contracts, for example through a personalised fund within a unit-linked policy, or directly held investments held through a SIPP trust, or a mixture of insured or non-insured assets. The test of a SIPP is whether the member is able to direct how contributions are invested.

Unlike conventional personal pensions where the pension provider as trustee has ownership and control of the assets, in a SIPP the member may have co-ownership of the assets (via an individual trust) as long as the scheme Administrator is a co-trustee to exercise control. In practice, most SIPPs do not work this way and simply have the provider as SIPP trustee.

The Personal Pension Schemes (Restriction on Discretion to Approve) (Permitted Investments) Regulations 2001 (SI 2001/117) came into force with effect from 6 April 2001. These regulations set out the investment conditions to be met by personal pension schemes to qualify for and maintain tax approval based upon the approval regime for the approval of pension schemes by HMRC relevant at the time.

SIPPs as registered pension schemes from 6 April 2006

[6.10] Self invested personal pension schemes became a form of registered pension scheme with effect from 6 April 2006. The main difference between a SIPP and other forms of registered pension scheme is that a SIPP has a more flexible approach to investments as set out above. A SIPP allows for much greater freedom in what may be invested in and for the SIPP to hold these investments directly rather than through some form of investment fund operated by an institution such as a life office.

The SIPP investor can have personal control over the investment strategy of his arrangement or can appoint a fund manager or stockbroker to manage the investments on advisory or discretionary terms.

Under the taxation regime associated with registered pension schemes generally a SIPP may invest in any asset but some assets will be subject to tax charges (see CHAPTER 5 relating to taxable property) and will therefore always be avoided.

SIPP providers will not allow investment to be made in such assets in any event as to do so would prejudice their status as registered pension schemes and in addition such action would risk incurring the wrath of the Financial Conduct Authority (FCA) who regulate SIPPs.

The assets that a SIPP may invest in which are not subject to any tax charge include:

- Stocks and shares listed on a recognised exchange.
- Futures and options traded on recognised futures exchanges.
- Authorised UK unit trusts, OEICs and other UCITS funds.
- Unauthorised unit trusts that do not invest in residential property.
- Unlisted shares.
- Investment trusts.
- Unitised funds issued by insurance companies in the EU.
- Bank deposits.
- Commercial property.
- Ground rents – so long as there is no relationship to residential property.
- Traded life insurance policies.
- Derivatives such as traded options and contracts for differences.
- Gold bullion.

The forms of investment which are 'permitted' but subject to heavy tax penalties include residential property, direct or indirect ownership of tangible movable property (where the market value exceeds £6,000), and other exotic assets such as vintage cars, fine wines, stamp collections, works of art, etc. As with any registered pension scheme a SIPP is allowed to borrow up to 50% of the net value of the fund in order to invest in any asset. In practice however SIPP trustees are only likely to permit borrowing when associated with commercial property purchase.

Not all SIPP providers will allow investment in all forms of assets – even where there are no adverse tax implications. According to the March 2012 *Money Management* survey only nine providers allowed investment in the full range of permitted investments. It is now likely to be even less than that.

SIPP providers and operators are regulated by the Financial Conduct Authority (FCA), and in recent times there are signs that the FCA is becoming more interested in the activities of relatively small SIPP operators in particular. The FCA sets rules and guidelines on how SIPPs are operated, communicated, marketed and advised on in line with the Financial Services and Markets Act 2000.

A thematic review into SIPPS in 2009 revealed for example 'a relatively widespread misunderstanding among SIPP operators that they bear little or no responsibility for the quality of the SIPP business that they administer, because advice is the responsibility of other parties, for example Independent Financial Advisers.'

The FCA has made it clear that whilst a SIPP provider is not responsible for determining whether a particular asset is suitable for an individual, it should take some responsibility for ensuring the investment is as it is described. Ensuring good title and an understanding of the investment would seem to be a minimum requirement for any asset.

SIPPS as a vehicle for syndicated property purchase

[6.11] As the SIPP market has evolved many individual SIPP members have wished to invest in the commercial property market but have been constrained from doing so because their individual fund may be insufficient to purchase a property, even allowing for a mortgage that is permitted to be raised.

Property syndication is where a number of unconnected individuals all buy a part of a property – and in this instance through their SIPPs. Individual SIPPS may decide to buy parts of properties across a number of different syndicates if they wish to do so.

Each SIPP has the ability to raise a mortgage of up to 50% of the net SIPP assets. Thus a SIPP fund of £100,000 could borrow up to £50,000 and therefore invest up to £150,000 into a property syndicate.

The exemption from tax on capital gains and rent is an obvious attraction of using a SIPP as the investment vehicle into a property syndicate.

Salary sacrifice arrangements – the background

[6.12] A salary sacrifice happens when an employee gives up the right to receive part of their pay due under their contract of employment. Usually the sacrifice is made in return for the employer's agreement to provide the employee with some form of non-cash benefit – for example registered pension scheme contributions coming from the employer. The 'sacrifice' is achieved by varying the employee's terms and conditions of employment relating to pay.

Salary sacrifice and its operation is a matter of employment law, not tax law as such. Where an employee agrees to a salary sacrifice in return for a non-cash benefit, they are giving up a contractual right to future remuneration.

Where a salary sacrifice has been put in place for the purpose of converting pay that is subject to tax and Class 1 NICs to a benefit that is not then HMRC has to be satisfied that the salary sacrifice is effective. The effect of the contractual change must be that the employee has given up the right to some of their pay in return for the benefit.

Salary sacrifice and pension contributions

[6.13] Most employers who operate Stakeholder or Group Personal Pension Schemes require employees to make contributions out of their net pay. This means that employees make their contributions from pay on which tax and national insurance has already been deducted. These contributions are 'net contributions from net pay', in the sense that the contribution paid by the member is net of basic rate income tax relief, the pension provider claiming the relief (to be credited to the member's fund), and the member claiming any higher rate income tax relief through their self-assessment return. The additional tax relief will be given either as a cash refund, or as an adjustment to their tax code.

The tax relief mechanism for members of occupational pension schemes is normally different in that member contributions are deducted from gross pay before tax is calculated on the remainder. Both higher and basic rate relief are therefore 'instant'.

Through a salary sacrifice arrangement associated with employed personal pension holders, there are no contributions from the employee out of their net pay. Instead, the employer contribution is increased, in return for the employee agreeing to an equivalent reduction in their gross salary (the salary sacrifice). If an organisation adopts a salary sacrifice scheme, the new employer contribution will normally be calculated to be at least equivalent to the sum of the previous employer's and employee's contributions.

There are some significant Tax and National Insurance savings available for employers and employees by operating a salary sacrifice pension scheme:

Savings for the employer

[6.14] The employer will make savings in employers' national insurance contributions, calculated at 13.8% of the value of the salary sacrificed. This is the most compelling reason for any employer to adopt a salary sacrifice scheme.

Employers can choose to use this saving to enhance pension contributions (in full or in part) or apply these savings elsewhere (perhaps to fund other benefits such as life insurance or health insurance.

Savings for employees – Basic-rate taxpayers

[6.15] There is no tax-saving for a basic-rate taxpayer but there is a saving in employees' national insurance at typically 12% of the salary sacrificed.

Savings for employees – Higher-rate taxpayers

[6.16] Although there is a limited national insurance saving for a higher-rate taxpayer, tax relief is effectively given immediately, typically at 40% or 45% as appropriate, on the salary sacrificed.

By contrast with making direct contributions there is no need to claim the difference between 20% and the member's highest rate of tax through their tax return – with the possibility of course that doing so may be omitted. In any event where the additional tax relief is received through the member's income tax return, the refunded amount is rarely invested into their pension fund.

The disadvantages of salary sacrifice

[6.17] Salary sacrifice results in the member having a lower salary. This could affect:

Life cover – the employer may provide earnings-related life cover as a multiple of salary. The employer may of course continue to provide life cover at the pre-salary sacrifice pay.

Refund of contributions – some occupational pension schemes offer a refund of employee contributions on leaving with less than two years' service. The contribution paid as part of the salary sacrifice arrangement is not an employee contribution so would not be available to be refunded.

Mortgage borrowing – mortgage lenders usually calculate the maximum borrowing level as a multiple of salary. As an individual's salary is lower as a consequence of salary sacrifice, mortgage borrowing may be affected.

Where relevant there may be an effect on state benefits including the state second pension.

Contributing to a Qualifying Non-UK Pension Scheme (QNUPS)

[6.18] QNUPS came about as a result of the Inheritance Tax (Qualifying Non-UK Pension Schemes) Regulations 2010 (SI 2010/51) which came into force on 15 February 2010. A QNUPS is not a 'product' as such but simply derives its name from these regulations.

These regulations were introduced because Finance Act 2004 restricted overseas pension schemes' protection from IHT. The Regulations ensured that the same inheritance tax protection given to registered pension schemes is available to QNUPS.

A QNUPS is a bona fide pension scheme and it is in most instances a requirement that at least 70% of the assets are used to provide the member with a retirement income for life and at not earlier than age 55. The exception is where the QNUPS is either established in an EU Member State or in a jurisdiction where pension schemes are regulated and the scheme is regulated by the relevant regulator.

To qualify as a QNUPS the Non-UK Pension Schemes must be available to residents in the country in which the QNUPS is based and provide that the maximum lump sum available should be no more 30% of the total fund value with the remainder used to provide an income for life from age 55 or later, subject to the exception set out above. In addition, the scheme must be recognised for tax purposes under the country or territory which it is established.

QNUPS offer high net worth individuals a vehicle that can be used for additional pension provision (particularly following the latest reduction in the lifetime allowance from £1.5m to £1.25m), but also as an asset protection tool in respect of capital gains and inheritance tax. There are no contribution limits but HMRC may challenge what it sees as abuse. Thus it is essential that an arrangement that meets the QNUPS definition is regarded as a pension arrangement in particular to ensure that the protection against IHT is not prejudiced.

There are no limits set out in the legislation but contribution levels may be prescribed in local pensions law for the jurisdiction in which the QNUPS is established. If broadly similar to UK pension rules these are likely to be considered reasonable. Another factor that HMRC are likely to consider is whether the payment of contributions to the QNUPS affected the individual's standard of living.

Within the 2014 Budget papers are the words: 'Qualifying non-UK pension schemes (QNUPS) – The Government will consult on ways to give equivalent treatment to QNUPS and to UK registered pension schemes to remove opportunities to avoid Inheritance Tax (IHT). (Finance Bill 2015)'. It is not yet clear how the Government plans to equalise the treatment of schemes, but it may perhaps be through an annual allowance on QNUPS. It is an oddity that QNUPS have no cash contribution limits so it makes sense for the Government to seek to create a level playing field.

Unlike Qualifying Recognised Overseas Pension Schemes (QROPS), see Chapter 9, which are primarily aimed at individuals planning to leave or who have already permanently left the UK, QNUPs can be used by UK resident individuals who have no intention of emigrating abroad. QNUPS are exempt from UK Inheritance Tax and there is no liability to Capital Gains Tax on the fund accrual. Existing assets can be transferred in specie. A QNUPS funded by contributions does not contain tax relieved pension fund so the QNUPS is not restricted by either the annual or lifetime allowance associated with registered pension schemes.

Any income taken from the QNUPS will be taxable under ITEPA 2003 s 575 – as foreign pension income. ITEPA 2003 s 573 applies to any pension paid by or on behalf of a person who is outside the United Kingdom to a person who is resident in the United Kingdom. ITEPA 2003 s 575 (as amended by IT(TOI)A 2005) provides that the taxable amount of a foreign pension is 90% of the actual amount arising in the tax year unless the income is charged in accordance with IT(TOI)A 2005 s 832 (relevant foreign income charged on the remittance basis). This means that 90% of the income will be chargeable to tax at the member's marginal rate. For example if monthly income of £10,000 is received £9,000 will be chargeable at the member's highest rate of tax.

From 6 April 2011, ITEPA 2003 s 574 also extends the charge under s 573 to an annuity purchased with sums or assets held under a relevant non-UK scheme and to an amount paid from a relevant non-UK scheme or from an overseas pension scheme which, if the scheme were a registered pension scheme, would be treated as drawdown income. The term 'overseas pension scheme' has the same meaning as in FA 2004 s 150(7). The term 'relevant non-UK scheme' should be read in accordance with paragraph 1(5) of Schedule 34 to FA 2004.

Depending upon where the QNUPS is invested, there may be further taxation relating to the underlying investment when realising the funds to provide the pension benefit.

Although any income drawn from the QNUPS is taxable on a UK resident there is no 55% tax charge on the residual pension fund on death. Neither does IHT apply but problems can be envisaged if the only reason for setting up a QNUPS is to avoid UK IHT. There is a danger, for example, that where the member is in ill health and sets up a QNUPS with the sole objective of avoiding IHT, HMRC could seek to attack the arrangement. They would do this by trying to claim the pension scheme was essentially a sham and was no different to a normal trust.

QNUPS providers have no obligation to submit information to HMRC. However providers may have to meet local tax reporting requirements depending on local jurisdictional requirements.

7

Schemes operating outside the registered pension scheme framework

Introduction

[7.1] Until 1989 the concept of a pension scheme which was outside the then regime for tax approval by the Inland Revenue did not exist.

The introduction of the earnings cap in 1989, as described in CHAPTER 6, limited the extent to which earnings counted for the purposes of measuring permitted pension scheme benefits or contributions. This created an environment where the Government of the day considered it necessary to allow schemes to operate which did not enjoy the tax privileges associated with what were then HMRC discretionary approved pension schemes, and later registered pension schemes.

In the period between 1989 and April 2006 schemes which were then unapproved were known as 'Funded Unapproved Retirement Benefit Schemes' (FURBS), or 'Unfunded Unapproved Retirement Benefit Schemes' (UURBS). The distinction between the two being somewhat obvious from the nomenclature.

Pension arrangements which in the period following 5 April 2006 are 'unregistered', are now known as 'Employer Financed Retirement Benefit Schemes' (EFRBS). From 6 April 2006 all schemes that were previously unapproved retirement benefit schemes (FURBS and UURBS) automatically became EFRBS.

EFRBS have in recent times become a major focus of Government attention leading to what many see as 'sledgehammer to crack a nut'. Legislation in Finance Act 2011 is associated with what is termed 'disguised remuneration'.

Funded Unapproved Retirement Benefit Schemes (FURBS)

[7.2] The 1989 Finance Act allowed employers for the very first time to establish unapproved retirement schemes. It was not possible to operate unapproved schemes before that time because a condition of operating an approved scheme was that any other scheme operated by the employer was also approved.

The introduction of the earnings cap in 1989 was accompanied by an abolition of this requirement and so the market for unapproved 'top up' schemes, in particular to provide benefits for those earning above the earnings cap, was created. Clearly an employer would first always wish to take maximum advantage of the tax privileges associated with what was then an approved scheme before looking at any alternative arrangements.

FURBS were set up under trust, as an individual arrangement between the employee and the employer. The employer generally acted as the trustee.

From a taxation perspective FURBS were relatively straightforward. Contributions made by the FURBS member did not attract income tax relief, employer contributions into a FURBS were normally taxed on the employee as a benefit-in-kind, and from the employer's perspective employer contributions would normally be allowable as a deduction from profits for corporation tax purposes under the usual rules associated with 'wholly and exclusively for the purposes of trade'.

The funding of a FURBS was almost always solely associated with contributions from an employer. Often because of the tax charge on the employee there would be some form of salary adjustment so as to compensate the member for the benefit in kind tax charge incurred.

There was no limit on the benefits payable nor on contributions, and if required, the entire fund accumulated prior to 6 April 2006 may be taken on retirement as a tax-free lump sum. The tax-free treatment of the benefits arose because the employer contributions had been taxed on entry in the hands of the member.

No investment constraints were associated with FURBS. All that was required was that the trustees of the FURBS operated the scheme in the best interests of the beneficiaries. In the event of the death of a FURBS member before the benefits were drawn, then so long as the fund was subject to the discretionary distribution of the trustees the fund normally escaped inheritance tax. The word 'normally' is used here because of the possibility of an inheritance tax charge being raised as a consequence of a 'failure to exercise a right'.

Since 6 April 2006 however the tax advantages previously given to FURBS (which have in effect become EFRBS – see below) have gone and all income and capital gains in a FURBS is taxed.

The FURBS fund was not in any event a tax-exempt fund. In the period up to April 2006 tax on income received into the fund was at a rate of 20% on savings income, and at 22% on other income (e.g. rental income on property owned by the FURBS). UK dividend income was received with a notional 10% tax credit and there was no further tax to pay. Tax on capital gains was at 34%, (this rate applied from 5 April 1998), was subject to taper relief, and a trustees' annual exemption (£4,250 for 2005–06) applied.

The first £1,000 of gross income (excluding capital gains), known as the Basic Rate Band, is now taxed at the previous preferential rates, being 20% on savings income and 10% on dividends, with any gross income above the Basic Rate Band being taxed at the higher rate tax levels. For the 2014–15 tax year, income above the Basic Rate Band is taxed at 45% (previously 50%) with the exception of dividends, which are taxed at 37.5% (previously 42.5%).

The Annual Exempt Amount (AEA) remains in respect of capital gains and for a FURBS, the level of AEA for most schemes for 2014–15 is £5,500, for 2013–14 it was £5,450. The Capital Gains Tax rate is 28%.

However one tax benefit did survive the 2006 reforms and subsequent changes, in that benefits paid on death from what was a FURBS and is now an EFRBS (see below) will normally still escape inheritance tax on that part of the fund arising from pre-6 April 2006 contributions.

A form of transitional protection was introduced in relation to FURBS contributions made before 6 April 2006. The position in respect of the period from 6 April 2006 onwards in relation to FURBS that then existed is that employer contributions will not be taxable or liable to NICs as they are made and the employer will not secure any tax relief on contributions until benefits start to be paid and are taxed on the former employee.

FURBS and National Insurance contributions

[7.3] This became an area of great controversy. There is no doubt that the intention of the Inland Revenue from 1998 onwards was that employer contributions to a FURBS would be subject to employer and employee National Insurance contributions (NICs).

In November 1997, a Contributions Agency Press Release announced that legal advice had confirmed that most payments into and out of FURBS were 'earnings' for NICs purposes. Prior to that date guidance issued to employers in respect of NICs did not make specific mention of FURBS. It was therefore decided not to collect any 'arrears' of NICs on payments paid into FURBS before 6 April 1998.

In the 1998 Finance Act, the then Chancellor sought to impose NICs on Employer's FURBS contributions. Although the drafting of the legislation was not thought by some to be watertight, most FURBS 'volunteered' to pay NICs on employer contributions paid after 5 April 1998. But in the face of some apparently robust legal advice that the levying of NICs post 5 April 1998 could be challenged in the courts, the Inland Revenue did make some NIC refunds in late 2003 before shutting the door again.

The HMRC view was that an employer contribution (or a contribution made by a third party) to a FURBS was earnings for NICs purposes because it was 'remuneration or profit derived from an employment' within the meaning of section 3(1) of the Social Security Contributions and Benefits Act 1992. There was (in the view of HMRC) a liability for NICs on the payment because it was 'paid to or for the benefit of an earner' as required by section 6(1) of that Act.

This was confirmed in Tax Bulletin 65 where as a result of the High Court decision in *Tullett & Tokyo Forex International Ltd*, and *Others v The Secretary of State for Social Security* (which did not directly relate to FURBS), the Inland Revenue announced that it had reconsidered its position on the National Insurance contributions liability on payments to FURBS. The tax bulletin confirmed the Revenue's view that such payments were liable for Class 1 NICs.

However many tax practitioners took the view that this remained incorrect. Despite that, the Revenue sought payment of any Class 1 NICs which had not been paid on employer contributions into a FURBS as well as interest on the unpaid amount. Between 1998 and 2006, HMRC's legal opinion was that any employer contributions into a FURB were liable for Class 1 NICs on the basis that section 6 of the Social Security Contributions and Benefits Act was satisfied because there was a payment of earnings 'to or for the benefit' of the employee.

The matter then went to the Upper Tribunal and specifically in relation to the case of *Forde and McHugh v HMRC*.

The question for the Upper Tribunal was whether Forde and McHugh Ltd (FML) were liable to pay Class 1 National Insurance contributions on certain payments made to the trustees of a FURB. Whether FML were liable depended upon whether the payments made to the scheme were 'earnings paid to or for the benefit of an earner' within the meaning of section 6(1) of the Social Security Contributions and Benefits Act 1992. There was no dispute that the payments were made 'for the benefit of an earner'. The dispute was whether they were 'earnings'. The HMRC position was that they were, the position of FML was that they were not.

The Upper Tribunal allowed the company's appeal against HMRC's decision that a company was liable to pay Class 1 National Insurance contributions on sums paid into a FURBS in respect of the sole member of the scheme. This was a lead case for a number of other appeals.

The tribunal decided that such contributions were not 'earnings paid' for 'the benefit of an earner' as required by the Social Security and Benefits Act 1992 s 6(1), and did not fall within the payments referred to in paragraph 2 of the Social Security (Contributions) Regulations 2001 Pt 2, with the effect that they were to be disregarded in the calculation of earnings. As a consequence (but subject to the outcome of any appeal – see 7.4 below) companies were able to recover NICs paid on FURBS contributions in some circumstances.

Claims for the year to 5 April 2005 had to be made by 5 April 2011. Exceptionally, it may have been possible to claim NIC refunds for years prior to 2004–05. This will depend on whether or not previous claims and/or settlements had been made, and the terms under which they were made. In addition, HMRC had the power to consider older claims.

The dispute continued . . .

[7.4] The controversy associated with NICs and FURBS rumbled on.

In April 2011 HMRC sought permission to appeal against the decision of the Upper Tribunal in *Forde and McHugh v HMRC*. Leave to appeal was granted and the Upper Tribunal's decision reversed – with one judge stating five reasons as to why these contributions constituted earnings paid to or for the benefit of Mr McHugh and were therefore subject to NICs.

The Court of Appeal, by a 2:1 majority, decided in favour of HMRC (*HMRC v Forde & McHugh Ltd* [2012] EWCA Civ 692). The Court thus reversed the Upper Tribunal's decision in favour of the taxpayer (and disapproved the High Court decision in favour of the taxpayer in *Tullett & Tokyo*).

Lady Justice Arden accepted HMRC's argument that 'earnings' carried a wider meaning under the National Insurance legislation than for income tax. As the contributions were 'paid to or for the benefit of an earner' they were therefore chargeable. Mr Justice Ryder gave a judgment agreeing with Lady Justice Arden.

Lord Justice Rimer would have upheld the Upper Tribunal's decision in favour of the taxpayer and dismissed the appeal. The contributions were in his view not 'earnings'; his reasoning was that the statutory derivation of earnings in the National Insurance Acts had long been linked to emoluments for income tax purposes, and it was accepted that the contributions were not emoluments.

The Court of Appeal refused Forde and McHugh's application for permission to appeal to the Supreme Court.

Unapproved Unfunded Retirement Benefit Schemes (UURBS)

[7.5] A reasonable definition of a UURBS would be 'an individual arrangement set up under a trust between an employer and employee to provide a top-up to the occupational pension scheme of which the employee is a member'.

These were often used by large employers in respect of high earning employees, in particular those earning in excess of the earnings cap introduced from 1989 onwards as set out earlier in this chapter.

UURBS were set up under trust, as an individual arrangement between the employee and the employer. The employer generally acted as the trustee.

The earnings cap (£60,000 when introduced in 1989), set a limit on the income that could be used for the purposes of defining pensionable pay for the purposes of pension provision within pension schemes generally.

The introduction of the earnings cap and the fact that it did not apply to then existing occupational pension scheme members but only to new members, meant that a new employee earning (say) £200,000 a year in 1989 would only be able to have occupational pension scheme provision provided for him based upon the then earnings cap of £60,000.

An existing employee earning the same amount of money could have their full salary subject to pension provision. So a highly paid individual could have been reluctant to move from one job to another where in the existing position he enjoyed pension rights based upon uncapped earnings, but where he would become subject to the earnings cap in the pension scheme of his new employer.

The UURBS enabled this 'gap' to be filled for employees that were subject to the earnings cap. No funds were actually set aside (as in the case of a FURBS), no tax implications arose at the time the benefit right was established simply because there were no contributions in respect of which a tax charge could arise. When income or lump sums were eventually paid to the member from the UURBS this was in effect in the form of pay from the employer taxed through the payroll in the normal way.

Instead of the fund being created as a discrete entity the liability for the eventual benefit to the member was registered in the employer's annual accounts. The weakness of an UURBS therefore was the lack of security for the member as it was just a promise to pay benefits at a future date. So if the employer went bust, the benefit might never be paid and the risk of this could extend for the remaining lifetime of the member.

This risk could however be dealt with by the employer granting the UURBS a charge over some of its assets or by arranging an insurance policy to cover the benefits if the employer became insolvent. Such arrangements became known as Secured Unfunded Unapproved Retirement Benefits Scheme (SUURBS) and although never common are for the sake of completion dealt with below.

Secured Unfunded Unapproved Benefit Schemes (SUURBS)

[7.6] It was possible to combine the two approaches (that is of FURBS and UURBS) by means of what is known as a Secured Unfunded Unapproved Retirement Benefits Scheme (SUURBS).

A SUURBS is in effect a type of UURBS. Employees are given a paper promise, and company assets are set aside (or insurance taken out) which are the subject of an equitable charge (not a trust) in favour of the employees. This provides the member with security and the employer with tax efficiency.

Many employers with high-earning executives who were subject to the earnings cap used a Funded Unapproved Retirement Benefit Scheme (FURBS) to provide retirement benefits on salary in excess of the cap. Others preferred an unfunded approach – thus UURBS as set out above. A SUURBS is an arrangement designed to provide security for an unfunded pension promise for an employee in a way that did not attract a benefit-in-kind tax charge for the employee in the way that a FURBS did. This was achieved by the employer making a benefit promise to the employee that is not funded for in advance of the payment of the benefit. Tax would arise on the member when the benefits were paid out.

A provision is built up in the employer's accounts against the accruing benefits and, when the benefits come into payment, they are paid out of the employer's normal trading resources and are tax-deductible for the employer as a normal expense. The member is taxed on the benefits in payment in a similar way as tax privileged pension schemes generally, the benefit being paid to the member through payroll and tax under PAYE.

At the same time, assets of the employer are designated as security for the benefits. The assets remain in the legal ownership of the employer. The SUURBS documentation specifies the events that trigger a charge on these assets. Normally, this would include the employer going into liquidation and the employer not paying benefits to the member in line with the promise made.

In the event that the charge on the assets is triggered, the assets are sold in order to pay the benefits due to the employee. Otherwise, the employer can continue to use the assets in the usual way and receives the benefit of any income or capital gains in respect of those assets. Usually the assets will never be called on and are not used to pay the benefits. As normally, benefits are and continue to be paid from the employer's own resources.

Employer Financed Retirement Benefit Schemes (EFRBS)

[7.7] The terminology associated with a pension scheme that is not a registered scheme is an Employer Financed Retirement Benefit Scheme (EFRBS). Since April 6 2006, the distinction between approved and unapproved pension schemes has been replaced with a distinction between registered and unregistered schemes.

The position as it applies with effect from 6 April 2006 relates equally to funded and unfunded arrangements. So both FURBS and UURBS became EFRBS. The rules for EFRBS are in fact rather closer to the rules as they previously applied to UURBS than to those associated with what were FURBS.

As unregistered schemes, EFRBS are not subject to the pensions taxation regime set out in Finance Act 2004. Thus contributions to an EFRBS are not subject to the Annual Allowance Charge and benefits from an EFRBS are not tested against the Lifetime Allowance. These rules apply equally to funded and unfunded arrangements, and so as existing FURBS and UURBS in effect became EFRBS with effect from 6 April 2006, the new rules apply to contributions after that date to FURBS established pre 6 April 2006 and to UURBS generally.

The employer will establish the EFRBS with a trust provider, who can be onshore or offshore, and the employer will then make contributions to the EFRBS in respect of individual employees, who each have an identifiable sub-fund within the structure of the EFRBS trust. The EFRBS must be established to provide retirement benefits for the employee, who can take pension benefits from age 55 onwards. The only investment restrictions will be those associated with the trust deed and rules governing the scheme.

No tax relief is available on employer contributions to an EFRBS until the benefits are actually paid to the member. However some tax practitioners and accountants took a more aggressive view seeking a corporation tax deduction associated with EFRBS contributions at the time of payment of the contributions.

The intention however from the HMRC perspective was that any contributions made to the EFRBS should obtain a deferred corporation tax deduction, which is triggered on the extraction of benefits by the member irrespective of whether the benefits are funded or not in the meantime. There is no benefit in kind tax charge on the member in respect of any employer contributions and employer contributions are not subject to National Insurance.

Instead the member of an EFRBS will be taxed in relation to benefits when taken, be it in lump sum form or an income form. The only exception is that any amount taken in lump sum form derived from the member's own contributions will be free from tax, as no tax relief will have been received on such contributions.

No relief from inheritance tax applies to EFRBS, nor in relation to any further contributions to what were FURBS from 6 April 2006. Protection from inheritance tax remains on pre 6 April 2006 funds – in other words relating to what were previously FURBS.

If the EFRBS is structured offshore, the fund can accumulate mainly tax-free, except for tax on UK source income, in respect of which investment returns (whether income or capital gains) are taxable at 45% with dividends taxed at 37.5%.

Where, in connection with an EFRBS, an individual's employer pays premiums under a life assurance policy in order to provide retirement or death benefits to the employee or their spouse/civil partner/children or dependants, the individual employee is eligible under section 266A of the Income and Corporation Taxes Act 1988 (ICTA), for tax relief. Legislation in Finance Act 2012 repeals ICTA 1988 s 266A.

EFRBS in the spotlight

[7.8] From 6 April 2006 onwards because of the relative generosity (compared to the previous era) associated with the extent to which tax privileged pension funds could be accumulated through a generous annual allowance, the need for using EFRBS was limited to the highest earners.

However the reduction in the annual allowance to just £50,000 with effect from 6 April 2011 put EFRBS in the spotlight – in particular as the usage of them in some cases had become somewhat controversial. Being a non-registered pension scheme and as a consequence with no restrictions whatsoever on the form of investment that may be utilised, in some cases loans to the member were provided with no real intention that any such loan would ever be repaid.

In addition as stated above some tax practitioners had adopted a view that it was possible for employers to claim corporation tax relief on EFRBS despite this being clearly an aggressive stance to take. As a consequence of both elements legislation was introduced in Finance Act 2011 to deal with what is seen as 'disguised remuneration' being provided through arrangements such as EFRBS.

There is no doubt that many EFRBS are properly used to provide pension arrangements for higher paid individuals similar to those that could be paid through a registered pension scheme. However no exception will be made to the new provisions applicable from 6 April 2011 and contributions to EFRBS by employers will be taxed on the member with effect from that time. However in order to avoid double taxation tax will not arise when benefits are received.

This by definition will make it much more difficult for those who exceed the £40,000 annual allowance to find tax efficient ways of investing. Unfunded arrangements however would seem to fall outside of the disguised remuneration rules.

EFRBS from April 2011 and 'disguised remuneration'

[7.9] In relation to EFRBS HMRC maintain that they have been used for the purposes of providing loans to members and so avoid tax. HMRC take the view that the 'creative use of EFRBS' to provide retirement benefits is not in keeping with their intention to create a 'more affordable' pensions tax regime.

On 6 December 2010 David Gauke (Exchequer Secretary to the Treasury), in a Written Ministerial Statement confirmed that:

> 'the Government will introduce legislation to tackle arrangements involving trusts or other vehicles used to reward employees, which seek to avoid or defer the payment of income tax or National Insurance Contributions (NICs), including to provide a tax-advantaged alternative to saving beyond the annual and lifetime allowances available in a registered pension scheme.'

Additional detail was published on 9 December 2010. This explained that the legislation would ensure that an income tax charge arose 'where a third party makes provision for what is in substance a reward or recognition, or a loan, in connection with the employee's current, former, or future employment.'

Draft provisions were published on 9 December 2010 so as to allow comment on the legislation that the Government intended to introduce. HMRC published a set of frequently asked questions associated with the proposals they had published and, following representations received, these were revised and republished in March 2011. The intention of the legislation was to impose an immediate income tax charge from 6 April 2011 where a 'relevant third person' takes steps to allocate or earmark cash assets or makes assets available by way of a loan or distribution.

The focus of the Treasury in putting forward these provisions was on 'employers, directors and employees who use arrangements involving trusts and other vehicles to avoid, reduce, or defer liabilities to income tax on rewards of an employment or to avoid restrictions on pensions tax relief'.

Legislation introduced in Finance Act 2011 ensures that where a third party makes provision for what is in substance a reward or recognition or loan in connection with the employee's employment, an income tax charge arises on its full value, that will be subject to PAYE and NIC.

The new legislation is in section 26 of, and Schedule 2 to, the Finance Act 2011 (FA 2011), and adds a new Part 7A to the Income Tax (Earnings and Pensions) Act 2003 (ITEPA 2003) (Part 7A).

Finance Act 2011 s 26 says:

> 'Schedule 2 contains provision about steps which are taken in pursuance of, or which have some other connection with, arrangements concerned with the provision of rewards or recognition or loans in connection with current, former or prospective employments'

In many cases, these third party arrangements allowed an employee to enjoy the full benefit of a sum of money paid, or assets provided, while arguing that, because of the structure of the arrangements, there was no legal right to the money or assets, and hence no charge to income tax.

Schedule 2 as drafted is highly complex and in the words of a CIOT response to the draft Bill in May 2011:

> 'the new exclusions are intricate and heavily qualified (running to nearly 60 pages compared with the original 25). . . . . The proposals still, essentially, tax the form (involvement of a third party) rather than the substance (reward or loans in connection with the employment) of the arrangement; they override the established rules under which benefits-in-kind are taxed and, notwithstanding the new exclusions, they could still impact in mainstream situations.'

For arrangements made prior to 10 December 2010 the legislation changed very little, as the tax treatment of benefits already provided are 'grandfathered' – i.e. they will not fall under the new regime. For example, if an employee has already received a loan on beneficial terms, the benefit-in-kind tax charge on the unpaid interest would still apply. The terms of the loan can be amended, and as long as no new money is paid out to the employee, then the loan will continue to fall under the old regime.

Income tax will be payable through PAYE, together with National Insurance contributions (NICs) as if the employer had paid employment income of equivalent value to the employee.

The disguised remuneration legislation in practice

[7.10] Part 7A the Income Tax (Earnings and Pensions) Act 2003 (ITEPA 2003) applies to arrangements put in place by an employer that are a means of providing an employment-related reward to its employee.

Where a third party (such as a trustee) then takes a 'relevant step' (see below) in relation to that arrangement after 6 April 2011, (see **7.11** regarding the anti-forestalling provisions which applied from 9 December 2010), the legislation imposes a tax charge (income tax and National Insurance contributions (NICs)) based on the value of the assets.

Importantly for pension arrangements, the third party can include the employer or employee where they are acting as a trustee of the arrangement. Actions taken by an employer (that is, when not acting in the capacity of a trustee) can also be treated as though they were being taken by a third party under Chapter 3 of Part 7A.

These provisions will be triggered where the employer gives a 'relevant undertaking' to pay a contribution to an arrangement in the future, and then either earmarks a sum of money to cater for that undertaking, or provides security for it. In practice, this is taken to mean that funded (or secured) unapproved retirement benefit schemes will be caught by the legislation, but that similar unfunded, unsecured promises will not.

The relevant steps

[7.11] The key issue is to determine whether or not a relevant step has been taken:

Payment or transfer. Where the third party pays a sum, or transfers an asset, to an individual, it will give rise to a tax charge. This step is the easiest to recognise in the pension context, as it catches the payment of benefits from the scheme. However, as such a payment was already subject to taxation before Part 7A came in, Part 7A prevents the double taxation of benefits received under an EFRBS.

Paragraph 14 of Schedule 2 to FA 2011 allows that relevant benefits provided by an EFRBS will only be taxed under ITEPA 2003 s 394 to the extent that the value of the benefits to be charged exceeds the amount already charged under Part 7A.

Also, the new section 554S of ITEPA 2003 provides that the tax charge on pension income under ITEPA 2003 Pt 9 will apply in priority to those in Part 7A (and so the remittance basis and the 10% abatement for foreign pensions in Part 9 will continue to apply). Where an earlier Part 7A charge applies, credit will be given when the later Part 9 charge then arises.

Making an asset available. Where a third party makes a particular asset available to a person to benefit from (as if the asset had been transferred to that person), it will also constitute a relevant step. This is less likely to be relevant in the pension context.

Earmarking. If a third party earmarks, or holds an asset or sum of money, with a view to taking a later relevant step, that will in itself be a relevant step. It does not matter if the third party does not know, or has not yet decided, what that later step will be. In the pension context, this can result in contributions that are paid into an EFRBS becoming subject to taxation (previously, it was only benefits being paid out of an EFRBS that were subject to some tax charges, and even then they were not subject to NICs).

The concept of earmarking has caused some difficulty, but could include, for example, the notional allocation of a sum held in the general assets of a defined contribution unregistered arrangement by a trustee for the benefit of a member.

Exclusions. Not all arrangements or relevant steps will result in a tax charge. There are a number of excluded arrangements in ITEPA 2003 s 554E, whilst later sections also include some specific steps and circumstances that would be excluded (in particular, ss 55Q–554Y). Most importantly, steps taken under a registered pension scheme, which have their own tax regime, are excluded from the ambit of Part 7A (see also the additional exemptions introduced by regulations laid towards the end of 2011).

Similarly, there is an exemption for steps taken under an arrangement whose sole purpose is to make 'authorised payments'. This is separate from the exemption for registered pension schemes (which are the vehicles that typically make authorised payments).

The example used by HMRC is where a registered pension scheme buys an annuity from an insurer. It is not aimed at (and does not exempt) arrangements that mirror the benefits provided by a registered pension scheme.

Other exclusions deal with very specific circumstances. For example, the right to receive an annuity or a lump sum outside of the registered pension scheme regime, acquired before 6 April 2011, can still be exercised without a Part 7A charge becoming payable.

Although there are a number of other specific exclusions, there is one other factor that is worth highlighting. When calculating the value of a relevant step for tax purposes, it is also necessary to check whether the employee is UK-resident in the tax year in question. If he is not, then the value of the relevant step will be reduced 'so far as it is not in respect of duties performed in the United Kingdom' (ITEPA 2003 s 554Z4). This has particular relevance to members of Income and Corporation Taxes Act 1988 s 615 pension trusts – typically a UK-based trust that provides retirement benefits for employees working outside the UK. These schemes are neither EFRBS, nor are they within the registered pension scheme regime.

HMRC Guidance on the Part 7A rules has been published in a new chapter of the Employment Income Manual (EIM) starting at EIM45000 (www.hmrc.g ov.uk/manuals/eimanual/EIM45000.htm).

This also includes changes to take account of regulations which provide a further exception to Part 7A – in connection with pension funds that have benefited from UK tax relief (including past unauthorised payments from registered pension schemes).

These are the Employment Income Provided Through Third Parties (Excluded Relevant Steps) Regulations, 2011/2696. These regulations prevent amounts from counting as employment income where the sums or assets in question (that are the subject of a relevant step – as defined in Part 7A) arise or derive from:

- a UK tax-relieved fund of a relevant non-UK scheme,
- a relevant transfer fund created by a transfer from a registered pension scheme, or
- an unauthorised payment made by a registered pension scheme.

The Regulations were laid on 10 November 2011 and came into force on 6 December 2011, but they apply retrospectively to relevant steps taken on or after 9 December 2010 to which the legislation on employment income provided through third-parties would otherwise have applied.

Anti forestalling provisions

[7.12] Anti-forestalling rules covered loans and assets provided between 9 December 2010 and 6 April 2011 to the extent that these remained outstanding at 6 April 2012. The anti-forestalling provisions were of limited application – primarily to the payment of a sum of money (including by way of loans) to a relevant person and the making available of readily convertible assets as security for back-to-back loans.

Having said this, if the benefit took the form of a loan made during the period that was repaid in full before 6 April 2012, this should not have given rise to a liability under the new provisions (the historic rules instead applied). However, anti-forestalling will also apply to some common benefits, such as the provision of education through the payment of school fees under arrangements entered into by a trustee where this followed a request from the employee beneficiary or a connected person.

A tax charge under the anti-forestalling rules will take precedence over any other charging provision; for example, a distribution to the employee beneficiary in cash that would be taxable as earnings under the previous rules. The 'tax point' was 6 April 2012.

8

Pensions and inheritance tax

Introduction

[8.1] Inheritance tax was introduced by the Inheritance Tax Act 1984 (IHTA 1984). The legislation has of course evolved since then but throughout there have been concessions and exemptions associated with pension schemes and inheritance tax (IHT).

Inheritance tax applies in relation to certain 'dispositions' or 'transfers of value', made during an individual's lifetime or following death. There are numerous exemptions associated with IHT and a nil rate band which for tax year 2014–15 is £325,000, unchanged since 6 April 2009.

IHT and pension contributions

[8.2] Under section 12 of the Inheritance Tax Act (as amended):

'(1) A disposition made by any person is not a transfer of value if it is allowable in computing that person's profits or gains for the purposes of income tax or corporation tax or would be so allowable if those profits or gains were sufficient and fell to be so computed.

(2) Without prejudice to subsection (1) above, a disposition made by any person is not a transfer of value if it is a contribution under a registered pension scheme, a qualifying non-UK pension scheme or a section 615(3) scheme in respect of an employee of the person making the disposition.'

This is very specific therefore in stating that there are no IHT considerations to be concerned about in relation to making pension contributions to a registered pension scheme (or other forms of pension scheme as stated above) which are tax relievable.

However an IHT charge may theoretically arise where a pension contribution is made for the benefit of another party.

This is because there will be a transfer of value between the estate of one party and another if a contribution is made to a registered pension scheme which provides benefit for someone other than the contributor (for example a child or grandchild).

However exemption from IHT will usually be available under the payment of contributions out of normal income rules, or through the usual spouse or civil partner exemption where a spouse or civil partner is the beneficiary of such contributions.

IHT and pension scheme benefits

[8.3] Although it is obvious to state it, death in the context of a member of a registered pension scheme will occur either before benefit has been taken, (in respect of a member of an occupational pension scheme often referred to as death in service benefits), or after benefit has been taken (in respect of an occupational pension scheme member generally referred to as death in retirement benefits).

A similar analysis can be made in respect of a member of a personal pension scheme.

Death is either going to occur before benefit has been taken in the form of a lump sum or dependants' pension, or after benefit has been taken by the scheme member. In the latter instance the benefits available will depend on the form in which benefit was taken. If for example benefit for the personal pension scheme member was secured by the provision of a pension annuity then following the annuitant's death a lump sum payment may arise (if death occurs for example within a guarantee period associated with the annuity) and / or if there was an ongoing annuity for the benefit of a surviving spouse or other dependant.

If however pension income was not secured (meaning following the provisions of the 2011 Finance Act benefit taken in the form of capped or flexible drawdown), then following the death of the member the remaining fund could be used to provide a lump sum or ongoing income (secured or otherwise) for a surviving spouse or other dependant, and if such income were not secured then on the eventual death of the dependant a lump sum would arise.

IHT and pension schemes following Finance Act 2011

[8.4] Finance Act 2011 significantly reduced the circumstances in which IHT could arise with regard to death benefits from registered pension schemes.

The major change in relation to pension benefits that Finance Act 2011 introduces is the effective abolition of the compulsion to buy an annuity by age 75 through the abolition of the Finance Act 2004 provisions relating to the alternatively secured pension (ASP). This was described in CHAPTER 4.

The latter facility where used in the past resulted in an IHT charge on the 'left over fund' following the member's death in ASP. This clearly now no longer applies. All IHT charges that arose on pension funds left over on death, or on unauthorised payments from pension schemes and annuities no longer apply. IHTA 1984 ss 151A–151E have been repealed by FA 2011 Sch 16 para 48.

Pre-Finance Act 2011 – failure to exercise a right

[8.5] In the pre-Finance Act 2011 era there was always the risk that the failure to exercise the right to take pension benefits could result in an IHT charge as a consequence of section 3 of IHTA 1984.

The relevant (edited) extract of IHTA states:

'(1) . . . , a transfer of value is a disposition made by a person (the transferor) as a result of which the value of his estate immediately after the disposition is less than it would be but for the disposition; and the amount by which it is less is the value transferred by the transfer.

. . .

(3) Where the value of a person's estate is diminished, and the value

(a)   of another person's estate, or
(b)   of any settled property, . . . to which a person is beneficially entitled,

is increased by the first-mentioned person's omission to exercise a right, he shall be treated for the purposes of this section as having made a disposition at the time (or latest time) when he could have exercised the right, unless it is shown that the omission was not deliberate.'

For IHT purposes, the general rule is that a transfer of value requires positive action by the person making it, such as the gift of an asset. However, in certain circumstances a failure to take positive action is treated as a disposition as well. In particular, the deliberate omission to exercise a right can be treated in this way. (IHTA 1984 s 3(3)) – as set out above.

This could for example have brought into the inheritance tax net the fund associated with a personal pension holder who, being beyond the age at which benefit could be taken, failed to exercise the right to do so whilst seriously ill to the extent of there being a significant short-term risk of death. Such an individual by deliberately leaving their pension fund untouched in an attempt to benefit from the discretionary disposal (and therefore IHT free treatment) of the lump sum benefit following death represented by the fund could be seen as omitting to 'exercise a right'. The failure to exercise this right would have the effect of increasing the estate of the recipient whilst diminishing the estate of the deceased.

Another instance that could be envisaged was the situation where an individual taking benefit through income drawdown and before the age of 75 became seriously ill.

Such an individual knowing that the residual fund following death would not be subject to inheritance tax (albeit subject to an income tax charge of 35% in accordance with the pre 6 April 2011 provisions), could have taken the deliberate action of reducing the level of income withdrawn to zero.

This would have had the effect of increasing the value of the fund eventually available for disposal following death through the failure to exercise the right to maintain income at the current level or indeed to increase it to the maximum permitted level. Death intervened and if the pension scheme member had reduced their level of income drawdown this could have triggered a IHTA 1984 s 3(3) claim. The reduction of the level of income withdrawn had the effect of increasing the value of the pension fund paid to others on death and was therefore not a 'genuine pension arrangement' for the benefit of the member himself.

The view of the Capital Taxes Office is that the circumstances in which an inheritance tax charge might be considered under section 3(3) IHTA 1984 are where decisions have been made with the aim of benefiting others on death rather than to make provision for the member's retirement.

If having elected to take income withdrawal at a certain level it could be shown that the member (or survivor, where applicable) was in normal health and that the option was elected for retirement planning reasons, a section 3(3) claim would not arise.

As a rule of thumb, if the pension scheme member made a decision (unless it was known that the member was in ill-health when making the decision), and lived for two years, this was accepted as sufficient evidence that the member was not suffering from ill-health when he made the decision. 'Ill-health' in this context was taken to mean terminal ill-health or such ill-health that the member's life was uninsurable.

When a claim under section 3(3) did arise it was based on the failure to take up the retirement benefits available to the member immediately before death. At that point in time the member had the right to use the entirety of the fund to purchase an annuity. The HMRC perspective was therefore to raise a claim for IHT based upon the value of an annuity guaranteed for ten years and payable monthly in advance which the balance of the fund could have purchased.

DM Fryer & Others (Personal Representatives of Patricia Arnold Deceased) v HMRC

[8.6] Although now of historical interest only the 'failure to exercise a right' in the context of a pension arrangement was the subject of *DM Fryer & Others (Personal Representatives of Patricia Arnold Deceased) v HMRC* (FTT [2010] UKFTT 87 (TC), TC00398).

In this case the executors appealed against a determination by HMRC that the deceased, Mrs Arnold, had made a disposition under IHTA 1984 s 3(3) by deferring her retirement benefits under a pension policy.

The pension age under the policy was 8 September 2002 (her 60th birthday), but Mrs Arnold was entitled to take benefits at any time between her 50th and 75th birthdays. In April 2002, Mrs Arnold was diagnosed with a serious illness, and died on 30 July 2003 without having taken benefits from the policy.

The tribunal held on the particular facts of the case that Mrs Arnold had omitted, throughout her lifetime, to exercise her pension rights, and that the omission had therefore continued until her death. The burden of proof was on the executors to show that the omission had not been deliberate. It was held that the deceased's omission was deliberate, and had as a consequence diminished her estate.

The tribunal considered that Mrs Arnold's estate had been diminished by her omission to exercise her pension rights, which increased the value of settled property (i.e., the payment of death benefits to the trustees of a discretionary trust).

For IHT purposes, a disposition is not a transfer of value if it is not intended to confer a gratuitous benefit (i.e., within IHTA 1984 s 10). However, the tribunal held that s 10 did not operate in Mrs Arnold's case to exempt her omission to exercise a right from an IHT charge (under IHTA 1984 s 3(3)).

There was, it was held, an intention to confer a gratuitous benefit on the beneficiaries of the trust, in the form of death benefits.

The Arnold case confirmed the previously and widely held view that the member of a registered pension scheme was effectively exposed to an IHT risk from the date when benefit could first be taken.

Extending the principles of the Arnold case when a member entered into income drawdown and whilst in income drawdown, ill-health intervened and the member reduced their level of drawdown, this would have the effect of increasing the value of the pension fund paid to others on death and so could easily have led to an IHT liability.

The position following 6 April 2011

[8.7] A potential IHT charge that previously arose where a member of a registered pension scheme omitted to take their benefit entitlements no longer applies.

IHTA 1984 ss 12(2A)–(2E) have been repealed and a new section 12(2ZA) inserted by FA 2011 Sch 16 para 47 specifically disapplies s 3(3) where a member of a registered pension scheme, or of a section 615(3) scheme (that is under Income and Corporation Taxes Act 1988) or of qualifying non-UK pension scheme, omits to exercise pension rights. Typically, this includes the failure to exercise a right where a member of a pension scheme is able to draw their retirement benefits, chooses not to do so whilst in ill-health and then dies.

This is of course a major change and removes at a stroke what had been seen as a risk which had been confirmed by the tribunal adjudication associated with the late Mrs Arnold as described above in 8.6.

IHT and registered pension schemes following 6 April 2011

[8.8] There do however remain circumstances where there is an IHT relevance in the context of registered pension scheme members. The most obvious is where a member dies before having taken benefit and has expressed a preference to the pension scheme trustees that the lump sum death benefit be payable to his estate, rather than using the facilities associated with discretionary disposal and so avoiding IHT.

Generally death benefits which are payable to the deceased's estate or personal representatives as at the date of death form part of the deceased's estate for IHT purposes. However where the trustees have discretion as regards to the payment of death benefits (meaning that the trustees can choose to whom death benefits will be paid) then the death benefits do not form part of the deceased's estate for IHT purposes. It should be noted that this applies even where the trustees have a discretion over the payment and exercise that discretion in favour of the deceased's estate – the lump sum death benefit is then not liable to IHT.

IHT potentially continues to apply to pension contributions made to registered pension schemes by the member or their employer within two years of the death whilst the member was in ill-health.

However HMRC will only consider raising such a charge where an established pattern of pension contributions over several years has been altered in the knowledge that the member would not survive to enjoy the retirement benefits associated with these contributions and as a consequence enhanced the benefit passing to the beneficiaries of any lump sum payment following the member's death.

IHT may also arise where there has been a transfer of pension benefits by a registered pension scheme member within two years of their death and whilst the member was in ill-health. This could be either by transferring from one scheme to another, including transfers to a Qualifying Recognised Overseas Pension Scheme (QROPS) (see **8.7** above), or by transferring the death benefits to a trust.

A member of a pension scheme has a 'statutory right' to transfer their pension fund between one registered pension scheme and another. On transferring the fund the member gives up their rights under the first scheme in return for rights under the receiving scheme.

An individual may make such a transfer even though they have given an irrevocable direction as to the payment of the death benefits under the first scheme (for example where under the first scheme the member irrevocably assigned the death benefits to a discretionary trust). That direction would not continue to apply to payment of the death benefit from the scheme to which benefits have been transferred.

The member can therefore transfer to a second scheme and direct (through making a nomination) that the death benefit be paid to anyone that they wish to benefit including their own estate. Having made the decision to exercise their right to transfer between schemes there is a loss to the member's estate unless they direct the death benefit to be paid to their own estate. Thus unless the member directs the benefit to be paid to their own estate a lifetime transfer arises under IHTA 1984 s 3(1).

The valuation of the lifetime transfer for this purpose is dependent on the member's state of health and therefore their life expectancy at the date of making the transfer. If the member is in normal health for their age and therefore likely to survive to enjoy the retirement benefits arising from the receiving scheme then the loss is nominal and will not result in a tax charge.

If, on the other hand, the health of the member who has transferred their pension rights is such that they are unlikely to survive to enjoy these benefits with a consequent payment of death benefits then the loss to the transferring member's estate is likely to be substantial.

The circumstances in which an IHT charge could continue to apply on the death of a registered pension scheme member are:

(1) Where the deceased could, right up to the date of their death, have signed a nomination which bound the trustees of the pension scheme to make a payment of the death benefits to a person nominated by the deceased. A binding power to nominate in this context means that the deceased could nominate anyone they wished including their own personal representatives. In these circumstances a claim to Inheritance Tax arises on the death benefits as an asset of the deceased's estate under IHTA 1984 s 5(2).

Inheritance tax will be charged on the sum received by the estate, which will be after deduction of the special lump sum death benefits charge of 55%. This will result in a composite charge of 73% tax overall.

Otherwise if the power is exercised irrevocably more than two years before the deceased's death (assuming the deceased was in good health at the time) then no Inheritance Tax claim normally arises.

This would it is emphasised not apply where the member simply made an expression of wish to the trustees which, although not binding on the trustees, would help guide them in the exercise of their discretionary disposal of the lump sum death benefit.

(2) In respect of guaranteed continuing payments from a registered pension scheme which continue to be paid to the deceased member's estate following their death.

Thus if the deceased remains entitled to pension annuity or scheme pension payments which continue after their death, these guaranteed payments will be liable to IHT if payable as of right to their personal representatives. This income stream then forms part of the death estate and IHT is payable on the open market value (that is the cost of buying the benefits in question) at the date of death.

This does not however apply where a pension continues for the benefit of a surviving spouse or other dependant following the member's death.

(3) Where the pension scheme trustees have no discretion over the payment of lump sum death benefits which are paid to the deceased's estate.

(4) Where the registered pension scheme includes protected rights, and there is no surviving spouse or civil partner, dependants or nominated beneficiaries. The lump sum is paid to the deceased's estate and therefore falls into the IHT net.

(5) Where the pension ceases on death then a claim to IHT might arise on any of the arrears of pension due at the deceased's death. Any such associated payment due would be an asset of the deceased's estate.

(6) On death before benefit is taken an occupational pension scheme may in addition to the usual scheme benefits pay a refund of member's contributions. Refunds of contributions are an asset of the estate and so are therefore potentially liable to IHT.

The two-year rule

[8.9] Where the registered pension scheme Administrators acting on behalf of the trustees have a discretion over to whom they pay the death benefits there was until April 2006 a two-year concessionary period in which to exercise that discretion. This concessionary treatment is now legislated for and can be found in IHTA s 58(2A).

If the discretion is exercised by payment of the death benefits to a private trust, that trust will be subject to the normal IHT charges which apply to mainstream discretionary trusts. It follows, for example, that any subsequent distributions from the recipient trust will be chargeable to IHT even if made within the balance of the two-year period following the member's death.

Where no discretion applies with regard to the death benefits, for example where the scheme trustees are bound to pay the death benefits to a private discretionary trust following the death of the deceased, then the 'two-year period' transfers to the trustees of the recipient discretionary trust. The recipient trustees therefore have the benefit of the two-year period, calculated from the date of the member's death, within which to distribute the funds without any exit charge applying.

Inheritance tax and non-registered pension schemes (EFRBS)

[8.10] There has been no change as a consequence of Finance Act 2011 to the Inheritance Tax charges that arise on unregistered pension schemes – Employer Financed Retirement Benefit Schemes (EFRBS) – see CHAPTER 7.

In relation to Funded Unapproved Retirement Benefit Schemes (FURBS) established before 6 April 2006, as these were occupational pension schemes established through an employer then the discretionary disposal of death benefits would be sufficient to ensure freedom from any charge to IHT. The relieving provisions for this purpose were to be found in IHTA 1984 s 151.

From 6 April 2006 'sponsored superannuation schemes' no longer qualified for the relieving provisions of IHTA 1984 s 151. The IHT relieving provisions are now restricted to Registered Pension Schemes and s 615(3) schemes (see CHAPTER 9).

This means that so far as contributions paid on or after 6 April 2006 are concerned, they will be regarded as 'settled property' and the FURBS/EFRBS is as a consequence treated as relevant property in the same way as any other discretionary trust.

This means that a charge to Inheritance Tax could arise:

- On the failure to take retirement benefits (in other words as a consequence of the failure to exercise a right). There is no obligation on the member of an EFRBS to take their retirement benefits at any particular time. So, in certain circumstances the provisions of IHTA 1984 s 3(3) may apply so as to give a charge to Inheritance Tax, where the member has died without taking retirement benefits and where as a result their beneficiaries have benefited from enhanced death benefits. This is a scenario where the member's estate is 'diminished' and the value of another person's estate is 'increased' by their omission to exercise a 'right'; the 'right' to take their retirement benefits. HMRC will look closely at a situation where the member of an EFRBS was in ill-health and died having made a deliberate decision not to take their retirement benefits.

- On chargeable events under the relevant property regime, as property in a EFRBS is settled property and subject to the normal periodic and exit charges to Inheritance Tax. At each ten-year anniversary there is a 'principal' charge of up to 6% on the value of the relevant property in the trust. The scheme member is regarded as the settlor for Inheritance Tax purposes. This applies with regard to contributions made by the member as an individual and contributions made by their employer as contributions to a pension arrangement by both employer and on the employee's behalf are 'delayed remuneration for their current work'.

Under the gift with reservation provisions – a disposition from an EFRBS may constitute a gift with reservation where the class of discretionary beneficiaries includes the member's personal representatives. The death benefits provision under an EFRBS is an item of property for Inheritance Tax purposes (IHTA 1984 s 272) and so can be the subject of a disposition by the scheme member either on joining the scheme or at any time during their lifetime before they retire. Therefore it is capable of being the subject matter of a gift.

Where no additional contributions are made to what was previously a FURBS and now an EFRBS from 6 April 2006, FA 2004 Sch 36 para 56(2)(b) provides transitional relief and IHTA 1984 s 151 continues to apply to the EFRBS and the trust funds are not relevant property for Inheritance Tax purposes.

Where additional contributions were made to what was previously a FURB (and now an EFRBS) FA 2004 Sch 36 para 57 applies and the value of the fund as at 6 April 2006, (indexed in line with RPI) is protected from periodic and exit charges. The excess of the fund over this protected amount will be subject to exit and periodic charges.

An Unfunded Unapproved Retirement Benefit Scheme (UURBS) – by definition originally set up before 6 April 2006 is as the name suggests a scheme that promises to pay a benefit in the future with no underlying employer contribution to a fund that is held on trust to provide the promised benefit.

As with EFRBS then after 6 April 2006 an UURBS is a relevant property trust and subject to periodic and exit charges. However, as there are no funds in the trust then there is no property on which to raise a charge to Inheritance Tax.

The inheritance tax treatment of non-UK pension schemes

[8.11] As we have seen above IHTA 1984 provides for inheritance tax charges on property held in a relevant property settlement. These may include charges when property is transferred into a settlement, periodic charges on property held under a settlement and charges when property is transferred out of a settlement.

Inheritance tax charges also arise on transfers of value out of an individual's estate. This can include property held when an individual dies, because the rules treat a person as having made a transfer of value of all the property in their estate immediately before their death.

Sums and assets held under a pension scheme may be subject to these inheritance tax charges. However, the Inheritance Tax Act 1984 contains provisions that generally exempt from the charges sums and assets held under a registered pension scheme or certain occupational pension schemes set up in the UK for an individual employed wholly outside the UK. These provisions are contained in IHTA 1984 ss 12(2), 58(1)(d), 58(2A)(b), 151 and 152.

Before changes were made to the pension taxation rules at 6 April 2006, protection from inheritance tax charges applied also to certain non-UK pension schemes. But changes included in the Finance Act 2004 (which had effect from 6 April 2006) restricted this protection to registered pension schemes and occupational pension schemes set up in the UK for an individual employed wholly outside the UK only. Overseas pension schemes were not included for the purposes of this protection. It was later recognised that this was an omission and HMRC undertook to correct it.

FA 2008 Sch 29 para 18 contained provisions to extend the protection from inheritance tax charges to qualifying non-UK pension schemes. The provisions gave a regulation-making power to prescribe the requirements an overseas pension scheme must meet to be a qualifying non-UK pension scheme. This includes Qualifying Recognised Overseas Pension Schemes (QROPS) – see CHAPTER 9.

The amendments made by FA 2008 Sch 29, together with Regulations made under IHTA 1984 s 271A, restored the inheritance tax protection to non-UK pension schemes that are broadly equivalent to registered pension schemes.

This created the intended position that any remaining fund within a QROPS (or other qualifying non-UK pension scheme) following the death of the scheme member and that of any dependants who are entitled to benefits following the death of the scheme member are free from IHT as for IHT purposes this does not comprise 'relevant property' – and so is free from IHT.

Consultation on uniformity of IHT treatment for UK registered pension schemes and qualifying non-UK pension schemes

[8.12] Within the 2014 Budget papers are the words: 'Qualifying non-UK pension schemes (QNUPS) – The Government will consult on ways to give equivalent treatment to QNUPS and to UK registered pension schemes to remove opportunities to avoid Inheritance Tax (IHT). (Finance Bill 2015)'.

To understand how curious this is we need to recall how it was that QNUPS came to exist in the first place. Perhaps then we might gain an insight as to what is meant by 'equivalent treatment to QNUPS and to UK registered pension schemes to remove opportunities to avoid Inheritance Tax (IHT)'.

A qualifying non-UK pension scheme is defined in IHTA 1984 s 271A (as inserted by FA 2008) as:

'(1) . . . a pension scheme (other than a registered pension scheme) which—

(a)   is established in a country or territory outside the United Kingdom, and

(b)   satisfies any requirements prescribed for the purposes of this section by regulations made by the Commissioners for Her Majesty's Revenue and Customs.'

The regulations were not published until January 2010 when HMRC issued The Inheritance Tax (Qualifying Non-UK Pension Schemes) Regulations 2010, SI 2010/51 which defined exactly what type of non-UK pension scheme would be exempt from IHT. This went beyond extending the IHT exemption to QROPS alone (see **8.11** above) and created (inadvertently) a new acronym into pensions terminology of QNUPS (also see Chapter 9).

The original purpose of SI 2010/51 was to rectify an error in Finance Act 2004 associated with QROPS. Due to an oversight the inheritance tax exemptions that apply to UK registered pension schemes were not extended to QROPS. The result was an unsatisfactory position where, according to the law, the exit charge and periodic charges associated with discretionary trusts would apply to a QROPS. When this was brought to HMRC's attention it was recognised as an error and SI 2010/51 was implemented in order to correct it.

The outcome is that a QNUPS benefits from a UK inheritance tax exemption in respect of:

*   UK tax-relieved funds that have been transferred to a QROPS;
*   contributions to a QNUPS by a UK-domiciled individual; and
*   UK-situated assets held by a QNUPS.

The key difference between a QROPS and a QNUPS is that a QNUPS does not have to be registered with HMRC and so it does not need to comply with the information reporting rules applicable to a QROPS – see Chapter 9.

The position as set out above means that:

*   a non-UK resident may transfer tax-relieved UK pension rights to a QROPS and on death, whether before or after age 75, no inheritance tax liability arises and no unauthorised payment charge applies, so long as the member has resided outside of the UK for more than five complete and consecutive tax years; and

- a non-UK resident or UK resident may contribute to a QNUPS, will not receive tax relief on the contributions, but on death no inheritance tax liability arises.

Which brings us neatly back to trying to understand what the words 'give equivalent treatment to QNUPS and to UK registered pension schemes to remove opportunities to avoid Inheritance Tax' actually mean, because funds held within QNUPS and within UK registered pension schemes are already outside the scope of IHT. In that sense the treatment is already equivalent.

The key difference arises with regard to contributions. The amount that can be paid into a UK registered pension scheme is of course limited by the annual allowance. However there is no guidance as to what might be construed as an acceptable level of contribution into a QNUPS that is consistent with contributing to a pension scheme and not first and foremost to an IHT planning vehicle.

Commentators on this have had something of a field day including the following:

'The government could strip qualifying non-UK pension schemes of their inheritance tax (IHT) exemption in a bid to curb avoidance.' (Citiwire)

'It is not yet clear how the Government plans to equalise the treatment of schemes, but it may be through an annual allowance on QNUPS. It is an oddity that QNUPS have no cash contribution limits so it makes sense for the Government to seek to create a level playing field.' (Money Marketing)

Effectively it seems the Treasury is looking at ways to plug the loophole they inadvertently created back in 2010.

9

Taxation of overseas pension scheme benefits and of non-UK resident members of UK pension schemes

Introduction

[9.1] In this chapter we will look at the tax regime associated with overseas pension schemes as it affects expats and UK residents. We will consider how it applies to those who go to abroad and work or retire overseas. Those who decide to emigrate may continue to be or become members of UK registered pension schemes subject to certain conditions. Others may be able to participate in an overseas scheme and may consider transferring their UK pension rights into such a scheme.

There is a relevance to certain overseas pension schemes to UK residents and this will be explored as well.

We will also describe Section 615 pension schemes which are used by certain non UK residents who are employed in the UK.

Living in the UK and participating in an EU pension scheme

[9.2] Most EU Member States tax occupational pensions according to the EET system (Exempt contributions, Exempt investment income and capital gains on the pension fund, Taxed benefits) or ETT principle (Exempt contributions, Taxed investment income and capital gains of the pension fund, Taxed benefits).

This means that in most EU countries that follow the EET basis:

- contributions by both employer and employee are tax deductible,
- the investment returns of the pension fund are usually tax exempt (they are taxed only in Denmark, Italy and Sweden), and
- benefits are taxed.

The European Commission supports this system of deferred taxation accepting that contributions to pension funds diminish a person's liability to pay taxes and it encourages citizens to save for their old age. However as we have seen in the UK the cost of this 'encouragement' has been seen as unacceptable at over 2% of GDP with measures taken to reduce it.

However, many Member States have not allowed a tax deduction for pension contributions paid to pension funds in other Member States. This effectively sealed off their national pension markets from competition from other Member States and created major obstacles to pan-European funds and the free movement of workers.

On the basis of the EU Treaty and the case-law of the European Court of Justice in Luxembourg (ECJ) the Commission concluded that Member States were not allowed to restrict the freedom to provide services and the free movement of workers by refusing tax deductibility for pension contributions paid to pension funds in other Member States.

Living overseas and retaining membership of or joining a registered pension scheme

[9.3] Since 6 April 2006 membership of a registered pension scheme has been open to anyone regardless of where they are resident. Nor is there any restriction on the amount that can be contributed by an overseas resident individual or by an employer in respect of overseas resident individuals. But relief from UK income tax on contributions may not be available, or may be restricted.

Member contributions

[9.4] The legislation is to be found in Finance Act 2004 s 188 et seq. Relief from UK income tax on contributions by an individual to a registered pension scheme is dependent on their being a 'relevant UK individual' during a tax year. The term 'relevant UK individual' relates to those who have earnings chargeable to income tax in the United Kingdom for the relevant tax year and who were tax resident in the UK at some stage during the tax year in respect of which tax relief is claimed, or were tax resident in the UK at some stage during the five previous tax years and at the time when the individual joined the registered pension scheme, or the individual (or the individual's spouse) has for the tax year, earnings from overseas Crown employment which are subject to UK tax.

Under Finance Act 2004 s 190 there is an annual limit for UK tax relieved contributions being the greater of 100% of UK relevant earnings which are chargeable to income tax in the UK (subject to the annual allowance of £40,000) and £3,600. So a relevant UK individual living overseas who has no relevant UK earnings may make pension contributions to a UK registered pension scheme of up to £3,600 in a tax year and enjoy income tax relief. The annual allowance applies in the same way as it applies to UK resident scheme members.

However it is only possible for contributions to qualify for income tax relief in the circumstances set out above in each of the five tax years after ceasing to be UK resident. In addition the value of the individual's tax relieved pension savings in any tax year is tested against the annual allowance in the usual way.

The annual allowance charge applies regardless of where the individual is resident. It is not covered by any double taxation agreement because it is not a tax on income but on excess pension tax relief. Being a non-UK resident does not therefore avoid the possibility of a tax charge arising on excessive contributions.

Individuals who don't fall into these categories are allowed to make unlimited contributions to a UK registered pension scheme but will not receive tax relief in the UK. They may be eligible for tax relief in their country of residence but that of course is beyond the scope of this book.

If the pension scheme member is a relevant overseas individual (see below), then any non tax-relieved personal contributions made by them, or perhaps more significantly contributions paid on their behalf by an overseas employer, can give rise to an enhanced lifetime allowance.

A relevant overseas individual is someone who is not a relevant UK individual, or who is a relevant UK individual only by virtue of their having been a UK resident, (or of their being in receipt of relevant UK earnings and being a member of a registered pension scheme), in the last five tax years, and are not at the same time employed by a UK resident employer (FA 2004 s 221).

To claim the enhancement to the lifetime allowance, the member will need to fill in form APSS 202 – the same as that which is required in respect of a transfer in to a UK registered pension scheme from a Recognised Overseas Pension Scheme.

Employer contributions

[9.5] A UK resident employer can make contributions to a UK registered pension scheme in respect of an overseas resident employee (whether or not the member is in receipt of UK earnings).

Therefore a UK employer can make a pension contribution in respect of an employee irrespective of where the employee is resident. Relief against Corporation tax will be given providing it can be demonstrated that contributions have been made 'wholly and exclusively for the purposes of the trade'. However the member will not be able to claim an enhanced lifetime allowance as they will not be classed a relevant overseas individual.

The conditions that must be met for the employer to claim Corporation tax relief are that the pension scheme member must be an employee or former employee of the UK business and the employer contributions may be treated as a deductible business expense if they are incurred wholly and exclusively for the purposes of the employer's trade or profession.

Corresponding relief – to 5 April 2006

[9.6] Before 6 April 2006 a non-UK domiciled employee who was in receipt of 'foreign emoluments', whilst working in the UK for a non-UK employer, could remain as a member of an overseas pension scheme. This was so long as

HMRC accepted that the overseas scheme 'corresponded' to a UK approved scheme, in which case 'corresponding relief' was available in respect of contributions (both member and employer) to that scheme.

If the individual was not in receipt of foreign emoluments, but participated in an overseas pension scheme which would qualify for corresponding relief, similar tax relief could be granted under the relevant Double Taxation Treaty.

In broad terms, an overseas scheme 'corresponded' with the UK regime if it:

- was established in the country where the employee either resided or worked immediately before coming to the UK, or was an international pension scheme for all expatriate employees; and
- was recognised by the relevant authorities in that country as a scheme which provides relevant benefits; and
- provided a reasonable amount of benefits (generally considered to be a maximum pension of 70% of final salary); and
- had as its primary purpose the provision of relevant benefits; and
- provided for reasonable employee and employer contributions to the scheme, in relation to the benefits to be paid.

From 6 April 2006, migrant member relief (Finance Act 2004 Sch 33) replaced corresponding relief.

Migrant member relief – from 6 April 2006

[9.7] As well as the option of obtaining tax relief via a participation in a UK registered pension scheme, if certain conditions are met migrant member relief allows UK tax relief on pension contributions made by or in respect of migrant workers who come to the UK as existing members of overseas pension schemes, and where they continue to make contributions to the overseas scheme whilst in the UK, just as if those contributions were made to a UK registered pension scheme.

This applies where the individual has come to the UK as an existing overseas scheme member and qualified for tax relief on contributions in respect of that scheme. However the scheme must be recognised by the Revenue as a qualifying overseas pension scheme, which involves it meeting prescribed conditions described below and the overseas scheme administrator making a number of undertakings via form APSS 250.

Qualifying overseas pension scheme

[9.8] To be a qualifying overseas pension scheme, the scheme must satisfy requirements relating to the regulation of the scheme in the country in which it is established, and the nature of the pension benefits it provides.

To be an overseas pension scheme (as defined in SI 2006/206 as amended) the scheme must be a pension scheme as defined in FA 2004 s 150(1), established outside the UK and not a registered pension scheme.

A qualifying overseas pension scheme is an overseas pension scheme that meets the qualifying conditions as set out in FA 2004 Sch 33 para 5 (see below).

The Schedule 33 qualifying conditions are:

'5(1) For the purposes of this Schedule an overseas pension scheme is a qualifying overseas pension scheme if:

(a)   the scheme manager has given to the Inland Revenue notification that it is an overseas pension scheme and has provided any such evidence that it is an overseas pension scheme as the Inland Revenue may require,

(b)   the scheme manager has undertaken to the Inland Revenue to inform the Inland Revenue if it ceases to be an overseas pension scheme,

(c)   the scheme manager has undertaken to the Inland Revenue to comply with any prescribed benefit crystallisation information requirements imposed on the scheme manager, and

(d)   the overseas pension scheme is not excluded from being a qualifying overseas pension scheme by sub-paragraph (3) . . .

(3) An overseas pension scheme is excluded from being a qualifying overseas pension scheme if the Inland Revenue has decided that:

(a)   there has been a failure to comply with any prescribed benefit crystallisation information requirements imposed on the scheme manager and the failure is significant, and

(b)   by reason of the failure it is not appropriate that relief from tax should be given in respect of contributions under the pension scheme . . . '

A qualifying overseas pension scheme is an overseas pension scheme as defined under the provisions of Finance Act 2004 s 150(7) and must also comply with The Pension Schemes (Categories of Country and Requirements for Overseas Pension Schemes) Regulations, SI 2006/206 as amended with effect from 6 April 2012. These amendments are substantial and are set out in **9.23**.

Obtaining migrant member relief

[9.9] Other conditions must also be met for migrant member relief to apply:

(a)   The individual must have relevant UK earnings chargeable to income tax.

(b)   The individual must be tax resident in the UK when the pension contributions are paid.

(c)   The individual must have notified the pension scheme manager that they intend to claim migrant member relief on their pension contributions.

So far as condition (b) above is concerned, an individual is treated as UK tax resident from their date of arrival in the UK until their date of departure. Matters relating to UK residence are covered below – in particular the introduction of a statutory residence test from April 2013.

The pension scheme member will be subject to both the annual allowance and the lifetime allowance limits in respect of contributions to the overseas pension scheme that have benefited from migrant member relief.

The overseas pension scheme administrator must have undertaken to provide details of benefit crystallisation events to HMRC in respect of funds relating to UK tax relieved contributions via form APSS252 in order to meet the Schedule 33 qualifying conditions as set out above.

The member's UK tax-relieved fund held in a relevant non-UK scheme is that part of the fund held in the scheme in respect of the member that is represented by any UK tax-relieved contributions paid, and any UK tax-exempt provision made under the scheme in relation to the member after 5 April 2006. Investment build-up within the scheme on such contributions and provision is not taken into account for the purposes of the member payment charges because it will not have benefited from UK tax relief.

Clearly the position can be complicated for contributions to an overseas scheme. Existing members of overseas schemes with relevant UK earnings may prefer to make relievable contributions to a new UK scheme.

Income tax relief for the member

[9.10] An individual may claim income tax relief on contributions to a qualifying overseas pension scheme if he:

- is a 'relevant migrant member' (see definition below) of a 'qualifying overseas pension scheme';
- has relevant UK earnings chargeable to income tax during that tax year;
- is resident in the UK when the contributions are paid; and
- has notified the scheme manager of an intention to claim relief.

Relief is given on up to 100% of the individual's relevant UK earnings which are chargeable to UK income tax for the tax year (subject of course to the annual allowance) or the fixed amount of £3,600. In addition, individuals are not subject to tax on any contributions made by their employer to that scheme in respect of that individual.

Tax relief on employer contributions

[9.11] Relief may also be available to the member's employer in respect of contributions made to a qualifying overseas pension scheme in respect of migrant members.

Employers may claim tax relief on contributions (to the extent that they are paid, and would be allowable under ITTOIA 2005 Pt 2 / CTA 2009 Pt 3) made to a 'qualifying overseas pension scheme' in respect of an employee who is a 'relevant migrant member' of the scheme, as if they were contributions to a UK 'registered pension scheme'.

Definition of relevant migrant member

[9.12] A 'relevant migrant member' is an individual who meets the following conditions:

- was not tax resident in the UK when they joined the overseas pension scheme;
- became UK tax resident whilst a member of the scheme;
- was entitled to tax relief on contributions to the overseas pension scheme either immediately before coming to the UK, or was entitled to tax relief on contributions whilst resident in an overseas country within the 10-year period before they became UK tax resident;
- has relevant UK earnings chargeable to income tax in the tax year in which they make contributions (this does not include earnings which are not taxable in the UK under a double taxation agreement);
- is tax resident in the UK when the contributions are paid;
- has notified the scheme manager of their intention to claim migrant member relief and has been notified by the scheme manager that information concerning their benefit crystallisation events will be given by the scheme when appropriate to HMRC.

Transitional provisions: members previously subject to corresponding relief

[9.13] Transitional protection allows individuals who were subject to corresponding relief prior to 6 April 2006 to continue to claim tax relief in respect of contributions to an overseas pension scheme after 5 April 2006 if certain conditions are met, even if those contributions would not otherwise be consistent with qualification for migrant member relief.

The transitional protections allow relief under section 355 of the Income Tax (Earnings and Pensions) Act 2003 (ITEPA) on contributions made by an individual to an overseas pension scheme in any tax year after 2005–06 if:

- they received 'corresponding relief' on contributions made to that scheme in the 2005–06 tax year.
- there has been no unacceptable change to the rules of the overseas pension scheme.
- HMRC is satisfied that the conditions set out in section 355 ITEPA are met (i.e. the employee is not domiciled in the UK, the employee is employed by a foreign employer, the employee has made a payment out of earnings from that employment, and that the payment does not reduce the employee's liability to UK income tax, but was made in circumstances corresponding to those in which it would do so).
- the scheme manager provides the same information about the individual's benefit crystallisation events as would be required if the individual was receiving migrant member relief (FA 2004 Sch 36 para 51).

In addition tax relief will also be available for an employee in respect of any contributions made by their employer to their benefit in the scheme (meaning there will be no benefit in kind tax charge) as if the pension scheme were a qualifying overseas pension scheme, and as if the contributions were relevant migrant member contributions.

Transferring UK pension rights overseas – pre April 6 2006

[9.14] Until 6 April 2006 transfers from UK pension schemes overseas were relatively unusual. This was because of HMRC restrictions and some transfers to overseas pension schemes required HMRC consent.

Even where HMRC consent was not required substantial written information needed to be obtained by and retained by the UK pension scheme making the transfer.

Unless all of the following conditions were met (which needed to be supported with written evidence) the transfer was not permissible.

(1)   The individual requesting a transfer value from the UK scheme to the overseas scheme had to leave the UK on a permanent basis with no intention of returning to the UK to work or to retire.

(2)   The individual had at the point of requesting transfer to be in employment or self-employment overseas.

(3)   The individual's UK employment arrangements had to have been completely severed, and the individual had no longer to undertake any self-employment within the UK.

(4)   The individual and the receiving pension scheme had to be resident/ established in the same country.

(5)   The overseas scheme had to be authorised or recognised as a pension scheme by the relevant tax or supervisory authority of the country in which it was established.

Finance Act 2004 changed this by allowing transfers from UK registered pension schemes to overseas pension schemes so long as they are recognised by HMRC as 'Qualifying Recognised Overseas Pension Schemes' (QROPS). Under FA 2004 s 169 a transfer from a UK registered pension scheme to a QROPS is a recognised transfer.

The conditions that needed to be satisfied for an overseas pension scheme to be recognised as a QROPS changed with effect from 6 April 2012. Further changes have been introduced in 2013 as it is clear that HMRC do not wish to see transfers to a QROPS providing the QROPS member with a more tax advantageous position as a consequence.

The sections which immediately follow (9.15–9.16) set out the position as it remained until 5 April 2012 relating to Recognised Overseas Pension Schemes (ROPS). The subsequent sections set out the position that currently applies and how it has changed since 2006.

This approach is adopted for the sake of completion and does involve some repetition as some of the new provisions (in fact most of them) carry forward from the old position despite the fact that the ordering in some instances is a little different.

Overseas pension schemes (OPS) until 5 April 2012

[9.15] If a scheme is designed to provide benefits in respect of retirement, ill-health, death or similar circumstances then it is a pension scheme. For a scheme to be classed as an overseas pension scheme under FA 2004 s 150(7), it must be a pension scheme that is established outside the United Kingdom. Normally a pension scheme will be treated as established in the country where its registered office and main administration is based.

Under The Pension Schemes (Categories of Country and Requirements for Overseas Pension Schemes and Recognised Overseas Pension Schemes) Regulations, SI 2006/206 (until amended from 6 April 2012) one of the requirements that a pension scheme had to normally satisfy to be an overseas pension scheme was that it was 'recognised for tax purposes' under the tax legislation of the country or territory in which it is established.

It had to meet the two primary conditions and also meet **one of** conditions A and B as set out in SI 2006/206 (pre-amendment):

'Primary condition 1

The scheme must be open to persons resident in the country or territory in which it is established.

Primary condition 2

The scheme is established in a country or territory where there is a system of taxation of personal income under which tax relief is available in respect of pensions, and:

Tax relief is not available to the member on contributions made to the scheme by that individual or, if the individual is an employee, by their employer in respect of earnings to which benefits under the scheme relate, or

The scheme is liable to taxation on its income and gains, and is a complying superannuation plan as defined in section 995-1 (definitions) of the Income Tax Assessment Act 1997 of Australia, [this was an amendment introduced in 2007 to the original SI to avoid Australian schemes not satisfying the requirements of SI 2006/206 as a consequence to a change in Australian legislation] or

All or most of the benefits paid by the scheme to members who are not in serious ill-health are subject to taxation.

Condition A

The overseas pension scheme is approved or recognised by, or registered with, the relevant tax authorities as a pension scheme in the country or territory in which it is established.

Condition B

If there is no such system for the approval, recognition, or registration of the overseas pension scheme as a pension scheme in the country or territory in which it is established, then the scheme must be resident there, and its rules must provide that:

at least 70% of a member's UK tax-relieved scheme funds will be designated by the scheme manager for the purpose of providing the member with an income for life, and the pension benefits payable to the member under the scheme (and any lump sum associated with those benefits) must be payable no earlier than they would be if pension rule 1 in section 165 Finance Act 2004 applied.' (see Appendix 1 regarding the pension rules).

Recognised Overseas Pension Schemes (ROPS) until 5 April 2012

[9.16] Under FA 2004 s 150(8) a recognised overseas pension scheme is an overseas pension scheme that met the following requirements prescribed under SI 2006/206 (pre amendment).

It must:

'(1)   Be established in a Member State of the European Union, Norway, Liechtenstein or Iceland, or

(2)   Be established in a country or territory with which the UK has a Double Taxation Agreement that contains exchange of information and non-discrimination provisions or

(3)   Satisfy the requirement that, at the time of the recognised transfer, the rules of the scheme provide that:

    (a)   At least 70% of the funds transferred will be designated by the scheme manager for the purpose of providing the member with an income for life, the pension benefits (and any associated lump sum) payable to the member under the scheme, to the extent that they relate to the transfer, are payable no earlier than under UK law — so age 55. (the 70% rule) — unless retirement is due to ill-health.

    (b)   Membership of the scheme is open to persons resident in the country or territory in which it is established.'

Overseas Pension Schemes (OPS) from 6 April 2012

[9.17] It remains the case that if a pension scheme is designed to provide benefits in respect of retirement, ill-health, death or similar circumstances then it is a pension scheme. Note the absence of the word 'pension' in this definition.

For a scheme to be classed as an overseas pension scheme under FA 2004 s 150(7), it must be a pension scheme that is established outside the United Kingdom. Normally a pension scheme will be treated as established in the country where its registered office and main administration is.

In addition, to be regarded as an overseas pension scheme the scheme must meet the requirements set out in The Pension Schemes (Categories of Country and Requirements for Overseas Pension Schemes and Recognised Overseas Pension Schemes) Regulations, SI 2006/206, as amended.

Important amendments were effective from 6 April 2012 through SI 2012/884. Alongside this were published numerous other documents including new forms, and guidance notes specifically aimed at UK pension scheme administrators, those intending to transfer their UK pension fund to a QROPS, and QROPS providers themselves.

Under the amended regulations to be an 'overseas pension scheme' as defined the scheme must meet the 'regulation requirements' test' and also the 'tax recognition test'.

The 'Regulation Requirements' test

[9.18] The regulation requirements look at whether there is a body in the country outside of the United Kingdom which regulates pension schemes. The test is aimed at identifying a regulator that oversees legislative guidelines which impact on the operation of the overseas pension scheme to ensure that it is administered soundly in order to protect members' interests.

Such regulation might extend to submitting accounts, investment guidelines, rules on trustees, etc. In considering this test, HMRC would expect the scheme to be fully subject to the regulation in that country that covers these aspects.

Dependent on the country or territory in which a scheme is established, it may be necessary to identify whether the scheme is an occupational pension scheme or some other type of pension scheme.

An occupational pension scheme is a scheme established by an employer to provide benefits for its own employees although it may also admit other types of member. For example, it may also admit employees of other companies.

The regulation test is met if **one** of the following requirements is satisfied:

Requirement (a):

(1)   The scheme is an occupational pension scheme,
(2)   There is in the country or territory in which it is established a body which regulates occupational pension schemes, and
(3)   The scheme is regulated by that body.

Requirement (b):

(1)   The scheme is not an occupational pension scheme,
(2)   There is in the country or territory in which it is established a body which regulates pension schemes other than occupational pension schemes, and
(3)   It is regulated by that body.

Requirement (a) or (b) here relates to the relevant pension regulator body of the relevant country or territory that regulates the scheme. This is not the same as the tax authorities test at condition 3 of the tax recognition test described later.

Requirement (c):

Neither requirement (a) nor (b) is met by reason only that no such pension regulatory body exists in the country or territory and, either,

(1)   The scheme is established in a Member State of the European Union or in Norway, Iceland or Liechtenstein, or

(2) The scheme's rules provide that at least 70% of a member's UK tax-relieved scheme funds will be designated by the scheme manager for the purpose of providing the member with an income for life. The pension benefits payable to the member (and any associated lump sum) must be payable no earlier than age 55 other than in ill-health.

'UK tax-relieved scheme funds' generally means the amount transferred from a UK registered pension scheme to the QROPS.

The 'Tax Recognition' Requirement

[9.19] The pension scheme needs to be 'recognised for tax purposes' under the tax legislation of the country or territory in which it is established. This requirement is met if **all** of the following conditions are met.

Condition 1

The scheme must be open to persons resident in the country or territory in which it is established.

Condition 2

The scheme is established in a country or territory where there is a system of taxation of personal income under which tax relief is available in respect of pensions, and test (a), (b) or (c) is met.

(a) Tax relief is not available to the member on contributions made to the scheme by that individual or, if the individual is an employee, by their employer in respect of earnings to which benefits under the scheme relate, or

(b) The scheme is liable to taxation on its income and gains, and is a complying superannuation plan as defined in section 995-1 (definitions) of the Income Tax Assessment Act 1997 of Australia, or

(c) All or most of the benefits paid by the scheme to members who are not in serious ill-health are subject to taxation.

Condition 2 means that either the contributions into the scheme or most of the benefit payments out of it (excepting serious ill-health benefits) must be taxable.

Condition 3

The scheme is approved or recognised by, or registered with, the relevant tax authorities as a pension scheme in the country or territory in which it is established. This condition is based on the other country or territory needing to have some mechanism for identifying pension schemes that can qualify for the tax relief that is available in the tax system as referred to in Condition 2.

Recognised Overseas Pension Schemes (ROPS) from 6 April 2012

[9.20] Under FA 2004 s 150(8) a recognised overseas pension scheme is an overseas pension scheme that meets the requirements prescribed under The Pension Schemes (Categories of Country and Requirements for Overseas Pension Schemes and Recognised Overseas Pension Schemes) Regulations, SI 2006/206 as amended by SI 2012/884.

It must satisfy:

(1)   The benefits exemption test, and
(2)   **One** of conditions (a), (b), (c) or (d).

The benefits exemption test

[9.21] Where an exemption from tax in respect of benefits paid from the overseas pension scheme is available to members of the scheme who are not resident in the country or territory in which the scheme is established, the exemption must:

(a)   also be available to members of the scheme who are resident in the country or territory; and
(b)   apply regardless of whether the member was resident in the country or territory, when the member joined the scheme, or for any period of time when they were a member of the scheme.

If there is no exemption from tax available to members who are not residents in the country or territory where the scheme is established then the benefits exemption test will be met.

The conditions

The overseas pension scheme must:

(a)   be established in a Member State of the European Union, Norway, Liechtenstein or Iceland, or
(b)   be established in a country or territory, other than New Zealand, with which the UK has a Double Taxation Agreement that contains exchange of information and non-discrimination provisions, or
(c)   satisfy the requirement that, at the time of the recognised transfer, the rules of the scheme provide that:

    (i)   at least 70% of the funds transferred from a UK registered pension scheme will be designated by the receiving scheme manager for the purpose of providing the member with an income for life,

    (ii)   the pension benefits (and any associated lump sum) payable to the member under the scheme, to the extent that they relate to the transfer, are payable no earlier than age 55,

    (iii)   membership of the scheme is open to persons resident in the country or territory in which it is established, or

(d)   satisfy the requirement that, at the time of the recognised transfer the transfer is made to a pension scheme which is a KiwiSaver scheme as defined in section 4(1)(interpretation) of the KiwiSaver Act 2006 of New Zealand.

Qualifying Recognised Overseas Pension Schemes (QROPS)

[9.22] Under Finance Act 2004 s 169 a Qualifying Recognised Overseas Pension Scheme is a Recognised Overseas Pension Scheme that meets the requirements to be a recognised overseas pension scheme and the scheme manager gives HMRC certain undertakings. The scheme manager is the person or persons administering or responsible for the management of the pension scheme.

This includes an undertaking to comply with prescribed information requirements found in The Pension Schemes (Information Requirements – Qualifying Overseas Pension Schemes, Qualifying Recognised Overseas Pension Schemes and Corresponding Relief) Regulations, SI 2006/208, as amended.

The scheme manager must:

(1)   Have notified HMRC that the scheme is a recognised overseas pension scheme, and have provided evidence of that if required,

(2)   Complete and submit form APSS 251 and supply the scheme rules if the scheme is not in the EU,

(3)   Inform HMRC of the name of the country or territory in which the scheme is established. If this is not an EU Member State, Norway, Liechtenstein, Iceland or a country or territory with which the UK has a Double Taxation Agreement which contains exchange of information and non-discrimination provisions the scheme manager must also provide evidence that the scheme satisfies the '70% rule',

(4)   Provide any other evidence required by HMRC,

(5)   Undertake to notify HMRC if the scheme ceases to be a recognised overseas pension scheme, and

(6)   Undertake to provide HMRC with certain information on making payments in respect of certain scheme members.

With regard to the provision of information to HMRC, a new 10-year reporting rule has been introduced that applies for 10 years following the date on which the transfer originally took place.

This applies to payments from a QROPS made on or after 6 April 2012 irrespective of when the transfer originally took place. The earliest date at which this obligation can fall away therefore is 6 April 2016 being 10 years from the date at which the concept of a QROPS was initiated.

QROPS jurisdictions affected by the 2012 revisions

[9.23] Pension schemes in **Guernsey** which used to meet the conditions necessary to be a QROPS before 6 April 2012 (in particular in relation to non-Guernsey residents) are known as retirement annuity trusts (RAT). An

RAT is open to local residents and there is a system of tax relief for pensions applicable to local residents. Although RATs are approved by the Guernsey income tax office there is no ongoing process of supervision. Guernsey is not in the EU but has a double taxation treaty with the UK.

When the draft legislation was published in December 2011 it was clear that Guernsey schemes would not be able to meet the provision that became known as the benefits exemption test. This was because local residents would be taxed on income from a Guernsey scheme whereas non-Guernsey residents would be tax exempt.

Guernsey responded to this by introducing an amendment to their legislation introducing new section 157E. A pension scheme approved under this section would be one which provided tax-exempt income for non-residents and local residents. HMRC took the view that this was a deliberate attempt to manipulate and passed a specific statutory instrument in order to take section 157E schemes out of QROPS recognition.

The statutory instrument involved was The Pension Schemes (Categories of Country and Requirements for Overseas Pension Schemes and Recognised Overseas Pension Schemes) (Amendment) Regulations, SI 2012/1221. The amendment was 'so as to provide that schemes established in Guernsey which are exempt pension contracts or exempt pension trusts under section 157E of the Income Tax (Guernsey) Law, 1975 cannot be recognised overseas pension schemes if they are open to non-residents of Guernsey'.

Guernsey was in effect forced out of the QROPS market.

Superannuation funds in New Zealand are open to local residents, and there is a system of tax relief for local residents. Superannuation funds are authorised and regulated by the Financial Markets Authority. Although New Zealand is not in the EU there is a suitable double taxation treaty in place.

New Zealand superannuation schemes, although no longer able to pay 100% cash commutation since 6 April 2102 as they have become subject to the '70% rule', do satisfy the benefits exemption test and, in the context of what has been said by HMRC, do so without making new legislation.

New Zealand schemes retain flexible benefit structures that can be useful for those who are long-term expats.

The Isle of Man Government introduced 'section 50C' into its tax law in October 2010. The Income Tax (Pensions) (Temporary Taxation) Order 2010 amended the Income Tax Act 1970 by inserting a new Section 50C.

These section 50C schemes (following an HMRC review) were until 5 April 2012 capable of being recognised by HMRC as a QROPS. Schemes established under 'Section 50C' schemes do not meet the new benefits exemption test. Legislation was expected in the Isle of Man so that benefits from such schemes would become tax-exempt to Isle of Man residents. But following the action of HMRC with regard to Guernsey and its section 157E arrangements, plans to amend the legislation in the Isle of Man were abandoned.

Schemes established in Malta as QROPS are unaffected by the benefits exemption test as the tax treatment of benefits for residents and non-residents is the same. An extensive set of double taxation arrangements means that in many instances tax will arise only in the member's country of residence on benefits when taken and not in Malta.

So far as Malta is concerned, their presence in the EU makes it much more difficult for HMRC to impose new legislation next year that will materially affect this jurisdiction because of the freedom of capital movement requirements applicable within the EU.

Further changes in 2013

[9.24] The 2012 budget report stated:

> 'The Government will introduce changes in primary legislation to strengthen reporting requirements and powers of exclusion relating to QROPS. They support the changes in secondary legislation published for consultation on 6 December 2011.
>
> The Government also announced that where the country or territory in which a QROPS is established makes legislation or otherwise creates or uses a pension scheme to provide tax advantages that are not intended to be available under the QROPS rules, the Government will act so that the relevant types of pension scheme in those countries or territories will be excluded from being QROPS. (Finance Bill 2013)'

These much anticipated changes were introduced in Finance Act 2013 and subsequent regulations.

Finance Act 2013 s 53 makes changes to the provisions for QROPS amending Finance Act 2004 Part 4.

The changes enable HMRC to require overseas pension schemes to provide information which is necessary to ensure the intended operation of the legislation relating to QROPS. In addition there are some new rules about when a pension scheme may be excluded from being a QROPS.

Finance Act 2013 s 53(1) amends Finance Act 2004 s 150 to clarify the power to make regulations setting out conditions that apply to recognised overseas pension schemes.

Finance Act 2013 s 53(4) inserts a new section 169(4) to Finance Act 2004 and introduces new sections 169(4A) and (4B). These provisions contain powers enabling HMRC to make regulations setting out information requirements; enable HMRC to require additional information from a new or existing QROPS; allow HMRC to obtain information from a pension scheme that has been a QROPS; and provide a power to apply the penalties set out in Finance Act 2008 Sch 36 Part 7 to a failure by a former QROPS to comply with the new information requirements.

Finance Act 2013 s 53(5) substitutes a new section 169(5)(a) of Finance Act 2004 to set out the circumstances in which it can be appropriate for a pension scheme to be excluded from being a QROPS.

Finance Act 2013 s 54 makes changes to the provisions for QROPS and former QROPS in Finance Act 2008 Sch 36. The changes ensure that the information and inspection powers for these pension schemes are similar to those applicable to UK pension schemes.

Finance Act 2013 s 54(2) amends Finance Act 2008 Sch 36 para 34B to ensure that a notice requiring information or a document in connection with a QROPS or former QROPS may be made in the same way as it is for UK pension schemes.

Finance Act 2013 s 54(4) confirms that any change in the application of the information powers in Finance Act 2008 Sch 36 paras 34B and 34C to former QROPS will affect all former QROPS, including those that ceased to be a QROPS before the paragraph was enacted.

The information and inspection powers set out in Finance Act 2008 Sch 36 apply both to pension schemes established in the UK and those established outside the UK.

The changes brought about by the section ensure that the same rules in relation to inspection and requiring information apply to all pension schemes, whether the scheme is registered in the UK or is a QROPS or former QROPS.

In addition to these legislative changes, a new online service is being introduced. Scheme managers will be able to send in notifications and other reports to HMRC using QROPS Online. This will be an optional process; paper forms will still be acceptable.

Requirements imposed by regulations made under FA 2004 s 169(4)

Currently these regulations are The Pension Schemes (Information Requirements – Qualifying Overseas Pension Schemes, Qualifying Recognised Overseas Pension Schemes and Corresponding Relief) Regulations 2006 (SI 2006/208).

These regulations now include the requirements to:

(a)   Re-notify the scheme's ROPS status to HMRC (regulation 3(1A) – see the QROPS re-notification process below).

(b)   Tell HMRC about payments made by the QROPS in accordance with regulation 3(2).

(c)   Fully respond to an HMRC request for information in respect of a transfer made under regulation 3A.

(d)   Notify HMRC of any changes or corrections to the information previously given to HMRC in accordance with regulation 3C.

The 2013 changes in detail

[9.25] The conditions that public service pension schemes or schemes set up by international organisations have to meet to be a recognised overseas pension scheme (ROPS) have changed. The effective date of this change for schemes that were already QROPS on the 5 April 2012 is 6 April 2012 (SI 2013/2259).

For all other schemes the change applies from 14 October 2013, the date on which SI 2013/2259 came into force.

The change is that neither an overseas public service scheme nor a scheme set up by an international organisation will have to satisfy the benefits tax relief test to be a ROPS.

An overseas public service pension scheme is a scheme set up outside the UK either under the legislation of its country or territory, or approved by the government of its country or territory.

The scheme must also be for the purpose of providing benefits to an individual in respect of services rendered to the scheme's country, territory or any political subdivision or local authority of the country or territory.

SI 2006/206 defines an 'international organisation' as an organisation to which International Organisations Act 1968 s 1 applies. This category includes the United Nations and the European Union. It doesn't include multinational companies that operate or have subsidiaries in several countries.

The circumstances in which HMRC can remove QROPS status from a scheme (called exclusion) are being extended. This change took effect from the date of Royal Assent to FA 2013, thus 17 July 2013.

HMRC can remove QROPS status from a pension scheme even though it continues to meet the conditions to be a ROPS. A scheme can be excluded if certain things happen and as a result HMRC consider that it's not appropriate for the scheme to continue to be able to receive recognised transfers from UK registered pension schemes.

The QROPS scheme manager can appeal against the decision to exclude the scheme. The appeal must be made in writing within 30 days of the date of the letter notifying the decision to exclude the scheme. HMRC can reverse their decision to exclude the scheme at any time. HMRC will notify the scheme manager if they do this.

From 17 July 2013 the following events may trigger a HMRC decision to exclude the scheme:

(a) The scheme has no scheme manager.
(b) There has been a significant failure to comply with a requirement imposed by regulations made under FA 2004 s 169(4). The scheme manager will have given an undertaking to provide the requisite information before the scheme could be a QROPS – SI 2006/208 as amended.
(c) There has been a significant failure to comply with the information requirements (information and documents) imposed by FA 2008 Sch 36.
(d) Any information given when complying with the above requirements is materially incorrect.
(e) Any declaration given when complying with the above requirements is false in a material respect.

There is a wide definition to what can be considered 'significant' in the above situations. A failure to comply with a requirement will be significant if it's a failure to give details (information or evidence) that may be of significance, or there are reasonable grounds to believe the failure may prevent HMRC receiving tax.

For the duration of the exclusion transfers from a registered pension scheme to the excluded scheme will be an unauthorised payment and taxable accordingly. And any transfer to the excluded scheme from an overseas pension scheme of funds that have received UK tax relief, thus where the funds were derived from a recognised transfer from a registered pension scheme, may be taxed as an unauthorised payment under the member payment provisions of FA 2004 Sch 34. This depends on whether or not the member is UK resident or has been UK resident in any of the previous five tax years.

A system to renew QROPS status is being introduced. This renewal process starts from 1 April 2015. The QROPS scheme manager has to re-notify the ROPS status of the scheme to HMRC. Renewal will normally be every five years. If a scheme manager doesn't successfully re-notify the status of their scheme as a ROPS, the scheme will be excluded by HMRC from being a QROPS.

The re-notification date for each QROPS will be set by the date of the letter sent by HMRC notifying the scheme manager of the QROPS reference number (the HMRC QROPS reference letter). The required renewal or re-notification date will depend on whether the HMRC QROPS reference letter was sent before April 2010 or on or after 1 April 2010.

The information needed to re-notify the ROPS status is broadly the same as that needed when a scheme first notifies it wishes to be a QROPS to HMRC. A scheme manager re-notifies the ROPS status of their scheme by submitting a re-notification using form APSS 251 together with a copy of the scheme rules if this is required by the APSS 251. The re-notification APSS 251 can be submitted in paper form or electronically using QROPS Online.

The reporting requirements for QROPS have been amended. These changes took effect from 14 October 2013, the date on which SI 2013/2259 introducing these requirements came into force.

The changes to the reporting requirements first appear to be extensive. However in practical terms the changes are minimal. HMRC has taken the opportunity to amend SI 2006/208 so that it lists the information that is currently required by forms APSS 251, APSS 251A, APSS 251B and APSS 253.

Reporting requirements have been introduced for former QROPS with effect from 14 October 2013. These requirements only apply to QROPS that lose or give up their QROPS status on or after 14 October 2013. There will be penalties if a scheme manager of a former QROPS fails to comply with these reporting requirements.

Previously when a scheme ceased to be a QROPS there was no longer a requirement to automatically report to HMRC payments from the scheme, or changes to information.

The new regulations extend many of the QROPS reporting requirements to former QROPS. These requirements only apply to schemes that ceased to be QROPS on or after 14 October 2013.

From 14 October 2013 former QROPS must:

(a)   Report payments from the scheme. When a scheme manager has to report, reporting deadlines, what they need to report, and how they report are the same as for QROPS.

(b)   Respond to a request for information issued under SI 2006/208 reg 3A within the same timelines as a QROPS.

(c)   Report changes or corrections to information. Scheme managers of a former QROPS should make reports, and can use form APSS 251A, just as if the scheme was still a QROPS. The deadline for reporting changes is within 30 days of the date of the change or when the inaccuracy/incompleteness became apparent, or such other date as may be agreed between HMRC and the scheme manager.

Scheme managers of former QROPS do not need to report changes to information if there are no relevant transfer funds in the scheme or the transfer to which the relevant information correction/change relates was made more than 10 years ago and the member is not a UK resident nor resident at any point earlier in the tax year or in any of the previous five tax years.

If the scheme manager of a former QROPS fails to make the reports within the required timescale penalties may be due. Penalties will apply as if the information and required reporting time had been specified in an information notice issued under FA 2008 Sch 36.

HMRC can issue an information notice to a QROPS or former QROPS asking for information to check the tax position of a member. HMRC can require the provision of information or the production of documents by issuing an information notice without needing either the consent of the taxpayer or the Tribunal.

Information notices can be sent to the taxpayer or to a third party.

Previously HMRC could issue an information notice to a third party without the agreement of either the taxpayer or the Tribunal if the notice asked for information relating to:

(a)   a registered pension scheme,

(b)   an annuity purchased from registered pension scheme (or pre 2006 scheme) funds, or

(c)   an employer-financed retirement benefits scheme (EFRBS).

Third party information notices issued in respect of other pension schemes required the consent of either the Tribunal or the taxpayer.

Now HMRC can issue an information notice to a third party without the agreement of either the taxpayer or the Tribunal if the notice asks for information relating to either a QROPS, a former QROPS, or an annuity purchased with funds held by a QROPS or former QROPS.

Requests for information relating to a QROPS or former QROPS can be made for information up to 10 years old. Requests for older information can be made if the information notice has been issued by, or with the agreement of, an authorised HMRC officer.

The Member Payment and Reporting Provisions (to 5 April 2012)

[9.26] The undertakings made by a ROPS when it seeks QROPS status relate to providing HMRC with specified information about payments in respect of certain scheme members. These are associated with the requirement under FA 2004 s 169 where the scheme manager of a recognised overseas pension scheme must have undertaken to comply with the information requirements imposed under regulation 3 of The Pension Schemes (Information Requirements – Qualifying Overseas Schemes, Qualifying Overseas Schemes and Corresponding Relief) Regulations 2006 (SI 2006/208) if the scheme is to be a QROPS.

The key information requirement is that the scheme manager notifies HMRC when they make a payment in respect of a 'relevant member'.

A relevant member is one in respect of whom there is a relevant transfer fund within the meaning of The Pension Schemes (Application of UK Provisions to Relevant non-UK Schemes) Regulations 2006 [SI 2006/207]. A member will have a relevant transfer fund within the overseas scheme if they have transferred sums or assets into it that relate to UK tax-relieved contributions.

However, the scheme manager does not have to notify HMRC when a payment is made if the relevant member is a person to whom the member payment provisions do not apply under FA 2004 Schedule 34 para 2.

The member payment provisions do not apply unless the member:

(a) Is resident in the UK when the payment is made; or
(b) Although not resident in the UK when the payment is made, was resident in the UK earlier in the tax year in which the payment is made or in any of the five tax years immediately preceding that tax year.

A payment includes a transfer from the scheme to another pension scheme. Where a non-pension payment such as a lump sum or a transfer was made, the scheme manager had to provide the information to HMRC by 31 January following the end of the tax year in which **each** payment was made.

Where a pension payment was made, the scheme manager had to provide the information by 31 January following the end of the tax year in which the first payment is made, but it was only necessary to do this in respect of the first such payment to any individual.

Important changes to the provisions set out above through changes to the relevant statutory instruments were introduced with effect from 6 April 2012 and are set out below.

The Member Payment and Reporting Provisions (from 6 April 2012)

[9.27] Important changes to strengthen the QROPS reporting regime were introduced from 6 April 2012 as follows:

If a QROPS ceases to be a QROPS, the scheme must provide HMRC with both:

(a)   the value at the cessation date of the 'relevant transferred sums and assets' relating to each 'relevant transfer fund' held by the scheme;

(b)   the name, residential address, date of birth and, if any, the National Insurance number of each member in respect of whom there is a 'relevant transfer fund' at the cessation date.

There is no time limit in respect of funds or members this cessation reporting requirement applies to.

There is no 10-year following the date of transfer rule (see below) and reporting is not limited to UK residents or recent non-residents.

This information must be provided within 30 days of cessation. (SI 2006/208 reg 3B as amended by SI 2012/884 para 9.)

The scheme manager must notify HMRC when they make a payment or are treated by tax law as making a payment, other than a non-reportable payment (see below), in respect of a 'relevant member'. A 'relevant member' is one in respect of whom there is a 'relevant transfer fund'.

The provisions under which a scheme manager is treated as making a payment are (see FA 2004 ss 172–174A):

•   assignment, surrender, and death,
•   the allocation of unallocated employer contributions,
•   certain increases in benefits,
•   on benefits that are not otherwise classed as payments,
•   value shifting.

A payment will also include any transfer out of the QROPS to another pension scheme. Where a non-pension payment (such as a lump sum or transfer) is made, notification is needed in respect of each payment.

Where the payment is part of a stream of pension payments, it is only necessary to send HMRC a notification in respect of the first such payment any individual receives.

Non-reportable payments

The scheme manager does not have to notify HMRC if:

•   the payment is made 10 or more years after the day of the transfer that created the 'relevant transfer fund', and
•   the 'relevant member' is a person to whom the 'member payment provisions' do not apply (FA 2004 Sch 34, para 2).

The member payment provisions apply if the member is resident in the UK when the payment is made (or treated as made), or although not resident at that time, has been resident in the UK earlier in the tax year the payment is made, or in any of the immediately preceding five tax years.

Details to report

Where reporting of payments is required, the scheme manager must provide HMRC with the following information:

- the name and principal residential address of the relevant member (as defined above),
- the relevant member's national insurance number, if any, and
- the date, amount and nature of the payment.

The above details must be provided within 90 days beginning on the day:

- on which the payment is made or treated as made; or
- by such other time as may be agreed between HMRC and the scheme manager.

Forms

HMRC forms APSS 253 and APSS 253 (Insert) are used for the purposes of reporting these payments. These forms and their processes have changed over time and there is a period of transition where:

- for each payment made or treated as made on or after 6 April 2012, the procedure as set out above applies. Reports should be made using the post-5 April 2012 versions of forms APSS 253 and APSS 253 (Insert). The reports should be made within the reporting time limits set out above;
- for payments made or treated as made on or before 5 April 2012, a report should be made using old forms APSS 253 and APSS 253 (insert). Reports for the tax year 2011–12 had to be submitted by 31 January 2013.

Other information that a QROPS may need to provide to HMRC

[9.28] The previous sections deal with information that a QROPS must automatically supply to HMRC when specific events happen. There are other circumstances where the trigger for information is a request from HMRC. (SI 2006/208, regs 3(5A) and 3A, as amended by SI 2012/884, para 9.)

There are two circumstances where HMRC may require information by sending a written notice, each with different reporting time limits. The first applies only where the scheme manager is a company, and HMRC may require the names and addresses of the directors of the company. This information must be provided by the time specified in the HMRC notice requiring it.

The second applies if there has been a transfer to a QROPS (whether from a registered pension scheme or from another QROPS). This request for information applies to the extent that any sums or assets transferred to the QROPS were at any earlier time held for the purposes of, or represented accrued rights under, a registered pension scheme.

The QROPS that is served the notice can be required to supply the following information within 90 days beginning on the day the notice is given by HMRC, or by such other time as may be agreed between HMRC and the QROPS:

(a) the date of the transfer to the QROPS,

(b) the name and address of any bank, and details of any bank account which the QROPS has used in relation to the transfer,

(c) details of the sums and assets transferred (and how they have been applied by the QROPS that received them if the notice is to that receiving scheme),

(d) where the transfer is from an RPS, the name and address of that scheme,

(e) the name, principal residential address, date of birth and the national insurance number, if any, of the member who is connected with the sums and assets,

(f) where the member is a person to whom the member payment provisions do not apply (under paragraph 2 of Schedule 34 – see 'Non-reportable payments' above), the date that the member ceased to be resident in the United Kingdom,

(g) the name and address of the body that regulates the QROPS and the reference number, if any, issued to the QROPS by that regulator,

(h) the name and address of the tax authority which administers the taxation of the QROPS and the reference number, if any, issued to the QROPS by that tax authority,

(i) evidence to show that the QROPS met at the time of the transfer and continues to meet, the ROPS conditions as specified in SI 2006/206 regs 2 and 3), and

(j) any other evidence relating to the transfer that HMRC requires.

Changes to information supplied

[9.29] If at any time after any information has been supplied to HMRC, it becomes apparent to the QROPS scheme manager that:

• there is a material change affecting the information that was provided to HMRC, or

• that the information provided to HMRC is incomplete or contains a material inaccuracy,

the QROPS must provide HMRC with details of the change, the complete information or correction of the inaccuracy, as appropriate and without undue delay.

The Pensions Schemes (Application of UK Provisions to Relevant Non-UK Schemes) (Amendment) Regulations 2012 (SI 2012/1795)

[9.30] These Regulations make amendments to the Pension Schemes (Application of UK Provisions to Relevant Non-UK Schemes) Regulations, SI 2006/207 ('the RNUKS Regulations') following amendments to FA 2004 (c. 12) made by FA 2011 (c. 11). The RNUKS Regulations modify FA 2004 Pt 4 in their application to relevant non-UK pension schemes to ensure that members of relevant non-UK schemes may receive the same payments with broadly the same tax treatment as members of registered pension schemes with effect from 6 April 2011.

From 6 April 2011, FA 2011 Sch 16 amended FA 2004 Pt 4 to remove certain tax rules that required members of registered pension schemes to secure an income, usually by buying an annuity, by age 75. The amendments replaced the concept of an 'unsecured pension' and an 'alternatively secured pension' with the concept of a 'drawdown pension'.

Further reforms permit an individual, with a minimum secure pension income of at least £20,000 a year, to draw unlimited amounts from their drawdown pension fund ('flexible drawdown') if certain conditions are met.

The Government announced in the Taxes Information and Impact Note published on 9 December 2010 entitled '*Removing the effective requirement to annuitise by age 75*' that:

> 'the changes made for members of registered pension schemes would also apply to members of non-UK pension schemes who have received either tax relief on contributions or funds transferred from registered pension schemes'.

Regulation 1 introduces the amendments which have retrospective effect to 6 April 2011.

Regulations 3 and 4 make amendments to regulations 6 and 7 of the RNUKS Regulations following the removal of certain pension and pension death benefit pension rules which imposed restrictions on the types of pensions that could be paid to members aged 75 and over.

Regulation 5 amends regulation 14(3) of the RNUKS Regulations so as to extend the modifications which replace the term 'scheme administrator' with a reference to a 'scheme manager' in accordance with provisions introduced by FA 2011.

Regulation 6 amends regulation 15 of the RNUKS Regulations. The amendments ensure that the scheme may pay out the same amount of lump sum once the member has reached the age of 75 as would have been permissible prior to the member reaching that age.

This brings the position of relevant non-UK schemes and relieved non-UK pension schemes into line with registered pension schemes following the changes made by FA 2011.

Payments from a QROPS and their taxation

[9.31] The position in respect of a payment from a QROPS to a member or in respect of a member is in general terms fairly straightforward.

As stated above, the member payment provisions are such that the reporting of payments (excepting as they arise in respect of taxable property where the QROPS is investment regulated – see below) is required during the member's first five full tax years of non-UK residence and in the ten years following the date of transfer – the latter provision introduced with effect from 6 April 2012.

In respect of payments made during the first five full tax years of non-UK residence where those payments are in excess of what would be permitted under UK law if such payments had been made from a registered pension scheme then an unauthorised member payment arises and so an unauthorised member payment charge applies at the rate of up to 40%. A 15% surcharge may also apply.

Any such payment outside UK rules beyond five complete tax years of non-UK residence remains an unauthorised payment but is not taxable in the UK.

It should always be borne in mind that any payments may also be subject to taxation in the member's country of residence. The position here depends on the country where the QROPS is established and the QROPS member's country of residence.

Examples

Malta – There are over 60 double taxation agreements (DTAs) between Malta and other countries. These generally provide that pension income from Malta is only payable in the member's country of residence. Maltese QROPS for the long-term expat can be paid from age 50 (as compared to age 55 in the UK) and can be drawn from the fund in a way that can be very tax efficient for some as it can be treated as if it were an annuity. This, for Spanish residents as an example, results in tax at no more than 3% depending on the member's age because of the way in which pension annuities are taxed in Spain. Schemes responded to the 27 March 2014 UK changes by allowing income withdrawals at up to 150% of GAD rates.

Gibraltar – Here there are no DTAs so there is reliance on unilateral relief. Tax is deducted at source on QROPS pension income at 2.5% and offset against the member's tax liability in his country of residence. As, for example, unilateral relief applies between Gibraltar and Portugal, any balance of income tax due in Portugal is payable there. Pension income from a Gibraltar QROPS can be drawn from the fund and the new UK style 150% of GAD rates limit has generally been adopted.

New Zealand – Here pension income is paid gross, that is without any deduction of tax in New Zealand. So DTA relief is irrelevant as is unilateral relief. Tax arises in the member's country of residence, and at least one scheme has followed the UK by increasing the permitted level of income withdrawal to 150% of the GAD rate.

UK resident or non-UK resident?

[9.32] One of the key issues for those who consider transferring to a QROPS and live overseas is whether or not they are actually non-UK resident, and if so when they became non-UK resident. There are many different factors which will determine whether an individual is or is not resident in the UK.

The circumstances in which individuals were treated as UK resident for tax purposes until 5 April 2013 included:

- They spent 183 days or more in the UK in any tax year;
- They went to the UK with the intention of living there permanently or to work there for an extended period, or with no particular end date;
- They went to the UK temporarily and spent 91 days or more per year in the UK on average over a four-year period;
- They went to the UK for a purpose, such as employment, that meant they remained in the UK for at least two years (whether or not, in a particular year, they spent 183 days or more in the UK); or
- They usually lived in the UK and went abroad for short periods, for example on business trips or holidays.

Whether an individual was regarded resident in the UK was not solely dependent on the amount of time that they spent there. The nature and quality of an individual's connections with the UK were important factors in determining whether or not they were resident in the UK.

For example, family, accommodation, and economic interests could be relevant. These rules and their impact on an individual's liability to UK tax were explained in leaflet HMRC 6 which provided a comprehensive statement on the HMRC interpretation of the application of the rules in practice. HMRC 6 replaced the previous guidance (IR20), the latter having been in place for many years and once reviewed in the context of preparing a replacement was found to contain a large number of errors and omissions.

The following were examples of instances that could be indicative of an individual who lives overseas actually being a UK resident. These and any other relevant factors had all to be considered together to give a complete picture. But the greater the number of these elements that were satisfied, the more likely it was that the individual should have been regarded as being UK resident:

- Family ties, including having a spouse, civil partner, children or other family members in the UK.
- Social ties including membership of clubs and societies and events that were regularly attended.
- Business ties including owning or being a director of a business based in the UK, or having employment, including self-employment, in the UK.
- Regular employment duties in the UK.

There was particular difficulty about the extent to which an individual could make and retain connections with the UK and still be considered non-resident. This affected those who visited the UK, had connections, such as employment, business, accommodation and social ties. There were no clear rules to indicate the point at which these connections were sufficiently strong to constitute being in the UK permanently or otherwise to make an individual UK tax resident.

Whilst for the overwhelming majority it was clear whether or not they were resident in the UK, for others this was not the case. This was because some of the key concepts within the rules were not defined. For example, no certainty existed over the concept of going to the UK temporarily. Whilst some would clearly have been in the UK on a temporary basis – for example a foreign tourist on a short holiday in the UK – for many others the answer could be less clearcut.

Decisions in court cases indicated the connections that may be considered relevant to residence status but this did not provide certainty on whether these connections applied in all cases, what weighting should have been given to different factors or precisely how they influenced residence status.

The Government announced in the 2011 Budget the intention to introduce a statutory definition of tax residence for individuals. The objective was to replace the uncertain and complex residence rules with a statutory residence test (SRT) that is simple for the taxpayer to use.

The SRT was introduced with effect from 6 April 2013 (Schedule 45 to Finance Act 2013).

The statutory residence test from 6 April 2013

[9.33] The new test for residence seeks to provide fairness and clarity in determining one's tax residence in the UK. The test has been designed to make it harder to become non-resident when leaving the UK, than it is to become resident when an individual comes to the UK. As such, distinction is made between arrivers to the UK and leavers.

The '**automatic overseas tests**', set out factors which are conclusive in themselves to make an individual non-resident.

The '**automatic residence tests**', set out factors which in themselves are conclusive to make an individual resident in the UK.

The '**sufficient ties tests**', set out factors and rules which will need to be considered where it is not possible to determine one's residence status under the automatic tests.

The 'automatic overseas tests' and the 'automatic residence tests' are summarised in the table below:

	'Automatic Overseas Test' – Conclusive Non Residence	'Automatic Residence Test' – Conclusive Residence
Arrivers to the UK – persons not resident in UK in any of the previous 3 tax years	In UK for less than 46 days	Present in UK for 183 days or more

| Leavers from UK – persons resident in UK in any of the previous 3 tax years | In UK for less than 16 days | Only one home and it is in the UK (or 2 or more homes and all are in the UK) and this remains the case for a total of 91 days in the year whether continuous or not |
| Full time work | Full time work abroad but in UK for less than 91 days, and working in UK for up to 20 days only | Full time work in the UK |

Where it is not possible to determine residence on the basis of the factors set out above, then the 'sufficient ties tests' set out five further factors which need to be considered in order to determine residence.

These take into account the number of days spent in the UK as well as five connecting factors. Broadly, the connecting factors are as follows:

Family – which includes spouses and civil partners and minor children resident in the UK (but with some relaxation for children in the UK because of their attendance at a UK educational establishment, and time spent in the UK outside term time is less than 21 days).

Accommodation – the individual has accommodation which is available for a continuous period of at least 91 days (ignoring gaps of less than 16 days) and he/she spends at least one night there.

Substantive work in the UK – 40 workdays or more.

UK presence in the previous two tax years – more than 90 days in the UK in either of the previous two tax years.

More time in the UK than any other country – this is only relevant for 'leavers'.

The following table summarises the 'sufficient ties tests':

Sufficient Ties Test

Days in the UK	Arrivers (Persons not resident in the UK in previous 3 tax years)	Leavers Persons resident in at least 1 of previous 3 tax years
Less than 16 days	Always non-resident	Always non-resident
16 – 45 days	Always non-resident	Resident only if at least 4 factors apply
46 – 90 days	Resident only if at least 4 factors apply	Resident only if at least 3 factors apply
91 – 120 days	Resident only if at least 3 factors apply	Resident only if at least 2 factors apply
121 – 182 days	Resident only if at least 2 factors apply	Resident only if at least 1 factor applies
183 days or more	Always resident	Always resident

Split year treatment

[9.34] Presently, where an individual becomes resident or non-resident during a tax year, split year treatment is available by way of extra statutory concessions. The Government proposes to put this on a statutory footing, broadly in line with the existing extra statutory concessions.

Transfers to USA pension schemes and in respect of USA residents generally

[9.35] As stated above under UK rules a registered pension scheme can transfer benefits to any Qualifying Recognised Overseas Pension Scheme (QROPS). Technically a USA pension scheme may be registered with HMRC as a QROPS. However, a US pension scheme will not normally be able to accept a transfer from a UK pension scheme in order to comply with USA Internal Revenue Service (IRS) rules.

There are conflicting views relating to the issues associated with the transfer of UK pension rights associated with US residents. However it is almost certain that any such transfer will be treated as a distribution under US law and be subject to US tax on transfer.

Transferring benefits in payment

[9.36] Benefits in payment, including those in income drawdown, may be transferred from a UK registered pension scheme to a QROPS subject to similar restrictions that would apply in respect of transfers of arrangements in drawdown taking place between UK pension schemes.

The sums and assets transferred are to be treated as remaining under the same arrangement that existed for UK tax purposes. The consequence is that where there is a transfer of benefits that are subject to income drawdown the receiving scheme should continue to observe the rules relating to maximum withdrawal limits and reference periods etc, that apply to funds in drawdown in UK registered pension schemes. (SI 2006/499 reg 2(1) and 12(2).)

Scheme reporting requirements and benefit crystallisation

[9.37] A transfer to a QROPS constitutes a reportable event and therefore the UK scheme administrator will be required to provide information regarding the transfer to HMRC as set out earlier in this chapter.

A transfer to a QROPS from a UK registered pension scheme is a benefit crystallisation event (BCE8) and so subject to a test against the lifetime allowance.

If the transfer results in the member's lifetime allowance being exceeded, the rate of tax chargeable is 25%. The 55% rate cannot apply, even though the payment in effect is a 'lump sum', because it is not being paid 'to the individual', so does not fall within the 55% rate charging provision.

Investment regulated QROPS

[9.38] HMRC published revised pages within the Registered Pension schemes manual in mid November 2009. This was as a consequence of a Statutory Instrument (SI 2009/2047) that came into effect in August 2009. SI 2009/2047 amends SI 2006/207. These changes were important and had retrospective effect back to April 2006. They need to be considered alongside another key 2006 Statutory Instrument (SI 2006/1960). SI 2009/2047 amends SI 2006/1960.

The purpose of this legislation was to introduce taxable property provisions (relating to investment in residential property, fine wines and the like) – and so to extend UK rules into QROPS where there is an investment in taxable property.

Until this statutory instrument was published a common view amongst some advisers and QROPS providers alike was that because after five complete tax years of non-UK residence when, as set out above, the member payment provisions fall away, it was possible to invest the fund held within a QROPS without reference to UK law but in accordance with the rules of the scheme and the relevant laws associated with the jurisdiction where the QROPS was based. So there was a view that this allowed for investment in residential property and the like if local law permitted.

However FA 2004 Sch 34 provided for regulations to be introduced that would apply the 'taxable property provisions' where funds have been transferred to a relevant non-UK scheme that is an investment-regulated pension scheme.

An investment-regulated pension scheme is one where the member is able to direct or influence the investments made. Transfers to an investment-regulated pension scheme of UK tax relieved funds since 6 April 2006 comprise a taxable asset transfer fund (TATF).

Any payments from the TATF are reportable to HMRC irrespective of when those payments are made. But no tax charge arises unless there has been an investment in taxable property.

So in respect of QROPS members who have a fund transferred in from a UK pension scheme where a TATF arises the statutory position provides for such a member to be liable to the taxable property unauthorised payment charges in the same or similar circumstances as would apply to a UK investment-regulated pension scheme as set out in CHAPTER 5.

The taxable property unauthorised payment charge is not a member payment charge under FA 2004 Sch 34. It therefore applies regardless of whether or not a transfer member has been non-resident for more than five complete tax years. Nor is there any time limit on the requirement that the manager of a QROPS reports to HMRC any payments that are referable to a transfer member's taxable asset transfer fund.

So if it is planned to use the QROPS fund to acquire taxable property it may be appropriate to transfer it to an overseas scheme that is not a QROPS (typically a QNUPS – see below), so long as the member has been non UK resident for five or more UK tax years.

The 2014 Budget announcements and QROPS

[9.39] The text below is drawn from an official statement from HMRC dated 6 December 2011.

'A QROPS is a pension scheme established outside the UK that is broadly similar to a UK RPS [registered pension scheme].

The criteria for what makes a foreign pension scheme similar to a UK RPS for the purposes of a transfer are set out in UK legislation. Schemes that notify HMRC that they meet the conditions and undertake to provide information to HMRC are "QROPS".

The purpose of the conditions is to ensure that the scheme is treated as a pension scheme for regulatory and tax purposes in the country in which it is established. It should be treated in the way that is usual for pension schemes in that country to be treated, particularly for members of the scheme who are resident there.

The Government provides generous tax relief on pension savings in UK RPSs. When an individual transfers their UK pension savings that have benefitted from those generous tax reliefs to another RPS or to a QROPS the transfer can be made free of UK tax (where it does not exceed the lifetime allowance).

The Government allows transfers to QROPS to be made free of UK tax because they enable people permanently leaving the UK to simplify their affairs by taking their pension savings with them to their new country of residence. This is intended to enable them to continue to save to provide an income when they retire.

An individual who leaves the UK and transfers their pension savings should be in broadly the same position as someone who remains in the UK with their pension savings.

The Government found that QROPS were being marketed extensively as a way of paying amounts or enabling the payment of amounts that are not allowed under UK rules (in particular 100% lump sums) once the UK tax rules no longer apply.

This is contrary to the policy rationale for allowing transfers of UK tax-relieved pension savings to be made free of UK tax to QROPS.'

It is hard to escape the irony that with effect from April 2015 UK-based defined contribution schemes will allow the 100% lump sums that HMRC took such offence to in 2011.

It will be fascinating to see therefore how the Government, having abandoned this principle for UK defined contribution schemes, amends the conditions that enable a recognised overseas pension scheme to achieve QROPS status.

UK law currently works as set out in The Pension Schemes (Categories of Country and Requirements for Overseas Pension Schemes and Recognised Overseas Pension Schemes) Regulations 2006 (SI 2006/206 as amended by SI 2012/884). Note the current application (where relevant) of the '70% rule' which seems inconsistent with the soon-to-be-implemented UK-based changes.

It was announced in the Government's response to the March 2014 pensions consultation that the provisions relating to QROPS would be consulted on late in 2014 with changes then introduced to ensure consistency with the UK regime starting from 6 April 2015 as described in CHAPTER 4.

Qualifying Non UK Pension Schemes (QNUPS)

[9.40] The Inheritance Tax (Qualifying Non-UK Pension Schemes) Regulations, SI 2010/051 introduced a new acronym into the pensions vocabulary, 'QNUPS'.

The draft regulations were first published in July 2008 and were eventually laid before Parliament in January 2010. The original purpose was to rectify an error that was within Finance Act 2004 associated with QROPS. Due to an oversight the inheritance tax exemptions that apply to UK registered pension schemes were not extended to QROPS. The result was an unsatisfactory position where strictly according to the law the exit charge and periodic charges associated with discretionary trusts would apply to a QROPS. When this was brought to HMRC's attention it was recognised that this was an error and the regulations referred to here were implemented in order to correct this.

The outcome is that a QNUPS will benefit from a UK Inheritance Tax exemption in respect of (a) UK tax-relieved funds that have been transferred to a QNUPS (see below), (b) contributions to a QNUPS by a UK-domiciled individual, and (c) UK-situated assets held by a QNUPS.

From the definition of a QNUPS, as set out in the Regulations, a QROPS will generally also be a QNUPS. It is also the case that a ROPS (a 'Recognised Overseas Pension Scheme') will also be a QNUPS because the set of conditions that a QNUPS needs to satisfy are the same conditions that define a ROPS.

In order to qualify as a QNUPS, a pension scheme must meet the following criteria:

- It must be established outside the UK; and
  - (a) be open to residents of the territory in which it is established; and
  - (b) be established in a territory where there is a system of taxation of personal income under which tax relief is available in respect of pensions; and either
    - (i)   tax relief is not available in respect of contributions and pension income is exempt from tax; or
    - (ii)   tax relief is available in respect of contributions and the pension income is taxable; or
    - (iii) the pension fund is taxable and the scheme is a qualifying Australian superannuation scheme.

The scheme must be approved, or recognised, or registered with, the relevant tax authorities as a pension scheme in the territory where it is established, or if no such system for approval exists:

(a)   the scheme must be resident there; and

(b)   the scheme rules must provide that at least 70% of a member's fund is used to provide an income for life; and

(c)   the pension does not become payable before age 55 unless retirement is due to ill-health.

There must be a body in the territory that regulates pension schemes and the scheme in question must be regulated by that body, but if no such body exists, then the scheme must be:

(a)   established in another European Economic Area (EEA) State; or

(b)   one where the scheme rules must provide that at least 70% of a member's fund is used to provide an income for life; and

(c)   one where a pension does not become payable before age 55 unless retirement is due to ill-health.

The key difference between a QROPS and a QNUPS is that a QNUPS does not have to be registered as such with HMRC and so it does not need to comply with the information reporting rules applicable to a QROPS. Thus any QROPS will be exempt from UK Inheritance Tax and on a retrospective basis to 6 April 2006 in accordance with the regulations.

QROPS / QNUPS and IHT planning

[9.41] The position as set out above means that:

(1)   A non-UK resident may transfer tax-relieved UK pension rights to a QROPS and on death, whether before or after age 75, no Inheritance Tax liability arises and no unauthorised payment charge applies, so long as the member has resided outside of the UK for more than five complete tax years.

(2)   A non-UK resident may contribute to a QROPS (which by definition is a QNUPS) or to a QNUPS (which is not a QROPS) and will not receive tax relief on the contributions, but on death no Inheritance Tax liability arises and there is no unauthorised payment charge.

(3)   After five complete and consecutive tax years of non-UK residence UK tax-relieved pension funds in a QROPS may be transferred to a ROPS (which is also a QNUPS) and freedom from Inheritance Tax will continue. In addition, there is investment freedom (including the ability for example to invest in residential property) as permitted by the rules of the QNUPS/ROPS and depending upon the legislation associated with such investments in the jurisdiction where the QNUPS/ROPS is held.

(4)   UK tax-relieved pension funds, once in a QNUPS/ROPS, may be supplemented by contributions without limit, other than those set by the jurisdiction where the QNUPS/ROPS resides, and assets held in the QNUPS/ROPS will not be subject to Inheritance Tax following the death of the ROPS member.

Transferring to a UK registered pension scheme from an overseas pension scheme

[9.42] Some individuals coming to work in the UK, or returning from secondment overseas, may wish to transfer benefits to the UK from an overseas pension scheme of which they have been a member. If the rules of the UK pension scheme allow it may be possible to transfer in rights from an overseas pension scheme.

The treatment of the transfer in the receiving scheme will depend on whether the overseas scheme is a Recognised Overseas Pension Scheme (ROPS) – see previous sections in this chapter for the relevant definitions.

Whether or not the overseas scheme is a ROPS, the UK scheme can accept the transfer and is under no obligation to check the status of the overseas scheme. However if the scheme is a ROPS the member may be entitled to claim an enhanced lifetime allowance in respect of their overseas membership of that scheme.

This can be done by completing form APSS202 no later than five years after the 31 January following the end of the tax year in which the transfer took place. However any enhancement will not include any part of the overseas transfer that was tax-relieved in the UK under the migrant member relief provisions as described earlier in this chapter.

HMRC will send the member a certificate confirming the enhanced lifetime allowance. This will be needed in the event of subsequent benefit crystallisation and should be given to the scheme Administrator to reduce or eliminate any possible lifetime allowance charges.

USA to UK transfers

[9.43] In order to comply with USA Internal Revenue Service (IRS) rules, a USA pension scheme will not normally be able to transfer funds to a UK registered pension scheme.

This is because the UK pension scheme would not be a qualified retirement plan under USA IRS rules. As an alternative to a transfer individuals might be able to withdraw funds directly from their USA 401K or IRA. However, this could give rise to a tax liability in their hands.

Taxation of UK Pensions received by non UK residents

[9.44] Overseas resident individuals receiving pension payments from a UK registered pension scheme are still generally subject to UK income tax under the usual PAYE rules. However they may be exempted from paying UK income tax by virtue of a double taxation agreement (DTA).

There is an internationally accepted principle that income should not be taxed both in the country that is the source of the income (the UK in this case) and in the country where the member resides. This is achieved either through the provisions of a DTA or where there is no such treaty through unilateral relief.

A DTA is an agreement between the UK and any territory outside the UK as set out in TIOPA 2010 s 2 (formerly ICTA 1988 s 788). Where pension income under the DTA is taxed in the member's country of residence then there is a mechanism through which double taxation relief is claimed. This is set out in the HMRC DTA manual. To apply for the UK pension to be paid gross, the member will need to complete a double taxation treaty relief form available from HMRC. The form confirms the claimant's tax reference number in their country of residence. These forms are in many instances country specific.

This has to be approved and countersigned by the tax authorities in the country of residence before being forwarded to the HMRC centre for non-residents. If authorisation is received the UK scheme administrator can pay the pension gross.

The UK has over 130 DTAs. Where there is a DTA between the UK and country X then, in most cases, pension income is taxed in country X and is not taxed in the UK. But not all DTAs work this way. Some DTAs are worded such that pension income may be taxed in the UK or may be taxed in country X. A few DTAs specifically say that pension income is taxed in the UK and not in country X.

Many non-UK residents with UK source income (pension or otherwise) simply pay tax in the UK. The 2014 Budget however proposes that the relatively generous UK personal allowances should not continue to apply to non-UK residents.

The fact that UK tax has been paid does not mean that the income does not have to be declared in the person's country of residence. The effect of not using the relief available under any DTA is such that income could be taxed twice.

Where there is no DTA then in most instances unilateral relief applies. This means that UK tax deducted at source can generally be offset against the person's tax liability in their country of residence. So if a person as a resident of country Y suffers tax of 20% in the UK, and in country Y tax at 25% would apply, then the balance of tax at 5% would be paid to the tax authorities of country Y.

Examples

In considering these examples it should be recalled that from April 2015 individuals as members of UK-based DC pension schemes will be able to withdraw the entire fund as a one-off payment or as a sequence of payments (see Chapter 4), 25% of the fund will be outside of the scope of UK tax and the balance will be taxed, it is proposed, as income at the member's marginal rate.

There is no DTA between the UK and the United Arab Emirates. So as there is no income tax in the UAE, UK source income (including pension income) is taxed in the UK with no ability to offset.

However for some non-UK residents the application of any DTA between the UK and the DC scheme member's country of residence can have wildly different effects.

There are thought to be about 55,000 ex-UK residents living in Thailand, many of whom will have deferred pension rights in UK pension schemes. There is a double taxation treaty between the UK and Thailand but unusually it has no article within it relating to pensions. So UK source pension income is taxable in the UK.

The double taxation treaty between the UK and the Philippines contains the OECD model standard wording, namely 'pensions and other similar remuneration paid in consideration of past employment to a resident of a Contracting State shall be taxable only in that State'.

Thus UK source pension income is taxed in the Philippines for a local resident. But pension income is exempt from tax in the Philippines as an 'exclusion from gross income'. Thus a UK national residing in the Philippines aged 55 will it seems be able to cash in the entirety of his UK defined contribution pension fund after April 2015 and pay no tax either in the UK or in his chosen country of residence.

Note: In the above example relating to Thailand, as the law currently stands a UK pension scheme member could transfer to a QROPS in New Zealand. The double taxation treaty between New Zealand and Thailand provides that pension income is taxed in Thailand. However pension income is subject to tax exemption in Thailand. Therefore UK tax relieved funds once transferred to a QROPS in New Zealand can be used to provide completely tax-free payments for a resident of Thailand.

Taxation of flexible drawdown and temporary non UK residents and of flexi-drawdown from April 2015

[9.45] If the member is not resident in the UK in the year of receipt of flexible drawdown and so not liable to tax on the drawdown under the terms of a double taxation arrangement with the UK, whether or not they have to pay tax depends on how long they are non-UK resident for.

If the member was UK resident for at least four of the seven tax years before the year of departure from the UK, **and** returns to the UK and becomes resident for tax purposes, **and** there are fewer than five tax years between the year of departure and the year of return then taxation applies on the amount taken as flexible drawdown as though it had accrued in the first year of becoming UK resident again for tax purposes.

The rules that apply for taxing flexible drawdown pension whilst temporarily non-resident will be changed from 6 April 2015 as set out in the (draft) Taxation of Pensions Bill 2014.

From then the types of pensions affected by these rules will be extended to include:

(1) Any drawdown pension (either as income withdrawals or short-term annuity) paid from a member's flexi-access drawdown fund (see CHAPTER 4).

(2) Any drawdown pension (either as income withdrawals or short-term annuity) paid from a dependant's flexi-access drawdown fund.

(3) The part of an uncrystallised funds pension lump sum (see CHAPTER 4) that is taxable as pension income.

(4) Any withdrawals from a drawdown fund or dependant's drawdown fund where the individual was entitled to flexible drawdown pension before 6 April 2015.

The pension will only be taxed when the member becomes UK resident again if the total of relevant withdrawals during the period of temporary non-residence exceeded £100,000.

If any relevant pension is not paid in sterling it is to be converted into sterling equivalent by using the average exchange rate for the year ending 31 March for all payments in the tax year containing 31 March. The average exchange rates are published on the HMRC website at www.hmrc.gov.uk/exrate/yearly _rates.htm.

Similar changes are being made to the rules that apply where the payment was from a relevant non-UK scheme except that the amendments apply as if the payment had been made from a registered pension scheme.

Tax-free benefits?

[9.46] Although payment of a pension commencement lump sum will be tax-free in the UK, some countries do not recognise this. It is therefore possible that the lump sum could be taxed in the country of residence – this is known to be an issue in France for example. This can perhaps be avoided by taking any pension commencement lump sum before leaving the UK.

The French tax authorities recently announced a new taxation regime for French residents who are settlors or beneficiaries of trusts, or where a trust owns French situated assets. Trust based QROPS may be caught by this new legislation.

In some cases another possible disadvantage of leaving pension benefits invested in the UK could be overseas 'wealth tax'. Some countries operate a 'wealth tax' on residents based on the value of their worldwide assets. It is therefore worth checking the tax position in the member's country of residence in respect of pension funds retained in the UK.

Section 615 pension schemes

[9.47] The Section 615 reference is to ICTA 1988 s 615. These pension funds are funds which may be established in the UK or offshore. Being trust based schemes the trustees may be UK trustees or offshore trustees. The application of this provision is relatively unusual and there are a handful of active trust company providers in the market.

The underlying legislation is so brief that it is worth setting it out here in edited form thus:

'Section 615 (3) Where an annuity is paid from a superannuation fund to which this subsection applies to a person who is not resident in the United Kingdom, income tax shall not be deducted from any payment of the annuity or accounted for . . . by the trustees or other persons having the control of the fund.

615 (6) Subsection (3) above applies to any superannuation fund which—

(a)   is bona fide established under irrevocable trusts in connection with some trade or undertaking carried on wholly or partly outside the United Kingdom;

(b)   has for its sole purpose the provision of superannuation benefits in respect of persons' employment in the trade or undertaking wholly outside the United Kingdom; and

(c)   is recognised by the employer and employed persons in the trade or undertaking; and for the purposes of this subsection duties performed in the United Kingdom the performance of which is merely incidental to the performance of other duties outside the United Kingdom shall be treated as performed outside the United Kingdom.'

Thus a Section 615 pension scheme exhibits the following features:

- No income tax liability to the employee as a benefit in kind on contributions paid by the employer.
- No National Insurance Contributions for the employer or employee.
- Pension rights may be taken entirely as a lump sum.
- 100% cash commutation by UK tax residents is tax-free (but see below).
- A minimum benefit age of 55, or earlier on leaving service.
- Complete investment freedom.
- Income arising from non UK investments and capital gains in the fund are tax-free.
- Inheritance tax efficient.
- Employer contributions are allowable against Corporation Tax in the UK subject to the 'wholly and exclusively test' as is usual in relation to pension contributions generally.

The taxation treatment of benefits if they are taken following a return to live in the United Kingdom (that is freedom from tax on annuity income or capital payment) have in the past been derived from extra statutory concession A10 (ESC A10).

ESC A10 provided for concessionary relief from taxation on a lump sum relevant benefit received from an overseas pension scheme where some or all of the lump sum relates to foreign service (broadly, to duties undertaken outside the UK while the individual was not UK resident).

HMRC announced on 31 March 2011 that ESC A10 was to be partially withdrawn from 6 April 2011. HMRC continued to apply ESC A10 to payments of lump sum relevant benefits, rights to receive which accrue to employees before 6 April 2011, whenever the lump sum is paid.

The Enactment of Extra-Statutory Concessions Order 2014 (SI 2014/211) puts these aspects of ESC A10 onto a statutory footing.

Finance Act 2011 insofar as it introduced legislation to deal with what is regarded as 'disguised remuneration' (see CHAPTER 7) has an effect on s 615 pension schemes, but only on members who are UK resident when benefit is taken from the s 615 scheme.

For Section 615 pension schemes this will impose tax charges on employment income when a 'relevant third person' takes or is treated as taking 'a relevant step' on or after 6 April 2011. HMRC will no longer apply the concession to relieve or exempt such benefits when they are provided in respect of rights accruing on or after 6 April 2011. In this context a 'relevant step' means the settlement of a contribution from the employer to the Section 615 scheme where the member is able to take benefit from it later.

So for the member of a Section 615 scheme who returns to live in the UK the effect of this provision is that the tax-exempt treatment of the fund arising from pre-6 April 2011 contributions continues, but benefit taken from the fund arising from later contributions may be taxed.

Section 615 scheme membership therefore works well as a tax planning vehicle in respect of employees (including shareholding directors) of UK employers where the employee carries out his or her duties entirely (or almost entirely) outside the UK – and in particular when the individual does not return to the UK as (in particular relating to post 5 April 2011 contributions), no UK tax will apply on the benefit taken.

There are broadly four categories of people who can benefit from a Section 615 pension scheme:

(1)   Any employee of a UK Limited Company whose duties are conducted wholly (or almost wholly) outside the UK.

(2)   Executives of multinational employers of overseas parentage with a United Kingdom presence.

(3)   Self-employed or contracting expatriates who are working outside the United Kingdom.

(4)   UK resident Executives of a UK Limited Company who conducts specific duties outside the UK amongst their other UK responsibilities.

10

Relationships with HMRC and the Pensions Regulator

Introduction

[10.1] In this chapter we look at the formation and maintenance of the relationship that exists between a registered pension scheme and HMRC. This 'relationship' is in the main fulfilled by the person or body who is appointed as the registered pension scheme Administrator.

It is the Administrator (appointed by the instrument that creates a pension scheme) who has to go through the process of registering the pension scheme with HMRC. The Administrator is responsible for ensuring that HMRC is provided as necessary with the information that it is entitled to receive (through event reports etc) by virtue of the legislation contained in Finance Act 2004 as amended and as a consequence of any secondary legislation – that is statutory instruments.

In this chapter we also consider the consequences of scheme de-registration and the circumstances that may lead to scheme de-registration. We also introduce the role of the Pensions Regulator and its interaction with occupational pension schemes.

Registering a pension scheme

[10.2] HMRC automatically treated most existing HMRC approved pension schemes as registered pension schemes from 6 April 2006. Other tax-privileged schemes and pension contracts (such as retirement annuity contracts) were also automatically treated as registered pension schemes from the same date.

These arrangements included:

(1) Any retirement benefit scheme approved under Chapter 1 of Part 14 of Income and Corporation Taxes Act 1988 (ICTA 1988) – commonly known as an approved occupational pension scheme. This included Additional Voluntary Contribution (AVC) schemes.

(2) Any personal pension scheme approved under ICTA 1988 Pt 14 Ch 4 (commonly known as an approved personal pension scheme) – including an approved stakeholder personal pension scheme – or an approved group personal pension scheme (GPP).

(3)   A retirement annuity contract or retirement annuity trust scheme approved before 1 July 1988 under ICTA 1988 Pt 14 Ch 3 (these were contracts for the self-employed or employees in non-pensionable employment). Policyholders are still able to contribute to these arrangements.

(4)   Relevant statutory schemes – more commonly known as public sector pension schemes. Examples included schemes such as those for employees of the NHS, civil service, police, fire service, armed forces, and teachers, and also schemes not established by statute but which have been treated as statutory schemes.

(5)   Certain deferred annuity contracts (typically used to buy out deferred pension benefits), which although not approved pension schemes before 6 April 2006, are automatically treated as registered pension schemes

With effect from 6 April 2006 new pension schemes, if they are to enjoy the associated tax privileges, must register with HMRC. Registration is undertaken through an online process.

Registered pension scheme providers

[10.3] For a pension scheme to be registered with HMRC between 6 April 2006 and 5 April 2007, it had to have been established by one of:

*   An employer or more than one employer – if the membership of the scheme is open to their own, or any other employees. Such a scheme is an occupational pension scheme even if other people may also join the scheme.
*   Government Departments or Ministers and UK Parliamentary bodies ('public service pension schemes').
*   An insurance company.
*   A unit trust scheme manager.
*   An operator, trustee or depositary of a recognised European Economic Area (EEA) collective investment scheme.
*   An authorised open-ended investment company (OEIC).
*   A building society.
*   A bank.
*   A European Economic Area investment portfolio manager.

The rules on who can establish a registered pension scheme that is not an occupational pension scheme were changed with effect from 6 April 2007. For such pension schemes seeking HMRC registration from that date, the scheme must be established by a person with permission under the Financial Services and Markets Act 2000 to establish in the UK a personal pension scheme or a stakeholder pension scheme.

Right to appeal

[10.4] An appeal against a decision must be brought within 30 days beginning with the day on which the scheme Administrator was notified of the decision. If it is determined that the pension scheme ought not to have been registered by HMRC the appeal must be dismissed. If however it is determined that the pension scheme ought to have been registered by HMRC the pension scheme is then to be treated as having been registered on such date as the Tribunal determines but subject to any further appeal.

Occupational pension schemes

[10.5] FA 2004 s 150 defines an occupational pension scheme as a pension scheme which has been established by an employer or employers, and which provides benefits to or in respect of employees of the employer who has established the scheme, or employees of any other employer.

An occupational scheme may under section 150 'provide benefits to or in respect of other persons'. In other words an occupational pension scheme is not restricted in terms of membership to employees of the sponsoring employer, it may under its own rules open its membership to other parties.

Non-occupational pension schemes

[10.6] The rules concerning who can establish a registered pension scheme that is not an occupational pension scheme were amended with effect from 6 April 2007.

Non-occupational pension schemes applying for registration with HMRC on or after that date must be established by a person or body who has the relevant permission from the Financial Conduct Authority (FCA) under the Financial Services and Markets Act 2000 to establish a personal pension scheme or a stakeholder pension scheme in the UK.

The pension scheme registration process (pre October 2013)

[10.7] Registration must take place 'online'. On receipt of an online application for a pension scheme to be registered, HMRC must decide whether or not to register the pension scheme. HMRC is obliged to register the pension scheme on application unless it appears that any information contained in the application is incorrect, or that any declaration accompanying it is false.

Until October 2013 this meant that HMRC processed the information and registered the scheme unless it was immediately obvious that it should not. HMRC could carry out checks later to ensure the scheme met and continues to meet the requirements for registration.

Thus the registration process was operated on a 'process now, check later' basis. In practice, the pension scheme was registered instantly if the scheme Administrator successfully submitted an online application. HMRC has the power to enquire into the scheme's affairs at a later date and may later withdraw the scheme's registration. The grounds on which HMRC can consider withdrawing registration include the discovery that any information or declaration given in the registration application was materially incorrect or false.

The declarations which HMRC may require to accompany an application for the registration of a pension scheme include a declaration that the instruments or agreements by which it is constituted do not entitle any person to unauthorised payments (FA 2004 s 153).

The Registered Pension Schemes and Overseas Pension Schemes (Electronic Communication of Returns and Information) Regulations 2006, SI 2006/570 provide for the use of approved methods of electronic communication for the purposes of the delivery of information under Part 4 of Finance Act 2004.

Under Regulation 6 a submission which is not accepted by HMRC's online system is treated as if it were not made. If these circumstances were to occur, then there would not have been a refusal to register the pension scheme, as no application has been made in the eyes of HMRC.

The pension scheme registration process (from October 2013)

[10.8] HMRC has made the pension scheme registration process more robust by moving away from a 'process now, check later' approach. Scheme registration is no longer confirmed on successful submission of the online form. This enables HMRC to conduct detailed risk assessment activity before making a decision on whether or not to register a scheme.

As part of HMRC's ongoing review of processes to combat pension liberation, since 21 October 2013 scheme registration is not confirmed automatically. HMRC reviews the application and may need to ask further questions or request additional information before deciding if the scheme can be registered.

If the pension scheme can be registered HMRC will write and confirm the date of registration (the date the decision is made by HMRC and from which the pension scheme qualifies for tax relief and exemptions). Otherwise HMRC will write giving the reason for their decision and there is a right of appeal against a decision not to register.

In reality the existing legislation did not give HMRC the powers to implement the above so Finance Act 2014 gives HMRC the necessary powers to help prevent pension liberation schemes being registered and makes it easier for HMRC to de-register schemes.

The new provisions (FA 2014 Sch 7) enable HMRC to refuse to register a new scheme where:

(1)   the scheme Administrator (generally in the case of an occupational trust-based scheme, this means the trustees) is not a 'fit and proper person'; and

(2)   the scheme has been established for purposes other than providing pension benefits.

HMRC now has greater information powers in connection with new applications to register a pension scheme in relation to scheme Administrators and third parties, and to make enquiries as to whether the scheme Administrator is a fit and proper person.

Similar powers will (by the time this edition has been published) have been introduced surrounding the circumstances in which HMRC can de-register a pension scheme.

HMRC now has powers to send information notices to the scheme Administrator and other persons, in order to help decide whether or not to register a pension scheme. Where the information notice is sent to another person, then there will be an appeals route and penalties may apply, which will be similar to those in Finance Act 2008 Schedule 36.

Where the information notice is sent to a scheme Administrator, if they don't respond within the specified period, HMRC may decide not to register the scheme. The scheme Administrator may appeal against that decision.

HMRC also has powers to enter business premises to inspect documents in order to help decide whether or not to register a pension scheme.

Where HMRC have not made a decision within six months of receiving an application to register a pension scheme, the scheme Administrator may appeal to a tribunal as if HMRC had decided to refuse to register the scheme.

There is a new requirement that the main purpose of a pension scheme must be to provide authorised benefits. HMRC may refuse to register or may de-register a pension scheme where it appears to HMRC that the main purpose of the scheme is not to provide authorised payments.

There are new penalties for providing false information or a false declaration in connection with a registration application.

Other measures introduced in Finance Act 2014

[10.9] Finance Act 2014 also introduces legislation to ensure that regulatory redress, for example in the form of transfers of sums and assets to registered pension schemes under certain court orders, are taxed and relieved (or not) appropriately.

Where the Pensions Regulator or a Court orders the repayment of pension funds into a registered pension scheme, the member and the scheme Administrator will be able to claim relief from tax on any earlier unauthorised member payment. However the member will not be entitled to tax relief on the payment to the registered pension scheme, even where the contribution is paid on the member's behalf.

A surrender of pension rights to fund an authorised surplus payment will be an unauthorised payment. A surrender of rights in favour of dependants will be treated as an unauthorised payment except where the dependants' newly-acquired rights are provided under the same pension scheme.

Measures in the Act ensure that independent trustees appointed by the Pensions Regulator will no longer be liable for tax that arose before they were appointed to the scheme in question. The previous scheme Administrator will instead retain liability for these tax charges. These provisions come into force on 1 September 2014 (FA 2014 Sch 7).

From 1 September 2014 the following changes came into effect:

(1)   The scheme Administrator of a registered pension scheme must be a fit and proper person to be the scheme Administrator.

(2)   HMRC will have powers to send information notices to the scheme Administrator and other persons in order to decide whether the scheme Administrator is a fit and proper person. HMRC may refuse to register or may de-register a pension scheme where it appears that the scheme Administrator is not a fit and proper person.

(3)   HMRC will also have powers to enter business premises to inspect documents in order to help decide whether the scheme Administrator is a fit and proper person.

(4)   There will be an appeals route and penalties for these information notices, similar to those set out in Finance Act 2008 Schedule 36.

Appealing a rejected application to register a pension scheme

[10.10] If an application to register a pension scheme is rejected by HMRC then the scheme Administrator (see below) will be notified. An appeal may be made to the First-Tier Tribunal except that the scheme Administrator may elect to bring the appeal before the Upper Tribunal (in accordance with TMA 1970 s 46(1)). These provisions are contained in FA 2004 s 156 which goes on to say:

> 'An appeal under this section against a decision must be brought within the period of 30 days beginning with the day on which the scheme administrator was notified of the decision.
>
> (6) The Commissioners before whom an appeal under this section is brought must consider whether the pension scheme ought to have been registered by the Inland Revenue.
>
> (7) If they decide that the pension scheme ought not to have been registered by the Inland Revenue, they must dismiss the appeal.
>
> (8) If they decide that the pension scheme ought to have been registered by the Inland Revenue, the pension scheme is to be treated as having been registered on such date as the Commissioners determine (but subject to any further appeal or any determination on, or in consequence of, a case stated).'

Legal structure of a registered pension scheme

[10.11] Interestingly the law does not specify any particular legal form that a registered pension scheme needs to take.

FA 2004 s 150 defines a pension scheme thus:

'"pension scheme" means a scheme or other arrangements, comprised in one or more instruments or agreements, having or capable of having effect so as to provide benefits to or in respect of persons—

(a) on retirement,

(b) on death,

(c) on having reached a particular age,

(d) on the onset of serious ill-health or incapacity, or

(e) in similar circumstances.'

A registered pension scheme may be established for example, by

- Establishing a trust – this would be the usual way of establishing an occupational pension scheme or a self-invested personal pension scheme.
- Putting in place a contract – this could be used for the purposes of establishing a pension annuity being purchased on the open market to provide a secure income.
- A board resolution – a small company may use this to establish a directors' pension scheme, or an occupational pension scheme for its employees generally.
- By deed poll – many personal pension providers choose to establish their schemes in this way.

The registered pension scheme may contain various categories of members (possibly defined benefit as well as defined contribution), who in turn will have 'arrangements' within the registered pension scheme. Definitions associated with pension scheme members and their arrangements are to be found in CHAPTER 2.

Trust law and trustees' duties

[10.12] In order to become a registered pension scheme there must be a Scheme Administrator.

Most pension schemes in the UK are set up under trusts. Thus the pension scheme's assets are legally separated from those of the sponsoring employer; they are, therefore, protected from creditors should the company go into liquidation.

Over the centuries trust law has evolved so as to impose high standards of behaviour upon those who are placed in positions of trust. In a pension scheme the trustees own the assets and administer the scheme, but they do so solely for the benefit of the scheme members and other beneficiaries.

Leaving aside the legislative and regulatory points that have already been made, the role of trust law in pension provision has frequently been questioned. After all, the concept of a trust dates from medieval times, and derives from equitable, rather than common law rules. Is such a device appropriate for the present day and age? Should not pension rights be incorporated into the contract of employment, for example?

The Goode Committee, which was set up by the Government to enquire into, and to propose regulations for, the operation of pension schemes in the wake of the Robert Maxwell affair, considered this question and concluded that:

'trust law in itself is broadly satisfactory and should continue to provide the foundation for interests, rights and duties arising in relation to pension schemes.'

There are several reasons for this, among them being:

(i)   while trust law is indeed of considerable antiquity, it has shown a remarkable ability to adapt to modern commercial requirements;

(ii) a trust is not only a means of segregating assets for the protection of the beneficiaries, thus insulating them from the bankruptcy of the settlor, i.e. the employer, but it also provides a mechanism for the collective protection and representation of a group of people linked by a common interest;

(iii) trust law provides for a high degree of fiduciary responsibility, i.e. the trustees have to act in good faith in the best interest of all the beneficiaries; it is surely right that this requirement be preserved; and

(iv) contract law is in fact not sufficient to take over the obligations under a trust. Individual employment contracts do not, of themselves, provide the security resulting from a segregation of assets nor the collective mechanism that is important for the running of pension schemes. Additionally, contract law does not provide protection to all the beneficiaries of a pension scheme, e.g. the dependants of current members and early leavers who have deferred pensions under the terms of the scheme.

This viewpoint was reinforced by the Pensions Act 1995. Thus, it can be confidently predicted that trust law will, with some modification, continue as the basis of mainstream occupational pension provision in the UK for the foreseeable future.

Pension scheme trustees can be individuals, but it is possible to have corporate trustees and trust corporations. It is also common, especially with executive benefit schemes, for the sponsoring employer to act as trustee. This is not generally to be recommended because of possible conflicts of interest.

All resignations and new trustee appointments have to be documented by means of deeds. This procedure, laborious though it may appear, is advantageous because it allows for the immediate vesting of the trust property in a new trustee.

Individual trustees are often directors or senior employees of the sponsoring organisation, but appointment of employee trustees who are selected, in some manner, by the scheme members is now required by legislation. Also, some schemes have appointed independent trustees either to act alone or in addition to company and member appointed trustees.

Trustees' duties

[10.13] Besides being responsible for ensuring that contributions are collected and that employees are admitted to membership when they become eligible to join the scheme, trustees have a wide range of other equally important duties. Their main duties can be summarised as follows:

(a)   familiarisation with the provisions of the scheme and with trust and pensions law (see **12.39**);

(b)   duty to carry out the provisions of the trust deed and rules of the scheme;

(c)   duty not to discriminate;

(d)   duty not to delegate unless authorised to do so;

(e)   duty to act jointly;

(f)   duty to invest;

(g)   duty to keep accounts and other records, e.g. payment and transfer details and minutes of meetings;

(h)   duty not to make a profit; and

(i)   duty to be discreet.

Trustees' powers

[**10.14**] Trustees are given limited powers under general law and statute, for example certain restrictive powers of investment and limited powers to insure the trust property and to delegate administrative functions. Wider powers are generally given in a pension scheme trust deed. Examples are as follows:

(a)   power of alteration;

(b)   power to invest;

(c)   power of delegation;

(d)   power to augment benefits;

(e)   power to accept incoming transfer values;

(f)   power to wind up schemes; and

(g)   discretionary powers.

There are certain discretionary powers which must be exercised by trustees. They can, and indeed must in some circumstances, call in advice, but must exercise the discretion themselves. Areas where trustees have to exercise discretion include:

(i)   payment of lump sum death benefits;

(ii)   approval of ill-health early retirements; and

(iii)   consenting to amendments proposed by the employer.

Trustees' hazards

[**10.15**] Remedies for errors by trustees are enforceable by court action by a beneficiary for breach of trust. Breach of trust can be deliberate, negligent or accidental but there can be no successful action unless the beneficiary has suffered some loss. The Trustee Act 2000 offers a degree of statutory protection to trustees.

The Pensions Ombudsman has made numerous published decisions against trustees. Some of these findings have resulted from complaints about malad-ministration where trustees have been ordered to reconsider decisions; others have resulted in trustees being forced to make compensatory payments. The Ombudsman can rule on complaints made by individuals against employers, trustees and administrators, e.g. insurance companies. Appeals against his decisions are to the High Court and can only be made on points of law.

Registered Pension Scheme Administrator

[10.16] In order to become a registered pension scheme there must be a Scheme Administrator.

The term Administrator here and throughout this text generally is capitalised so as to differentiate between the duties of the scheme Administrator as required by the legislation, and providers of administration services to pension schemes.

In respect of pension schemes that were approved by HMRC by 5 April 2006 under the previous provisions associated with HMRC 'discretionary approval', the Administrator was that applicable under the tax legislation then in force. So an earlier scheme Administrator was assumed to continue in that capacity.

This in relation to occupational pension schemes meant a person or persons resident in the UK who had been appointed as the Administrator. Often this would be the scheme trustees collectively, or the sponsoring employer. In relation to personal pensions and retirement annuity policies, it would be the provider or insurance company respectively who would act in the capacity of Administrator.

Under FA 2004 the role and duties of the pension scheme Administrator are defined in Section 270:

'(1) . . . the scheme administrator, in relation to a pension scheme, [is] the person who is, or persons who are, appointed in accordance with the rules of the pension scheme to be responsible for the discharge of the functions conferred or imposed on the scheme administrator of the pension scheme by [Finance Act 2004 Part 4] . . . [and] . . . has made the required declaration to the Inland Revenue . . .

'The required declaration' is a declaration that the person:

(a) understands that the person will be responsible for discharging the functions conferred or imposed on the scheme administrator of the pension scheme.'

The pension scheme Administrator must be resident in the United Kingdom, in the European Union, or the wider EEA (that is the EU with the addition of Liechtenstein, Iceland and Norway):

'(2) But a person cannot be the person who is, or one of the persons who are, the scheme administrator of a pension scheme unless the person—

(a) is resident in the United Kingdom or another state which is a member State or a non-member EEA State . . . '

Registering for Pension tax relief at source

[10.17] Registered pension scheme Administrators can at the same time as they register a new pension scheme with HMRC, register to operate pension tax relief at source. This means that member pension contributions are deducted from net pay and the pension provider claims the associated tax relief from HMRC periodically. This is the usual approach adopted by personal pension schemes. Personal pension scheme members who are eligible for higher rate income tax relief then claim the balance of the tax relief due through their self-assessment tax return.

Occupational pension schemes however typically adopt procedures whereby gross contributions are deducted from gross pay meaning that tax relief at basic and higher rate as applicable are available immediately for the members. After the details for the new scheme have been provided online, scheme Administrators are given the option of also registering for relief at source.

Duties of the registered pension scheme Administrator

[10.18] The Administrator must declare to HMRC when making the application for registration that they understand their responsibility for discharging their functions under FA 2004.

The duties of the registered pension scheme Administrator include:

(1) Registering the pension scheme with HMRC.
(2) Operating tax relief on contributions under the relief at source system where appropriate.
(3) Reporting events relating to the scheme to HMRC as required by the legislation.
(4) Making returns of information to HMRC again as required.
(5) Providing information to scheme members, and others, regarding the lifetime allowance, benefits and transfers.

A registered pension scheme Administrator can appoint a practitioner to act on their behalf in relation to some of these duties. In other words some of the 'administration services' that are duties of the pension scheme Administrator as set out in FA 2004 above may be delegated to a third party provider of administration services.

Pension Scheme Inspections

[10.19] HMRC Pension Scheme Services (PSS) have put in place an 'Inspections' regime associated with registered pension schemes. This regime involves visits to scheme Administrators but the scheme will be asked to provide information in advance. This information will be provided by the scheme Administrator in the form of a pre-inspection questionnaire. The purpose of this questionnaire is to assist the investigator so as to better understand how the scheme is administered in advance of a visit and to identify specific areas where assurances may be required.

The pre-inspection questionnaire will ask for information on key issues such as:

*   What IT systems are used to operate the pension scheme.
*   How Relief at Source (RAS) and repayment of tax claims are administered.

- How data is identified, extracted from scheme records, and reported at the appropriate time to make the necessary returns to HMRC.
- Scheme investment policy.

The investigator will plan an Inspection visit using this information which will help reduce the length of the visit. Any compliance issues arising from the information provided can be addressed quickly and tax charges raised where necessary. The pre-visit questionnaire will also provide the opportunity for the investigator to give advice on compliance matters where there is any uncertainty relating to any scheme issues generally.

Anti Fraud Unit

[10.20] The HMRC Pension Scheme Services Anti Fraud Unit set up during 2010 has been focusing its activity in the following areas:

- Stopping abuse – particularly targeting the promotion of the so-called 'liberation' of pension scheme funds. The term 'pension liberation' (also known as 'trust busting' or 'freeing up your pension') describes the process by which people release their pension funds before retirement and convert them partly or entirely into cash.
- Restricting the use of tax avoidance schemes.
- Tackling and preventing criminal attack on PSS systems.

The Anti Fraud Unit works closely with other enforcement teams within HMRC in tackling a number of issues involving potential abuse.

Event reports

[10.21] Where certain events occur in a tax year the scheme Administrator is required to provide an event report giving details of those events. There are 20 'reportable events' as set out in The Registered Pension Schemes (Provision of Information) Regulations, SI 2006/567 and a further event 21 introduced from 2012–13 relating to flexible drawdown arrangements. Event report 22 is applicable from 2014–15 when the scheme Administrator is required to give a pension savings statement to a scheme member automatically.

These are:

1. **Unauthorised payments** – The scheme makes an unauthorised member payment or an unauthorised employer payment.

2. **Payments exceeding 50% of the standard lifetime allowance** - The scheme makes a lump sum death benefit payment following the death of a scheme member, and that payment, either alone or when aggregated with other such payments from the scheme, amounts to more than 50% of the standard lifetime allowance applicable at the time of the member's death.

3. **Early provision of benefits** – The scheme provides benefits to a member who is under age 55 when the benefit was paid and where the member was, either in the year in which they were provided with benefits or in any of the preceding six years a director or a person connected with the director of an employer sponsoring the scheme (or of an associated company).

4. **Serious ill-health lump sum** – A scheme pays a member of the scheme a 'serious ill-health lump sum' and where the member was, either in the year in which they were provided with benefits or in any of the preceding six years a director or a person connected with the director of an employer sponsoring the scheme (or of an associated company).

5. **Suspension of ill-health pension** – An ill-health pension which has been paid is not now paid (other than in respect of death), because the ill-health condition is no longer met.

6. **Benefit crystallisation events and enhanced lifetime allowance or enhanced protection, or fixed protection** – A benefit crystallisation event occurs in relation to a member and the amount exceeds the standard lifetime allowance (either alone or together with other crystallisation events associated with that member) and where the member relies on entitlement to either an enhanced lifetime allowance or enhanced protection, or (from 6 April 2012) fixed protection, in order to reduce or eliminate any liability to the lifetime allowance charge.

7. **Pension commencement lump sum** – this relates to certain payments of pension commencement lump sums that exceed 7.5% of the standard lifetime allowance.

8. **Pension commencement lump sum relating to primary and enhanced protection under provisions of FA 2004 Sch 36** – this relates to payments of pension commencement lump sums where the scheme member benefits from primary or enhanced protection and is able to take a lump sum exceeding £375,000 arising from the protection of pre 6 April 2006 lump sum rights.

[An amendment arising from The Registered Pension Schemes (Provision of Information) (Amendment) Regulations, SI 2008/720 created event 8A which relates to stand-alone lump sum payments exceeding the levels associated with event 8 or in some circumstances where the sum paid exceeds 7.5% of the standard lifetime allowance.]

9. **Transfers to Qualifying Recognised Overseas Pension Schemes (QROPS)** – applicable where the pension scheme makes a recognised transfer to a QROPS (as permitted by FA 2004 s 169).

10. **Member able to control scheme assets** – this relates to a pension scheme acquiring or losing the status of being an investment regulated pension scheme. Such a scheme is where a member of the scheme, whether alone or with others, has the ability to control or influence the way in which scheme assets are invested.

11. **Changes in scheme rules** – the pension scheme changes its rules to either permit the making of unauthorised payments or to permit investment other than in contracts or policies of insurance.

12. **Changes to the rules of a 'pre-commencement scheme' treated as more than one scheme** – this refers to a pension scheme which became a registered pension scheme as a consequence of being an HMRC approved scheme as at 6 April 2006 and was treated as two separate schemes under the provisions of Section 611 Income and Corporation Taxes Act 1988 and where such a scheme changes its rules.

13. **Change in legal structure of the pension scheme** – The legal structure of the scheme changes from one form to another as set out in the regulations.

14. **Change in number of members** – The number of scheme members is in a different band (as set out below) at the end of a tax year to the band in which it fell at the end of the previous tax year.

The bands are:

(a)   0 members;
(b)   1 to 10 members;
(c)   11 to 50 members;
(d)   51 to 10,000 members; and
(e)   more than 10,000 members.

15. **Alternatively secured pension** – It is not possible for reportable event 15 to occur from 6 April 2011 as alternatively secured pensions ceased on that date. From 6 April 2011 an individual would go into a form of drawdown pension.

16 **Transfer lump sum death benefit** – this reporting event has not applied since 6 April 2008 from which date the transfer lump sum death benefit payment was removed from the list of authorised payments.

17. **Lump sum payment after the death of a member aged 75 or over** – This event ceased to be reportable for lump sums paid on or after 6 April 2011.

18. **Scheme chargeable payment** – the remaining circumstance where this report is necessary (following the abolition of the alternatively secured pension), relates to income or capital gains arising from a scheme investment in taxable property.

19. **Country or territory of establishment** – where a pension scheme changes its place of establishment.

20. **Occupational pension schemes** – where during the course of the tax year a registered pension scheme ceases to be, or becomes, an occupational pension scheme.

21. **Flexible drawdown arrangements** – This event is only reportable on the event report for the 2012–13 tax year onwards. It occurs where a drawdown pension or dependants' drawdown pension is paid to a member or a dependant who has a flexible drawdown arrangement during the tax year.

It will be apparent that the number of reportable events in force has changed over time. The definition of what has to be reported may also have changed from one tax year to the next.

22. **Annual allowance** – This event is only reportable on the event report for the 2014–15 tax year onwards. It occurs when the scheme Administrator is required to give a pension savings statement to a scheme member automatically. This requirement applies in relation to pension savings statements for pension input periods ending in 2013–14 and subsequent tax years.

The event report must be made for the tax year in which the pension savings statement is actually given to the member. The event report is, therefore, likely to be for a later tax year than the tax year for which the pension savings statement relates.

The event report is required only when the scheme Administrator is required to give the pension savings statement automatically for the purpose of regulation 14A(1) of the Registered Pension Schemes (Provision of Information) Regulations 2006, SI 2006/567.

Deregistration of a registered pension scheme and withdrawal of registration

[10.22] HMRC may withdraw the registration of a pension scheme. There is no provision for voluntary de-registration by a registered pension scheme itself, so a scheme remains registered unless or until HMRC deregister it. HMRC will only withdraw registration from an entire pension scheme, and not just from any arrangement that exists within the scheme.

If HMRC decide to withdraw the registration of a pension scheme then HMRC must notify the scheme Administrator – this may be done by electronic means.

If there is no scheme Administrator, (which is one of the possible grounds for deregistration) the notification of de-registration must instead go to the person who is responsible for the discharge of any obligations relating to the pension scheme and who it is reasonably practicable for HMRC to identify. The term 'obligation' in this context means an obligation that the Administrator (were there one) would otherwise be responsible for carrying out.

Clearly HMRC must have proper grounds for scheme de-registration and any scheme faced with de-registration has the right of appeal as set out in FA 2004 s 159, and within 30 days of the day on which the scheme Administrator (or the person performing the obligations of the Administrator) is notified of deregistration.

The registration of a pension scheme may only be withdrawn under FA 2004 s 157 if it appears to HMRC:

(a)   That the amount of scheme chargeable payments (that is payments that are in one form or another unauthorised - such as an unauthorised member payment) made by the registered pension scheme during any period of 12 months exceeds the de-registration threshold. The dereg-istration threshold for this purpose is represented by unauthorised payments exceeding 25% of the registered pension scheme fund value.

(b)   That the scheme Administrator fails to pay a substantial amount of tax (or interest on tax) due to HMRC.

(c)   That the scheme Administrator significantly fails to provide informa-tion that is required on the part of the scheme Administrator to be provided to HMRC.

(d)   That any information contained in the application to register the pension scheme or otherwise provided to HMRC is found to have been materially incorrect.

(e)   That any declaration made in respect of the application to register the pension scheme or the provision of other information to HMRC associated with the application contains information that is materially false.

(f)   That there is no scheme Administrator.

The scheme Administrator (or whoever it was that received the notification of withdrawal of registration because there was no scheme Administrator) may appeal against HMRC's decision to de-register the scheme. And any appeal must be made within 30 days of the notification of the decision to de-register the scheme issued by HMRC.

Instead of making a formal appeal an alternative course of action could be to seek to have the decision to deregister overturned by the HMRC official who was responsible for making the decision to deregister the scheme. Alternatively a review of the decision by HMRC may be sought. Otherwise a written appeal to the HMRC tribunal would need to be made. This option remains open even once a review process by HMRC has been undertaken without any reversal of the original decision.

As set out in **10.8** and **10.9** under new powers introduced in Finance Act 2014, HMRC may de-register a pension scheme where it appears that the scheme Administrator is not a fit and proper person.

HMRC also has powers to enter business premises to inspect documents in order to help decide whether the scheme Administrator is a fit and proper person.

Consequences of scheme deregistration

[10.23] A tax charge applies on the deregistration of a pension scheme. The purpose of this tax charge in general terms is to recoup the tax relief that was enjoyed by the scheme on employer and member contributions, investment returns, etc. during its period of registration. The amount of the tax charge is 40% of the assets of the scheme measured immediately before the withdrawal of registration. It is the scheme Administrator (jointly and severally where there is more than one) who is liable for the deregistration tax charge. Following deregistration the scheme is no longer able to benefit from the tax privileges associated with registered pension schemes – and in effect becomes an EFRB. If the scheme is not wound up it may continue to exist in the form of a non-registered scheme.

Relationships with the pensions regulator

[10.24] The Pensions Act 1995 established the Occupational Pensions Regulatory Authority (OPRA) as the principal authority for the regulation and supervision of occupational pension schemes in the UK. It had wide powers to deal with breaches of legislation by trustees but was criticised for being too reactive.

The Pensions Act 2004 therefore established a proactive Pensions Regulator to replace OPRA from 6 April 2005. The Regulator aims to focus on tackling fraud, bad governance and poor administration, and to encourage best practice through an increased education and guidance role. The Regulator has wider powers and a more proactive and risk-based approach to the regulation of occupational pension schemes.

As part of its educational role, the Regulator issues codes of practice (see **10.26**) containing practical guidance on meeting the requirements of legislation. Breach of a code does not, of itself, result in legal proceedings, but the code is admissible in evidence in any legal proceedings.

The Pensions Regulator (tPR) has a clear set of objectives:

- to improve confidence in occupational pensions by protecting the benefits of scheme members;
- to reduce the risk of situations arising that may lead to claims for compensation from the Pension Protection Fund (PPF);
- to promote the effective administration of occupational pension schemes; and
- to maximise employer compliance with their duties, including the requirement to automatically enrol eligible employees into a qualifying pension provision with a minimum contribution, and with certain employment safeguards.

To meet these objectives, tPR employs a risk-based approach, concentrating its resources on schemes which pose the greatest risk to the security of members' benefits. The regulator also promotes high standards of scheme administration and works to ensure that those involved in running pension schemes have the necessary skills and knowledge.

Registration with tPR

[10.25] Registered pension schemes have three months from the date of registration with HM Revenue & Customs (HMRC) to register the scheme with the regulator. The scheme trustees or scheme managers could face a fine if they don't do this on time.

For many schemes the information required is very straightforward, such as the name and pension scheme tax reference number, details of the trustees, employer(s), insurer (if appropriate) and the number of members.

Codes of practice

[10.26] The Pensions Regulator targets its resources on those areas where members' benefits are at greatest risk. The Pensions Regulator has a number of regulatory tools, including issuing codes of practice, to enable it to meet its statutory objectives. The Pensions Regulator's 12 codes of practice give practical guidelines on how to comply with the legal requirements of pensions regulation.

The codes of practice provide practical guidelines on the requirements of pensions legislation and set out the standards of conduct and practice expected of those who must meet these requirements. The intention is that the standards set out in the code are consistent with how a well-run pension scheme would choose to meet its legal requirements.

The codes of practice are not statements of the law and there is no penalty for failing to comply with them. It is not necessary for all the provisions of a code of practice to be followed in every circumstance. Any alternative approach to that appearing in the code of practice will nevertheless need to meet the underlying legal requirements, and a penalty may be imposed by tPR if those requirements are not met. When determining whether the legal requirements have been met, a court or tribunal must take any relevant codes of practice into account.

Pensions legislation also imposes duties to report to the regulator in some specific circumstances, for example changes in registrable information, a failure to pay contributions due to the pension scheme, and certain failures in relation to the funding of defined benefit schemes.

Additionally, there are requirements placed on trustees and employers to notify tPR about certain events that may affect the pension scheme and the sponsoring employer.

Trustees and tPR

[10.27] The Pensions Act 2004 ss 247–249 requires trustees to have knowledge and understanding of the law relating to pensions and trusts and the principles relating to the funding of occupational schemes and the investment of scheme assets.

Trustees are also required to be conversant with their own scheme documents. The regulator has taken the phrase 'conversant with' to mean having a working knowledge of those documents such that the trustees are able to use them effectively when carrying out their duties as a trustee.

The 'scope guidance' (broadly speaking a list of items that the pensions industry considers that trustees need to know and understand and a list of the documents containing policy with which trustees may need to be familiar) has been available since 2005.

There are now three documents which comprise the 'scope guidance', which sit alongside the code:

(1)   a full version for defined benefit (DB) schemes,

(2)   a separate and shorter document for trustees of defined contribution (DC) schemes,

(3)   a new and much reduced scope document for the benefit of trustees of small (12–99 members) fully insured DC schemes.

Each document is designed to be appropriate to a different group of trustees defined by scheme size and type. The code sets out how to use the scope guidance appropriately.

Areas where there is increased emphasis include:

* the importance of good administration;
* a reference to the forthcoming auto enrolment regime;
* developments in investments over recent years;
* the importance of the employer covenant and trustees' understanding of their powers;
* buy-out issues (including scheme abandonment and inducements); and
* a new emphasis on the importance of recognising the possibility of wind-up where appropriate and being aware of sensible preparatory steps.

The Trustee toolkit

[10.28] TPR see it as important that trustees recognise that the requirement for knowledge and understanding, as described in the code of practice, applies equally to all trustees.

The code of practice was revised and reissued in November 2009. It contains help and practical guidance about how trustees might set about fulfilling the requirement. It also recognises the value of the Trustee toolkit, a free e-learning programme from tPR, in helping trustees identify and remedy any gaps in their knowledge and understanding. Although designed primarily with trustees in mind, the toolkit is available to anyone who wishes to use it. As an additional tool, tPR has produced an index for the toolkit to show where learning material covering each scope item can be found in the toolkit.

The core learning programme consists of 11 modules, covering the whole of the scope guidance. Largely based on case studies, it is highly interactive, with the learning delivered using a variety of techniques such as audio or video snippets, and self-assessment. It allows for a different path for each trustee according to the type of scheme and their own experience.

The first few modules cover the basics, preparing the ground for a more in-depth exploration of such matters as scheme funding. The final module is set over a typical scheme year and looks at the practices involved in running a trust-based scheme.

The programme should be sufficient for most trustees to meet the knowledge and understanding requirements and, as is made explicit in the code, the regulator expects trustees to use the Trustee toolkit to do this, unless they can find an alternative learning programme.

Those from large or complex schemes, however, may feel they need to supplement the toolkit with further learning of their own. Additionally, for trustees who find themselves in specific circumstances, such as facing wind-up or considering bulk annuity purchase, the toolkit contains additional 'just-in-time' learning resources.

The Pensions Regulator and auto enrolment

[10.29] Auto-enrolment began in October 2012 and will be fully phased in by 2018. By then every employee aged between age 22 and State pension age earning over £10,000 per year (this is the figure for 2014–15) will need to be enrolled into a workplace pension scheme. Contributions will be payable on annual earnings between £5,772 and £41,865. There will be a major reliance upon 'inertia', where people will simply be enrolled into a pension arrangement and accept the cost almost as if it were a form of additional taxation despite the right to 'opt out'.

Each employer has been allocated a date from when these new duties will apply to them known as their 'staging date'. The staging dates are in The Employers' Duties (Implementation) Regulations, SI 2010/4 – albeit with a later amendment as set out in CHAPTER 14.

The staging dates are based on the number of people in an employer's PAYE scheme. Employers with the largest numbers of workers in their PAYE schemes will have the earliest staging date.

Employers will need to:

- automatically enrol certain workers into a pension scheme;
- make contributions on their workers' behalf;
- register with tPR;
- provide workers with information about the changes and how they will affect them.

CHAPTER 14 looks at auto enrolment in depth.

11

Pensions and divorce (marriage or civil partnership breakdown)

Introduction

[11.1] After taking account of the value of the matrimonial home the value of pension rights may be the next largest asset held by a married couple or civil partners. In fact for those who have been long-term members of private or public sector defined benefit schemes the value of accrued pension rights may prove to be the largest single asset to be dealt with.

The courts have long had the power to take pensions into account in dividing up matrimonial assets. Frequently it is the case that the husband has substantial pension provision and the wife might have little or limited pension provision because, for example, she has given up her job in order to look after the children. Such a wife on divorce is likely to wish to be 'compensated' for her lack of pension entitlement.

While the spouses remain married the wife might legitimately expect that when her husband retires she will benefit from his pension and, in the event that anything happens to him, she might expect to receive a surviving spouse's pension. When they divorce these benefits are lost and the wife may understandably be concerned that she has no provision in her own right and that she has little chance of being able to rectify that within any working life that may be left to her.

Pensions and divorce is a question which has assumed greater importance especially since the implementation of the relevant provisions of the Pensions Act 1995 and of the Welfare Reform and Pensions Act 1999.

The Matrimonial Causes Act 1973, gave courts in England and Wales the power to take private pensions (both occupational and personal) into account when structuring the financial settlement of a divorce. Similar provisions were introduced in Northern Ireland in the Matrimonial Causes (Northern Ireland) Order 1978.

The Family Law (Scotland) Act 1985 treated pension rights as part of the 'matrimonial property' which had to be divided up between the divorcing parties. In Scotland the value of pension benefits had to be taken into account by the courts on divorce, whereas there was no such compulsion in England, Wales and Northern Ireland. However, over time the courts outside Scotland, encouraged by divorce solicitors generally, have paid increasing attention to the value of pension rights.

In this text the terms husband and wife may be seen as interchangeable with the term 'civil partners'. And in the same context the term 'marriage' may be seen as being interchangeable with the term 'civil partnership'. References to divorce generally include dissolution of a civil partnership.

The Matrimonial Causes Act 1973

[11.2] In making financial provision orders associated with divorce (which can be in the form of a lump sum payment or periodical payments), the courts are in the main guided by the provisions of the Matrimonial Causes Act 1973 s 25 (as amended by the Matrimonial and Family Proceedings Act 1984).

This provides that the factors which the court must have regard to include the income, earning capacity, property and other financial resources which each of the parties to the marriage has or is likely to have in the foreseeable future. This includes in the case of earnings capacity any increase in capacity which it would be in the opinion of the court reasonable to expect a party to the marriage to take steps to acquire.

When deciding what Orders to make, the court has a very wide discretion. Under Section 25 of the Matrimonial Causes Act 1973, all the circumstances of the particular case must be taken into account and first consideration must be given to the welfare of any minor child of the family who has not attained the age of 18.

The Matrimonial Causes Act made a specific reference to pensions in section 25 stating:

> 'in the case of proceedings for divorce or nullity of marriage the value to which either the parties to the marriage of any benefit (for example a pension) which by reason of the dissolution or an annulment of the marriage that party will lose the chance of acquiring.'

The procedure by which financial issues (transfers of property, maintenance etc) are resolved within the context of a divorce is known as 'ancillary relief'.

Prior to the Pensions Act 1995 and the Welfare Reform and Pensions Act 1999, the court's powers to intervene in pensions matters on divorce were limited.

The three main powers were:

(1)   to make an order for periodical payments to a spouse or in respect of the children of the marriage. Any payment in relation to the spouse comes to an end on the death or remarriage of the spouse.

(2)   to order the payment of a lump sum immediately or at a later date. For example an order could be made awarding a lump sum to be payable following the retirement of the husband if the (ex) wife were still alive.

(3)   to order the transfer or settlement of property.

Options in relation to pensions on divorce

[11.3] Through the court, a divorcing couple can choose to:

- balance pension rights against another asset or assets, such as the matrimonial home (this is known as Pension Offsetting);
- arrange that when one party's pension eventually comes into payment, a portion of it will be paid to the other party (this is known as Pension Earmarking); or
- divide the pension at the time of the divorce to give both parties their own pension pot for the future (this is known as Pension Sharing).

It is up to the respective parties and their lawyers to agree on the most equitable way of dividing up all the matrimonial assets, not just the pension, and offsetting may still be appropriate in some cases particularly where the pension fund is small.

Earmarking is uncommon in practice and when offsetting is not used pension rights are dealt with more often by a pension sharing order.

Pension offsetting

[11.4] Under this method all the divorcing couple's assets are taken into account and the value of pension benefits are offset against other assets (e.g. the matrimonial home). The party with the pension rights keeps them for him/herself and the other party is given the benefit of other assets, such as the right to live in the matrimonial home.

It can be difficult to achieve a fair share of a couple's total assets by offsetting a pension rights against other assets. This may be because pension rights can by far be the greater in value.

Also pension values tend to fluctuate more than, say, property values. If it turns out to be difficult to achieve offsetting, one or other of the alternative bases is then likely to be used.

This process of offsetting is still the most common method used even now by the courts, in spite of the introduction of earmarking and pension sharing (see below).

There were exceptions to the normal practice of offset in a very limited number of cases. In *Brooks v Brooks*, (see below) for example the court held the pension scheme to be a post-nuptial settlement under the Matrimonial Causes Act 1973. This Act gave the court the power to vary the scheme as a post-nuptial settlement to provide a pension for the wife on divorce.

The background to this case was that the divorcing couple married in 1977 and the case was first considered by a District Court in October 1992. The couple ran a family business where the assets held in a small self administered scheme (SSAS) represented a significant part of the matrimonial assets. The company had established the SSAS in 1980 for the benefit of the husband which entitled the husband, on retirement, to surrender a portion of his pension entitlement for the benefit of a spouse or dependant. Mrs Brooks was employed by the company.

The court held that the SSAS was a post-nuptial settlement and therefore formed part of the matrimonial property. The district Judge treated the pension scheme as a post-nuptial settlement which was capable of being varied under section 24(1)(c) of the Matrimonial Causes Act 1973, and varied it to give the wife a modest pension. The Judge thus awarded non-member pension benefits to Mrs Brooks of £76,000 from the SSAS. On appeal the High Court, then the Appeal Court and finally the House of Lords all upheld the decision.

Attachment orders (Earmarking)

[11.5] The Pensions Act 1995 inserted a new Section 25B into the Matrimonial Causes Act 1973 which introduced the concept of 'earmarking'. Pension Earmarking was introduced as an option for divorce petitions filed on or after 1 July 1996 (or on or after 19 August 1996 in Scotland).

This provided for the ability of the courts to make an 'attachment order' on pensions when they come into payment. Until the introduction of earmarking in 1996, the position had been throughout the UK that in theory, the relevant law should have meant that the pension-owning spouse (usually, but not always, the husband) was directed to pay over a greater share of other (i.e. non-pension) assets than would otherwise have been the case if no pension rights had existed – in other words through offsetting as set out above.

Earmarking and offset in practice

[11.6] In practice, the indivisibility of pension rights as compared to many other assets meant that the non-pension owning spouse would commonly be left with no pension benefits, but instead would receive an offsetting capital sum (often in the form of the family home). The courts generally had no power to order payments to be made to an ex-spouse out of the ex-spouse's pension benefits when they fell due.

So in addition to the practice of 'offset', where the value of the parties' pension rights would be taken account of in the context of the overall financial settlement, the earmarking principle gave the courts the power to make an award of a periodical payments order against the pension when it came into payment (despite the fact that this could be many years hence). This could include an order which would compel the member of a pension scheme to commute his or her pension rights for a lump sum to the maximum extent available passing some or all of that to the (ex) spouse.

Under an earmarking order the member's pension rights continue within the pension scheme but part of the member's pension or lump sum entitlement is earmarked for the former spouse. The benefit becomes payable to the former spouse from the same date as a member's benefits become payable.

The courts could also require the pension scheme trustees to pay part or all of any lump sum death benefits in the event of the member of the registered pension scheme dying before retirement (or otherwise whilst taking benefit) to be payable to the ex-spouse to the extent of even overriding any nomination letter or expression of wish provided by the pension scheme member for the guidance of the trustees in determining the destination for pension scheme death benefits.

Orders could be made in percentage terms or in monetary terms, and needed to bear in mind that tax would be payable by the member before payment of the earmarked amount to the ex-spouse. As the member's pension payment would cease on his or her death, earmarking of the member's pension rights represented what was largely seen as an unsatisfactory solution. For example the ex-spouse might well have needed to consider insuring the pension scheme member against their death.

The main objection however to the principle of earmarking was that it was not consistent with any desire to adopt a clean break on divorce. The absence of a clean break was exacerbated by the fact that since earmarking orders were always variable the divorced ex-spouse could return to court later to seek a variation in the order.

Valuing pension rights on divorce

[11.7] The Pensions Act 1995 gave the Lord Chancellor the power to make regulations which would prescribe the method for valuing pension rights the purposes of making financial provision awards on divorce under the Matrimonial Causes Act 1973. The prescribed method of valuation was the Cash Equivalent Transfer Value – (CETV). (see CHAPTER 12.)

The court is obliged to consider the CETV calculation but it may be necessary to make adjustments to it. For example the CETV does not include the value of any lump sum death in service benefits. In relation to defined contribution arrangements including personal pension plans then the transfer value provided by the personal pension provider is the prescribed method of valuation of the policy for divorce purposes.

The regulations do not prevent the parties providing additional information as to future pension expectations and do not prevent the courts from taking account of that information where it deems that the CETV method of valuation provides an inappropriate or inadequate indication of pension value.

Earmarking – procedure

[11.8] As stated above the Pensions Act 1995 gave the courts the power to earmark pensions. The Act requires the court to have regard to pension rights in determining a financial settlement. The system (known as deferred maintenance, earmarking or attachment) has been available for divorces petitioned for since 1 July 1996 (19 August 1996 in Scotland).

The sequence of events in putting in place an earmarking order runs as follows:

(1) The court instructs the pension benefits holder(s) to obtain a cash equivalent transfer value (CETV) in respect of pension benefits accrued to date. Outside Scotland, this measure of benefits includes those accrued before the marriage took place, which could have serious consequences for those who marry late in their working life. In

Scotland, the benefits to be taken into account are those accrued whilst the couple were married up to the date of the divorce petition, or when they stopped cohabiting if that was earlier.

(2) The pension scheme or provider must provide the CETV at a valuation date that is within three months of the date of the request.

(3) The court issues the ex-spouse with an earmarking order to be served on the pension holder's scheme(s) or insurer(s). This must be recorded by the pension provider. The order potentially has three components:

(a) The court can direct that a specified part of an individual's pension benefits must be paid to the ex-spouse, from the date on which the individual begins to draw benefits.

(b) The court can order the pension holder at retirement to commute part of their pension for a pension commencement lump sum to the extent that HMRC and/or the scheme rules permit; and pay all or part of the lump sum that has been realised to the ex-spouse.

(c) The court can override the usual trustees' discretion and require that the ex-spouse should be included as a beneficiary of any lump sum death benefits. While the Pensions Act 1995 does not extend this power to include the redirection of dependants' pensions, it does envisage that the value of such 'lost' benefits would be taken into account in reaching the overall financial settlement.

(4) If the pension holder subsequently transfers benefits to which an earmarking order attaches, then the order must be passed to the receiving scheme or provider for future implementation unless the transfer is only a partial transfer. The ex-spouse must be informed of transfers by the transferring scheme or pension provider within 14 days of the date of transfer. There is no requirement on a scheme or provider to accept transfers which are subject to an earmarking order on the benefits.

(5) In England and Wales, the earmarking order automatically lapses on the ex-spouse's remarriage or on the pension holder's death. This provision applies even if payments have already started after the pension holder's retirement.

Pension sharing

[11.9] Even before the provisions of the Pensions Act 1995 came into force, it was recognised that earmarking was a far from perfect solution. The introduction of pension sharing arose because of the disadvantages and difficulties associated with earmarking both in principle and in practice.

The then Government suffered a number of setbacks in its attempts to place the legislation on the statute book. In the end, pressure from virtually all parties concerned with pensions and divorce forced the Government to promise that the topic would be revisited with the aim of achieving what was originally termed 'pension splitting', but now referred to as 'pension sharing'.

An enabling clause to this end was included in the Family Law Act 1996, and legislation was included in the Welfare Reform and Pensions Act 1999. This came into effect on 1 December 2000.

The coming into law of the Welfare Reform and Pensions Act 1999 paved the way for the introduction of pension sharing. Pension sharing is available in all cases where a divorce petition was issued after 2 December 2000.

Under pension sharing, the member's benefits are valued and 'shared out' between the pension scheme member and the former spouse at the time of divorce. As a consequence two separate pension entitlements arise. Where the individual whose pension is subject to a sharing order is a member of a defined benefits scheme it can be possible for both the member and the former spouse to retain those rights within the scheme – the former spouse is in effect treated as a member of the scheme but one who has deferred pension rights.

A member of a pension scheme who enters into an arrangement on divorce to pension share or in respect of whom a court has made a sharing order is subject to a pension debit. The ex-spouse receives an equivalent pension credit. The member's rights which are being shared are calculated in value terms using the CETV and the court will award a percentage share to the ex-spouse based on the CETV.

The Pension Credit is therefore based on the member's CETV. The pension credit will be expressed as a percentage of the CETV, rather than as a fixed sum of money. The CETV is calculated as that applicable on the day before the Pension Sharing Order takes effect, so it can be higher or lower than the value disclosed at the start of the divorce proceedings. The Pension Sharing Order takes effect from

> 'the date on which the Decree Absolute of Divorce or nullity is pronounced or if later, either (a) 21 days from the date of this Order, unless an appeal has been lodged in time, in which case (b) the effective date of the Order determining that appeal'.

A pension sharing order requires the pension scheme to 'split' the member's pension so that both husband and wife have separate and independent pensions. The clear advantage is that the former spouse no longer has to wait for her ex-partner to take pension benefits but may make their own arrangements and the shared pension will not be lost if the ex spouse dies before reaching pensionable age. Sharing is undertaken at a set point in time and thereafter the ex-spouse will not benefit from any further pension contributions or accrual earned enabling the party whose pension has been shared to rebuild his own pension provision.

The administration of pension sharing

[11.10] As set out in the previous section, a pension sharing order states the portion of the value of a member's benefit rights that is to be awarded to the member's ex-spouse or former civil partner. When a pension sharing order is made, the member's benefit rights in the registered pension scheme are valued so as to provide a CETV.

The CETV associated with the member's benefit rights is then reduced to the extent of that which prevails in the pension sharing order. This is known as a pension debit.

The CETV reduction in the registered pension scheme member's benefit rights is then allocated to the ex-spouse (or former civil partner) so as to provide benefit rights in his or her own name. These new benefit rights are known as a pension credit.

The pension credit might be retained in the same scheme as the original member or it might be transferred into another pension scheme in the name of the former spouse. The pension credit is transferable to a pension arrangement of the ex-spouse's choosing, as long as that pension arrangement is able and willing to accept the transfer.

The court will make an order stating how much of an employee's pension benefits must be shared with the ex-spouse, although in some cases, in particular court orders under Scottish law, the pension sharing arrangements will be set out in a legally recognised 'qualifying agreement' between the divorcing couple.

If the ex-spouse makes no choice as to the destination of their pension share, the trustees/scheme managers of the scheme in which the member whose rights are subject to an order participates, can choose whether or not to offer the ex-spouse membership of their scheme. That is, schemes are permitted if they wish to insist on a transfer out (an 'external transfer'), which will typically be to an insurance contract such as a personal pension. However, any transfer to a contracted-out scheme of contracted-out Pension Credit benefits (termed 'safeguarded rights' — see below) required the consent of the ex-spouse.

The Pensions Act 2008 however abolished safeguarded rights from 6 April 2009 and an amendment to the Pension Sharing (Pension Credit Benefit) Regulations, SI 2000/1054, made by the Occupational and Personal and Stakeholder (Miscellaneous Regulations) Regulations, SI 2009/615, allows pension schemes to pay pension credit benefits in accordance with the same provisions as applied to pension benefits generally.

Registered pension schemes are permitted to charge for dealing with the administration of pension sharing. Basically the cost involved in administering pension sharing should not be borne by the scheme generally, other members of the scheme or for that matter the taxpayer.

The scheme must supply a schedule of charges to the couple involved on their first enquiry. Any cost not directly relating to implementing a specific divorce order (e.g. amending the scheme rules, training administration staff, altering computer systems etc) will be borne by the scheme. The National Association of Pension Funds (NAPF) maintains a table of recommended charges to be used as a guide to the industry. This can be found on the NAPF website.

Pension sharing and taxation – the recipient of a pension credit

[11.11] The beneficiary of a pension sharing order does not need to take account of the value of the share received for the purposes of their annual allowance. As a consequence the receipt of a pension share as a consequence of the pension sharing order has no bearing on the member's capacity to make contributions to a registered pension scheme.

How a pension credit might affect the recipient's lifetime allowance depends on when the pension sharing order was awarded and whether or not the pension credit derives from benefit rights that were in payment at the time of the pension sharing order.

Where the pension sharing order was awarded before 6 April 2006, the associated pension credit will not be tested against the recipient's lifetime allowance when the benefits resulting from the pension credit come into payment. An enhanced lifetime allowance will be awarded to the recipient.

Where the pension sharing order was awarded on or after 6 April 2006 and where the benefit rights of the member subject to the order (that is of the party whose pension rights are subject to a pension debit) are not yet in payment, or were in payment before 6 April 2006, the pension credit will be tested against the recipient's lifetime allowance when the benefits relating to the pension credit come into payment.

Where the pension sharing order was awarded on or after 6 April 2006 and the benefit rights subject to the order (that is of the party who is subject to a pension debit) came into payment on or after 6 April 2006, the pension credit will not be tested against the recipient's lifetime allowance when the benefits relating to the pension credit come into payment. An enhanced lifetime allowance will be awarded to the recipient.

Where the pension credit is derived from benefits that were in payment at the time of the pension sharing order then the recipient of the pension credit cannot receive a pension commencement lump sum as part of the benefits that are eventually paid to the recipient in respect of the pension credit.

Pension sharing and taxation – the recipient of a pension debit

[11.12] A member whose benefit rights are reduced as a consequence of a pension debit is able to rebuild pension rights by making contributions subject to the usual rules associated with the annual allowance.

Consistent with this, it is the reduced benefits as a consequence of suffering a pension debit, together with any fund rebuilding associated with further contributions, that is tested against the lifetime allowance when benefits are taken.

Pension sharing associated with drawdown funds

[11.13] Where the capped drawdown fund of a registered pension scheme member is reduced as a consequence of a pension sharing order then a review of the maximum drawdown pension payable in the remaining years of the reference period is triggered. The scheme Administrator is required to recalculate the maximum drawdown pension on the date that the pension sharing order comes into effect.

The revised drawdown limit does not however take effect until the pension year following the one in which the pension sharing order was issued. As a consequence the recalculation is not necessary if the pension debit takes place during the final year of the relevant reference period.

12

Pension transfers

Introduction

[12.1] In the period up to 1986 (when the available forms of pension scheme were occupational schemes, retirement annuity policies, and buy-out policies), the concept of a pension transfer generally only applied in respect of the ability to transfer pension rights from one occupational pension scheme to another.

Although in this time period most occupational schemes allowed early leavers to take a transfer value to the scheme of a new employer as an alternative to a deferred pension (or in some circumstances a refund of member contributions), some schemes only used to permit transfers with the consent of the employer or the trustees and others did not permit a transfer value at all.

Even fewer occupational pension schemes were prepared to allow the buy-out of deferred rights with an insurance company. However the relevant legislation now gives the member of an occupational pension scheme whose pensionable service terminated on or after 1 January 1986 the statutory right to take the transfer value – referred to in the legislation as a 'cash equivalent' – and generally known as a cash equivalent transfer value or CETV, as an alternative to leaving accrued rights to be preserved in the scheme.

This right of transfer to another registered pension scheme must normally be exercised at least one year before the member's normal retirement age specified in the scheme rules, although even in these circumstances many schemes will still allow a transfer value despite the fact that they have no statutory obligation to do so.

There is however no obligation on a pension scheme to receive a transfer payment. If a member of a pension scheme decides to transfer his rights to another arrangement he must normally transfer all of those rights.

In some circumstances it may be appropriate for an individual considering a transfer to look at transferring his pension rights to more than one arrangement. For example if the transfer value is particularly large so as to spread the available investment opportunities by transferring to more than one new arrangement. Many pension schemes will however only permit the transfer value to be taken across to a single new arrangement.

Cash equivalent transfer values

[12.2] The cash equivalent transfer value (CETV) is the cash value of pension benefits which have accrued to or in respect of a member of a pension scheme at the date their pensionable service terminates, or if later, at the date the member applies to the trustees for the cash equivalent. The CETV represents the expected cost of providing the member's benefits within the scheme.

In the case of defined benefit pension schemes, the CETV is a value determined using actuarial principles, which requires assumptions to be made about the future course of events affecting the scheme and the member's benefits in the scheme.

Calculating the CETV

[12.3] In straightforward terms a transfer value in relation to deferred benefits in a final salary scheme is calculated by estimating the amount of a member's future pension payments (benefits accrued to pension age), taking account of the amount of the entitlement which the member has built up to the date of leaving the scheme, assumed rates of future pension increases (before and after pension age) and life expectancy. This is then given a current value.

Benefits accrued to pension age, means those benefits accrued under the scheme rules to the date of leaving, plus the revaluation of benefits to the date that the transfer value is requested. Then the calculation process takes account of the future revaluation of benefits to pension age and of any post-retirement escalation of benefits associated with the deferred pension rights. These are given a lump sum value at pension age.

The second step of the calculation involves discounting the value of these expected future payments to a present day value. This represents the amount which, if invested now, the scheme would expect to be sufficient on the assumptions made to meet the benefit payments as they fall due. The discount rate used should therefore broadly equal the return expected from the assets held by the scheme to back the member's pension entitlement.

This method of calculation is of course that associated with deferred pension benefits available as a consequence of membership of a defined benefit pension scheme. If the individual were instead a member of a defined contribution or money purchase pension scheme (occupational or personal) then the transfer value would simply be represented by the fund value less any 'penalty' that the pension provider may apply because the transfer value has been taken earlier than the anticipated date on which the fund would be used to provide retirement benefits.

CETV – scheme specific basis (best estimate and alternative option)

[12.4] Since October 2008, it has been the responsibility of registered pension scheme trustees to take the decision regarding the basis on which the calculation of the CETV is to be based. Previously, the calculation had to be certified by the scheme actuary as consistent with a professional technical standard.

The Occupational Pensions (Transfer Values) (Amendment) Regulations, SI 2008/1050 (the amending regulations) amended SI 1996/1847, and thus changed the basis upon which transfer value calculations are made, and came into effect on 1 October 2008. Cash equivalent transfer values associated with defined benefit schemes are now calculated on a 'scheme specific basis' with a methodology that is deemed to provide members with a fair valuation of their pension rights in accordance with the regulations as set out above.

If the defined benefit scheme is however underfunded and therefore in deficit then the law permits for a transfer value to be reduced as to do otherwise would prejudice the interests of the remaining members of the scheme.

The regulations referred to above established a framework which provides for the calculation of an 'initial cash equivalent' (ICE) which is then adjusted if necessary to arrive at the cash equivalent transfer value which is available for the member to transfer. The ICE must place a value on the member's accrued benefits together with any options and discretionary benefits that the trustees decide should be included. This is known as the 'best estimate' method and is based on a best estimate of the expected cost of providing the member's benefits in the scheme.

This is a best estimate of the amount of money needed at the effective date of the calculation which, if invested by the scheme, would be just sufficient to provide the benefits. When deciding on the assumptions for this best estimate, and to put them in a position to make informed decisions, trustees must seek advice from the scheme actuary.

Most defined benefit schemes give members some benefit options, usually at retirement, other than the 'standard' benefits. For the purpose of calculating CETVs, an option is something which can be exercised by the member without needing anyone else's consent (trustees or employer).

Common options are:

- to exchange a part of the member's pension for a lump sum at retirement. However, unless the commutation terms are such as to increase the expected value of a member's benefits, commutation may not be included as an option within the ICE;
- to take a pension earlier or later than normal pension age (which might be subject to a reduction or an increase, respectively, in the amount) – there may, for example, be the option to take benefit before normal pension age without the need for trustee or employer consent. If so, and the early retirement factors increase the actuarial value of the benefit, the legislation requires the trustees to include an allowance for early retirement within the benefits to be valued for ICE purposes;

- to exchange a part of the member's pension in for a higher dependant's pension on death.

Only those options that would increase the value of benefits may be included within the benefit for cash equivalent purposes under the best estimate method.

The amending regulations inserted a new regulation which states that:

> ' ... the trustees must determine the extent of any options the member has which would increase the value of his benefits under the scheme; of any adjustments they decide to make to reflect the proportion of members likely to exercise those options; and to which any discretionary benefits should be taken into account, having regard to any established custom'.

Where including options in the calculation, trustees do not have to assume that the member will select the option. They may allow for the chance that the member will not take up the option, which could be based on their view of past experience of the proportion of members taking up the options available.

Many schemes also have some benefits which are not automatic, but which can be awarded at the trustees' and/or the employer's discretion. Trustees must decide on whether, and if so to what extent, discretionary benefits are to be included within the benefits to be valued. In doing so, they must have regard to any established custom for awarding them and any consent requirements needed (which will usually involve the employer).

A typical discretionary benefit is the award of pension increases over and above what the rules of the scheme automatically provide; another is early retirement on favourable terms with consent. Once a discretionary benefit is awarded, it becomes part of a member's accrued benefit. Awarding discretionary benefits sometimes requires the consent of the sponsoring employer.

Trustees must have regard to their investment strategy when choosing assumptions. This includes the appropriate investment returns to be expected, which in turn will influence the choice of interest rates with which future expected cash flows are discounted.

To inform their decision-making, trustees should:

- discuss with the scheme actuary the relevance or otherwise of the scheme's funding plan as set out in the statement of funding principles (or any similar document where their scheme has not completed its first valuation under the funding regime of the Pensions Act 2004). For example, where a scheme's funding plan implicitly assumes that the investments underpinning benefits (for example with an increasing percentage associated with gilts or other forms of fixed interest or cash investment) change at or approaching retirement, it might be appropriate to take this into account in deriving discount rates; and
- consider consulting the scheme investment adviser on the financial landscape and its implications for choosing a best estimate of future investment returns.

Trustees should monitor and regularly review the appropriateness of the assumptions underlying the calculation of the ICE.

An alternative method is where trustees want to pay CETVs which are above the minimum amount.

Although the legislation sets a floor on the minimum level of transfer values, it also provides a basis which allows for schemes deciding to pay higher amounts. Trustees might set CETVs at a higher level than that calculated through the 'best estimate' basis where, for example:

- the scheme's rules require it;
- the scheme is in surplus;
- the employer asks the trustees to do so;
- the trustees and the employer agree that it would be more cost effective to adopt assumptions which are likely to produce higher CETVs than under the best estimate, rather than to go into the level of detail necessary to ensure a best estimate; or
- the trustees consider it is reasonable to do so after consulting with the employer.

If the employer has asked the trustees to calculate CETVs at higher than 'best estimate' values, the trustees must still consider whether it is proper to do so. They may need to take legal and actuarial advice before deciding whether to proceed on this basis.

One consideration for the trustees should be whether the scheme is fully funded and, if not, the pace at which any underfunding is due to be made good.

The precise way of determining alternative, higher, CETVs is a matter for the trustees. They will need to discuss it with the scheme actuary.

One possible method is to use one or more assumptions that are on the prudent side of a 'best estimate' but otherwise adopting the same approach to options and discretions as under the best estimate method.

If this approach is adopted, the trustees will need to have gone through the process of deciding what options to allow for and which of any discretionary benefits to take into account as set out above in respect of the best estimate method.

Whatever approach is adopted, the trustees must be able to check that the resulting CETV is higher than it would have been under the best estimate method.

Where the trustees decide to use an alternative method for calculating CETVs, they may take the view that paying them at full value would prejudice the security of remaining members because of the current state of funding of the scheme. In these circumstances, the trustees may commission an insufficiency report but with the scheme liabilities calculated based on the chosen assumptions.

Substantive guidance on this subject is available to pension scheme trustees from the Pensions Regulator (tPR). Schemes in a Pension Protection Fund assessment period are not normally permitted to pay transfer values.

Exercising the right to a cash equivalent

[12.5] The statutory right to a cash equivalent transfer value is exercised by the member requiring the scheme trustees to transfer his pension rights to another registered pension scheme.

The receiving scheme may be another registered pension scheme (typically an occupational pension scheme, or a personal pension scheme), or a qualifying recognised overseas pension scheme (see CHAPTER 9). Note however that there is no statutory right to transfer to a qualifying recognised overseas pension scheme.

The trustees or managers of the destination scheme must be able and willing to accept the transfer payment.

Another option may be for the member to look to buy out their benefit by using the cash equivalent fund to buy an annuity from a life office.

A pension scheme member may exercise the right to a cash equivalent transfer value at any time following the cessation of pensionable service until one year before the date on which they reach the scheme normal pension age. Section 93A of the Pension Schemes Act 1993 requires the salary related pension scheme to provide the scheme member with a statement of entitlement to a cash equivalent transfer value within three months of the member applying for same.

Where the trustees of the scheme are, for reasons beyond their control, unable to obtain the information required to calculate the cash equivalent transfer value (this may for example be because it is necessary to have any Guaranteed Minimum Pension confirmed) they must do so within six months of the date of the member's application. It can be possible to seek an extension to the relevant timescales from the Pensions Regulator.

The cash equivalent transfer value once provided from a defined benefit scheme is guaranteed for a period of three months. A member who has made an application for a statement of entitlement including a CETV may not within the following 12 months make a further application to be informed of the transfer value unless the rules of the pension scheme provide otherwise or the scheme trustees permit the member to do so. Generally further transfer values will be provided by schemes but it is common practice for a small administrative charge to be made.

Taxation and pension transfers

[12.6] Under FA 2004 s 169 a 'recognised transfer' (that is one which is an authorised payment) is defined as:

> 'a transfer of sums or assets held for the purposes of, or representing accrued rights under, a registered pension scheme so as to become held for the purposes of, or to represent rights under
>
> (a)   another registered pension scheme, or
> (b)   a qualifying recognised overseas pension scheme,

in connection with a member of that pension scheme.'

A recognised transfer is therefore a type of authorised payment and so no tax charges or sanctions apply to recognised transfers. A transfer does not represent a contribution and therefore does not receive any form of tax relief. It is merely a transfer of the value of pension rights between one registered pension scheme and another registered pension scheme or to a Qualifying Recognised Overseas Pension Scheme (QROPS).

Enhanced Pension Transfers

[12.7] The increased desire by trustees and sponsoring employers to reduce and remove the risks associated with their pension scheme liabilities has led to the 'offer' of Enhanced Transfer Values (ETVs) to incentivise deferred members to leave the scheme. This may be particularly attractive for employers/schemes that believe the cost of the transfer value in addition to any enhancement is less than the associated liability and taking into account ongoing management costs.

ETVs offer an incentive for members to leave a defined benefit pension scheme, in favour of, that is by making a transfer to, a personal (that is a defined contribution) arrangement. This is achieved via an enhanced payment that is above the value of the underlying cash equivalent transfer value, yet still below the full cost of funding the member's pension entitlement.

For example, it may cost an employer £200,000 to fund the cost of an individual's pension compared to a transfer value of £150,000. If they successfully encourage that member to take an enhanced transfer value of £180,000, therefore, the organisation will have reduced the cost of its liability by £20,000.

Many defined benefit schemes are closing to future benefit accrual, resulting in a significant increase in their liabilities associated with deferred pensioners. ETVs can provide defined benefit pension schemes with a cost effective solution for reducing their risk exposure relating to deferred members. The 'enhancement' may be offered via a cash sum, or as an increase to the member's cash equivalent transfer value. The Pensions Regulator (tPR) has provided guidance on such transfers and employers, trustees and scheme members should take this into consideration.

Employers that want to reduce pension liabilities in this way should be mindful of tPR's guidance on offering inducements and incentives designed to encourage employees to transfer out of a scheme, published in 2007. This was intended to advise against employers making unfair offers and poorly communicating these arrangements to pension scheme members. The guidance stipulates that trustees and employers must give scheme members full and proper information in order that the members may properly understand the implications of transferring out of a defined benefit scheme.

Transfers to QROPS (see Chapter 9)

[12.8] A transfer from one registered pension scheme to another is not generally a benefit crystallisation event requiring a test against the lifetime allowance. However if the transfer is made to a Qualifying Recognised Overseas Pension Scheme (QROPS) this is a benefit crystallisation event, (BCE8), and a lifetime allowance charge may arise if the fund transferred exceeds the lifetime allowance (£1.25 million from 6 April 2014 – unless enhanced through protection) at the time of transfer.

Although a transfer to a QROPS is a recognised transfer there is not quite the same degree of certainty of that in practice as there is regarding a transfer to another registered pension scheme. If the transfer were not a recognised transfer then unauthorised payment charges would apply.

This arises because although registration as a QROPS scheme is subject to some degree of HMRC oversight it largely relies upon self certification. This is clear from the preamble to the regularly published list of QROPS published by HMRC which states:

> 'This list is based on information provided to HMRC by non-UK schemes when they notify HMRC they meet the conditions to be a QROPS. Publication on the list should not be seen as confirmation by HMRC that it has verified all of the information supplied by the scheme in its notification. The purpose of this list is merely to help UK registered pension schemes carry out their due diligence when transferring pension savings to another pension scheme that is not a registered pension scheme. The list is not to be taken as a recommendation for a particular scheme or product. Nor should it be taken that any scheme featured on the list is approved or backed by HMRC ...

> Absence of a scheme name from the list should not be seen as a statement of scheme status. For example, some schemes choose to opt out of this public listing even though they may have notified HMRC of their status. Pension schemes also have 30 days to inform HMRC they no longer meet the conditions to be a QROPS and that they need to come off the list.

> The conditions have changed over time so schemes need to ensure that they continue to meet the conditions to be a QROPS. If you have any doubts that a pension scheme that is listed meets, or continues to meet the conditions to be a QROPS, you should check with the scheme manager of the relevant pension scheme. HMRC cannot provide assurances of QROPS status . . .

> If a scheme has been included on this published list, but did not or no longer meets the conditions to be a recognised overseas pension scheme – any transfer that has been made to that scheme when the conditions were not met, could mean that the member has to pay an unauthorised payment charge. This charge seeks to recoup some of the UK tax relief previously given where the transferred sums are no longer being retained in a pension scheme that is sufficiently equivalent to a UK registered pension scheme funding an income for life. Such a transfer could also give rise to a scheme sanction charge on the scheme making the transfer and to an unauthorised payments surcharge on the member ...

> Where the scheme administrator has relied on the fact that the overseas pension scheme is included on the latest published list (and can demonstrate if required that it checked the list no more than one day before the transfer was made) and did so in good faith, this should normally provide just and reasonable grounds for HMRC

to discharge any liability of the scheme administrator to the scheme sanction charge... This should also normally provide just and reasonable grounds for HMRC to discharge any liability of the member to the unauthorised payments surcharge. However, as mentioned above there may still be an unauthorised payment charge liability for the member in these circumstances.'

This is something of an unsatisfactory position as it suggests that the individual considering a transfer to a QROPS should only do so having done some due diligence (or having taken professional advice that can be relied upon), to be as sure as possible that issues will not arise in the future if it is determined that the scheme in question did not satisfy the relevant conditions.

Similarly any registered pension scheme that is requested to make a transfer value out to a QROPS would be well advised to undertake its own due diligence to ensure that they are satisfied that the QROPS is operating in such a way that does not later risk its removal from the HMRC list with retrospective effect.

Transfers which may result in a tax charge

[12.9] A transfer from a registered pension scheme to a non-registered pension scheme, or to an overseas pension scheme that is not a QROPS is not a recognised transfer and will lead to tax charges.

A transfer from a registered pension scheme to a UK pension scheme that is not a registered pension scheme is not a recognised transfer and is therefore an unauthorised member payment. Such a transfer incurs a tax charge on the member at 40% of the payment.

This tax charge is designed to recoup the tax relief already given in respect of the contributions made by or on behalf of the member. If the transfer payment and any other unauthorised payments to the member in a 12-month period exceed 25% of the member's rights under the pension scheme, the member is liable to an unauthorised payment surcharge of a further 15% of the payment.

A scheme sanction charge of up to 40% may also apply, for which the registered pension scheme administrator is liable. If the scheme administrator has deducted the member's tax charge from the transfer payment and paid the tax charge to HMRC on the member's behalf, the scheme administrator may reduce the amount of the scheme sanction charge by the lesser of 25% and the amount of member's tax charge deducted as a proportion of the transfer payment.

A transfer from a registered pension scheme to a non-UK pension scheme that is not a QROPS is also not a recognised transfer. Such a transfer is therefore an unauthorised member payment and the tax consequences will be the same as those set out above relating to a transfer from a registered pension scheme to a non-registered pension scheme.

If the amounts transferred equate to 25% or more of the registered pension scheme fund value, HMRC may withdraw the transferring scheme's registration. This involves a de-registration charge of 40%.

Transfers of pension rights when in payment

[12.10] When pension rights have been 'secured' either through the provision of a 'scheme pension' or through the purchase of an annuity, then it is generally no longer possible for these rights to be transferred to another scheme.

However where there is a transfer of the sums and assets relating to an annuity from one life insurance company to another, the Transfer Regulations (The Registered Pension Schemes (Transfer of Sums and Assets) Regulations, SI 2006/499, and as amended) prescribe the circumstances in which a surrender of rights is not treated as an unauthorised payment as a consequence of FA 2004 s 172A (and as a consequence no tax charge arises). This is achieved by treating the new annuity as if it were the original one provided by the original annuity provider.

In addition a transfer of assets between one registered pension scheme and another representing a scheme pension is treated as a recognised transfer so long as within the receiving scheme these rights are also used for the purposes of providing the member with a scheme pension. The new scheme pension is treated as if it were the original scheme pension.

When pension benefits are being taken in an unsecured fashion through what in terms of Finance Act 2004 is described as an unsecured pension, but in terms of Finance Act 2011 is represented by 'flexible drawdown', or 'capped drawdown' then the fund associated with benefits being drawn in these ways may be transferred from one registered scheme to another.

Transfer of benefits in 'drawdown' – Finance Act 2011

[12.11] Under the provisions of Finance Act 2011, the terms 'unsecured pension income' and 'alternatively secured pensions income' have been abolished and replaced with the term 'drawdown'.

Under the rules operational from 6 April 2011 the operation of drawdown applies before and after age 75, unlike the previous position with 'unsecured pension income' which was able to continue to age 75 (age 77 under transitional provisions prior to the introduction of the new legislation), and the 'alternatively secured pension' which operated from age 75. From 6 April 2011, benefits are either 'secured' (through an annuity or a scheme pension), or provided from the registered pension scheme fund in the form of 'capped drawdown' or 'flexible drawdown'.

Under the new drawdown rules a transfer from one arrangement to another may still take place but the transfer must be made to a new arrangement which does not contain any existing pension rights. Ongoing benefits provided from the new arrangement must be provided on a like-for-like basis. So if the original arrangement was providing benefits under 'capped drawdown' then the new arrangement must also provide benefits as 'capped drawdown'.

Failure to comply with these conditions will result in an unauthorised payment taking place with the taxation consequences as previously described. These provisions are therefore entirely consistent with those in place before 6 April 2011.

The Registered Pension Schemes (Transfer of Sums and Assets) Regulations, SI 2006/499, and in particular Regulation 12 sets out the conditions that must be met in respect of such a transfer. It is a requirement that in order to qualify as a recognised transfer (and so for there not to be any tax charges), the cash and any other assets transferred must become held in a single arrangement in the receiving registered pension scheme.

This new arrangement must be dedicated for the purpose of the transfer. The purpose of this is to avoid 'mixing' the assets associated with the provision of an unsecured pension benefit with other assets associated with the scheme member which are not associated with such a provision of benefits.

The effect therefore is to treat the fund transferred in exactly the same way as it would have been treated as if it had remained in the original registered scheme. Thus the rules associated with ongoing reviews of the level of unsecured pension rights continue in exactly the same way as if the transfer had not taken place.

Transfer of benefits in payment to a QROPS

(See also Chapter 9)

[**12.12**] Unlike the position on a transfer between one registered pension scheme and another where benefits are already in payment, a transfer in the same circumstances between a registered pension scheme and a QROPS is a further benefit crystallisation event and will result in a test against the lifetime allowance.

A further requirement is that the receiving overseas scheme must continue to provide benefits on a like-for-like basis in the same way that benefits were being provided before the transfer took place. In other words the same rules apply so far as benefit provision is concerned as they would apply in the previous section associated with a transfer of pension rights in payment to a UK registered pension scheme and once again a failure to adhere to these conditions results in the possibility of an unauthorised member payment charge.

However the unauthorised member payment tax charges following a transfer to a QROPs are only applicable in relation to those who are UK resident at the time the unauthorised member payment arises, or who were UK resident earlier in the same tax year or in any of the five previous UK tax years.

Thus a failure to meet these conditions following a transfer to a qualifying recognised overseas pension scheme for an individual who has been non-UK resident for more than five complete tax years will result in an unauthorised member payment arising, but no tax charge arises.

Transfers from 6 April 2015

[12.13] The changes being introduced from April 2015 and in particular the availability of flexi-access drawdown (see CHAPTER 4) created a concern in Government that there would be a far greater demand for transfers from defined benefit schemes to defined contribution schemes in order to take advantage of the possibility of accessing up to 100% of the available fund in lump sum form albeit with 75% of any such lump sum being subject to income tax.

Although at the time of finalising this text (August 2014) the changes we are about to set out are yet to be legislated for, we know the associated policy from the Government's response to the March 2014 consultation document; this response was published in July 2014.

In summary:

(1)   Transfers from unfunded public sector pension schemes will be banned from 6 April 2015.

(2)   Transfers from funded public sector pension schemes (meaning the Local Government Pension Schemes) will continue to be available but are likely to be adjusted (downwards) to reflect their funding position.

(3)   All transfers from defined benefit schemes to defined contribution schemes will need to be accompanied by advice given by an FCA regulated financial adviser who is independent from the defined benefit scheme. Responsibility for paying for the financial advice will fall on the employer if the transfer is from defined benefit to defined contribution schemes within the same scheme, or as a result of an employer-led incentive exercise.

(4)   The requirement for professional financial advice will not apply to small pension pot holders with pension savings below £30,000 as the trivial commutation rules would still apply as described in CHAPTER 4.

Although it is unlikely that the number of members of defined benefit schemes wishing to transfer would be sufficient to destabilise any individual scheme, this was nonetheless a concern raised by some who responded to the consultation document.

At present pension fund trustees have the power to ask the Pensions Regulator for a longer time to make transfer payments if the interests of the members or the scheme generally will be prejudiced by making the payments within the usual period. Trustees are also able to reduce the transfer values offered to individual members to reflect the scheme's current funding position.

The Government's view is that these current powers available to trustees are sufficient to keep schemes viable under the new flexible pensions regime. However the Government wants to ensure that trustees are fully aware of these powers and are prepared to use them should the need arise. The Government therefore announced an intention to ensure that there is new guidance to trustees on the powers available to them to maintain the sustainability of schemes.

Safeguards akin to those in the private sector will be introduced in relation to funded public service schemes. This will include the Local Government Pension Scheme (LGPS), which is the largest of the funded public service pension schemes. Unlike the other funded public service pension schemes, the LGPS is not a trust-based scheme. The Government will therefore ensure appropriate safeguards are introduced to the Scheme which give due consideration to the interests of both scheme members and the taxpayer.

Automatic transfers of small pension pots

[12.14] On 23 April 2013 the Government published proposals for the automatic transfer of small money purchase pension pots, up to £10,000. It also confirmed that short service refunds for occupational money purchase pension schemes would be abolished in 2014.

The Government intends to introduce a 'pot follows member' system whereby if a member changes jobs having accrued only a small pension 'pot' in his old employer's scheme, that pot will be automatically transferred to his new employer's scheme unless the member decides not to transfer.

A pot will be eligible for automatic transfer if:

(a)   it is less than £10,000;
(b)   it comprises only money purchase benefits;
(c)   contributions to the scheme in respect of the member have ceased. This may be coupled with a requirement that the member is no longer working for the employer; and
(d)   the pot first began to accrue after a certain date, yet to be specified. It may be that the automatic transfer system will be extended over time to cover older pots.

The Government originally proposed that the automatic transfer system would only apply to pots created in automatic enrolment schemes. However, it now proposes to apply the system more broadly so that in practice it will cover small money purchase pots in respect of most individuals who start to accrue benefits after the specified date.

Initially the automatic transfer regime will only apply where the receiving scheme provides only money purchase benefits, although the regime may in future be broadened to cover schemes capable of providing money purchase benefits.

The Government has yet to make a fundamental decision about how the automatic transfer system will work, ie whether via a central IT system, with schemes under a duty to both upload and search for relevant information, or whether via a system more akin to the current P45 system whereby a member leaving his employer has to be given information to pass on to his new employer.

No date is specified for the introduction of automatic transfers of small pots. The Government has previously stated that it sees 2015–16 as the earliest date from which it would be possible to introduce automatic transfers. The Pensions Act 2014 contains legislation to enable the introduction of the automatic transfer regime, but nearly all the detail has been left to regulations, which have not yet been published.

13

Charges and penalties associated with registered pension schemes

Introduction

[13.1] Finance Act 2004 as we have seen introduced a framework for pension scheme registration. It also introduced a set of benefit rules (lump sums and pensions) as described in previous chapters, an annual allowance, and a lifetime allowance.

It also introduced circumstances in which taxation charges and penalties may arise. The overwhelming majority of individuals and schemes generally will not encounter circumstances where tax charges will occur. In fact schemes and individuals will tend to behave in such a way so as to deliberately avoid the possibility of any such tax charges and penalties because they are relatively onerous where they do apply.

Although reference has been made in earlier chapters to the circumstances in which unauthorised payment charges may apply, the purpose of this chapter is to bring together the circumstances in which charges and penalties will apply, and to set out the extent of those charges.

Unauthorised member payments

[13.2] The legislation associated with unauthorised member payments is to be found in Finance Act 2004 from section 172 onwards. In the simplest terms an unauthorised member payment is any payment from a registered pension scheme which is not an authorised member payment.

Section 172 relates to the assignment of benefits from a registered pension scheme. This is for example to prevent an individual borrowing money from a third-party in return for offering security by virtue of assigning the benefits that may later be taken from the scheme. An exception however arises in relation to pension benefits effectively being assigned to an ex spouse or civil partner as a consequence of a pension sharing order.

The value of the unauthorised member payment in the event of an assignment:

'is the greater of:

(a)   the consideration received in respect of the assignment or agreement, and
(b)   the consideration which might be expected to be received in respect of the assignment or agreement if the parties to the transaction were at arm's length and any power to reduce the entitlement to the benefit or right did not exist.'

In the simplest terms however an unauthorised member payment is any payment from a registered pension scheme which is not an authorised member payment.

Section 173 is concerned with payments, other than for the purposes of providing benefits which are authorised under the legislation generally, any other payments not being authorised.

Authorised member payments

[13.3] Authorised member payments are as set out in FA 2004 s 164:

'The only payments a registered pension scheme is authorised to make to or in respect of a member of the pension scheme are—

(a)   pensions permitted by the pension rules or the pension death benefit rules to be paid to or in respect of a member [set out in sections 165 and 167 of the Act], [see Appendices 1 and 2]

(b)   lump sums permitted by the lump sum rule or the lump sum death benefit rule to be paid to or in respect of a member [see sections 166 and 168 of the Act], [see Appendices 1 and 2]

(c)   recognised transfers [see section 169 of the Act],

(d)   scheme administration member payments [see section 171 of the Act],

(e)   payments pursuant to a pension sharing order or provision, and

(f)   payments of a description prescribed by regulations made by the Board of Inland Revenue.'

Payment outside of these provisions will be unauthorised member payments and taxed as set out later in this chapter.

Short service refund lump sum charge

[13.4] This arises from FA 2004 s 205, and is applicable to members of occupational pension schemes who on leaving service after less than two years' membership are allowed to take a refund of their own contributions. Any benefit arising from employer contributions is therefore lost.

The rate of the tax charge applicable in the period to 5 April 2010 was:

'(a)   20% in respect of so much of the lump sum as does not exceed £10,800, and

(b)   40% in respect of so much (if any) of it as exceeds that limit.'

However as a consequence of The Taxation of Pension Schemes (Rates. Etc) Order, SI 2010/536, the amount of tax due for a short service refund lump sum made in the 2010–11 tax year or later is:

•   20% in respect of the first £20,000 of the payment, and

•   50% in respect of any remainder.

The Treasury can amend these rates and the thresholds by order from time to time. However the 20% and 50% levels and thresholds remain in place for tax year 2014–15.

The tax charge is the liability of the registered pension scheme Administrator, but may be deducted from the member's refund of contributions before payment of the balance to them – which of course is what will happen in practice.

In 2011, the Department of Work and Pensions announced its intention to abolish short service refunds of contributions from defined contribution (DC) trust based arrangements, as this works against the Government's efforts to encourage the accumulation of pensions savings.

The Pensions Act 2014 provides that short service refunds will be abolished for members with more than 30 days of qualifying service and this will apply to individuals who join a DC pension plan after the date that the legislation comes into force. This is designed to ensure that members retain savings within a pension scheme.

Special lump sum death benefits charge

[13.5] Before amendment by FA 2011 Sch 16 para 41 the original legislation (FA 2204 s 206) referred to:

'A charge to income tax, to be known as the special lump sum death benefits charge, arises where—

(a)   a pension protection lump sum death benefit,
(b)   an annuity protection lump sum death benefit, or
(c)   an unsecured pension fund lump sum death benefit,

is paid by a registered pension scheme.'

From 6 April 2011 the 35% tax charge that the original legislation refers to associated with the special lump sum death benefit charge was increased to 55%.

Paragraph 37(1) of FA 2011 Sch 16 introduced amendments to paragraph 17 of FA 2004 Sch 29 so that a drawdown pension fund lump sum death benefit can be paid, rather than an unsecured pension fund lump sum death benefit, which will be taxed at 55%.

It remains the case that lump sum death benefits payable on death before the age of 75 and before benefits have been taken are free from tax. But if the pension scheme member chooses not to take benefit by age 75, then irrespective of whether or not benefit has been at a later stage prior to death the remaining fund following death will be taxed at 55%. The 55% rate is to be reduced, and the new rate is to be announced in the 2014 Autumn statement.

For the sake of completeness associated with the contents of Section 206 a pension protection lump sum death benefit arises where a pension annuity has been set up on the basis that if the beneficiary should die before having received an amount of gross pension income that at least represents the purchase price of the annuity there will be a payment of the balance – this also being known as value protection. Previously available up until age 75, from 6 April 2011 value protection is available beyond age 75 under Finance Act 2011 and the introduction of 'drawdown'.

An annuity protection lump sum death benefit refers to any payment that would be made following the death of an annuitant within any minimum benefit payment guarantee period associated with a pension annuity.

Serious ill-health lump sum charge

[13.6] Since April 2006 the entirety of an individual's pension fund may be commuted for a single lump sum payment in the event of the member's serious ill-health. Serious ill-health is taken as meaning the member's life expectancy (based upon the information provided by a medical practitioner) is so seriously impaired that death may be expected within the next 12 months.

Payment of a serious ill-health lump sum is an authorised member payment and resulted in no tax charge under the provisions of Finance Act 2004. A further condition however is that on taking the serious ill-health lump sum the member's lifetime allowance has not been used in its entirety (including the value of the serious ill-health lump sum benefit) and that the benefit once paid extinguishes the member's rights under the arrangement.

However Finance Act 2011, which allows for the possibility of benefits not having been secured by age 75, introduces the serious ill-health lump sum charge where the member's fund is commuted for a lump sum in the same circumstances as those described in the previous paragraph. The key difference however is that beyond age 75 the serious ill-health lump sum benefit is taxed at 55%.

Unauthorised member payments and tax charges arising

[13.7] When a member receives or is deemed to have benefited from an unauthorised member payment then that payment is subject to:

(1)   An unauthorised member payment charge at the rate of 40% of the unauthorised member payment.

(2)   An unauthorised member payment surcharge if during a period of 12 months unauthorised member payments exceed 25% of the fund value. This surcharge amounts to a further 15% of the unauthorised member payment.

(3)   In the same circumstances that would result in an unauthorised member payment surcharge then a scheme sanction charge will also apply of typically a further 15%. The scheme sanction charge is actually set at 40% but reduced by the extent of the unauthorised member payment charge settled to HMRC.

Unauthorised employer payments and tax charges arising

[13.8] An unauthorised employer payment, is a payment made by an occupational pension scheme to the sponsoring employer which is not regarded as an authorised employer payment.

Authorised employer payments include:

(1)   **Scheme surplus payments** – excepting those where the employer is a charity.

(2)   A **scheme administration employer payment** – where the payment is made to the employer from the scheme but only for the purposes of operating the registered pension scheme. A good example would be to pay the salaries of those engaged in administering the pension scheme.

Unauthorised employer payments are taxed in the hands of the employer at the rate of 40%, and as with unauthorised member payments increasing by a further 15% in the same circumstances. In addition a scheme sanction charge would apply of typically a further 15%. Once again the scheme sanction charge is actually at a rate of 40% but reduced by the extent of the taxation on the unauthorised employer payment.

Value shifting

[13.9] A further source of unauthorised payments arises from FA 2004 s 181 which relates to 'Value shifting' and specifically with regard to occupational pension schemes.

The legislation states:

'(1)   A registered pension scheme that is an occupational pension scheme is to be treated as having made an unauthorised payment to a person who is or has been a sponsoring employer if, in connection with any of the events mentioned in subsection (2) or a change in the value of a currency—

(a)   the value of an asset held for the purposes of the pension scheme is reduced or a liability of the pension scheme is increased, and

(b)   the value of an asset held by or for the benefit of the person is increased, a liability of the person is reduced, or a liability of another person is reduced for the benefit of the person.

(2)   The events are—

(a)   the creation, alteration, release or extinction of any power, right, option or liability relating to assets held for the purposes of the pension scheme (whether or not provided for in the terms on which the asset is acquired or held),

(b)   the creation, alteration, release or extinction of any power, right or option relating to a liability of the pension scheme (whether or not provided for in the terms on which the liability is incurred),

(c)   the exercise of, or failure to exercise, any power, right or option in relation to assets held for the purposes of the pension scheme or a liability of the pension scheme, or

(d)   the exercise of, or failure to exercise, any power, right or option which constitutes an asset held for the purposes of the pension scheme, in a way which differs from that which might be expected if the parties to the transaction were at arm's length.'

Value shifting is therefore seen as a means of passing value from a registered pension scheme to a scheme member, a connected party or the scheme's sponsoring employer.

Value shifting occurs where a benefit is extracted from a pension scheme on terms which would not be available under an arm's-length or commercial transaction i.e. buying or selling assets at other than their true market value.

Where value shifting takes place, any benefit acquired by the member, connected party or sponsoring employer, will be an unauthorised payment with tax consequences on the member or sponsoring employer, and the scheme.

Value may be shifted by either increasing the value of an asset, or decreasing a liability of a scheme member or sponsoring employer without actually creating a payment.

Where value is passed from the scheme to either a member (or a person who has been a scheme member) or a sponsoring employer (or a person who has been a sponsoring employer), the amount of the value shifted out of the scheme is treated as an unauthorised payment if the amount passed is other than what can be expected on arm's-length terms. A scheme sanction charge will also be made on the scheme.

Authorised surplus payments charge

[13.10] Under FA 2004 s 207:

'A charge to income tax, to be known as the authorised surplus payments charge, arises where an authorised surplus payment is made to a sponsoring employer by an occupational pension scheme that is a registered pension scheme.'

This relates to the position where an occupational final salary scheme finds itself to have a surplus of assets over liabilities and seeks as a consequence to make a payment associated with that surplus to the sponsoring scheme employer.

The rate of tax applicable to this authorised payment is at 35% and is a liability of the pension scheme Administrator.

The tax charge however does not apply if the scheme sponsoring employer is a charity or if it is made with regard to a pension scheme that is being wound up where the winding-up process began before 19 March 1986. A further exemption from the tax charge applies where the sponsoring employer receiving the payment is otherwise exempt from Income tax and Corporation tax in respect of the payment.

Scheme chargeable payment

[13.11] A registered pension scheme is regarded as having made a scheme chargeable payment in the following circumstances:

1. The scheme borrows money beyond the permitted limit of 50% of the fund value (having taken into account any existing borrowings). The registered pension scheme will as a consequence be subject to a scheme sanction charge of 40% on the amount of borrowing over the 50% threshold.

Where there has been previous borrowing, the amount of the scheme sanction charge will depend on whether the original loan was below the 50% limit immediately before the new borrowing takes place. If the amount of the original borrowing was below the 50% limit then only the amount of the new loan that exceeds the 50% limit will be chargeable.

Example 1

A self-invested personal pension scheme (SIPP) borrowed £75,000 on 1 December 2011 to purchase a property. The net value of the personal pension scheme arrangement as at 30 November 2011 was £160,000.

On 1 December 2014 the amount outstanding relating to the original loan was £70,000 and the SIPP has a net value of £250,000. The scheme then proceeds to borrow a further £60,000.

The borrowing limit is 50% of the net value of the arrangement, (£125,000) and as £70,000 of the previous borrowing is still outstanding only £55,000 of the limit remains.

As the new borrowing is £60,000 the scheme is liable to a sanction charge on the £5,000 excess at a rate of 40% thus £2,000.

If on the other hand the amount of the original borrowing exceeded 50% of the value of the scheme immediately before the new borrowing takes place (for example if there had been a fall in the value of the scheme assets after the original borrowing was taken out) the scheme sanction charge will be charged on the whole amount of the new borrowing.

Example 2

A SIPP borrowed £50,000 on 1 December 2011 to purchase shares. The net value of the SIPP as at 30 November 2011 was £100,000.

On 1 December 2014 the scheme borrows a further £20,000.

The amount outstanding from the original borrowing is £45,000. However the SIPP is now only valued at £80,000 due to the shares dropping in value.

As the amount outstanding on the original borrowing (£45,000) exceeds 50% of the fund value (£40,000) immediately before the new borrowing takes place, the scheme is liable to a scheme sanction charge on the entire amount of the new borrowing of £20,000. This is once again at the rate of 40% resulting in a scheme sanction charge of £8,000.

Income arising from 'taxable property' and gains from 'taxable property'

[13.12] FA 2004 ss 174A, 185A to 185I, 273ZA and Sch 29A impose tax charges where an 'investment regulated pension scheme' holds investments that are taxable property.

Taxable property consists of residential property and the majority of tangible moveable assets. Residential property can be in the UK or overseas and is defined as a building or structure, (including associated land), that is used or suitable for use as a dwelling. Tangible moveable property comprises things that can be touched and moved. It includes assets such as works of art, antiques, jewellery, and fine wine. The provisions apply to directly held taxable and also to indirect holdings of property except through genuinely diverse commercial vehicles.

An investment regulated pension scheme is a pension scheme where a member is able to direct or influence the investments the scheme makes.

The acquisition of taxable property by an investment regulated pension scheme will create an unauthorised payment in respect of which there will be a tax charge on the member whose arrangement acquires the asset. In addition the scheme Administrator will be liable to a scheme sanction charge in respect of income arising from the taxable assets and any capital gains arising on their eventual disposal.

A particularly onerous burden arises where the net income from the property (income less expenses) is less than 10% of the value of the property. In these circumstances then instead of being taxed on the actual income the scheme Administrator will be taxed on deemed income represented by 10% of the value of the property.

Any capital gain arising on the disposal of taxable property will also be taxed on the scheme administrator in accordance with the provisions associated with scheme sanction charges and so at 40%.

Accounting for tax due by the registered pension scheme Administrator

[13.13] The methodology for accounting for and settling tax due is set out in FA 2004 s 254 under which The Registered Pension Schemes (Accounting and Assessment) Regulations 2005, SI 2005/3454, became effective from 6 April 2006.

The legislation is very straightforward in stating:

'(1)   A scheme administrator of a registered pension scheme must make returns to the Inland Revenue of the income tax to which the scheme administrator is liable ...

(2)   A return is to be made for each period of three months ending with 31st March, 30th June, 30th September or 31st December if tax has been charged on the scheme administrator ... in that period.

(3)   A return for any period must be made before the end of the period of 45 days beginning with the day immediately following the end of that period.

(4)   A return must—

        (a)   show the income tax to which the scheme administrator is liable, and

        (b)   include such particulars of the events or other circumstances giving rise to the liability . . . '

if the payment is made late then interest is added.

Other penalties

[13.14] The registered pension scheme Administrator is responsible for fulfilling certain functions. These include:

* registering the pension scheme with HMRC;
* operating tax relief on contributions under the relief at source system;
* reporting events relating to the scheme to HMRC;
* making returns of information to HMRC;
* providing information to scheme members, and others, regarding the lifetime allowance, benefits and transfers.

Where the scheme Administrator fails in respect of a particular duty, a penalty may be imposed on the scheme Administrator.

Some examples of the penalties that may apply to the scheme Administrator are set out in the table below.

Cause of penalty being imposed	Penalty
Failure to comply with a notice to complete a pension scheme return.	£100
Continuing failure to comply with a notice to complete a pension scheme return.	Up to £60 per day.
Fraudulent or negligent return or provision of incorrect documents.	Up to £3,000
Late tax return.	An amount from £100 upwards depending on the number of members in the scheme and the length of the delay.
Producing an incorrect document or certificate or providing false information in connection with any matter registered in accordance with the Enhanced Lifetime Allowance regulations.	Up to 25% of the relevant excess
Making a false statement or representation to obtain tax relief or a tax repayment.	Up to £3,000.

When the scheme administrator has to make an event report to HMRC it must be made by 31 January following the end of the tax year to which the event report relates. If the scheme administrator fails to submit the report in respect of any reportable event by the required date then the scheme administrator may be liable to pay an initial penalty of up to £300.

If the failure continues the scheme administrator may be liable for further penalties of up to £60 a day. As soon as the failure is remedied no further penalties will be imposed in respect of that failure.

If the scheme administrator fraudulently or negligently makes an incorrect event return then the scheme administrator may be liable to a penalty of up to £3,000.

The same range of penalties as for the event report apply where the scheme administrator is required to provide information to a person other than HMRC. The occasions where the scheme administrator has to provide information to someone other than HMRC are:

- information to a scheme member;
- information following a member's death;
- information to other scheme administrators;
- information to insurance companies.

Change to the penalties for failure to submit an Accounting for Tax Return

[13.15] Changes were made to the penalties for failure to submit an Accounting for Tax Return (AFT) for periods ended 31 March 2010 onwards. An Appointed Day Order coming into force on 1 April 2011 (SI 2011/702) was laid on 11 March 2011 and repeals FA 2004 s 260(1)–(260(5).

Failure to submit an ATF will be brought within Schedule 55 Finance Act 2009 for returns due after 1 April 2011. The first return due after this date was the return for the quarter ended 31 March 2011 which was due by 15 May 2011.

Under the new penalties a scheme administrator will be liable to a £100 penalty if the AFT is made late. But if the return is made more than three months late the registered pension scheme will be liable for daily penalties of £10 per day for a period of up to 90 days.

Where the failure continues for a period of six months after the first penalty date the administrator will be liable to a penalty of the greater of 5% of any liability to tax on the AFT and £300. Where the failure continues after 12 months from the first penalty date the administrator will be liable to a further penalty of the greater of 5% of any tax due on the return and £300. But if by failing to make a return for more than a year the administrator deliberately withholds information which would enable or assist HMRC to assess the administrator's liability to tax, higher penalties apply.

In such cases, the penalty is the greater of 100% of the tax and £300 if the withholding of information is deliberate and concealed, or the greater of 70% of the tax and £300 if the withholding of information is deliberate but not concealed.

Changes to penalties for failure to submit a self-assessment tax return

[13.16] Trustees of registered pension schemes need to file a tax return (SA970) in the following circumstances:

- The scheme or the investment manager the trustees have authorised to act on their behalf have made requests for and/or received repayment of tax deducted at source from any pension schemes investments.
- The pension scheme has taxable income to declare.

If HMRC are aware of circumstances that would require a return then the submission of a tax return will be requested from the trustees or the scheme Administrator. If the scheme has not been asked to complete a tax return in circumstances where it is known that one should be required then the scheme should contact the Pensions Scheme Helpline and request a self-assessment tax return if any of the following apply:

- a belief that the scheme has a liability for Income Tax or Capital Gains Tax.
- a need to claim a refund of tax that has been deducted from scheme investments.
- if the scheme has already claimed a refund of tax deducted during the tax year.

The return must be completed and submitted even if there is no tax to pay or if no refund is due. The deadline for sending in the return is 31 January following the end of the tax year of assessment. So the tax return due in respect of the tax year 2013–14, must be submitted to HMRC by 31 January 2015.

However if the scheme wishes that HMRC calculate any tax liability and perform the relevant tax calculations, the return must be submitted by the previous 31 October. The trustees must ensure that the appropriate records are kept to enable the return to be completed accurately.

From April 2011 if the return is filed late or there is a failure to pay any tax due on time, the penalties that will have to be paid have changed. The greater the delay then the greater the penalty as follows:

- A single day late and the scheme will be charged an initial penalty of £100 (even if there is no tax to pay or if all the tax paid due has been paid).
- A delay of three months late results in an automatic daily penalty of £10 per day, up to a maximum of £900.
- A delay of six months late will result in further penalties, which are the greater of 5% of tax due or £300.
- If the return is submitted 12 months late yet more penalties then apply, which are the greater of 5% of tax due or £300.
- In particularly serious cases the scheme may face higher penalties of up to 100% of the tax due.

14

The Road to Auto — enrolment and its implementation

Introduction

[14.1] Up until the late 1980s employers operating occupational pension schemes were able to make membership compulsory in the sense that membership of the scheme was, subject to satisfying the relevant eligibility conditions, generally a condition of employment. This had been the traditional position for many years. As most employers with a pension scheme operated a defined benefit scheme this basis underpinned the provision of a decent pension for most.

There is little doubt that the abolition of this provision was a major feature in the diminution of occupational pension scheme membership in the UK, and indeed of a general lack of sufficient retirement planning across-the-board. The abolition of compulsory occupational scheme membership was alongside the introduction of personal pensions with an expectation that the public generally with the benefit of freedom of choice would fund their retirement provision. With the benefit of hindsight this 'voluntarist approach' (as it was later described) may be seen as a somewhat naïve position.

The Pensions Green Paper 2002

[14.2] On 17 December 2002, the Government published a Pensions Green Paper following the Pickering report on the simplification of the pension system. *A Simpler Way to Better Pensions – An Independent Report* by Alan Pickering which, in July 2002, had put forward suggestions for simplifying the occupational pensions system. These reviews took place against a background of increasing concern over the adequacy and security of pension provision.

The Green Paper reaffirmed the government's commitment to what it called the 'voluntarist approach' which required a renewal of the partnership between the Government, individuals, employers and the financial services industry, but also announced the establishment of another Commission to keep this under review.

According to the Green Paper, estimates suggested that there were likely to be around 3 million people who were seriously under-providing for their retirement. Depending on their expectations and circumstances, a further group of between 5 and 10 million people *'may wish to consider saving more or working longer'*. In 2001-02, more than half of all employees were contributing to a private pension. Most – nearly 11 million people – were in occupational pension schemes.

293

Interestingly the Green Paper stated that 'the Government is not proposing to set a general minimum level of employer contributions to pensions'. But on the other hand the Government was wondering whether employers, on a voluntary basis, ought 'to be able to make membership of their occupational scheme a condition of employment for all new employees'. This followed the thinking of the Pickering report where it was considered that the possibility of compulsory membership of workplace pension schemes should include 'traditional occupational pensions and other employer-sponsored pensions such as stakeholder personal pensions, personal pensions, or group personal pensions where the employer is making a contribution of at least, say, 4% of the employee's pensionable salary'.

The Green Paper announced the establishment of:

'a Pensions Commission to assess trends in occupational and private pensions and long-term saving, and to advise whether there is a case for moving beyond the current voluntarist approach'.

The Pensions Commission and its first report

[14.3] The Pensions Commission was appointed in December 2002 with the remit of keeping under review the adequacy of private pension saving in the UK, and advising on appropriate policy changes, including about whether there was a need to 'move beyond the voluntary approach'.

The first report of the Commission, published in October 2004, was a formidable piece of analysis. The report was 346 pages long and contained more than 250 graphs, tables and diagrams.

The report painted a stark picture of the problems of the UK pensions system. Traditionally, the UK had relied on a highly developed private pensions system offsetting a relatively ungenerous State pension system. The proportion of men in occupational pension schemes had declined from a high of 58% in 1958 to 34% by 1995.

Relatively generous defined benefit (DB) private pensions had survived until the late 1990s on the unsound foundations of a stock market boom and inaccurate forecasts of life expectancy increases. Outside the public sector such schemes were clearly in decline as they were simply not affordable by the overwhelming majority of private sector employers.

Between 1995 and 2004, the Commission estimated a 60% reduction in the number of active members in private sector DB schemes, with further reductions predicted. There had also been a shift to less generous defined contribution schemes.

Due to increasing life expectancy and a low predicted birth rate, the Pensions Commission predicted that the percentage of the population aged over 65 would double by 2050, putting further strain on the UK pension system. However, perhaps the most shocking finding was that 60% of employees over age 35, were on course to have inadequate pensions. Private savings into pensions or other forms of savings were not responding on anything near the scale required to offset these developments and were, in any case, highly unequally distributed meaning that low to medium income earners were the least likely to save into a pension.

The combined result of all this was that, on a business as usual path, pension accrual in the UK generally was *'both deficient in total and increasingly unequal'*. The report established what Commission Chairman Adair Turner referred to as three *'killer facts'*.

The first of these was that the proportion of UK private sector workers relying entirely on the State pension was 46% in 1995 and had risen to 54% by 2004. This powerfully illustrated the failure of private sector pensions and the weight of responsibility under which the State pension was labouring.

The second *'killer fact'* was that only about 0.5% of people make pension saving decisions on a rational basis of the type economists use to model and predict behaviour, taking into account interest rates, discount rates and the net present value of their assets.

Rather, they enter into pension arrangements if they are compulsorily enrolled by the state, if they are automatically entered into a scheme as a by-product of employment, or if a pension provider goes to them direct to sell them a pension.

The third fact was that it was near impossible for small- and medium-sized enterprises to offer occupational pensions without administrative fees so high that they ended up consuming a punitive proportion of the employee's contributions. The cost of operating a pension scheme for a small employer was 1.5%–2.0% a year that ate up 30% of the potential pensions entitlement for an employee.

The central thrust of the first report was to make it quite clear that the nation faced an unavoidable choice between four possible options:

* stick with the business as usual option and allow pensioners to become poorer relative to the rest of society;
* increase the amount of tax revenue devoted to State pensions;
* increase private savings; or
* raise the average retirement age.

The report argued that the first option seemed unattractive and, given that the proportion of GDP transferred to pensioners would have to rise from 10% to 15% to maintain pensioners' living standards, none of the other options would be able to shoulder the load on their own.

This analysis helped define the problem in a very different way to the Government's initial intent. From being an issue of the divide between those with defined benefit scheme membership versus defined contribution, the Commission's analysis showed that the real cliff edge was between those in the private sector enrolled in an occupational scheme of any sort and those with no provision at all.

Before the Pensions Commission report came out, changes to the State pension age was something regarded as unmentionable, but the evidence in the report made discussion of it unavoidable. Including the pension age in the policy mix opened up the option of a better pension at a later age.

Consensus building and depoliticising of the issue were still at the forefront of the Commission's strategy. Though the Commission had become clear on the overall direction of travel by the summer of 2004, a little over a year after its establishment, they stuck to a two stage report process.

The Commission was careful to avoid pointing the finger at anyone in particular for the then perceived state of private sector pension policy, instead stressing the cumulative effects of past policies. But their analysis meant that the State pension had to come into play in order to prevent the spread of means testing becoming too strong a disincentive to private savings.

It also meant that new approaches were needed to change the entire approach to private pension provision and the Commission's 'big idea' was to use the insights of behavioural economics to understand why people saved so little and to frame proposals for auto-enrolment in employer schemes, 'the last piece in the jigsaw'.

The Pensions Commission — its second report

[14.4] The Commission's second report, published in November 2005, made recommendations for reform that went well beyond its initial limited remit. The first recommendation was for the creation of a low cost, funded pensions saving scheme, which all individuals would automatically be enrolled into, with the option of opting out. This would help overcome the problem of inertia and the inefficiency of small and medium enterprises-provided occupational pension schemes.

The second recommendation was to make the pensions system less means tested, in order to minimise disincentives to saving, financed partly by an increase in taxes devoted to pensions.

Lastly, the Commission recommended re-linking the basic State pension to average earnings growth financed in part by a steady increase in the State pension age designed to keep the proportion of life spent in retirement constant.

The impact of the Pensions Commission reports and their legacy

[14.5] By the 2005 General election, both the Conservative Party and Liberal Democrats had pledged to re-link the State pension to earnings. The Labour manifesto, on the other hand, made few if any specific proposals on further reform.

The Pensions Acts of 2007 and 2008 (see below) enjoyed broad cross-party support though there was some criticism of the means-tested elements in PA 2008. Since the last election, the Coalition Government has continued with the reforms recommended by the Commission (most of which took effect in 2012), but has accelerated the raising of the State retirement age taking account of the increase in life expectancy from the projections on which the Commission's original recommendations were based.

The actual impact of the changes will not be seen until they are finally implemented. The state of the stock market (and tumbling annuity rates) has undermined the value of many people's pension savings and, as a Pensions Commission policy reunion participant pointed out, perhaps brought into question the wisdom of tying people into the stock market.

The process of implementation: Pensions White Paper 2006

[14.6] In May 2006, the Government published a Pensions White Paper, *Security in Retirement: Towards a New Pensions System*. The report signalled the Government's commitment to the Commission's proposals and set the stage for two pieces of legislation to make them law.

In the White Paper tackling pensioner poverty was highlighted as a key priority for the Government over the coming years. The paper estimated that 7 million working people of working age were making insufficient provision for their retirement.

The White Paper announced that the Government's first priority was to make it easier for more people to save more for their retirement. To achieve this, in 2012 the following were to be introduced:

- A new scheme of personal accounts, which will provide a straightforward opportunity to contribute to a high-quality, low-cost savings vehicle.
- Automatic enrolment for employees into either the new personal accounts scheme or their own employer's occupational scheme providing it meets a minimum standard; employees will be able to opt out of this provision, in which case the employer would not contribute.

The view of the Pensions Commission was that personal accounts should be delivered through a National Pension Savings Scheme (NPSS), so that all personal accounts were provided by a single organisation. The alternative solution then under consideration was that 'branded providers' should be used so the pension saver then had a choice from a limited number of providers who would administer their pensions account. A White Paper associated with personal accounts was promised for publication in December 2006.

The concept of personal accounts of course eventually evolved into the development of NEST.

The responses to the White Paper with regard to auto enrolment were extremely positive. One respondent said:

'Auto-enrolment will overcome the inertia many consumers demonstrate by not tackling the need to save for their retirement, and reduces the costs of acquiring business. Research shows that 80 per cent of consumers support personal accounts operating through auto-enrolment with an opt-out option.'

Proposals were also introduced to increase State pension age as well as to make other structural changes to the State pension system.

Personal accounts: a new way to save – White Paper published December 2006

[14.7] The opening words of the White Paper are instructive:

> 'Automatic enrolment is one of the most effective ways of combating people's tendency not to act when faced with difficult financial decisions. It is central to tackling the problem of undersaving . . . Personal accounts will extend the benefits of private pension saving to those on moderate to low incomes who do not have access to a good employer pension scheme.'

Although since 1988 it had not been possible for employers to require membership of their pension scheme many employers in the period that followed used the principle of auto enrolment where the individual employee had to make a deliberate decision to opt out of the scheme. The White Paper reminded us that the Employers' Pension Provision Survey 2005 findings showed a link between automatic enrolment and increased levels of pension scheme membership.

Within private sector firms with 20 or more employees, the proportion of employees that were in a pension scheme averaged 60% where the firm used automatic enrolment. This compared with 41% where the member had to make a conscious decision to join.

The White Paper announced that with effect from 2012, everyone with annual earnings above approximately £5,000 would be automatically enrolled, either into a personal account or an exempt work-based pension scheme. The minimum contribution to be 8% of gross earnings above the earning threshold comprising a minimum 3% employer contribution, an employee contribution of around 4% and a State contribution of around 1% in the form of income tax relief. A minimum age of 22 for auto enrolment was selected.

Continuing with the concept of relying upon inertia, and dealing with a lack of inertia to join a pension scheme in relation to those who had decided to opt out a process of continuous auto enrolment was decided upon. In the words of the White Paper:

> 'Individuals may choose to opt out of personal accounts at the outset, perhaps because they do not believe they can afford to save. A year or two later, their circumstances could be completely different but inertia may prevent them from doing anything about it.'

The Pensions Commission had earlier recommended that employees who opted out should be automatically re-enrolled every three to five years or on changing employers. The Government agreed that employees who opted out of personal accounts should be automatically enrolled again periodically and settled on a three-year period at which point auto enrolment would occur again (with a further opportunity to opt out), with a repetition of this time period for those who remained opted out.

Legislation associated with the development of the 'delivery authority' for personal accounts was introduced in the Pensions Act 2007 – the remit for the delivery authority to be one of:

- providing advice and making recommendations – supporting the Government in understanding the operational and commercial implications of policy options; and
- developing the commercial strategy – taking forward the financial, technical and commercial development work prior to commencement of the procurement process.

A second Act would include provisions to give the delivery authority executive powers, in order to allow the authority to enter into formal negotiations, finalise contracts, and manage the development of the systems and structures needed before the scheme could go live.

It was also announced that the Government would allow employers as an alternative to offer pension schemes that were equivalent to, or which provided more generous benefits than, personal accounts and which were able to automatically enrol their employees into those schemes rather than personal accounts.

In developing the exemption tests two guiding principles were proposed:

simplicity – any exemption test should be as straightforward as possible for employers, promoting understanding and avoiding unnecessary burdens; and

participation – to ensure that the overall strategy maximised the number of employees with good pension coverage.

Employers should therefore be able to seek exemption through self-certification, based on a small number of clear criteria.

The diversity of the structure of employer provision generally reflects the choices that employers have made about how they want to support their employees' pension savings and reflects the needs of their businesses.

The White Paper indicated that the Government had developed tests that reflected and supported that diversity. Tests were proposed for occupational defined benefit and defined contribution schemes and consultation took place on how these tests could be adapted for employers who had chosen to provide hybrid schemes or to make personal pension based provision available.

The basic principle underlying the exemption proposals was that the level of employer contributions and the emerging benefits for exempt schemes should be broadly equivalent to those applicable to personal accounts. The earnings bands on which contributions were to be paid would also need to be the same to ensure parity for individuals.

The Government decided that the exemption test for a defined benefit scheme should be based on the rate of benefit accrual applicable to the scheme operated by the employer.

There were of course two types of defined benefit schemes – contracted-in and contracted-out, which needed to be considered separately. At the time the White Paper was published around 95% of active members in defined benefit schemes were in a scheme that was contracted out of the State Second Pension (previously SERPS). As a result their scheme had already been subject to a test – the Reference Scheme Test. There were about 6,000 private sector contracted-out defined benefit schemes with around 3 million scheme members.

Schemes that satisfy the Reference Scheme Test typically offer benefits which accrue at a rate of 1/80th of pensionable earning in respect of each year of membership and are recognised as high-quality schemes. The Government therefore saw no value in setting an additional test for these schemes and proposed to use the Reference Scheme Test with the inclusion of automatic enrolment as the exemption test for contracted-out defined benefit schemes. Many schemes already operated on this basis.

For contracted-in defined benefit schemes, which are not subject to the Reference Scheme Test, the Government focussed instead on finding a level of benefit accrual supported by analysis from the Government Actuary's Department, that provided a reasonable comparison with what individuals could expect to see delivered to them by way of a pension from personal accounts.

Analysis from the Government Actuary's Department suggested that a $1/120$ accrual rate broadly equated to an 8% contribution level each year into a personal account throughout the working life of the average income earner.

The Government therefore concluded that suitable contracted-in defined benefit schemes should satisfy the automatic enrolment condition and have a pension accrual rate of at least $1/120$ of pensionable earnings in respect of each year of service with the employer in order to gain exemption from having to provide automatic enrolment into personal accounts.

For a 'contracted-in' defined benefits scheme, the quality requirement imposes the 'test scheme standard' in relation to the jobholder concerned. The test scheme standard is conceptually similar to the reference test for contracted-out schemes and can be satisfied if the benefits are as valuable as those under a 'test scheme' for at least 90% of the relevant members.

A test scheme is one that provides a pension from age 65 (gradually rising to 68 over the 20-year period from 6 April 2024 to 6 April 2044) of $1/120$th of average qualifying earnings in the last three tax years preceding the end of pensionable service, for each year of pensionable service (not exceeding 40 years).

Defined contribution occupational schemes were already becoming an increasingly important element of workplace pension provision. As personal accounts were to be structured in the same way as an occupational defined contribution scheme it was easier to draw direct comparisons between the two.

The test in respect of an occupational defined contribution scheme should, it was proposed, be carried out at the level of the scheme, that is to say in respect of the benefits applying to the scheme in general and be based on the principle of offering automatic enrolment and two other criteria:

- Contributions paid into the scheme were proposed to be at least equal to the minimum level of contributions that was required to be paid into personal accounts. This meant that schemes that offered a minimum default contribution for individual scheme members of 8% with a minimum of 3% from the employer, should be exempt from having to auto enrol into a personal account.
- In order to be exempt the occupational defined contribution scheme must in addition offer a default investment option but would be able to offer an additional choice of funds if they want to do so.

Note that the scheme must require the 8% 'joint' level of contributions to be paid. It is not enough for the employer to be required to pay 3% (or even as much as 7%) and for the jobholder to have the ability to make good the difference. To be a qualifying scheme, it must impose a requirement on the jobholder to contribute whatever is needed to bring the total of his and his employer's contributions up to the 8% level.

It follows from this that, if the employer's contributions alone reach or even exceed the 8% level, then there is no requirement for the jobholder to have to contribute. This leaves the way open for salary sacrifice arrangements.

Evidence suggested that most occupational defined contribution schemes had charges broadly equivalent to an annual management charge (AMC) of under 0.6%.

This level was broadly comparable with that which was anticipated for personal accounts so the Government decided that charges should not form part of the exemption test. The Government proposed to take legislative powers to reconsider this question if charges in exempted occupational defined contribution schemes ceased to be comparable with those offered by personal accounts.

Employer-sponsored personal pension provision, where an individual secures membership of a contract-based personal pension (typically through a life office) and receives a contribution to their personal pension from their employer (including stakeholder pensions and 'Group Personal Pensions'), was already a significant part of the existing market for pension provision.

Under European law pure automatic enrolment could not be used with these contract-based schemes since the employee's written consent to be enrolled was required. But the Government did not want this to be an obstacle to exempting participation in such arrangements from having to provide for automatic enrolment into personal accounts.

The guidance on automatic enrolment issued to employers in 2005 for workplace personal pensions outlined a modified type of automatic enrolment which could be used. The end result was that personal pensions operated and administered through an employer is a perfectly acceptable alternative to personal accounts.

The question of transfers between personal accounts and other forms of pension arrangements was a subject it was proposed that required careful consideration. The ability of individuals to transfer pension funds to and from personal accounts could have an important influence on how the market responded to the introduction of automatic enrolment and personal accounts. The Government's view was that there was a strong case for prohibiting transfers between personal accounts and other forms of pension arrangements and schemes.

A prohibition on transfers between personal accounts and other schemes could help, it was thought, to minimise any market disturbance during the transitional period of introducing personal account provision. It would remove the possibility of existing schemes moving funds into personal accounts. This measure would help to ensure that personal accounts remain focused on the target market of moderate to low income earners who did not have access to good pension provision in the workplace.

The thinking was that prohibiting such transfers would remove the need for employers and individuals to make complex and possibly costly decisions about pension transfers. Making a pension transfer can often involve more than just moving funds. Many pension schemes offer a range of features that could not be easily translated into the simple, straightforward structure of personal accounts that was envisaged. Obvious examples are death and disability benefits.

The Government proposed that these arrangements should be reviewed in 2020 to assess the market impact of the reforms and to see whether this prohibition remained appropriate.

Pensions Bill 2007 – DWP research exercise

[14.8] It was decided that the introduction of the recommendations of the Pensions Commission should be a two-stage process through Pensions Bills that would of course become PA 2007 and PA 2008, the auto enrolment part of the legislation to be primarily introduced in the second stage. The first stage introduced the formation of the Personal Accounts Delivery Authority which would be tasked with making personal accounts happen.

Following the Pensions Commission proposals that all qualifying employers should contribute a minimum of 3% of an employee's salary into a workplace pension scheme and automatically enrol all employees into this, the DWP recognised the need to understand why some employees currently chose not to join their company pension scheme.

Key reasons for employees not joining their employer operated scheme were then investigated.

This investigation found that employees' attitudes towards retirement fell between two extremes:

- that it would be a time to pursue personal interests, travel and spend time with family; or
- it would be boring, due to ill-health and inactivity.

Regardless of personal expectations, most employees assumed they would have sufficient savings to live on, or that they would continue working during a period that one would normally associate with retirement. Disturbingly many had not made any provision for their retirement at all. A lack of interest in retirement issues meant that employees' knowledge of the different options available for saving for retirement was, to say the least, fairly limited.

Many at the time the research was undertaken assumed that they would invest in property, though few had seriously looked into this option let alone done anything about it. Typically, little was known about the benefits available from company pension schemes generally, and they were often seen as inferior to property investment, which was perceived as being both tangible and a guaranteed form of investment.

Employees tended to recall receiving information about their company pension scheme, but many had merely skim-read it or filed it away to review at a later date (which in practice they rarely did). In general there was no active decision to not participate in a pension scheme. Apathy was the key reason for respondents' non-participation in a pension scheme.

On further consideration employees also gave a number of other reasons for non-participation, as follows.

- Perceived low levels of understanding about financial matters and pensions specifically – this may have been partly a result of a lack of employee engagement with the information provided.
- Perceived risks – the intangible nature of pension schemes and a lack of guaranteed future returns.
- Other spending priorities – e.g. saving towards a deposit for buying a house or paying off a credit card debt.
- Feeling too young or old to join a pension scheme – younger employees had often set themselves an age to think about joining a pension scheme; whereas those who were older felt they had left it too late and were looking for alternative forms of investment.
- Concerns about affordability, in particular the reduction in spendable income that pension savings would result in.
- Having other forms of savings or investments to provide for their retirement, including ownership of a second property.
- Perceptions associated with a lack of flexibility and portability of pension savings.
- Concerns about the joining process, including the length of application forms, the complexity of forms and the information requirements on joining.

The research confirmed a number of issues that DWP considered important in relation to encouraging employees to save for their retirement, namely:

- Changing employees' perceptions of retirement. Most employees interviewed during the research exercise did not see their retirement as an immediate concern and some were reluctant to think about retirement because of the negative images this conjured up. Those who had positive images assumed they would have sufficient savings by the time they reached old age but few had made any provision for this.
- The content and timeliness of information surrounding company pension schemes also played an important role in scheme participation. Ensuring that information was salient, understandable and meaningful to employees was likely to have a positive impact on scheme participation.
- Simplifying the joining process it was found may also help to encourage scheme participation. Employees who had decided to join a pension scheme quickly lost the momentum to do so when faced with a complicated application process.
- Many felt that if they were automatically enrolled it was unlikely they would opt out as this would require effort on their part. This finding of course supported one of the key features of the proposals of the

Pensions Commission, later enshrined in PA 2008, which requires employers to automatically enrol their qualifying employees into a workplace pension scheme, rather than them needing to make a conscious decision to join.

Addressing the perceived risk associated with pensions will be an important step towards overcoming employees' reluctance to save. The lack of guaranteed returns on investment was a commonly cited issue among employees, many of whom were disinclined to invest money in something they knew little about and had little control over.

Finally, overcoming employee apathy towards retirement issues and pension schemes in general would play an important role in encouraging people to save. Lack of understanding and negative views of pension schemes appeared to feed into this apathy but were also a result of it. The reforms laid down in PA 2008 are of course likely to help address this apathy, particularly as automatic enrolment will require employees to opt out of their workplace pension scheme if they do not wish to participate.

Pensions Act 2007

[14.9] PA 2007 was the first stage in implementing the changes arising from the main findings of the all-party Pension Commission in 2006.

The main provisions were:

- reduction of the qualifying years for a full basic State Pension from 44 years for men and 39 years for women to 30 years for both;
- linking cost of living increases in respect of the State pension to earnings rather than prices;
- changing the contribution conditions for the basic State Pension so that it was easier for everyone to build up some entitlement;
- replacing Home Responsibilities Protection (HRP) with a new system of weekly credits for parents and carers;
- raising the pension age for women to 65 by 2020;
- raising the pension age for both women and men from 65 to 68 between 2024 and 2046;
- introducing National Insurance credits for parents and carers so that they could build up some entitlement to the additional State Pension (SERPS) which had later become the State second pension); and
- ending the option to contract out of the additional State Pension.

Pensions Act 2008

[14.10] Further legislation setting out a framework for personal accounts and automatic enrolment followed in a second Pensions Act in 2008 which put in place measures to address the lack of pension provision in the private sector, including the creation of new low cost savings vehicles and an obligation on employers to enrol all employees into workplace pension schemes.

PA 2008 introduced a series of private pensions reforms to enable and encourage individuals to save more for retirement, building on the foundation of the State Pension elements of which had already been modified in PA 2007.

In PA 2008 the 'stakeholder designation requirement' is removed (PA 2008 Chapter 7).

Stakeholder personal pensions were originally introduced in April 2001 as a part of earlier initiatives to encourage pension savings for low and medium earners. They are a form of personal pension in respect of which the Government set minimum standards in areas such as the costs charged by providers.

PA 2008 contained a number of measures aimed at encouraging greater private pension saving and introduced new duties on employers to provide access to a workplace pension scheme for most employees. It was designed to bring about a substantial increase in the number of people saving towards their retirement. PA 2008 in accordance with the lengthy process of consideration and consultation already set out put in place new requirements on employers to automatically enrol employees into, and to contribute to, a qualifying workplace pension scheme. This requirement was introduced from October 2012.

Employers will, over a staged period, need to enrol most of their employees into a workplace pension scheme that meets certain standards, or instead in personal accounts made available through the National Employment Savings Trust (NEST).

Auto-enrolment will apply this to all employers who employ one or more UK-based workers. The term 'worker' (or 'jobholder') is used rather than 'employee' in order to follow the definitions used in PA 2008.

Under PA 2008 para 1:

' . . . a jobholder is a worker—

(a)   who is working or ordinarily works in Great Britain under the worker's contract,

(b)   who is aged at least 16 and under 75, and

(c)   to whom qualifying earnings are payable by the employer in the relevant pay reference period . . . '

A worker is defined as any individual who works under a contract of employment (an employee), or has a contract to perform work or services personally (i.e. they cannot send a substitute or sub-contract the work) and is not undertaking the work as part of their own business.

This may include agency workers. Broadly, these are individuals who are supplied by an agent to work for a third party (the 'principal') under a contract or arrangement between the agent and the third party, e.g. a person taken on by a recruitment agency that gives that person a temporary assignment to work for someone else.

The physical location of the employer, or the worker, is not a determining factor when considering an individual's status as a worker, e.g. the employer may be based outside of the UK. Individuals working on secondment from another company will usually remain a worker for the company they are on secondment from.

PA 2008 s 2 prevents an employer in any way facilitating the end of a jobholder's active membership of a qualifying scheme without putting the member into another qualifying scheme. For example, an employer will not be able to withhold information from the scheme if by that action of the employer the jobholder ceased to be a member.

This means that employers have an ongoing duty to ensure that jobholders always have access to a qualifying scheme. This duty does not apply if the jobholder ends membership of his or her own accord, and the duty only applies so long as the employer employs the jobholder.

Under PA 2008 Ch 1 s 3 automatic enrolment into a workplace pension scheme:

> 'applies to a jobholder who—
>
> (a)   is aged at least 22, and
> (b)   has not reached pensionable age.'

And:

> 'The employer must make prescribed arrangements by which the jobholder becomes an active member of an automatic enrolment scheme with effect from the automatic enrolment date.'

PA 2008 s 3 thus introduces the employer obligation to automatically enrol jobholders aged between 22 and state pension age into a scheme that fulfils the criteria for an 'automatic enrolment scheme' (as defined in PA 2008 s 17).

Under PA 2008 s 9 the pension scheme may be either an occupational pension scheme, or a personal pension scheme registered under FA 2004. Also, a personal pension scheme must have direct payment arrangements between the worker and the employer.

'*Direct payment arrangements*' are either where the employer makes a contribution and sends it to the worker's scheme or where the employer deducts contributions from the worker's earnings and forwards these to the worker's scheme on behalf of the worker.

Automatic enrolment must take place when the individual first meets the relevant criteria (i.e. is a jobholder and is over 22) in that employment. This is known as the automatic enrolment date.

With regard to personal pensions and the fact that automatic enrolment could not be accommodated as the employee's written consent to be enrolled was required is dealt with as a consequence of PA 2008 s 3(6) which states:

> 'For the purposes of arrangements made under subsection (2) in relation to a personal pension scheme, regulations may deem an agreement to exist (subject to section 8) between the jobholder and the provider of the scheme for the jobholder to be an active member of the scheme on terms and conditions determined in accordance with the regulations.'

PA 2008 s 4 provides for the possibility of delaying initial automatic enrolment in circumstances described in the regulations.

Employers that are permitted to delay automatic enrolment may be required to ensure that members remain in such a scheme for a prescribed period of time, unless the jobholder leaves that employment or chooses to leave the scheme. This will enable the member to make up pension savings foregone during the initial period associated with the delay.

PA 2008 ss 5–6 set out the duty and the timing for employers to periodically automatically re-enrol into an automatic enrolment scheme jobholders who are aged at least 22 and under pensionable age and who are not already members of qualifying schemes.

As with automatic enrolment, this obligation does not apply if the jobholder chose to end membership in the same employment, within a prescribed period before the re-enrolment date (PA 2008 s 5(4)) or gave notice to opt out under PA 2008 s 8. This enables the delay of re-enrolment if it falls soon after the jobholder has chosen to leave the scheme.

PA 2008 s 6 required regulations to determine that re-enrolment will not occur more frequently than once every three years. The three-year interval may be by reference to the jobholder or the employer. The section then goes on to set out exceptions whereby regulations may be made to enable re-enrolment to take place more frequently than once in a three-year period.

PA 2008 s 7 is concerned with a jobholder's right to opt in. There may be jobholders who are not participating in workplace saving because they opted out or cancelled their active membership, or do not qualify for automatic enrolment because they are aged between 16 and 22 or between pensionable age and age 75.

PA 2008 s 7 allows such jobholders to require their employer to make arrangements to enrol them into an automatic enrolment scheme by giving the employer notice. The jobholder can give notice to opt in under this section more than once in a 12-month period, although the employer is not obliged to accept more than one notice in 12 months. Therefore employers are not required to keep enrolling a jobholder who has opted out a number of times in the same year. This process, the details of the notice required and the date from which membership must be effected were to be prescribed in regulations.

PA 2008 s 8 established the right of a jobholder who has been automatically enrolled (or re-enrolled) into an automatic enrolment pension scheme to opt out of that membership by providing a signed notice to their employer within a prescribed period indicating that they choose not to participate. The form and content of this notice is to be set out in regulations, as will the prescribed period during which they can choose to opt out, to whom the jobholder must give notice of opt-out and arrangements which must be made to give effect to an opt-out decision.

The opt-out notice must include information relating to the effect of opting out on the jobholder. Opting out in this context refers to the specific decision not to participate in a pension scheme from the point of enrolment. Once in a scheme, an active member is free subsequently to cancel membership at any time and this section does not interfere with that established right.

Once a jobholder has opted out they will be treated as if they had never become a member of the qualifying scheme through automatic enrolment. In effect this means that they will not have any rights in the scheme and any contributions collected from the jobholder and the employer will be refunded. However, when a jobholder chooses to opt out after being enrolled or re-enrolled in a pension scheme, any refund of contributions due is only for the current period of membership and not for previously accrued rights from earlier periods of active membership.

PA 2008 s 9 deals with people who do not qualify for automatic enrolment and who are not participating in workplace pension saving. This is because although they ordinarily work in the UK and are aged at least 16 and under 75 they do not have qualifying earnings, as defined in PA 2008 s 13.

PA 2008 s 9 allows such workers to require their employer to make arrangements to enrol them into a pension scheme by giving notice. The worker may give notice to opt in under this section as many times as they like, although once again the employer is only obliged to act on one request in a 12-month period. This does not prohibit the employer allowing workers to join the scheme at other times by agreement. An employer is not obliged to make any matching contribution but may choose to do so.

PA 2008 s 10 is concerned with the information to be given to workers. This section required regulations to set out the circumstances in which a prescribed person (in effect meaning an employer) must give information to individuals about how the employer's duty may affect them. This will include information about the effect of automatic enrolment, re-enrolment, postponement of automatic enrolment, giving notice to opt in and the right to opt out.

PA 2008 s 11 enables the process by which employers will be required to register with the Pensions Regulator and allows for regulations requiring employers to provide information to the Regulator about how they are complying, or intend to comply, with the employer duties, including information relating to the pension schemes that are to be used for the purposes of automatic enrolment.

PA 2008 s 12 allows for the introduction of the employer duties to be staged over a period of time.

PA 2008 s 13 defines qualifying earnings. Subsection (1) defines them by reference to an earnings band (the qualifying earnings band), with lower and upper limits which were later reviewed and amended. 'Earnings' are defined as sums comprising: wages/salary, commissions, bonuses, overtime and certain statutory benefits.

Under PA 2008 s 14 the value of the 'qualifying earnings' lower and upper limits must be reviewed annually against the general level of earnings and must be amended if they have not maintained their value measured against earnings.

PA 2008 s 15 sets out the pay reference period which is the period of earnings over which the calculation is made to calculate:

- whether the jobholder should be automatically enrolled (i.e. because they have earnings that exceed the lower limit); and

- to calculate the level of contributions that the jobholder and employer need to pay into money purchase schemes.

While the qualifying earnings band is expressed in annual terms this section allows for other periods to be used for calculation purposes. Because of the different types of workers and different pay periods used by employers, there was a need to enable the pay reference period to be tailored to specific workers and payment types. For example, agency workers might require a much shorter calculation period than salaried employees.

PA 2008 s 16 defines a qualifying scheme. Qualifying schemes are those that meet minimum standards and quality requirements, which can be used by employers in discharging their auto enrolment obligations as prescribed by PA 2008 s 2. A qualifying scheme can be either an occupational pension scheme or a personal pension scheme. Qualifying schemes must meet the quality requirement for the scheme type and must also be registered pension schemes under FA 2004 Ch 2 Pt 4.

Schemes established outside the UK may also qualify if they meet further requirements, in particular schemes with members who will receive UK tax relief on their contributions.

Under PA 2008 s 17 schemes that are used for the purposes of automatic enrolment, automatic re-enrolment and allowing those eligible to opt in must be qualifying occupational pension schemes or qualifying personal pension schemes and must enable automatic enrolment to take place. The scheme must not require jobholders who are enrolled to express a choice, or provide information, in order to remain active members of the scheme. For example, the jobholder participant will not be required to make a choice about the fund into which their contributions may be invested. The scheme cannot refuse membership on the grounds that the jobholder has not provided information.

PA 2008 s 18 defines occupational pension schemes as those which fall within the relevant definitions from UK or European legislation or are of a prescribed description if they are based outside the European Economic Area (EEA).

Personal pension schemes as set out in PA 2008 s 19 are defined as schemes which fall outside the definition of an occupational pension scheme.

Under PA 2008 s 20 there is a quality requirement to be satisfied for a money purchase scheme to be deemed a qualifying scheme. It must require an employer contribution equivalent to at least 3% of qualifying earnings and total contributions paid by the employer and jobholder equivalent to be at least 8% (including tax relief).

PA 2008 s 21 defines the quality requirement for defined benefit schemes and provides that the quality requirement for defined benefit schemes depends on whether or not the jobholder is in contracted-out employment, as defined under the Pension Schemes Act 1993 (PSA 1993).

If a jobholder is in contracted-out employment, evidenced by a certificate issued under PSA 1993 s 7(1), the scheme satisfies the quality requirement in relation to that jobholder. The quality requirement may be changed should this prove necessary in the future so that the scheme no longer qualifies on the evidence of contracting out alone but is required to meet a modified version of the test scheme standard with an accrual rate of no more than $\frac{1}{80}$th.

For jobholders who are members of a defined benefit scheme and not in contracted-out employment, the scheme must meet the standard associated with a test scheme.

PA 2008 s 22 provides that a contracted in scheme satisfies the test scheme standard if it provides benefits that are broadly equivalent to or better than the benefits provided by a model test scheme as set out in PA 2008 s 23.

The model test scheme in respect of which the comparison is made is set out at PA 2008 s 23. It provides a pension for life based on no more than 40 years of accrual at an annual rate of $1/120$th of average qualifying earnings.

PA 2008 s 24 deals with a quality standard for hybrid schemes, which have a mix of defined benefit and money purchase elements. In order to qualify they will be required to satisfy the quality requirement for either money purchase schemes or defined benefit schemes as set out above.

PA 2008 s 25 enables regulations to be made about the quality criteria of non-UK based occupational pension schemes.

PA 2008 s 26 provides the conditions which a personal pension scheme must meet in order to satisfy the quality requirement. In order to qualify the employer must be required to contribute an amount equivalent to at least 3% of qualifying earnings and the jobholder must be required to make up any shortfall in contributions up to a contributions total of an amount equivalent to 8% of qualifying earnings in the pay reference period. There need to be agreements between the scheme and the employer and the jobholder confirming the contributions required.

PA 2008 s 27 allows secondary legislation to prescribe the quality requirements for non-UK personal pension schemes.

PA 2008 s 29 sets out how employers operating qualifying occupational money purchase schemes and personal pension schemes will be able to phase in their contributions over two transitional periods. This is achieved by setting lower contributions in the quality requirements over two transitional periods. Both transitional periods to last at least one year and the exact duration of both to be later prescribed in regulations.

In the first period the scheme rules must require employer contributions of at least 1% and a total contribution of at least 2% of the jobholder's qualifying earnings in the pay reference period. For the second period, the minimum contributions will increase to 2% from the employer and 5% overall.

PA 2008 s 33 allows for permission to deduct the jobholder's contributions from the jobholder's pay from the date on which they are to become active members and to pay these contributions to the scheme. This means that a deduction from earnings made by an employer in order to comply with the employer duty is not otherwise an unlawful deduction from earnings under the Employment Rights Act 1996 s 13.

PA 2008 Chapters 5 and 6 then turn to compliance matters in respect of which the Pensions Regulator is the sole body responsible for taking action against such breaches.

In summary Chapters 5 and 6:

- introduce powers for the Pensions Regulator to issue compliance notices where the Regulator is of the opinion that a contravention of the employer's duties has occurred. A compliance notice will direct the recipient to put right their breach of the employer duty;
- provide the Pensions Regulator with the power to issue an unpaid contributions notice to an employer if it is of the opinion that an employer has failed to pay the required contributions on time;
- provide the Pensions Regulator with powers to issue penalty notices where the Regulator is of the opinion that there has been a failure to comply with a compliance notice. A fixed penalty notice will require the person to whom it is issued to pay a penalty of up to £50,000 within a specified timeframe;
- provide for an escalating penalty notice where there is continuing failure to comply – such as where a fixed penalty notice has been ignored. The penalty may be up to £10,000 per day;
- provide that a person who has received a fixed or escalating penalty notice may submit an appeal to the Pensions Regulator Tribunal against the issue of the notice and/or the amount of the penalty;
- make it a criminal offence for employers wilfully to fail to comply with specified duties. These duties are automatic enrolment, re-enrolment of eligible jobholders into an automatic enrolment scheme and the requirement to enrol jobholders into an automatic enrolment scheme at the jobholders' request;
- provide that a person who commits such an offence could face imprisonment for up to two years and/or a fine; and
- present a package of pre-employment and employment safeguards to ensure that individuals' entitlements under PA 2008 can be protected.

This package contains three key elements:

- a prohibition on employers attempting to screen out job applicants on the basis that they want to be a member of a pension scheme. The prohibition is contravened if, in an application for employment, an employer makes a statement or asks a question that indicates that the application might be conditional on whether or not an applicant might opt out of auto-enrolment. A typical example would be if it was found that a job advertisement indicated that the applicant might stand more chance of success if he was prepared to opt out of auto-enrolment;
- a prohibition on employers acting or attempting to act so as to induce employees to opt out from, or cease, membership of a qualifying workplace pension scheme. An employer contravenes this prohibition if they take any action for the sole or main purpose of inducing a worker or jobholder to give up membership of a relevant scheme, without becoming an active member of another relevant scheme. For example this protects a worker who might have been denied promotion or training opportunities because of their decision not to opt out of pension scheme membership; and

- providing employees with a range of employment rights to enable them to present a complaint to an employment tribunal if they feel they have been put at a disadvantage or dismissed as a result of their pension choices. If the tribunal upholds a claim, it can make an award of compensation to be paid by the employer to the worker.

PA 2008 Ch 5 from s 67 places a duty on the Secretary of State to establish a pension scheme.

That scheme to be a trust based occupational pension scheme tax registered under FA 2004 Pt 4 Ch 2, which will allow tax relief on pension contributions and investment returns. The scheme must be an automatic enrolment scheme in relation to any jobholder who is employed by an employer who chooses to participate in the scheme and who must be enrolled.

The scheme must require the trustees of the scheme to make arrangements for consulting the scheme members and participating employers about the ongoing operation, development and amendment of the scheme. These arrangements must include the establishment of members' and employers' panels to represent the interests of members of the scheme and participating employers.

The Secretary of State may set a maximum amount which a member of the scheme can contribute (including the employers contribution and income tax relief) in any tax year. This allows for a contribution limit of £3,600 (by reference to the level of earnings in 2005). The £3,600 figure is derived of course from the minimum contribution limit that enables even those without earnings to contribute to a personal pension scheme. For this purpose the £3,600 figure has been uprated to £4,600.

The Personal Accounts Delivery Authority's functions were to take forward the implementation work to establish the scheme described in PA 2008 Ch 5 and to work with the Pensions Regulator to create the infrastructure to enable employers to register and comply with their new duties.

This led of course to the establishment of the National Employment Savings Trust (NEST). Thus for qualifying employees employers must either pay a minimum contribution into a defined contribution scheme such as NEST or provide a minimum level of benefits from a defined benefit scheme.

This package of reforms focused on the use of auto-enrolment into workplace pension schemes, from which an individual would need to actively opt-out, to build private saving. This was combined with a minimum employer contribution, and the creation of a pension scheme – now known as the National Employment Savings Trust (NEST) – that could be used by any employer.

Regulations

[14.11] The 'final rules' governing auto-enrolment into workplace pension schemes from 2012 were laid before parliament on 12 January 2010 by then Work and Pensions Secretary Yvette Cooper.

Ms Cooper said the reforms were the most radical change to workplace entitlements since the introduction of the National Minimum Wage and the fact that employers of all size would be joining employees in paying into a pension scheme for the first time was a massive step.

The Department for Work and Pensions said the regulations have increased flexibility and removed some of the burdens that had been identified, without compromising the intentions or undermining protection for individuals such as:

- start-up businesses created from 2012 to be given until 2016 to start enrolling staff into a workplace pension arrangement;
- businesses employing 120,000 or more staff to start enrolling in October 2012, with smaller businesses phased in over a further period through to 2016; and
- phasing in employer contributions from 1% in 2012 to 2% in October 2016 and the full 3% by 2017.

The Occupational and Personal Pension Schemes (Automatic Enrolment) Regulations 2010 (SI 2010/772) set out the practical arrangements employers must make to automatically enrol eligible jobholders into a workplace pension scheme, as required by PA 2008, including the set minimum contributions.

In accordance with the primary legislation individuals who do not want to participate in pension savings have the right to opt out. The instrument also provides those people not eligible for automatic enrolment with the ability to opt into pension saving voluntarily. Where an employer operates a higher quality scheme, the Act enables the employer to postpone automatic enrolment for a period of time. This statutory instrument sets out the practical arrangements underpinning the scheme including the process and time limits for employers to achieve active membership for jobholders and the information flows required between employers, pension schemes and jobholders.

Regulations also extend the due date by which an employer must pay over employee contributions deducted from earnings to a pension scheme. By allowing the employer to keep the contributions until after the opt out period has passed, the need for the scheme to refund contributions to the employer if the jobholder opts out will be minimised.

The Employers' Duties (Implementation) Regulations 2010 (SI 2010/4) phase in the requirements on specific dates according to the description of the employer. The implementation approach has been designed to help small employers adjust to the costs of reform gradually and minimise costs to small employers during the implementation period.

The Employers' Duties (Registration and Compliance) Regulations 2010 (SI 2010/5) set out the safeguards designed to prevent an employer persuading or forcing a jobholder to opt out or leave pension saving and prevent recruitment arrangements that are intended to screen out job applicants who want to save in a pension.

The establishment of the National Employment Savings Trust (NEST)

[14.12] PA 2008 imposed a duty on the Secretary of State to establish a pension scheme, treated as if established under a permanent trust (like many other occupational pension schemes) through legislation. The aim of the scheme is to address pension saving amongst moderate to low earners who do not have access to a quality workplace pension scheme and it includes a public service obligation to accept any employer who wishes to use the scheme to fulfil their duty under the automatic enrolment requirements.

NEST is a State-established pension scheme with the following characteristics:

- it has a public service obligation, meaning it must accept all employers who apply;
- it has been established by Government to ensure that employers, including those that employ low to medium earners, can access pension savings and comply with their automatic enrolment duties; and
- it has a maximum contribution limit of £4,600 for 2014–15.

As a consequence of The National Employment Savings Trust Corporation Naming and Financial Year Order 2010 (SI 2010/3): 'The name of the body corporate referred to in section 75 of the Pensions Act 2008 shall be the National Employment Savings Trust Corporation'.

Statutory instruments and Orders of relevance are as follows.

- National Employment Savings Trust Order 2010 (SI 2010/917) — This instrument establishes the first set of rules for the scheme.
- Transfer Values (Disapplication) Regulations 2010 (SI 2010/6) – These regulations prohibit the transfer of pension funds out of NEST, except in certain circumstances relating to pension sharing on divorce.
- Application of Pension Legislation to The National Employment Savings Trust Corporation Regulations 2010 (SI 2010/8) and the National Employment Savings Trust (Consequential Provisions) Order 2010 (SI 2010/9) – these provide that certain parts of trustee legislation relating to the trustees' knowledge of the scheme and the auditing requirements will apply to the National Employment Savings Trust scheme in a modified form.
- National Employment Savings Trust Corporation Naming and Financial Year Order (SI 2010/3) – This order names the body which will run the scheme, and the Draft Personal Accounts Delivery Authority Winding Up Order 2010 winds up the Personal Accounts Delivery Authority and makes arrangements for the transfer of its property, rights and liabilities to either the National Employment Savings Trust Corporation (the NEST Corporation) or the Secretary of State.

The Personal Accounts Delivery Authority was set up on a time-limited basis to assist and advise the Secretary of State on setting up a new pension scheme and ceased to exist when NEST took over on 5 July 2010.

Coalition Government independent review

[14.13] The Coalition Government which came into power in May 2010 undertook an independent review of the above proposals which had of course been put in place by the previous Labour administration. This independent review of workplace pension reform, *Making Automatic Enrolment Work*, examined the scope of auto-enrolment policy (and as part of which, whether NEST was necessary).

As part of this, the review team undertook a consultation on the scope of reforms and looked at options for amending those reforms.

Although the Government's aim is to provide an incentive for individuals to save towards their retirement there will be something of a reliance on employee 'inertia' as has been made clear throughout this chapter.

The review document referred to above states this using the following words:

> 'The purpose of the automatic enrolment policy is to increase the numbers of people saving for their pension by ensuring that inaction on their part will lead to pension saving occurring, just as inaction at present leads to no saving.'

The review was concerned with four broad areas:

- Was there a case for excluding a substantial additional tranche of workers from automatic enrolment, for example those earning below a particular threshold or those above a certain age?
- Was there a case for excluding any group of employers, in particular the very smallest employers, from the additional responsibilities implied by the policy?
- Would any changes to the proposed regulations, implementation and details surrounding automatic enrolment enhance the policy?
- Was NEST necessary for the successful implementation of automatic enrolment and are there changes to the rules surrounding NEST which would be helpful?

The conclusions of the review and its recommendations in these broad areas were as follows.

The review argued that the proposed contribution threshold was very low, and well below the current income tax threshold. In addition, contributions were due from the first pound earned above that threshold. This would mean that people on very low earnings will as a consequence build up very small pension pots indeed, potentially damaging the credibility of the reforms. It was however also recognised that those with very small pension funds would be able to take advantage of the ability to commute those sums for a single lump sum payment rather than receive a meaningless pension.

The review proposed that people should only be automatically enrolled once they reach the income tax threshold but that contributions should be on earnings in excess of the National Insurance earnings threshold.

The review reached a similar 'no change' conclusion on whether to change the upper age threshold for automatic enrolment.

The review identified that the vast majority of employers are very small. Two thirds of employers, that is around 800,000 of them, have fewer than five employees. Very few of these had any experience of any kind associated with making pension provision available to their employees.

But the review came down against excluding small employers for three main reasons:

- to do so would exclude approximately 1.2 million employees from automatic enrolment;
- there would be substantial practical problems in enforcing boundaries. And incentives to hide or distort the number of employees could be considerable so as to prevent going over whatever threshold was set; and
- a significant disincentive to business growth would be created. The employer pension costs alone of moving from four employees to five could come to more than £1,500.

The review proposed two further major changes:

Firstly giving employers the opportunity to have a waiting period of up to three months. This would allow employers to automatically enrol their employees at any point in the first three months of their employment (although workers who wished to opt in and receive an employer contribution in this period would be able to do so).

This would avoid automatically enrolling the large numbers of workers who leave very quickly after starting employment, including many seasonal workers, and would allow employers flexibility to align enrolment dates with their own payroll and other systems. It would also allow workers more opportunity to decide whether they wanted to opt out.

Secondly automatic enrolment requires minimum contributions based on a very particular definition of pay, total pay between a floor and a ceiling. Most existing pension schemes involve contributions defined as a percentage of all basic pay without setting a lower level nor a ceiling threshold. Employers were asking for certainty over whether contributions based on these existing scheme definitions would meet the legislative requirements.

So the review recommended that any pension scheme which met one of the following criteria could be certified as meeting the requirements of being a qualifying scheme for the purposes of auto enrolment:

- a minimum 9% contribution of pensionable pay (including a 4% employer contribution);
- a minimum 8% contribution of pensionable pay (with a 3% employer contribution) provided pensionable pay constitutes at least 85% of the total pay bill; or
- a minimum 7% contribution of pensionable pay (3% employer contribution), provided that the total pay bill is pensionable.

This was seen as being consistent with the overall objective of a required contribution at the level of 8% of qualifying pay, and in what follows where the 8% level is stated then it should be taken as read that this is satisfied as a consequence of these alternative measures that were later introduced by regulation.

The review concluded that NEST would provide a pension scheme that would be appropriate to most small employers, and one which will be very easy for them to use. The review saw no alternative if automatic enrolment was to be introduced at anything like the currently envisaged scope and within the envisaged timescale.

The review argued that two particular policy variables also needed to be considered in the context of NEST.

The first being the proposed limit on contributions, set at £3,600 a year in 2005/06 terms. This was imposed in the interests of ensuring that NEST remain focused on its target market, those employers and individuals the pensions market currently finds too difficult to serve, and did not compete unfairly with the existing pensions industry. The review did not recommend any change to the cap in the short run, but did recommend that it be removed once the staging in of employers is complete.

Secondly concerning transfers: According to the review people move between employers about 11 times on average during their working lives. If they moved between employers operating different pension schemes (outside of NEST), they could easily end up with 11 or more different pension pots on retirement. Regulation can make transferring pension pots between one scheme and another difficult, and few people do in practice. The review argued that for the reforms to be truly effective it would need to be straightforward, indeed the norm, for people to move their pension pot with them as they move employer. It is in this context that the review recommended that NEST should be able to receive transfers in and pay transfers out, but only once automatic enrolment had been fully established.

Pensions Act 2011

[**14.14**] PA 2011 received Royal Assent on 3 November 2011 and included measures to implement the findings of the independent review of automatic enrolment into workplace pensions referred to above.

Among other provisions, PA 2011 makes amendments to PA 2008 and at last finalises the primary legislation for workplace pensions reform. These changes had been anticipated for more than a year after the Government accepted the findings of the *Making Automatic Enrolment Work* review in summarised above.

The major amendments introduced by PA 2011:

- raise the earnings threshold that workers will need to earn to trigger the employer duty to automatically enrol them in a workplace pension scheme. The amount will be reviewed annually and may be changed by the Secretary of State for Work and Pensions;
- introduce an optional waiting period that allows employers to defer a worker's automatic enrolment date for up to three months (but the worker can opt-in at any time during this deferral period);
- permit a new certification regime that will allow employers to certify that their pension schemes meet or exceed certain criteria; and
- provide greater flexibility for employers dealing with automatic re-enrolment by allowing them to pick a date three months either side of their re-enrolment date.

The aim of these changes was to try and introduce a degree of flexibility for employers. The three months grace period in particular will help those employers who have a high turnover of seasonal or temporary staff. There were no plans however to change the timetable for auto-enrolment.

PA 2011 also includes minor amendments that refine the automatic enrolment legislation, which will have minimal or no impacts to the overall costs or benefits of automatic enrolment. These measures concern:

- continuity of scheme membership, to clarify the duty on employers to re-enrol employees following a change to or closure of a scheme (PA 2011 s 4);
- transitional arrangements for defined benefit and hybrid pension schemes, to allow employers a choice as to whether they use these arrangements (PA 2011 s 14);
- use of a personal pension scheme so that employers may meet their employer duties, where certain conditions of defined benefit and hybrid transitional arrangements cease to apply, and the employer has chosen not to use a money purchase or defined benefit or hybrid scheme to meet that duty (PA 2011 s 15);
- power to modify occupational pension schemes, to provide that managers, as well as trustees, of schemes are to modify the scheme so that it complies with the requirements for an automatic enrolment scheme or the requirements as to payment of contributions (PA 2011 s 16);
- no indemnification for penalties and fines, to ensure that trustees or managers of pensions funds cannot take money out of scheme funds to pay for penalties and fines (PA 2011 s 17); and
- rules that govern the service of any compliance notices and documents sent by the Pensions Regulator (PA 2011 s 36).

PA 2011 also extends or modifies powers relating to automatic enrolment. These measures concern:

- extending an existing reserve power to regulate cap charges in respect of deferred members of qualifying schemes, as well as active members as the power currently provides (PA 2011 s 10);
- provisions to be made in regulations for the details of the test scheme (PA 2011 s 11); and
- a power to make regulations that would exclude from automatic enrolment individuals that fall under Cross Border Regulations (PA 2011 s 18).

Automatic enrolment earnings thresholds

[14.15] Under PA 2008 Ch 1 para 13(3):

"'earnings", in relation to a person, means sums of any of the following descriptions that are payable to the person in connection with the person's employment—

(a)   salary, wages, commission, bonuses and overtime;

(b)   statutory sick pay under Part 11 of the Social Security Contributions and Benefits Act 1992 (c. 4);

(c)   statutory maternity pay under Part 12 of that Act;
(d)   ordinary statutory paternity pay or additional statutory paternity pay under Part 12ZA of that Act;
(e)   statutory adoption pay under Part 12ZB of that Act;
(f)   sums prescribed for the purposes of this section.'

PA 2011 provides flexible powers to review the automatic enrolment earnings trigger and the lower and upper limits of the qualifying earnings band each tax year. According to the Government, the breadth of the power allows the Government to ensure that automatic enrolment continues to target the right group of individuals while carefully weighing the cost to business and the impact on the pensions industry generally.

The lower and upper limits of the qualifying earnings band were set (in 2006/07 earnings terms) in the Pensions Act 2008 at £5,035 and £33,540.

The automatic enrolment earnings trigger (the level of earnings from which people are automatically enrolled) was set at £7,475 (in 2011–12 terms) in the Pensions Act 2011. This has been set at £10,000 for 2014–15.

The lower and upper limits of the qualifying earnings band are set at £5,772 and £41,685 (2014–15) respectively. So, for example, for someone who earns £18,000 a year, the minimum percentage is based on earnings between £18,000 and £5,772, which is £12,228.

The Government is required to review these figures ahead of each tax year and, taking into account a number of factors, to decide whether or not the lower and upper limits and the earnings trigger should be changed.

The Government has retained flexibility to review the trigger and thresholds in future. For 2014–15 they mirror the personal allowance and lower and upper earnings limits for tax and national insurance respectively. But this may not be the case in future years.

Implementing auto enrolment

[14.16]   Auto-enrolment began in October 2012 and will be fully phased in by October 2018. By then every employee aged between age 22 and State pension age earning over £10,000 per year (2014–15 level) will need to be enrolled into a workplace pension scheme. There is a major reliance upon 'inertia', where people will simply be enrolled into a pension arrangement and accept the cost almost as if it were a form of additional taxation despite the right to 'opt out'.

Each employer has been allocated a date from when these new duties will apply to them known as their 'staging date'. The staging dates are spread over four years (see below). The staging dates are in The Employers' Duties (Implementation) Regulations 2010 (SI 2010/4) – albeit with a little later amendment.

The staging dates are based on the number of people in an employer's PAYE scheme. Employers with the largest numbers of workers in their PAYE schemes will have the earliest staging date.

Employers will need to:

- automatically enrol certain workers into a pension scheme;
- make contributions on their workers' behalf;
- register with The Pensions Regulator (tPR);
- provide workers with information about the changes and how they will affect them.

Staging dates

[14.17] The staging dates were set out in The Employers' Duties (Implementation) Regulations 2010 (SI 2010/4) but as later amended:

List of staging dates by PAYE scheme

PAYE scheme size

Staging date

PAYE scheme size	Staging date
120,000 or more	1 October 2012
50,000-119,999	1 November 2012
30,000-49,999	1 January 2013
20,000-29,999	1 February 2013
10,000-19,999	1 March 2013
6,000-9,999	1 April 2013
4,100-5,999	1 May 2013
4,000-4,099	1 June 2013
3,000-3,999	1 July 2013
2,000-2,999	1 August 2013
1,250-1,999	1 September 2013
800-1,249	1 October 2013
500-799	1 November 2013
350-499	1 January 2014
250-349	1 February 2014

Source: The Pensions Regulator

Staging time bands for employers with fewer than 250 persons in their PAYE scheme

[**14.18**]

	Staging date	
	From (inclusive)	To (inclusive)
50 to 249	1 April 2014	1 April 2015
Test tranche for fewer than 30	1 June 2015	30 June 2015
30 to 49	1 August 2015	1 October 2015
Fewer than 30	1 January 2016	1 April 2017
Employers without PAYE schemes	1 April 2017	
New employers who set up from April 2012 to March 2013	1 May 2017	
New employers who set up from April 2013 to March 2014	1 July 2017	
New employers who set up from April 2014 to March 2015	1 August 2017	
New employers who set up from April 2015 to December 2015	1 October 2017	
New employers who set up from January 2016 to September 2016	1 November 2017	
New employers who set up from October 2016 to June 2017	1 January 2018	
New employers who set up from July 2017 to September 2017	1 February 2018	
New employers who set up from October 2017 onwards	Immediate duty	

Source: The Pensions Regulator

Amendment to the staging dates and transitional arrangements

[**14.19**] On 25 January 2012 a written ministerial statement was released whereby:

' . . . the Government announced that the timetable for the implementation of automatic enrolment will be adjusted so that small businesses are not affected by the reforms during this Parliament . . .

. . . all employers with an existing staging date of on or before 1 February 2014 are unaffected . . .

Medium sized employers will be re-allocated automatic enrolment dates between 1 April 2014 and 1 April 2015. This means that the implementation dates of some of these employers will be up to nine months later.

. . . Small employers will be allocated automatic enrolment dates between 1 June 2015 and 1 April 2017. New employers setting up business from 1 April 2012 and up to and including 30 September 2017 will have automatic enrolment dates between, and including, 1 May 2017 and 1 February 2018.'

And:

'We propose to delay from October 2016 to 1 October 2017 the increase in the minimum rate of employer pension contributions from 1% to 2% of banded earnings. Contributions will increase to 3% from 1 October 2018.'

Transitional periods

[14.20] Regulation 5 of SI 2010/4 sets the length of the two transitional periods during which the quality requirement for UK money purchase and personal pension schemes is less than what is provided for in PA 2008 ss 20 and 26.

'For the purposes of section 29 of the Act (transitional periods for money purchase and personal pension schemes)—

(a)   the first transitional period is four years, beginning with the coming into force of section 20 (quality requirement: UK money purchase schemes); and

(b)   the second transitional period is one year, beginning with the end of the first transitional period.'

At the expiry of the two transitional periods, the quality requirement for these types of scheme will be what is provided for in PA 2008. But note the 26 January 2012 ministerial statement which delays the transitional period by a further 12 months.

Regulation 6 prescribes the length of the transitional period for defined benefits and hybrid schemes. Where the conditions in PA 2008 s 30(2) are satisfied and continue to be satisfied during that transitional period, an employer is under a duty to make arrangements for jobholders to become active members of an automatic enrolment scheme from the end of that period.

'For the purposes of section 30 of the Act (transitional period for defined benefits and hybrid schemes), the transitional period for defined benefits and hybrid schemes is four years, beginning with the day on which section 3 (automatic enrolment) comes into force.'

For ease of reference the conditions referred to in PA 2008 s 30(2) are:

' . . . that —

(a)   the jobholder has been employed by the employer for a continuous period beginning before the employer's first enrolment date,

(b)   at a time in that period before the employer's first enrolment date, the jobholder became entitled to become an active member of a defined benefits scheme or a hybrid scheme,

(c)   the jobholder is, and has always since that time been, entitled to become an active member of a defined benefits scheme or a hybrid scheme, and

(d)   the scheme to which that entitlement relates is a qualifying scheme, and any scheme to which it has related on or after the employer's first enrolment date has been a qualifying scheme.'

Transitional arrangements in summary: money purchase schemes

[14.21] For a money purchase scheme (whether occupational or personal) to be a qualifying scheme (and, therefore, an automatic enrolment scheme), the employer's and jobholder's combined contributions must eventually be at least 8%, of which the employer must pay at least 3%. Of course this means that if an employer is generous enough to pay 8% of qualifying earnings, then the employee need not contribute at all if they do not wish to do so.

However, for the first five years from 1 October 2012 (in accordance with the ministerial statement) these percentages are replaced by combined contributions of 2% of which the employer must pay at least 1%; for the year after that (1 October 2017 to 30 September 2018), they move up to 5% and 2% respectively.

From 1 October 2018, the full 8% (combined contribution) and 3% (minimum employer contribution) levels apply.

Testing contribution levels

[14.22] A money purchase scheme which uses a different earnings definition from the statutory 'qualifying earnings' definition, and which sets out different contribution rates from those stated above, can still be a qualifying scheme so long as the end effect is to reach the 3% and 8% thresholds when applied to statutory qualifying earnings.

Schemes therefore which have different rates or different earnings definitions (and wish to continue using them) will need to consider whether these will result in contribution levels that satisfy the quality requirement. This should not present a problem in those instances where the scheme's contribution rates and earnings definitions are so generous that the quality requirement will always be met or exceeded.

The more usual scenario, however, will be that such a scheme cannot be certain of reaching the statutory level of contributions in every case. In these schemes, a periodic test will need to be carried out to compare the contributions actually paid with those necessary to meet the quality requirement and, if need be, ensure that a further contribution is paid to make good the difference.

In most cases, the test will have to be carried out by reference to a 12-month period. The test should be conducted at a late enough date to make it possible to form a reliable view as to whether the statutory level over that period has been reached, and soon enough for the employer to be able to pay any further contribution that may be required promptly. The legislation does not set a clear deadline for this payment, but it is safest to pay it within the 12 months or, failing that, by the due date of the employer's final regular contribution in respect of that 12-month period.

So far as the period itself is concerned, the 12 months run from the employer's staging date and each anniversary of it. However, a shorter period will apply if the jobholder was not an active member for the whole of the 12 months concerned. This 12-month cycle may present practical difficulties for employers whose schemes have a year-end date which bears no relationship to the statutory staging date set out for them in the legislation. Employers in these circumstances may be able to address the problem by bringing their staging date forward to a date that will work better for them.

Transitional arrangements: defined benefit schemes

[14.23] Where there are defined benefit arrangements, there is scope for automatic enrolment to be delayed beyond the date when automatic enrolment would otherwise have applied to the employer concerned ('the starting date').

Where before the starting date a jobholder was entitled to become a member of a defined benefit scheme which is a qualifying scheme, then automatic enrolment can be delayed for up to four years (or until the jobholder ceases to be entitled to join that scheme or it ceases to be a qualifying scheme under the legislation).

Defaults

[14.24] In addition to the quality requirement, it is also important that the scheme does not require the jobholder to make a choice in order for him to remain a member; if he is required to make a choice, then the scheme cannot be used as an automatic enrolment scheme.

This means that a DC scheme will need to have a default investment approach and default contribution rate, and that DB schemes will need to have a default benefits structure, so that members are not required to make a decision on these points. Employers whose schemes do not already incorporate these defaults will need to address the position in advance of their staging dates.

According to DWP guidance:

> 'It is likely that the vast majority of individuals being automatically enrolled will end up in the default option. Therefore the design, governance and communication of the default option will play an important role in securing good outcomes for members.'

The default option should take account of the likely characteristics and needs of the employees who will be automatically enrolled into it. It is likely that employees in the default fund will not be engaged in financial decisions. Decisions will need to be taken for them about their risk profile. As such there should be an appropriate balance between risk and return for the likely membership profile and the charging structure should reflect this balance.

Early automatic enrolment

[14.25] To support the Government's aim of getting more people into pension saving, employers can bring forward their automatic enrolment date to an alternative specified date. This is known as early automatic enrolment.

The use of early automatic enrolment is conditional on an employer having:

- put in place a pension scheme which it considers could be used to comply with the employers' duties;
- secured agreement from the scheme that it can be used to discharge those duties from that early auto enrolment date; and
- notified The Pensions Regulator (tPR) in writing of their intention to bring forward their duty date at any time, but at least one month, before their new proposed date.

Flexible benefit schemes

[14.26] Flexible benefit schemes raise a number of possible issues.

Employers are prohibited from taking any action for the 'sole or main purpose' of inducing a worker to give up membership of a relevant scheme or opt out of an automatic enrolment scheme (without becoming a member of another such arrangement). Employers with flexible benefits schemes who annually invite workers to reconsider their arrangements do not normally have this as their 'sole or main purpose', but care should be taken to ensure that matters cannot be interpreted in that way.

If an employee does opt out for alternative benefits, this needs to be done in a way that makes it very clear that this is the individual's choice. An employer is not permitted (except at the jobholder's request) to end a jobholder's membership of a qualifying scheme.

Timing considerations will also be an issue for many employers operating flexible benefits schemes. The 2012 changes generally provide for automatic enrolment to take place on the employer's staging date (or when the individual becomes a jobholder of that employer aged at least 22 but under State pension age, if later), and for automatic re-enrolment then normally to occur at three-yearly intervals. Most flexible benefits schemes will probably find that this does not coincide with their existing time cycles. Some employers may be able to mitigate the last of these points by exercising their right to bring the staging date forward to one that works better with their existing processes.

Assessing the workforce

[14.27] Employers will need to assess their workforce to see what their duties will be in relation to each of their workers. Employers will need to provide their workers with certain information, which will be identified by this assessment. Once an employer has identified that they have a worker, the next step is to ascertain what type of worker they have. It is only in respect of certain types of workers that an employer will have duties.

There are two main categories of worker for which the employer duties apply:

- jobholders; and
- entitled workers.

The first category of jobholder then further subdivides into two groups:

- eligible jobholders; and
- non-eligible jobholders.

The employer duties therefore apply in respect of:

- eligible jobholders;
- non-eligible jobholders; and
- entitled workers.

Eligible jobholders

[14.28] Eligible jobholders are 'eligible' for automatic enrolment. These are workers who:

- are aged between 22 and State pension age;
- are working, or ordinarily working, in the UK;
- have qualifying earnings payable by the employer in the relevant pay reference period that are above the earnings trigger for automatic enrolment (currently £10,000).

Non-eligible jobholders

[14.29] Non-eligible jobholders are not eligible for automatic enrolment but can choose to opt in to a pension scheme. They are also entitled to employer contributions.

These include workers who are either:

- aged at least 16 and under age 75 working or ordinarily working in the UK, and have qualifying earnings payable by the employer in the relevant pay reference period that are above the lower earnings level for qualifying earnings (currently £5,772) but below the earnings trigger for automatic enrolment (currently £10,000); or
- aged at least 16 and under age 22, or between State pension age and under age 75, who are working, or ordinarily working, in the UK and have qualifying earnings payable by the employer in the relevant pay reference period that are above the earnings trigger for automatic enrolment.

Together, non-eligible jobholders and eligible jobholders make up the jobholders group.

Entitled workers

[14.30] Entitled workers are 'entitled' to join a pension scheme. These are workers who are aged at least 16 and under 75; are working or ordinarily working in the UK and have qualifying earnings payable by the employer in the relevant pay reference period that are below the lower earnings level for qualifying earnings currently £5,772 (2014–15).

Pension schemes that may be used for auto-enrolment

[14.31] As we have seen employers must operate one or more qualifying auto-enrolment pension schemes. These can be occupational pension schemes including DC, DB and hybrid schemes, workplace personal pension schemes and/or NEST.

Employers must automatically enrol into a qualifying auto-enrolment scheme all eligible jobholders who work or ordinarily work in the UK and who are not already active members of a qualifying scheme. Non-eligible jobholders can opt into a qualifying auto-enrolment pension scheme, if they are not already members of such a scheme and work or ordinarily work in the UK. They are entitled to contributions from the employer.

Employers who already have a pension scheme can confirm that it is suitable for automatic enrolment by a process called 'certification'. The qualifying auto-enrolment scheme may be an existing or new occupational or personal pension plan. Employers are not restricted to using a single scheme; they can use different schemes for different parts of their workforce.

Where a scheme does not meet the requirements of the statutory minimum test, employers can certify that it meets alternative quality requirements. Qualifying DB schemes may defer the start of auto-enrolment until 2016 for any existing jobholders at the staging date who have previously chosen not to join that scheme despite being eligible to do so in the past.

Criteria that schemes must meet

[14.32] Whether the scheme an employer uses for automatic enrolment is new or not, it must meet certain, specific criteria set out in the legislation.

The scheme cannot:

- impose barriers, such as probationary periods or age limits for members but there is an optional three-month window (known as 'postponement') for employers to auto-enrol joiners who are eligible jobholders;
- require staff to make an active choice to join or take other action, e.g. putting in place a requirement to sign an application form for membership or by requiring that employees give information to the scheme themselves, either prior to joining or to retain active membership of the scheme.

Each pension scheme will of course have its own rules, but all employers will need to provide the particular scheme they are operating with certain information about the individuals who are automatically enrolled. All employers will need to register with the Pensions Regulator (tPR). This will be an online process.

Every employer will have to make pension contributions to a qualifying auto-enrolment pension scheme for two groups of employees: eligible jobholders (unless they opt out) and non-eligible jobholders who opt in.

Informing employees

[14.33] Information must be provided telling employees about their right to opt in (that is in respect of non-eligible jobholders) to an automatic enrolment scheme. For those being automatically enrolled information must be provided about automatic enrolment, what it means for them, and about their right to opt out.

Opting out (PA 2008 Ch 1 para 7)

[14.34] The Department for Work and Pensions (DWP) suggests one in four of those who are eligible for auto enrolment into a pension scheme may opt out of membership. Employees who have been automatically enrolled into a pension scheme have a one-month period after their automatic enrolment during which they may choose to opt out.

The effect of opting out is that the jobholder is treated as never having been a member of the pension scheme. Any deductions made from their salary will be refunded. The worker can choose to cease membership at any time, although they may not be entitled to a cash refund of contributions after the end of the one-month opt-out period.

To opt out, workers must give notice via a document called an 'opt-out notice' to the employer. These notices will usually only be available from the pension scheme provider and not the employer, so that workers do not feel pressured into opting out as a consequence of such documentation being made available to them by their employer.

When employers receive a valid opt-out notice within the one-month period, they must pay back any contributions that have been deducted from the employee's pay. Equally, any contributions that the employer has made must be refunded to the employer by the pension scheme. There is therefore a significant reliance on inertia in maintaining scheme membership.

It is important that any worker's decision to opt out of a scheme, or stop saving for retirement altogether, should be taken freely and without influence by the employer. Employers cannot induce employees to opt out of a pension scheme. Individuals have up to six months to register a complaint if they believe that they have been 'encouraged' to opt out. Employees who do not opt out also have protection against being treated less favourably by their employer generally than employees who do opt out.

Every three years (within a six-month window) employers must re-enrol all eligible jobholders who have opted out (unless they have opted out within the previous 12 months). Once again the option to give notice to opt out comes into play.

Opting in

[14.35] As well as automatically-enrolling eligible jobholders, employers must also put certain other workers into a pension scheme, if these individuals ask.

Under PA 2008 Ch 1 para 7:

> 'The jobholder may by notice require the employer to arrange for the jobholder to become an active member of an automatic enrolment scheme.'

What the employer will need to do depends on the type of worker.

Entitled workers can opt in if they are not already members of a scheme and work or ordinarily work in the UK but do not have rights to employer contributions.

Some workers as we have seen have a right to 'opt in' to an automatic enrolment scheme and the employer is required to arrange this and make employer contributions. Others have a right to 'join' the scheme but there is no requirement on the employer to make employer contributions in respect of these workers; although the employer must set up the deduction of the worker's contributions from pay.

Changes announced on 11 October 2013

[14.36] We are at the time of finalising this edition two years into auto-enrolment and without doubt it has met with a positive response. More than 1.6 million employees have signed-up to join auto-enrolment company pension schemes.

After a consultation exercise it was announced on 11 October 2013 that several changes to the auto-enrolment rules will take effect from 1 November 2013.

The changes include:

- Extending the deadline for employers to provide information to individuals on their opt-in and joining rights from one month to six weeks.
- Alternative definitions of pay reference periods for both assessing jobholder status and determining whether a scheme is a qualifying scheme.
- Extended deadlines for registration and postponement notices fit with the extended joining window.
- An extended deadline for passing worker contributions to a pension scheme applies to all new joiners (including contract joiners).

See https://www.gov.uk/government/consultations/workplace-pensions-proposed-technical-changes-to-automatic-enrolment.

Changes to State pension age

[14.37] State Pension age will increase to 67 between 2026 and 2028. This decision was taken in the light of increasing life expectancy and will help keep the cost of state pensions sustainable.

These proposals will mean that people born after 5 April 1961 but before 6 April 1969 will have a State Pension age of 67 and people born after 5 April 1960 but before 6 April 1961 will have a State Pension age between 66 and 67.

This change to the timetable has been implemented in the Pensions Act 2014.

15

Miscellaneous changes, conclusions and what the future may hold

Introduction

[15.1] In this book we have attempted to set out in as accessible a fashion as possible how the system of pensions taxation operational in the United Kingdom works. We have seen how it was that in the period between 1970 and 2004 no less than eight different taxation regimes associated with pensions developed. These developments were often with what seemed like scant regard for the consequences of developing such a complicated set of regimes that few people understood in totality and with many inconsistencies and contradictions.

Thus when the so-called pension simplification project began in the late 1990s/early 2000s it seemed to all in the industry at that particular point in time a very welcome breath of fresh air.

As you by now know the attempt at Pensions simplification and the introduction of a single tax regime associated with pensions led to the provisions of the Finance Act 2004 and a multitude of changes and amendments in subsequent years that belie the original intention.

Arguably as we approach 2015 we have a pensions taxation framework which is no less complicated than it was previously. Even the published HMRC guidance which attempts to translate the legislation into more accessible English can on occasions seem impenetrable, although efforts are being made at the current time to improve this.

Pensions taxation, its effect on scheme design and 'unintended consequences'

[15.2] From a personal perspective when I began to work in the pensions business in the mid-1970s the norm was that employers, even small ones, tended to operate a final salary scheme. Schemes operating on a defined contribution basis were from my recollection extremely unusual except where associated with individual arrangements for company directors or senior employees. The latter were often referred to in by now defunct terms such as 'Top Hat schemes', 'Individual Pension Arrangements' and the like. These were generally insured plans usually invested on a 'with profits' basis with massively over optimistic projections of the eventual outcome.

By 1997 successive years of stock-market growth had led to a situation where many final salary schemes were in surplus. They had more assets invested in them than the present value of their liabilities. Many large employers were taking advantage of this by having 'contribution holidays'. Thus when the then Chancellor of the Exchequer (Gordon Brown) eliminated the ability of pension funds to reclaim the tax deducted at source on UK dividends it was against the backdrop of a scenario where it was felt that this would do no great harm.

With the benefit of hindsight however perhaps this was amongst the early nails in the coffin of defined benefit schemes. Now outside of the public sector most employers who still operate final salary schemes would rather that they didn't with a continuous movement away from what are perceived as 'gold plated' schemes to the uncertainty associated with defined contribution arrangements.

There also remains at the heart of policy what seems to the author as being a dogmatic approach along the lines of on the one hand being willing to reward pension savings with a reasonably generous framework of tax incentives whilst on the other hand placing restrictions on how the accumulated pension fund might be used from the perspective of investment and of benefits.

Perhaps a major lost opportunity arose when in December 2005, after the passage of the Finance Act 2004 but before its implementation in April 2006, the Government removed at a stroke the unfettered investment flexibility that the pension simplification team foresaw.

The intention was originally to allow people to invest their pension fund as they wished, including investment in assets such as residential property, works of art, antiques, stamp collections, and the like. But the dogmatists came forward and removed the viability of such possibilities by imposing tear inducing tax charges at the 70% mark which made such investment, although permitted, impossible from a practical perspective.

It seemed that policymakers could not tolerate the thought that during the period between making tax privileged pension contributions and benefiting at retirement that the pension scheme member might invest in something which might give him some form of personal enjoyment that did not suffer a sufficient burden of taxation.

Yet for many people this approach denies them the opportunity of investing (within the framework of a pension fund anyway) in areas where their personal skill and knowledge could enable them to grow a fund decent enough to allow a good standard of living in retirement, represented by an income which of course at that time would be taxed.

The meddling has continued. Any so called 'unintended' consequence of the legislation is swiftly snuffed out. How are we as practitioners supposed to know whether any particular permitted behaviour were intended or not? It may be more accurate to refer to 'unforeseen' behaviour (which the legislation permits) rather than 'unintended'. What we can be sure of however is that the cost burden of the tax privileges associated with registered pension schemes will continue to be eroded.

For example the attack on so called 'family pension plans'. The Government announced in the 2012 Budget that it would take action to prevent an existing exemption from being exploited in a way that was 'not envisaged when the legislation was introduced'.

Some employers not only offer pension plans to their employees but are also willing to make contributions to a registered pension scheme for family members as part of their employees' flexible remuneration package. In response to the lower annual allowance limits placed on the individual employee from 2011–12 onwards these types of arrangement were sometimes used to side step an income tax charge on contributions in excess of the lower then £50,000 limit, now £40,000.

Employer contributions paid into employees' registered pension schemes are deductible as an expense for corporation tax purposes so long as they meet the requirements of the wholly and exclusively test for the purposes of the employer's trade as detailed in Income and Corporation Taxes Act 1988 s 74(1)(a) and Income Tax (Trading and Other Income) Act 2005 s 34. Such contributions are also disregarded in the calculation of earnings in respect of all contributions paid by an employer to which Income Tax (Earnings and Pensions) Act 2003 s 308 (ITEPA) applies. Therefore such contributions do not attract employers' NICs (SI 2001/1004, Sch 3).

So under the pre-April 2013 legislation, a higher rate taxpayer could sacrifice some of their income and the employer would then make commensurate contributions into a family member's personal pension plan – regardless of whether they were an employee of the firm or not. The individual sacrificing their salary effectively received full tax and national insurance contribution relief, with the employer also making a saving in national insurance contributions.

Finance Act 2013 s 11 amends ITEPA s 308 to restrict the employees' exemption from income tax on pension contributions made by their employer to a registered pension scheme. This ensures that the exemption will only apply to contributions made by an employer to their employee's arrangements under a registered pension scheme, rather than contributions made to any registered pension scheme – such as that for a family member. So with effect from 6 April 2013 employees no longer enjoy exemption from income tax and national insurance on such contributions into a family member's pension scheme.

Miscellaneous changes introduced in 2013

[15.3] The 2012 budget papers included specific announcements relating to pensions tax relief and amendments which were introduced in Finance Act 2013.

Pensions tax relief – Legislation was introduced to amend the rules which allowed employers to pay pension contributions into their employees' family members' pensions as part of their employees' remuneration package to remove the tax and NICs advantages from these arrangements as detailed above.

A regulation making power was introduced by FA 2013 s 47 to allow changes to be made to the lifetime allowance fixed protection legislation. SI 2013/1740 (The Registered Pension Schemes and Relieved Non-UK Pension Schemes (Lifetime Allowance Transitional Protection) (Amendment) Regulations 2013) make amendments to the fixed protection 2012 legislation to ensure that individuals do not lose this protection inadvertently. They also ensure that an individual's UK tax relieved savings in UK and non-UK pension schemes are subject to the same qualifying conditions for the purposes of fixed protection.

Technical improvements were also made to the annual allowance rules through secondary legislation. Schedule 22 sets out the detail of the fixed protection 2014 regime, and sets out how individuals can apply for FP2014. Schedule 22 also makes a number of consequential amendments to FA 2004 relating to the reduction in the lifetime allowance.

FA 2013 s 49 introduced the new annual allowance for the tax year 2014–15 and subsequent tax years. This reduces the annual allowance to £40,000 for year 2014–15 and subsequent years.

Drawdown pensions and dependants' drawdown pensions – FA 2013 s 50 raised the maximum amount of pension income a pensioner can withdraw from a drawdown arrangement from 100% to 120% of an equivalent annuity (150% from 27 March 2014). The change applies to all drawdown pension years beginning on or after 26 March 2013.

Pensions tax: abolition of contracting out – Contracting out through a defined contribution scheme was abolished with effect from 6 April 2012. Legislation introduced in FA 2013 s 52 brings the tax legislation in line with Department for Work and Pensions legislation. The Registered Pension Schemes (Authorised Payments) (Amendment) Regulations 2013 (SI 2013/1818) amended the existing authorised payment regulations as a consequence of the abolition of contracting out for defined contribution pension schemes.

Bridging pensions – Legislation was introduced to amend the legislation associated with bridging pensions to reflect changes in state pension age. A power was created to allow for regulations to be made changing the tax rules on bridging pensions to fit with any further changes to state pension rules. FA 2013 s 51 means that pension schemes can continue to pay a bridging pension up to a member's state pension age without incurring unauthorised payment tax charges. Previously any reduction in a bridging pension had to be made by age 65, but with the increase in state pension age, this is no longer appropriate. The reduction must now be made by the time the member is 65 or reaches pensionable age whichever is later.

Qualifying Recognised Overseas Pensions Schemes (QROPS) – Changes in primary legislation were introduced in FA 2013 to strengthen reporting requirements and powers of exclusion relating to the QROPS regime. These have been described in detail in CHAPTER 9.

Where a country or territory in which a QROPS is established makes legislation or otherwise creates or uses a pension scheme to provide tax advantages that are not intended or available under the QROPS rules, the Government will act so that the relevant types of pension scheme in those countries or territories will be excluded from being QROPS.

Miscellaneous regulations introduced in 2014

[15.4] The Registered Pension Schemes and Relieved Non-UK Pension Schemes (Lifetime Allowance Transitional Protection) (Individual Protection 2014 Notification) Regulations 2014 (SI 2014/1842) – This sets out how an individual must give notice to HMRC if they intend to rely on individual protection 2014 ('IP14') to reduce or eliminate any potential lifetime allowance charge from April 2014 when the lifetime allowance for UK tax relieved pension savings was reduced from £1.5 million to £1.25 million for tax year 2014–15 onwards.

The Registered Pension Schemes (Accounting and Assessment) (Amendment) Regulations 2014 (SI 2014/1928) – This amends the Registered Pension Schemes (Accounting and Assessment) Regulations 2005 (SI 2005/3454), ('the principal Regulations') to allow HMRC to assess persons in respect of certain tax liabilities and remove the requirement for these liabilities to be included on a tax return. Section 273ZA of FA 2004 provides that regulations may be made in connection with certain non-UK schemes that hold an interest in taxable property (as defined in Part 2 of Schedule 29A to FA 2004). Regulations made under section 273ZA may make provision for the member to be liable for certain tax charges that may arise. Paragraph 19 of Schedule 7 to the Finance Act 2014 amends FA 2004 to insert new section 272C which sets out who is liable for tax charges where the Pensions Regulator appoints a new scheme administrator following an intervention.

Section 255 of FA 2004 enables HMRC to make regulations for and in connection with the making of assessments for certain prescribed tax charges. Section 255 was amended by paragraph 17 of Schedule 7 to the Finance Act 2014 to include any liability arising under new section 272C. The regulations are made under this amended power.

The Registered Pension Schemes (Provision of Information) (Amendment) Regulations 2014 (SI 2014/1843) – This amends the Registered Pension Schemes (Provision of Information) Regulations 2006 (SI 2006/567), as a consequence of the introduction of IP14. This instrument prescribes the information requirements for scheme administrators and individuals where an individual wants to rely on IP14 to reduce or eliminate a lifetime allowance charge.

The April 2015 changes and beyond

[15.5] In this section of last year's edition we said that at the time of writing we remain in what feels like a relatively quiet interlude within what are undoubtedly highly abnormal economic conditions. Not much has changed in that regard.

It is impossible not to feel that politicians will see the soft underbelly of pension funds as being a potential source of tax revenue. Indeed the April 2015 introduction of flexible access to defined contribution pension funds (see CHAPTER 4) will raise tax revenue.

From 6 April 2015 the Government expect around 130,000 people to access their pension flexibly every year with the following additional income tax arising:

2015–16	£320m
2016–17	£600m
2017–18	£910m
2018–19	£1,220m
2019–2020	£810m

And here perhaps lies the nub of the problem, politicians tend to (despite their protestations to the contrary) think rather more about the short-term – perhaps literally the period up until the next general election or at best the one after, whereas a cohesive pensions policy needs collective planning and thinking over a period of time which spans at least a generation.

Time after time we see headlines claiming how we as a community are collectively sleepwalking towards a pensions disaster. As the population ages the disaster becomes ever closer. And yet Governments still wish to meddle in order to deal with short-term needs associated with the economy as a whole whilst unwittingly doing immense damage to the long-term prosperity of a future generation of pensioners.

The Office for National Statistics (ONS) suggests that the number of people in company pension schemes is at an all-time low – the number of people in occupational pension schemes fell from 8.2 million in 2011 to 7.8 million in 2012 (the peak being 12.2 million in 1967), most of these are employed in the public sector.

Whilst auto-enrolment has celebrated its second birthday, the coming years will be much more challenging. We are all living longer and patterns of work are changing.

Increasing life expectancy is one of the many elements that continue to put pressure on final salary schemes in particular. Alongside that there is a gradual movement away from the concept of compelling retirement at a fixed chronological age. It only takes a visit into your local do-it-yourself store to become aware of the extent of those who are of an age where historically retirement from the working population would have been expected and in some instances many years ago.

In past times people could simply not afford to retire. In 1881 for example, nearly 75% of males over the age of 65 were still in work. By the 1920s this had fallen to less than 50%, and by the 1980s to around 10%. An expectation of retiring at 65 for males had been put in place by a reduction in state pension age to age 65 in 1928. The 1909 introduction of a state pension at 70 was more on financial grounds rather than any expectation that individuals were generally capable of working to that age. The reduction in state pension age for women to age 60 in 1940 has been consigned to history.

According to the Office for National Statistics (ONS) a 65-year-old can expect to live on average into their early to mid 80s. More than 95,000 people celebrating their 65th birthday in 2012 can expect to survive to receive a congratulatory message from the then Monarch on reaching 100.

Again, the ONS show that in 1981 there were 2,420 people aged over 100 in England and Wales but by 2012 this figure had soared to 12,320, a fivefold increase. Add this to the ONS figure that over one million people over the age of 65 are still in active employment. We are living longer, patterns of work are changing and, for many, retirement aspirations are simply too high.

Every now and again policymakers' eyes turn to what used to be called the tax-free lump sum which the legislation refers to as a pension commencement lump sum.

The option of taking a tax-free lump sum on retirement has been part of the pension system for many years. David Blake in 'Pension schemes and pension funds in the United Kingdom', Second Edition, 2003, p 41–2 explains its origins as follows:

'One interesting anomaly which has remained purely for historical reasons is the tax-free lump sum that is available on retirement. Civil servants were granted a lump sum on retirement in return for a lower pension thereafter as a result of the Superannuation Act of 1909. The Inland Revenue (whose civil servants could also have the lump sum) was asked whether the lump sum would be taxable, and it said that it would not be. It gave no reason for this decision, although presumably the reason was that the lump sum was a capital payment, not income, and hence not taxable (in 1909). While there is no real logic to this argument, the lump sum (where a lump sum has been permitted) has remained free of tax ever since, although there have been legislative measures to deal with the permissible size of the lump sum.'

The current treatment of the lump sum of course remains tax-free but I really do wonder how long this will last for. It would not surprise me at all if (with another echo from the past) at some stage the pension commencement lump sum remains tax-free but only up to a certain threshold and taxed beyond that at what will be claimed as being a 'concessionary rate' because it is lower than the (then) lowest rate of taxation on income.

The economic travails of the Republic of Ireland resulted in the introduction of a policy there which will surely not have gone unnoticed in the corridors of Whitehall. On 10 May 2011 the Irish Government announced that it would:

'impose a temporary levy on domestic private pension savings to fund a jobs plan aimed at cutting unemployment and aiding the economic recovery.

"The government plans to apply an annual 0.6% charge over four years on pension assets, excluding funds providing benefits to non-resident employers and members".'

Finance Minister Michael Noonan announced saying that 'the move should generate 470 million euro a year'. It will be interesting to see if this tax burden extends beyond the four-year period envisaged. For 2014 the rate of the levy has increased to 0.75%.

According to the 2010 Towers Watson survey UK the UK, the third-largest pension market after the US and Japan, has grown to US$2.3tn (£1.44trn). The UK has as about as much invested in pension funds as the value of its GDP.

The personal pension and fund management industry generally has managed to prosper with annual management charges that over the years have crept up on average to approximately 1.5% of individuals' pension funds, and in this context it is hard to think that the Government have not at the very least toyed with the idea of imposing a fund based tax charge, which ironically could have the effect of pension providers reducing their charges.

A 0.5% tax rate on UK pension funds would generate annual revenue of around £7 billion a year. About as much again as the annual effect associated with the inability of pension funds to reclaim the tax on UK source dividends.

The major development in the UK has been the introduction of auto enrolment with effect from October 2012. A welcome move given that the total number of active members of private sector occupational pension schemes fell from 6.3 million in 1991 to 2.9 million in 2010.

A reasonably detailed summary of the development of the concept of auto enrolment is contained in CHAPTER 14, and you will see that it has been over 10 years in the making. Government at last have recognised that funding towards a decent pension on the part of many requires the application of inertia where individuals are entered into a pension scheme automatically and have to make a conscious decision to opt out. A process of automatically being opted back in respect of those who do opt out takes advantage of the concept that later inertia may be prompted at the point that the associated member contributions can be readily afforded.

The auto enrolment contributions on the part of the member and on the part of the employer have been hugely watered-down again as will be apparent from CHAPTER 14. But the concept seems a sound alternative to that of requiring occupational scheme membership as a condition of employment and is certainly a big change from the 'voluntarist' approach that has been adopted for over 20 years.

Rapid reductions in annuity rates in recent years (relevant to those who have defined contribution based pensions) and the decline in membership of final salary schemes have played their part in increasing the financial pressures on those who may wish to retire from active work but simply cannot afford to do so. Around 50% of the working population no longer expect to be able to afford to retire at the age of 65 and an astonishing 20% of the working population have no pension savings put aside at all.

All told we can expect that in general people will need to work longer and save more towards their pension provision, a fairly bleak prospect for many!

Restricting income tax relief on contributions and more to come

[15.6] I remember very well speaking at various conferences in the period from late 2004 onwards when it was very clear to me that the astonishing generosity of the Government in allowing tax relieved pension contributions eventually amounting to up to £255,000 in a single year could not possibly last. I remember thinking it would last for five years and take no pleasure in not being far wrong.

Given that the top rate of income tax in the UK is now 45% (reduced from 50%) it comes as no surprise to learn that the Government have in the past been reported to be considering restricting the extent of tax relief on pension contributions.

The following is extracted from a Daily Telegraph article published on 18 June 2011 under the heading 'George Osborne plots £7bn pensions "raid" on better off':

> 'Discussions have begun at the Treasury over the move which would see the axing of tax relief currently paid out on pension contributions by people who pay income tax at the higher rates of 40 per cent and 50 per cent.
>
> The money saved could go towards cutting the budget deficit or – in what would be a more politically popular decision – be used to provide a significant increase to the value of the basic state pension.
>
> Ministers last year studied similar plans but instead decided to reduce the amount of tax-free income that savers can put into pensions. That total was cut from £255,000 to £50,000 in a move which came into force in April.
>
> However, The Telegraph understands that the plans for ending so-called "higher-rate" relief have restarted as Mr Osborne targets immediate cash flow savings as easy "wins".'

This policy is claimed to have been supported before the last general election by the Liberal Democrats.

Currently people paying into an occupational pension have their contributions deducted by their employer before tax is deducted – enabling them to get full income tax relief straightaway.

Those making contributions into a private pension – out of earned income – get immediate tax relief from the government at 20%, the basic level of income tax.

Higher-rate taxpayers can claim the difference through their tax returns or by contacting HMRC – a form of relief that surely remains under threat as we approach 2014.

Some expect an axing of higher-rate relief to be merely the first stage in a more extensive and radical plan which would end up with all tax relief – including on contributions made by people paying the basic 20p rate of income tax – being abolished, saving £22 billion a year in total.

Such a raid would be greeted with howls of protest by the pensions industry. However, experts estimate that the abolition of all tax relief on pension contributions could be used to boost the value of the basic state pension by up to half.

Although it is not the official policy of either of the Conservative Party or the Liberal Democrats the Pensions Minister has stated that he sees a logic in the tax relief on pension contributions being at a common rate of 30% irrespective of earnings. This is consistent with the recommendations of a report published by the Pensions Policy Institute in July 2013.

The Pensions Minister has further suggested that flat rate relief at this level could enable the abolition of the lifetime allowance. It will be interesting to see if this idea develops further over the next year or two as it would represent another massive form of simplification, albeit one with significant administrative difficulties. For example it may be necessary on implementation that those paying tax at more than 30% would have to pay a benefit in kind tax charge on any employer contribution. In the July 2013 analysis from the Pensions Policy Institute (PPI) referred to above it was suggested that there is 'little evidence' that the cost of tax relief on pension contributions actually encourages pension saving among low and medium earners.

Furthermore, the PPI said that pension tax relief is 'poorly understood' by savers and favours higher rate taxpayers. The report examines a range of alternative pension tax regimes, including introducing a single-rate of tax relief at 30% and capping the tax-free pension commencement lump sum to £36,000.

'Tax relief for pension saving in the UK' was sponsored by Age UK, the Institute and Faculty of Actuaries, and the TUC and can be accessed in full at https://www.pensionspolicyinstitute.org.uk/uploadeddocuments/20130715_T ax_Relief_for_Pension_Saving_in_the_UK.pdf.

In a speech at the Labour Party conference in September 2013 Shadow Chancellor Ed Balls outlined plans to restrict pension tax relief 'for the very highest earners to the same rate as the average taxpayer'.

Shadow pensions minister Gregg McClymont signalled that Labour will propose reforms of pensions tax relief before the next general election. Speaking at the September 2013 Labour party conference McClymont said the debate on the future of pensions tax relief will continue and to 'watch this space' for Labour's proposals. Watch we will indeed as we said last year, and in August 2014 we continue to do so.

Some hints have emerged:

Daily Telegraph 20 June 2014:

> 'Middle class pensioners face a £2 billion tax raid on their savings, under plans endorsed by Ed Miliband.
>
> The tax free lump sum that workers can withdraw on retirement will be capped at £36,000, under proposals being studied by the Labour leader.
>
> The move would raise £2 billion for the Treasury to be spent on funding four weeks of paid paternity leave for every new father and ensuring for a third of nursery staff are educated in childcare to degree level.
>
> . . .
>
> Ed Balls has already pledged new taxes on pension savings of 300,000 wealthier Britons.
>
> The shadow chancellor has said those earning more than £150,000 should only receive basic rate relief on their retirement savings, with the revenue spent on a work scheme that would effectively pay private firms to hire unemployed youngsters.
>
> That would mean wealthy retirees could only get tax relief of 20 per cent on their savings, compared with 45 per cent today.'

The Independent 19 June 2014:

'Labour is to consider a plan to reduce tax relief on pensions by £2bn a year by ending people's automatic right to take a quarter of their pension pot tax-free.

The move was recommended today in a blueprint for a "good society in tough times" which was launched by Ed Miliband and will heavily influence Labour's manifesto at next year's general election.

In its "Condition of Britain" report, the IPPR think tank argued that the £24bn a year spent on tax relief on pension contributions – which is worth 40 per cent for taxpayers on the 40p tax rate – "disproportionately benefits those on higher incomes rather than those who need a stronger incentive to save."

The IPPR said a review was needed because of George Osborne's sweeping pensions reforms, which will abolish the requirement to buy an annuity on retirement to provide a guaranteed annual income for life. The think tank argued that this made the tax-free lump sum "the biggest anomaly" in the pensions system, saying it costs the Government between £2.5bn and £4bn a year.

"Now that savers can withdraw all their pension pot from the age of 55 without penalty (other than paying income tax at their marginal rate), the justification for this policy is weak," said the report. "Capping the value of this lump sum at £36,000 from April 2015 would increase tax revenues by around £2bn a year." The IPPR proposed that the savings be invested in early-years support for families.

Labour has already announced plans to reduce pension relief for people earning £150,000 a year from 45 to 20 per cent to raise £1.3bn for its jobs guarantee scheme for the long-term unemployed.'

Early access?

[15.7] As mentioned in the introduction to this book the UK pension system is based on one which provides welcome tax privileges. What has evolved with that though are mechanisms, rules and restrictions that are designed to restrict those privileges in terms of when the end result (a lump sum and/or pension) may be enjoyed. For some to have to wait until they are 55 to access benefit from their pension fund is too long – serious ill-health can allow earlier access but not a prolonged period of unemployment nor the threat of repossession of the family home.

Whereas the company director can 'self invest' through having a loan from his self-administered pension scheme to his company, the self-employed and those in dire need for some reason or another have no such opportunity.

A Government discussion document on 'early access to pension funds' was rather half-hearted – a close read of it revealed no real intent and other than to meet a coalition agreement one had to wonder why it was produced at all.

The discussion paper said:

'The Government believes that any new flexibility should be considered in line with the following principles:

The purpose of tax-relieved pension saving is to provide an income in retirement;

Any change to pensions tax rules should be affordable, sustainable and maximise the value for money of Exchequer tax relief, and should not create opportunities for tax avoidance;

Any changes to pensions tax rules should not add undue complexity or place disproportionate burdens on individuals, providers, schemes, including defined benefit (DB) schemes, HMRC or others.'

Early access clearly was not going to happen. The Government later 'concluded that early access to pension savings should not be considered at the present time,' adding that 'overall there was no consensus in favour of change.' The consultation found that the risks to the sustainability of a pension outweighed the benefits of potentially persuading more people to pay into a pension fund by broadening early access rights.

But the consultation was with the pensions industry – ask the man in the street and I promise you will get a different answer.

The impact of auto enrolment introduces a fundamental reform to the UK pension system in an effort to increase the number of people in the UK saving towards a pension. As we have seen earlier there is already a process in train that will lead towards the accessibility of pension rights being linked to State pension age.

Others however have argued that some degree of earlier access could further encourage pension savings in particular amongst the young where the prospect of taking benefit at age 55 or later is so distant. Now that the genie associated with the removal of the purpose of a pension fund being to provide an income for life principle has been released from the bottle (at least where that purpose is met from within the fund) we wonder if it will end there or whether particular circumstances might allow for earlier access.

There is no doubt that in the March 2014 consultation the Government had taken note of the pensions systems operated in other countries. In the Chancellor of the Exchequer's Foreword to the 'Freedom and Choice in pensions' consultation document specific mention is made of the fact that in some other countries such as the USA, Australia and Denmark the Government does not impose restrictions on how people are able to access their pension savings at the point of retirement. These are not the only jurisdictions where such freedom is available. The Republic of Ireland, Jersey and New Zealand are additions to this list that immediately come to mind.

For those who have accumulated what to them are reasonable sums in pension funds it must be galling that in times of acute need there is no possibility of earlier access before (currently) age 55 unless subject to a 55% tax charge and a deregistration risk so far as the scheme itself is concerned in permitting such an unauthorised payment.

These issues are dealt with elsewhere by allowing earlier access subject to constraints as to quantum, on the grounds of financial hardship or, as in the case of New Zealand Kiwi saver schemes to assist in first-time house purchase. The early access argument is clearly a trade-off between making pension savings more attractive whilst discouraging practices which could leave insufficient funding available to provide a decent income in retirement.

Other countries instead of allowing a degree of early access based upon permanent withdrawal allow for loans from the member's pension pot. This example is permitted within the section 401(k) model for pension savings in the USA. Many 401(k) arrangements allow early access options in the form of loans and hardship withdrawals and it is left to individual providers to decide whether such options will be offered. Loans from 401(k) accounts are not taxed but the capital must be repaid with interest within five years although loans taken to assist in house purchase can be repaid over up to 15 years. Permanent hardship withdrawals are permitted but where taken are taxed as income plus an additional 10%.

As it is up to the individual 401(k) provider as to whether or not they offer such a facility it has been possible to establish whether or not those offering such facility attract higher contribution levels. This has in practice been the case with such arrangements receiving contributions which can be higher on average by up to 3% of participant's remuneration.

Perhaps a model which allowed for loans from defined contribution pension funds which have to be repaid within a specific period with interest (from which the fund benefits) where failure to repay or permanent withdrawals would result in an income tax charge is something which many would find highly attractive.

Borrowing from financial institutions would become possible based upon the ability of early access to facilitate loan repayment at age 55 or later if it was permitted for a lender to take some form of security over a defined contribution fund. In any event some lenders may be willing to lend on an interest only basis in order to allow people to invest in residential property for example whilst taking a charge on the property in the usual way and in the knowledge that the means of repayment through defined contribution pension fund cash access is in place.

Early access was extensively debated in a House of Lords Pensions Bill committee session in June 2008. It was then stated that in the Government's view early access would not be consistent with the key policy objective of increasing pension savings because 'tax relief on pension contributions is provided so people can save for an income in retirement, not for other purposes'. Well that all changes as we have seen from April 2015.

We wonder whether this entire subject is one that may therefore be revisited at some stage. Allowing some form of earlier access may for example reduce the opt out rate associated with auto enrolment.

Some studies suggest that allowing early access to pension savings could encourage people to contribute higher percentages of their income to pension provision even if they do not necessarily intend to withdraw funds earlier. As stated above this has been the experience of 401(k) schemes in the USA. Knowing that an early access option is available might incentivise those who would otherwise save in an alternative savings vehicle to invest in a defined contribution pension arrangement instead.

Arguably however the recent increase in the ISA contribution limit to £15,000 from July 2014 provides a savings alternative where ready access is available. This could form the basis of a 'feeder fund' where individuals accumulate savings in an ISA without the benefit of tax relief using the accumulated fund to feed pension contributions in the future when it becomes apparent that early access to the capital for other purposes is not going to be required.

And in extremis?

[15.8] The ultimate would be policy which was tantamount to state confiscation – at least in part. This would be the effect for example of a compulsion for pension funds to invest a percentage of their assets in Government issued securities. It has happened in other countries.

It is pretty hard to envisage this actually happening in the UK but on the other hand an awful lot has happened in the last few years which no right minded person would have considered remotely possible 20 years ago.

Conclusion

[15.9] The United Kingdom does seem these days to be a follower rather than a leader in pensions reform. The principle of auto enrolment for example has been in place for many years in Australia and New Zealand. The concept of flexible access to pensions savings from pension age has been present in some other countries for some years.

No doubt we will continue to see more and ongoing restrictions. It seems to me that the first steps have already been taken down a path that may eventually lead to basic rate tax relief alone on pension contributions made by individuals or at some composite flat rate.

The tax leakage associated with pension contributions has now been addressed through the restricted annual allowance. If restrictions on the tax relief were associated with a dismantling of the complexity and greater flexibility for scheme members (for example being able to use pension rights as security for a loan from a mainstream bank to deal with financial distress, house purchase or whatever) then I think that the majority of pension scheme members would welcome this. However it would not surprise me at all if we end up with a different scenario of less tax relief and more restrictions. It is time for the short-termism to come to an end and for a long-term system associated with fairness and certainty to be put in place and not to be met with. Time for another go at 'pensions simplification' perhaps?

Appendix 1

Pension and lump sum rules

The purpose of this appendix is to set out in one place for ease of reference the pension and lump sum rules as set out in Finance Act 2004.

The pension rules are to be found in Finance Act 2004 s 165 (with further explanation in Schedule 28) – comments are in square brackets, and later amendments are noted as appropriate.

Pension rule 1

'No payment of pension may be made before the day on which the member reaches normal minimum pension age, unless the ill-health condition was met immediately before the member became entitled to a pension under the pension scheme.'

[Normal minimum pension age was 50 until 5 April 2010, and 55 thereafter. There are earlier than normal permitted minimum pension ages for those in occupations that traditionally retire earlier]

Pension rule 2

'If the member dies before the end of the period of ten years beginning with the day on which the member became entitled to a scheme pension, an annuity or alternatively secured pension, payment of the scheme pension, annuity or alternatively secured pension may continue to be made (to any person) until the end of that period.

But no other payment of the member's pension may be made after the member's death.'

[This rule changed with effect from 6 April 2011 as a consequence of the abolition of the alternatively secured pension, and its replacement by flexible drawdown and capped drawdown. It will further change from April 2015 when the ten-year limitation on the guarantee period is removed]

Pension rule 3

'No payment of pension other than a scheme pension may be made in respect of a defined benefits arrangement.'

[As a consequence if a defined benefit scheme member wishes for example to enter into flexible or capped drawdown, or to establish a flexi-access drawdown fund from April 2015, it is necessary first to transfer into a personal pension type of arrangement]

Pension rule 4

'If the member has not reached the age of 75, no payment of pension other than—

(a)   a scheme pension,
(b)   a lifetime annuity, or
(c)   unsecured pension,

may be made in respect of a money purchase arrangement; but a scheme pension may only be paid if the member had an opportunity to select a lifetime annuity instead.'

[The age 75 restriction in this rule disappeared with effect from 6 April 2011 – and the term unsecured pension was replaced by the two forms of drawdown – capped and flexible]

Under the provisions of Finance Act 2011 (Schedule 16) the rule becomes:

'no payment of pension other than—

(a)   a scheme pension,
(b)   a lifetime annuity, or
(c)   drawdown pension,

may be made in respect of a money purchase arrangement; but a scheme pension may only be paid if the member had an opportunity to select a lifetime annuity instead.'

Pension rule 5

'The total amount of unsecured pension paid in each unsecured pension year in respect of a money purchase arrangement must not exceed 120% of the basis amount for the unsecured pension year.'

[With effect from 6 April 2011 unsecured pensions were replaced by the forms of drawdown, where capped drawdown applied the limit became 100% of the basis amount and reverted to 120% from March 2013, where flexible drawdown applies there is no limit associated with this rule]

So under the provisions of Finance Act 2011 (Schedule 16) the rule became:

'The total amount of drawdown pension paid in each drawdown pension year in respect of a money purchase arrangement must not exceed 100% (and is now 150%) of the basis amount for the drawdown pension year'

Pension rule 6

'If the member has reached the age of 75, no payment of pension other than—

(a)   a scheme pension,
(b)   a lifetime annuity, or
(c)   alternatively secured pension,

may be made in respect of a money purchase arrangement; but a scheme pension may only be paid if the member had an opportunity to select a lifetime annuity instead.'

Under the provisions of Finance Act 2011 (Schedule 16) this rule is omitted.

Pension rule 7

'The total amount of alternatively secured pension paid in each alternatively secured pension year in respect of a money purchase arrangement must not exceed 70% of the basis amount for the alternatively secured pension year.'

Under Finance Act 2011 (Schedule 16) this rule is omitted.

Lump sum rules

The lump sum rules are to be found in section 166 Finance Act 2004 – comments are in square brackets. The meanings of these lump sums are to be found in Finance Act 2004 schedule 29.

'No lump sum may be paid other than—

(a)   a pension commencement lump sum, [Under Finance Act 2011 this can now be paid after age 75]

(b)   a serious ill-health lump sum, [Following Finance Act 2011, if this benefit is paid beyond age 75 it is taxed at 55%]

(c)   a short service refund lump sum,

(d)   a refund of excess contributions lump sum,

(e)   a trivial commutation lump sum, [may also now be payable beyond age 75]

(f)   a winding-up lump sum, or

(g)   a lifetime allowance excess lump sum.'

A further form of lump sum, the stand-alone lump sum, arises when it is possible because of pre- 6 April 2006, transitional protection provisions, it is possible for all of the registered pension scheme members fund to be taken as a lump sum.

As a consequence of the protection of lump sum rights exceeding £375,000 for those with primary protection a monetary amount of lump sum is protected. So it may be possible in these circumstances for the member for take all the benefits as a stand-alone lump sum.

Appendix 2

Pension Death benefit rules and Lump sum Death benefit rules

The purpose of this appendix is to set out in one place for ease of reference the pension death benefit rules as set out in Finance Act 2004, as amended.

These rules are to be found in Finance Act 2004 ss 167 and 168 (Schedule 29 should also be referred to) – comments are in square brackets.

Pension death benefit rule 1

'No payment of pension death benefit may be made otherwise than to a dependant of the member.'

Pension death benefit rule 2

'No payment of pension death benefit other than a dependants' scheme pension may be made in respect of a defined benefits arrangement.'

Pension death benefit rule 3

'If a dependant has not reached the age of 75, no payment of pension death benefit to the dependant other than—

(a)   a dependants' scheme pension,
(b)   a dependants' annuity, or
(c)   dependants' unsecured pension,

may be made to the dependant in respect of a money purchase arrangement; but a dependants' scheme pension may only be paid if the member or dependant had an opportunity to select a dependants' annuity instead.'

[The age 75 provision is irrelevant with effect from 6 April 2011. Dependants' unsecured pension is replaced by dependants' drawdown pension. Dependants' flexi-access drawdown will be applicable from April 2015]

Pension death benefit rule 4

'The total amount of dependants' unsecured pension paid to a dependant in each unsecured pension year in respect of a money purchase arrangement must not exceed 120% (now 150%) of the basis amount for the unsecured pension year.'

[With effect from 6 April 2011, dependants' unsecured pension is replaced by dependants' drawdown pension which, as in the case of the members' own drawdown pension is in two possible forms capped or flexible, with the same provisions applying. Dependants' flexi-access drawdown will be applicable from April 2015]

Pension death benefit rule 5

'If a dependant has reached the age of 75, no payment of pension other than—

(a)   a dependants' scheme pension,
(b)   a dependants' annuity, or
(c)   dependants' alternatively secured pension,

may be made to the dependant in respect of a money purchase arrangement; but a dependants' scheme pension may only be paid if the member or dependant had an opportunity to select a dependants' annuity instead.'

[This rule has no effect beyond 6 April 2011.]

Pension death benefit rule 6

'The total amount of dependants' alternatively secured pension paid to a dependant in each alternatively secured pension year in respect of a money purchase arrangement must not exceed 70% of the basis amount for the alternatively secured pension year.'

[This rule has no effect beyond 6 April 2011.]

Lump sum death benefit rule

'No lump sum death benefit may be paid other than—

(a)   a defined benefits lump sum death benefit, [Finance Act 2011 allows for this to be payable beyond age 75 but on payment of such a lump sum beyond age 75, 55% tax will apply, but the 55% rate is under review]

(b)   a pension protection lump sum death benefit, [this lump sum can only be provided where the member was in receipt of a scheme pension from a defined benefits arrangement and on death after 5 April 2011 is taxed at 55%, but the 55% rate is under review]

(c)   an uncrystallised funds lump sum death benefit,

(d)   an annuity protection lump sum death benefit, [on death after 5 April 2011 tax at 55% will apply, but the 55% rate is under review]

(e)   an unsecured pension fund lump sum death benefit, [this now becomes a drawdown pension fund lump sum death benefit and tax at 55% applies, but the 55% rate is under review]

(f)   a charity lump sum death benefit, [the tax-free status of this benefit continues to apply]

(g)   a transfer lump sum death benefit, [this was abolished following the abolition of the alternatively secured pension]

(h)   a trivial commutation lump sum death benefit, [the whole lump sum is taxable as pension income of the dependant]

(i)   a winding-up lump sum death benefit.' [abolished from 6 April 2015]

[The whole lump sum is taxable as pension income of the dependant]

Appendix 3

Pension schemes, VAT and Stamp Duty Land Tax

Introduction

Most occupational schemes are set up under trust deed and the appointed trustees control the funds which are invested in order to provide for the members' benefits in accordance with the scheme rules.

Each party (the employer and the trustees) has separate responsibilities, duties and activities, and needs to consider their own ability to treat VAT incurred as input tax. In addition the operation of running a pension scheme involves engaging various professional services (for example, solicitors, fund managers, actuaries), who will be registered for VAT and who allowed VAT when invoicing the scheme.

It can sometimes be difficult to decide to which person these services are supplied, that is to the employer who sponsors the scheme or to the scheme trustees. In addition to the traditional trust based scheme mentioned above an employer may provide pensions to his employees by means of:

- an insurance based scheme whereby benefits are secured through an insurance policy – to insure lump sum benefits and dependants' pensions for example;
- an 'unfunded' scheme where no specific funds are set aside to pay pensions; or
- a scheme where the employer makes provision for the payment of pensions by a segregated reserve fund in the balance sheet, represented by specific assets.

In these cases the normal VAT rules apply, that is supplies are made to the employer and input tax is claimable in the usual way subject to any necessary partial exemption restrictions.

Where the employer makes VAT exempt supplies the amount of input tax which may be deducted may be restricted. The entitlement is to deduct the input tax incurred on costs that are used in making taxable supplies. It is not normally possible to deduct input tax incurred on costs that relate to exempt supplies. If input tax relates to both taxable and exempt supplies, it is normally possible only to deduct the amount of input tax that relates to taxable supplies.

The management of a company pension scheme is a part of the business's normal activities So if the employer is VAT registered, and sets up a pension fund for its employees under a trust deed, the VAT incurred in both setting up the fund and on its day-to-day management is the employer's input tax. This applies even where responsibility for the general management of the scheme rests (in accordance with the terms of the trust deed) with the trustees, or where the trustees pay for the services supplied.

Management costs and investment costs

A distinction is made between 'management costs' and 'investment costs'.

Except where the sponsoring employer is the sole trustee of the pension fund the fund itself is not a part of the employer's business activities. So when the trustees make investments, acquire property and collect rents from property holdings, etc. these activities are quite separate from the employer's business. It follows that VAT incurred in carrying on investment activities is not the employer's input tax even if the employer pays such expenses on behalf of the pension trust.

The employer may however act as sole trustee of its pension fund and, in this case, any activities carried on, or supplies made by the fund, will be made by the employer. In this case the employer will be entitled to treat all tax incurred on supplies received in connection with the fund as input tax.

Management services giving rise to input tax

The VAT registered employer as the pension scheme sponsor can claim as input tax:

- VAT incurred in making arrangements for setting up a pension fund;
- VAT incurred in the management of the scheme, that is for example the collection of contributions and payment of pensions;
- VAT incurred in receiving advice relating to the scheme and in implementing changes to it;
- VAT incurred in accountancy and auditing relating to the management of the scheme, such as preparation of the annual scheme accounts;
- VAT incurred in obtaining an actuarial valuation;
- VAT incurred in receiving actuarial advice connected with the fund;
- VAT incurred in receiving statistical information in connection with the performance of a the fund's investments or properties; and
- VAT incurred associated with legal costs, general legal advice, including drafting trust deeds etc.

Investment services which do not give rise to input tax

The VAT registered employer as the pension scheme sponsor cannot claim as input tax VAT incurred in respect of:

- advice connected with making investments;
- stockbroker charges and fees,
- rent, and service charge collection in respect of property holdings;
- the production of records and accounts in connection with property purchases, lettings etc;
- trustee services, that is the cost of engaging services of a professional trustee in managing the assets of the fund;
- custodian charges.

This inability to avoid incurring input tax in full is currently the subject of a dispute which is summarised later.

How this operates where a third party manages the scheme

A fund manager, property manager or professional trustee may be appointed to manage the pension scheme and usually their charges will cover both management as well as investment services associated with the pension scheme.

In this case the employer is required to apportion the input tax on their services because only the tax connected with the management of the scheme may be treated as the employer's input tax.

However if the supplier issues only one inclusive invoice for both kinds of services the employer may be able to treat 30% of the VAT charged as input tax – but see below. If on the other hand the employer does not consider that this correctly reflects the proportion of the supply attributable to management, and wishes to claim a higher proportion, they will have to provide evidence to support this.

The third party manager may themselves apportion their supply between investment and management services and issue separate invoices – in which case the employer should treat the whole of the tax incurred on 'management' services as input tax.

HMRC and the '30/70' rule

HMRC was concerned that in some cases the 30:70 split referred to above is applied even where fund managers provide a low value or no administrative services to the employer.

There has therefore been modification as follows:

(1) Third parties in providing both investment and administration services, who are able to determine the actual values of each, must provide separate invoices to employers and trustees showing the actual value of services provided;

(2) Where third parties are genuinely unable to determine separate values for their supplies the continued application of the 30:70 split will be permitted, but only where the third parties are administering the pension scheme fully or providing the bulk of the administration of the scheme;

(3) Where third parties do not administer fully or the bulk of the administration of the scheme, employers will be required to agree with HMRC a fair and reasonable apportionment that is 'robust, transparent and able to be tested'; and

(4)   An apportionment must also be agreed with HMRC in the unlikely event that employers consider that the administration work performed by a third party amounts to more than 30% of the total services provided.

How VAT works where the pension scheme provides benefits for the employees of more than one employer

Note that this paragraph does not apply where employers are members of the same VAT group registration

Some pension schemes provide pension benefits for the employees of several employers who may have a commercial link or may in fact be entirely separate from each other – for example an industry wide scheme. In such cases each employer can only treat as input tax that proportion of the management services associated with their own employees.

Where the provider of management services to the fund issues a single invoice to one of the employers the recipient employer may act as 'paymaster' and treat all the VAT on management services as input tax provided they recharge each of the other employers with their share of the costs plus VAT. A person acting as paymaster must issue a VAT invoice to each of the respective employers who, in turn, can treat the tax as their input tax.

Ceasing to trade

If the employer ceases trading, by definition they no longer have any entitlement to input tax on the management of the pension scheme. Where, however, the pension scheme trustees are themselves VAT registered they may treat the tax incurred on services connected with the continuing management of the scheme as their input tax, subject to the normal rules. This means that where the trustees are required to restrict recovery of input tax because they make exempt supplies not all the tax on the management services may be recovered.

Trustees and claiming input tax

A pension fund has no legal status in itself being represented by its trustees. If the trustees make taxable supplies, for example following an election to waive VAT exemption in relation to supplies of property, they must consider whether they need to be VAT registered. Guidance is available from HMRC in this regard.

If the pension fund is VAT registered the trustees can treat as input tax VAT incurred on goods and services used. VAT incurred on supplies connected with the management of a pension scheme is normally not counted as input tax as these supplies are regarded as being the responsibility of the scheme sponsoring employer. In making exempt supplies the trustees' recovery of input tax may be restricted.

Disputes regarding investment management services and VAT

A dispute over whether occupational defined benefit (DB) pension schemes should have to pay VAT on investment management services was referred to the European Court of Justice (ECJ).

The challenge against HM Revenue & Customs (HMRC) was brought by the National Association of Pension Funds (NAPF) and the £6bn multi-employer Wheels Common Investment Fund (WCIF) together with its underlying Ford pension schemes.

If the legal challenge had been successful, pension schemes would have been entitled to claim back at least £300m in VAT paid over the past three years, but might also be able to apply for refunds of tax paid in previous years. An adverse ruling would cost the Treasury £100m annually in the future.

The legal action, which started in 2008, followed a European ruling that investment trusts had special status and should not pay VAT on investment management services. Under European Union law, certain investment funds are entitled to claim exemption from VAT on management fees. However, member states are given some latitude to decide which type of funds are covered by the law and the UK had until recently restricted the exemption to unit trusts and open-ended investment companies (OEICS).

The action was initiated following a ruling in the European Court on JP Morgan Fleming Claverhouse Investment Trust plc. The Court stated then that investment trusts were special investment funds and should be exempt from paying VAT on investment management services. The NAPF and WCIF brought the case because they believed that pension funds have similar characteristics and should have a similar exemption.

The NAPF claimed that the same benefits should also be offered to final salary pension schemes which, like investment trusts, unit trusts and OEICS, have segregated investments managed by asset managers. Most other pension schemes already qualify for the VAT exemption, because they typically access investment management through unit trust and OEIC structures, or via insurance products that are also exempt. Pension schemes' VAT bills are significant because the tax charge is payable at the full 20% rate on investment management fees.

The Court of Justice of the European Union (CJEU) ruled in March 2013 that UK workplace DB pension funds are not special investment funds and are therefore not exempt from paying VAT on investment management services.

The judgment meant that pension schemes will continue to pay about £100m a year in VAT and will not be able to make backdated claims to 1990 that could have totalled £2bn.

However in March 2014, Danish pension provider ATP won its case against its tax authority over whether occupational defined contribution (DC) management costs should be exempt from VAT charges, in a ruling by the European Court of Justice (ECJ).

Following the advice of its Advocate General, the ECJ ruled that DC schemes, under certain conditions, can be classed as special investment funds (SIFs), thus exempting the management costs from VAT.

ATP, which administers DC pension funds in both investment and administration, mainly for Pension Danmark, challenged its tax authority, Skatteministeriet, suggesting it should not be charging its clients VAT for its services.

This was based on the notion that DC funds, unlike DB schemes, shared enough characteristics with UCITS funds and SIFs to receive similar tax treatment.

In a landmark ruling for the DC industry, the ECJ has agreed with this view and said ATP should not be charging VAT to its clients for investment and administrative services. This also includes the cost of payment services it provides to scheme members.

The Court, however, placed certain conditions on DC schemes for this VAT exemption, centralised around risk sharing between the member and employer.

In his opinion to the Court late last year, the Advocate General, Pedro Cruz Villalón, concluded that DC funds do share characteristics with UCITS funds and fulfil the purpose of the directive's original exemption. As the Court's highest adviser, he said that the VAT exemption applied to UCITS and SIFs in general must also apply to occupational DC funds, where pooled assets are spread over a range of securities. However, he stipulated it should only be the case where the beneficiary, and owner of the assets, bears all the risk of the investment, as is the case in pure-DC funds.

This was always the key debating point in previous challenges over occupational pension schemes paying VAT on management costs.

In the previous case referred to above brought by the Wheels Common Investment Fund, backed by the UK's National Association of Pension Funds (NAPF), the ECJ ruled in favour of the UK tax authority and said DB schemes could not be exempt from VAT, as the beneficiary neither owns the assets, nor bears all the investment risk.

In the ATP ruling, the Court said member states should exempt VAT on DC funds without prejudice, providing said funds meet certain criteria.

It listed the following charges to be exempt: 'Transactions, including negotiation, concerning deposit and current accounts, payments, transfers, debts, cheques and other negotiable instruments, but excluding debt collection and factoring and management of special investment funds as defined by member states.'

The win for ATP brings to a close a number of cases between tax authorities and occupation pension schemes and sponsors.

In a landmark ruling for DB scheme sponsors, Dutch company PPG won its case against the Dutch government, with the ECJ ruling that companies that pay for investment management costs of DB schemes should also be exempt from VAT charges.

VAT and property investment

Many properties are subject to VAT, meaning VAT at currently 20% must be added to the purchase price when calculating the funding for a pension scheme property purchase. Normally vendors will have 'opted to tax' the building or land being sold. By 'opting to tax' the vendor must charge VAT on top of the sale price, unless the sale includes the rights to sub leases in place. Then the sale is known as a Transfer of Going Concern (TOGC).

The reason why a TOGC is preferred by a purchaser is that they will not have to pay any VAT on the purchase (giving a cash flow saving) and also there is a stamp duty saving (if applicable), because stamp duty is payable on the VAT inclusive price of the building.

If the purchaser is a SIPP or a SSAS it can register for VAT and reclaim any VAT paid on the property purchase. However this may create a cashflow issue as the reclaim can take several months to be repaid. If a SIPP or a SSAS is purchasing a TOGC it can register for VAT and 'opt to tax' the purchase before exchange of contracts resulting in no VAT being charged on the purchase price.

Where the pension scheme is registered for VAT, it must then be charged on the rent paid to the pension scheme, and quarterly VAT returns submitted to account for this (less any VAT charged on property repairs and expenses).

It is possible for the pension scheme to register for VAT online via the HMRC website. VAT returns are then also online, and VAT liability paid by direct debit on the pension scheme's bank account. Where this applies in relation to a self invested personal pension scheme, it is therefore advisable to have a separate property rental bank account from which the direct debits are taken.

It is possible for more than one SIPP to acquire a stake in a particular property (subject to any borrowing restriction linked to fund value). That being so, such investments are usually via a Limited Liability Partnership ('LLP') which would itself register for VAT. Each of the investing SIPPs would have a stake in the LLP, which might also include private investors.

If investment in commercial property is via a LLP there would be no benefit in registering the SIPP for VAT as the LLP would itself be registered if it wished to reclaim VAT or purchase a TOGC.

At the point of completion, the solicitor will arrange for payment of the VAT, and will request sufficient funds to cover this when providing the completion statement.

Stamp duty Land Tax

It is essential that Stamp Duty is included in the purchase price when calculating the required funding of a pension scheme property purchase, and applies to commercial property transactions exceeding £150,000 unless the annual rent exceeds £1,000.

The tax rate applied for commercial properties in 2014–15 is as follows:

Up to £150,000 and annual rent less than £1,000 – 0%;

Up to £150,000 and annual rent over £1,000 – 1%;

Over £150,000 to £250,000 – 1%;

Over £250,000 to £500,000 – 3%;

Over £500,000 – 4%.

Appendix 4

Benefit crystallisation events from registered pension schemes

Introduction

The concept of 'benefit crystallisation' was, in terms of its introduction in Finance Act 2004, entirely new.

In the period before 6 April 2006 benefits were payable from pension schemes of whatever type in particular circumstances (for example on retirement or on death).

Legislation and the so-called 'practice notes' (IR12 in relation to occupational pension schemes and IR76 in relation to personal pension schemes) set out the limits associated with benefits and timing of same so as to be consistent with the discretionary approval of pension schemes by HMRC as then applied.

The application of benefit crystallisation events

An individual may have several benefit crystallisation events throughout their working life. The benefit crystallisation framework is designed to make sure that the lifetime allowance applied to the total of an individual's benefits across all registered schemes.

Benefit rules set out the circumstances in which authorised payments may be settled from a registered pension scheme. These events will also trigger a test against the lifetime allowance, arising from benefit crystallisation and if the lifetime allowance is exceeded (bearing in mind the existence of primary protection and enhanced protection) taxation charges ensue.

This is clear from the legislation set out at Finance Act 2004 s 214 which states:

'A charge to income tax, to be known as the lifetime allowance charge, arises where:
- (a) a benefit crystallisation event occurs in relation to an individual who is a member of one or more registered pension schemes, and
- (b) either the first lifetime allowance charge condition or the second lifetime allowance charge condition is met.

(2) The first lifetime allowance charge condition is that—
- (a) the whole or any part of the individual's lifetime allowance is available on the benefit crystallisation event, but
- (b) the amount crystallised by the benefit crystallisation event exceeds the amount of the individual's lifetime allowance which is available on the benefit crystallisation event.

(3) The second lifetime allowance charge condition is that none of the individual's lifetime allowance is available on the benefit crystallisation event.'

For an individual who has been a member of only one registered scheme and for whom all benefits are paid at the same time (either on death or retirement), the comparison against the lifetime allowance will be fairly straightforward.

But, where an individual takes benefits in stages whether from one or more registered schemes, the latter allowance test becomes more complicated. Each benefit crystallisation event uses up some of the individual's lifetime allowance, leaving less against which the remaining benefits can be tested.

The set of benefit crystallisation events

The benefit crystallisation events (BCEs) and how the lifetime allowance test is dealt with are set out in Finance Act 2004 s 216 alongside Schedule 32 to the Act.

There are currently 11 different BCEs, following the addition of BCE5B from 6 April 2011.

The circumstances where these may apply are described below together with how the test against the lifetime allowance then takes place:

BCE 1. When funds are designated to provide an unsecured pension (see note below) for the registered pension scheme member. Designation may be based on a member decision, or occur automatically when a member with uncrystallised funds in a money purchase arrangement reaches age 75.

Valuation is based on the size of the fund designated for this purpose, which is then tested against the member's remaining lifetime allowance.

Note – Finance Act 2011 replaced the concepts of 'unsecured' (and indeed 'alternatively secured' pensions) with the concept of a 'drawdown' pension.

BCE 2. Commencement of a scheme pension.

Valuation is determined by the amount of the scheme pension multiplied by a 'valuation factor'. The valuation factor remains as originally set out in Finance Act 2004 as a multiple of 20, (unless there has been an agreement between HMRC and the pension scheme Administrator that a higher valuation factor should apply).

BCE 3. When a scheme pension, being already in payment, increases above a permitted level.

The permitted level of increase for this purpose is 5% per annum, or retail prices index if less – and a valuation is determined by adopting a multiple of 20, unless the circumstances set out in BCE2 above apply. Increases of up to £250 are ignored.

Finance Act 2008 introduced retrospective changes to BCE3 so that they were deemed to take effect from 6 April 2006. Where a registered pension scheme provides an increase to all scheme pensions in payment (although not necessarily any dependants' scheme pensions in payment) above the permitted margin, BCE 3 would not be triggered if the scheme in question has 50 or more pensioner members who are in receipt of a scheme pension or dependants' scheme pension.

Any scheme where there are at least 50 pensioner members, and at least 20 of those pensioner members are receiving increases to their scheme pension at the same rate, will be exempt from BCE3, regardless of the size of the increase or whether or not the increase applies to all pensioners under the scheme. However, if an individual who has two such pension increases in a 12-month period, where the second increase was included in a different group of pensioners from the first, and this was specifically to allow the increases to become exempt, then the subsequent increase will not be exempt from the BCE test.

BCE 4. Commencement of a lifetime annuity.

Valuation is represented by the lifetime annuity purchase price.

BCE 5. When a member of a defined benefit scheme reaches age 75 with uncrystallised benefits remaining in the scheme.

Valuation is based upon the amount of income that could be secured at age 75 multiplied by a valuation factor of 20, plus any additional lump sum.

BCE 5A. A member reaches age 75 with an unsecured pension fund. Note however that Finance Act 2011 replaced the concepts of 'unsecured' (and indeed 'alternatively secured' pensions) with the concept of a 'drawdown' pension. Individuals who commenced drawdown (unsecured pension) before 6 April 2006 are exempt from BCE 5A in respect of the funds that were placed into drawdown at that time.

Finance Act 2011 inserted:

BCE 5B

"The individual reaching the age of 75 when there is a money purchase arrangement relating to the individual under any of the relevant pension schemes". The valuation to be "The amount of any remaining unused funds".

From 6 April 2011, the requirement to secure pension benefits at age 75 by purchase of an annuity or designation of any uncrystallised pension funds as a drawdown pension ceased. BCE5B was introduced to cater for members wishing to retain their uncrystallised funds after age 75. BCE5B takes place when the member reaches age 75 and (apart from BCE3) no other BCE will take place when benefits are crystallised at a later date, or on the member's death.

BCE 6. Payment of lump sums. As set out in schedule 32 Finance Act 2004:

'For the purposes of benefit crystallisation event 6 a lump sum is a relevant lump sum if it is:

$E+W+S+N.I.$

(a)   a pension commencement lump sum,
(b)   a serious ill-health lump sum, or

(c)   a lifetime allowance excess lump sum.'

(a lump sum payment where the member has no remaining lifetime allowance)

Valuation is straightforward, simply being the amount of lump sum that is paid.

Under the provisions of Finance Act 2011 and with effect from 6 April 2011 this BCE will not apply if the individual becomes entitled to a pension commencement lump sum before age 75 and it is not paid until after age 75.

BCE 5 (defined benefit schemes) and the revised BCE 5A (money purchase schemes) ensure that the sum involved is tested against the lifetime allowance.

The payment of a trivial commutation lump sum is not a Benefit Crystallisation Event and does not require a lifetime allowance test. The member would not be eligible for trivial commutation if the total value of their retirement benefit provision (including both crystallised and uncrystallised benefits), exceeds £30,000 on the nominated date.

Where entitlement to a lump sum payable on the grounds of serious ill-health arises on or after 75 a tax charge of 55% is applicable.

BCE 7. Payment of a lump sum death benefit.

The valuation for the purposes of the lifetime allowance test, is the amount of the lump sum death benefit paid.

BCE 8. A transfer to a Qualifying Recognised Overseas Pension Scheme.

The valuation is simply the amount of the transfer value paid. This means in effect the cash transfer value paid plus the market value of any assets transferred in specie.

BCE 9. Payment of certain lump sums (as prescribed by SI 2009 No. 1171).

This further BCE was introduced as a consequence of Finance Act 2008. BCE9 occurs:

'if regulations under section 164(1)(f) so provide, the happening of an event prescribed in the regulations in relation to a payment prescribed in the regulations. The amount of the BCE being such amount as determined in accordance with regulations.'

Payments captured under BCE9 fall into two broad categories. Firstly lump sum payments that would not be otherwise permitted as authorised member payments under the provisions of Finance Act 2004, and pensions lump sums paid or overpaid in error.

One example is to introduce as an authorised member payment a payment made after the death of a registered pension scheme member, who died on or after 6 April 2006 but before reaching age 75, representing arrears of scheme pension that were due to be paid to that member before death, but were not so paid because entitlement to those pension instalments could not be established before the member's death.

BCE9 also allows for certain small payments not exceeding £10,000 which would otherwise be unauthorised, to escape an unauthorised payment charge.

Appendix 5

HMRC guidance

Introduction

In the era before the reforms introduced in April 2006, as stated in the main text, pension schemes of one form or another that benefited from tax privileges were approved by the Inland Revenue. The form of approval provided was known as 'discretionary approval', and so that pension schemes generally knew what was expected of them as a condition of retaining that discretionary approval the Inland Revenue published what were colloquially referred to as 'practice notes'.

In relation to occupational pension schemes these were under the reference IR 12, and in relation to personal pension schemes were under the reference IR 76. These were very much the 'bibles' of the pensions practitioner because the practice notes, together with the associated background legislation, gave guidance as to how schemes were expected to behave in particular circumstances.

The way in which pension schemes operate as 'registered pension schemes' with effect from 6 April 2006 under the provisions of Finance Act 2004 is very different. No longer do we have a framework of legislation associated with the discretionary approval of schemes supported by practice issued by the Inland Revenue, instead we have a detailed and quite complex statutory framework to which schemes must adhere. Failure to adhere to the statutory rules leads to a system of tax on penalties that has been set out in the main text.

HMRC recognised however that it was unreasonable to expect practitioners to dip into the legislation every time something emerged on which information or guidance was required. Thus the concept of developing and putting in place HMRC guidance in what is now known as the Registered Pension Schemes Manual (RPSM). The first issue of the RPSM was available in printed form as well as online, but the RPSM is now available only online at www.hmrc.gov .uk/manuals/rpsmmanual/index.htm.

The manual is updated regularly and so as to enable practitioners to be aware of what has changed any amendments or additions to the manual get a mention on the HMRC website in the 'what's new' section which can be found at www.hmrc.gov.uk/news/index.htm. News and updates for pension schemes specifically can be found at www.hmrc.gov.uk/pensionschemes/index.htm.

In addition HMRC regularly issue newsletters online known as 'pension scheme newsletters' in order to provide detailed information updates.

The Registered Pension Schemes Manual (RPSM)

The RPSM is divided into sections as follows:

RPSM00100000   Technical Pages
RPSM00200000   Member Pages
RPSM00300000   Scheme Administrator Pages
RPSM00400000   Employer Pages
RPSM00500000   Overview of the International Pensions Regime
RPSM20000000   Glossary

You will for example see immediately why it was thought unnecessary to prepare a glossary associated with this particular publication where a definitive glossary is easily accessible.

For any practitioner the Technical Pages will generally be the starting point, whereas a member of the public or a pension scheme member will probably find it easier to begin by looking at the Member Pages. The content of the Scheme Administrator Pages is specifically targeted at the Administrators of registered pension schemes and includes detailed helpful information, for example about the sanctions on penalties associated with failing to make particular reports as required by the legislation on time.

Until you get used to the way that the manual works it can be quite difficult to navigate through to the particular page that you want. Trial and error, patience and experience are what is required.

The RPSM pages make frequent references to the associated legislation – but above all the guidance is what it says it is, HMRC's interpretation of the legislation and it is not always correct and up to date needing amendment from time to time.

Appendix 6

Annual allowance calculation examples in relation to defined benefit scheme members

In order to assist practitioners with how the annual allowance calculations work, in other words how the pension input amount is calculated in relation to members of defined benefit schemes, HMRC have provided a substantial set of helpful examples.

A sample of these are reproduced below for ease of reference.

All the examples assume:

- CPI (consumer prices index) is 3%;
- the scheme is a defined benefits arrangement;
- normal pension age under scheme rules is 65;
- the individual joins the scheme at age 25 and is 40 at the start of the pension input period (PIP);
- their pensionable pay is £50,000 at the start of the PIP and £52,000 at the end of the PIP.

Example 1 - Standard accrual

The rules of A's scheme for defining the pension at NRD give an accrual rate of 1/60 for every year of service.

The member's pension input amount is:

$(16/60 \times £52,000 \times 16) - (15/60 \times £50,000 \times 16 \times 1.03) = $ **£15,866.**

Example 2 - Variable accrual - low start, high finish

The rules of the scheme in which the member participates defines the pension entitlement normal retirement date to be 1/80 of final pay in respect of the first 30 years of service and 1/40 of final pay for each year in excess of 30.

The member's pension input amount is:

$(16/80 \times £52,000 \times 16) - (15/80 \times £50,000 \times 16 \times 1.03) = $ **£11,900**

At age 58 the member has built up 33 years' pensionable service, the calculation would reflect a new accrual at the rate of 1/40.

Assuming his opening pensionable pay was £60,000 and closing pensionable pay was £61,000 the pension input amount is:

$[(30/80 + 3/40) \times £61,000 \times 16] - [(30/80 + 2/40) \times £60,000 \times 16 \times 1.03] = $ **£18,960**

Example 3 – Limited number of years

The rules for defining the pension at NRD give 1/45 for each year of service, subject to a maximum number of years service of 30.

The member's pension input amount is:

$(16/45 \times £52,000 \times 16) - (15/45 \times £50,000 \times 16 \times 1.03) = £21,155$

At age 58 when the member has built up 33 years' pensionable service he has exceeded the maximum number of years he can count toward his pension benefits and, apart from an adjustment for increases to his pensionable pay, is not accruing any further 1/45.

Assuming his opening pensionable pay was £60,000 and closing pensionable pay was £61,000, the pension input amount is:

$(30/45 \times £61,000 \times 16) - (30/45 \times £60,000 \times 16 \times 1.03) = 0$

Example 4 – Adjustment for early leaver

The above type of normal retirement rule might be combined with different rules if a member leaves before retirement or takes their benefits before the normal pension age for the scheme.

The accrual rate for the member's scheme is 1/45 for each year of service, subject to a maximum number of years service of 30.

However, under the scheme rules if the member leaves employment before reaching normal pension age an adjustment is made to the pension entitlement at the point the member ceases active membership of the scheme.

On leaving the pension entitlement is adjusted so it becomes pensionable pay × actual service/potential service to normal pension age × (fraction of pensionable pay applicable on staying to normal pension age – in this case 2/3).

The outcome for a PIP in which the member was an active member at opening and closing would be identical in principle to example 3 above– and the member's pension input amount is:

$(16/45 \times £52,000 \times 16) - (15/45 \times £50,000 \times 16 \times 1.03) = £21,155$.

At age 53, after building up 28 years' pensionable service, if the member stayed an active member throughout the PIP and assuming opening pensionable pay of £60,000 and closing pensionable pay of £61,000, the pension input amount is:

$(28/45 \times £61,000 \times 16) - (27/45 \times £60,000 \times 16 \times 1.03) = £14,008$

In fact, the member leaves the job and ceases to be an active member of the pension scheme at aged 53.

The pension input amount becomes:

$(28/40 \times 2/3 \times £61,000 \times 16) - (27/45 \times £60,000 \times 16 \times 1.03) = 0$

Example 5 – N/NS adjustment for an active member

The rules of the member's pension scheme for retirement at normal pension age provide that he is entitled to a pension of $^2/_3$ salary subject to an adjustment of (N/NS × $^2/_3$) each year, where N equals service to date and NS equals prospective service from joining the scheme to normal pension age.

This adjustment is made each year even though he remains an active member because it is not contingent on some future event, such as his becoming a deferred member.

His pension input amount is:

(16/40 × $^2/_3$ × £52,000 × 16) – (15/40 × $^2/_3$ × £50,000 × 16 × 1.03) = **£15,866.**

The exact conclusion from a particular case depends on the precise wording in the rules.

Not all scheme rules are written in the way described above. For example the rules of a scheme might be expressed as:

'On retirement at Normal Retirement Date (NRD), the member is entitled to a pension of pensionable salary × $^2/_3$. However if the member leaves employment before reaching NRD, his pension entitlement becomes pensionable salary x some formula (which might for example be N/NS × $^2/_3$)'.

Written this way, the scheme rules provide for a reduction in the pension entitlement contingent on the member leaving before NRD.

Therefore the member's pension input amount in his first PIP would reflect accrual of a full $^2/_3$ current pensionable salary arising from the point the joined.

After the first PIP the $^2/_3$ fraction would continue – that is there would be no accrual as far as the $^2/_3$ fraction is concerned, although there could still be accrual by reference to salary linkage. Such an immediate accrual of the full $^2/_3$ pension could mean a significant pension input amount in the first PIP after joining.

Example 6 – where unused annual allowance is carried forward.

Chris is a teacher. The teachers' pension scheme provides benefits of a pension of $^1/_{80}$ final pay and a lump sum of $^3/_{80}$ pensionable pay for each year of service. Pensionable pay is pay received over the last 12 months.

At the start of 2013–14 Chris's pensionable pay was £45,000.

Chris successfully applied for a job as deputy head of a secondary school. He started his new job at the start of the new school year in September 2013. Given his promotion and a move to the inner London area, the pay rate for Chris's new job is £70,000. However, Chris's pensionable pay at the end of 2013–14 was £59,600 as his pensionable pay is pay over the last 12 months.

At the start of the year Chris had 24 years' pensionable service.

Opening value – year 1

The value of Chris's pension benefits (opening value) is calculated as:

(1) calculate amount of annual pension accrued
   $24/80 \times £45,000 = $ **£13,500**
(2) multiply annual rate of pension by flat factor of 16
   $£13,500 \times 16 = $ **£216,000**
(3) add amount of separate lump sum
   $£216,000 + (24 \times {}^3/_{80} \times £45,000) = $ **£256,500**
(4) increase by CPI (for this example assumed to be 3%)
   $£256,500 \times 1.03 = $ **£264,195**

Chris's opening pension benefits value is **£264,195.**

Closing value – year 1

The value of Chris's pension benefits (closing value) at the end of the PIP is calculated as:

(1) calculate amount of annual pension accrued
   $25/80 \times £59,600 = $ **£18,625**
(2) multiply annual rate of pension by flat factor of 16
   $£18,625 \times 16 = $ **£298,000**
(3) add amount of separate lump sum
   $£298,000 + (25 \times {}^3/_{80} \times £59,600) = $ **£353,875**

Chris's closing pension benefits value is **£353,875.**

Calculating the pension input amount – year 1

The increase in Chris's benefits under his scheme is £89,680. This is £39,680 more than the annual allowance of £50,000.

Carrying forward unused annual allowance – year 1

The reason that Chris's pension input is so high is because he has had a very large pay rise following his promotion.

Chris's pension input amount is normally much lower. In fact for the previous three years his pension input amounts (using the new calculation method) were:

2012–13 = **£10,135**
2011–12 = **£10,250**
2010–11 = **£10,330**

Chris has unused annual allowance from the previous three tax years of £119,285 that he can carry forward, worked out as:
2012–13 = £50,000 – £10,135 = **£ 39,865**
2011–12 = £50,000 – £10,250 = **£ 39,750**
2010–11 = £50,000 – £10,330 = **£ 39,670**

Total unused allowance available to be carried forward = **£119,285**

Together with the £50,000 annual allowance for 2013–14 Chris could have pension savings in 2013–14 of £169,285 without being subject to an annual allowance charge.

Chris's pension input amount for 2013–14 is **£89,680**. This is less than his available annual allowance of **£169,285**. So Chris does not have to pay the annual allowance charge on his pension input for 2013–14.

Chris has not used up all his available annual allowance. He has used up his annual allowance from 2013–14 and also respect of 2010–11, and just £10 of his available annual allowance from 2011–12.

Chris still has **£79,605** unused annual allowance to carry forward to 2014–15.

Opening value – year 2

At the end of 2014–15 Chris's pensionable pay has risen to £70,500.

But now his pensionable pay figure now includes all the large pay rise he received last year plus part of his normal annual pay increase.

Chris's opening value is calculated as:

(1)   calculate amount of annual pension accrued
$25/80 \times £59,600 = $ **£18,625**

(2)   multiply annual rate of pension by flat factor of 16
$£18,625 \times 16 = $ **£298,000**

(3)   add amount of separate lump sum
$£298,000 + (25 \times {}^3/_{80} \times £59,600) = $ **£353,875**

(4)   increase by CPI (assumed to be 3%)
$£353,875 \times 1.03 = $ **£364,491.25**

Chris's opening pension benefits value is **£364,491.25.**

Closing value – year 2

The closing value is calculated as:

(1)   calculate amount of annual pension
${}^{26}/_{80} \times £70,500 = $ **£22,912.50**

(2)   multiply annual rate of pension by flat factor of 16
$£22,912.50 \times 16 = $ **£366,600**

(3)   add amount of separate lump sum
$£366,600 + (26 \times {}^3/_{80} \times £70,500) = $ **£435,337.50**

Chris's closing pension benefits value is **£435,337.50.**

Working out the pension input amount – year 2

The increase in pension saving over the year is **£70,846.25** (£435,337.50 – £364,491.25).

This exceeds the annual allowance of £40,000. But Chris still has unused annual allowance that he can carry forward.

Carrying forward unused annual allowance – year 2

The amount of Chris's unused annual allowance from earlier years that he can carry forward is **£79,605.**

This is broken down as:

2013–14 = £ 0
2012–13 = £39,865
2011–12 = £39,740

This unused annual allowance together with this year's annual allowance of £40,000 is **£119,605**.

This is more than enough to cover Chris's pension input for 2014–15.

There is no annual allowance charge on the pension input of **£70,846.25.**

Chris has used up his annual allowance from 2014–15 and £30,846.25 of his available annual allowance from 2011–12.

Chris cannot carry forward any remaining unused annual allowance from 2011–12 to the following year as it falls out of the three-year limit.

Chris has **£39,865** unused annual allowance to carry forward to 2015–16. This is broken down as:

2014–15 = £ 0
2013–14 = £ 0
2012–13 = £39,865

Index

Q